To His GRACE the

Duke of DORSET,

Lord High Steward of His Majefty's Houfhold,

Conftable of Dover Caftle,

Lord Warden of the Cinque Ports,

Knight of the moft Noble Order of the Garter,

AND

One of His Majefty's moft Honourable Privy Council.

My LORD,

I Hope Your Grace will not condemn my begging Your Protection for a Work that can have no Patron but Your Self. The Charters, Cuftoms and Liberties of the *Cinque Ports*, are fo nearly related to their *Confervator*, that any Declaration of them

would

would be improperly addrefs'd elfewhere. The Love You have at all Times fhown to Your Country, affures me this Inquiry into fome of its Privileges can't be unacceptable to Your Grace.

May You long continue the Delight of Your Friends, an Ornament of Your Country, and a *Confervator* of Liberty.

I am, My LORD,

With the greateft Refpect,

Your Grace's *moft obedient,*

moft humble, and moft

devoted Servant,

S. JEAKE.

CHARTERS

OF THE

CINQUE PORTS,

Two Ancient Towns,

AND THEIR

MEMBERS.

Tranflated into *Englifh*, with

ANNOTATIONS

Hiftorical and Critical thereupon.

Wherein divers old Words are explain'd, and fome of their
ancient Cuftoms and Privileges obferv'd.

By, SAMUEL JEAKE, *fen.* of *Rye*, one of the faid Ancient Towns.

L O N D O N:

Printed for BERNARD LINTOT, at the *Crofs-Keys* between the
Temple-Gates in *Fleet-Street*. MDCCXXVIII.

Advertisement.

THIS Book was wrote in 1678. and had then the Approbation of the Lord Chief Justice North; but the Author soon after dying, it was not printed; and perhaps never had been, if the late Lord Chief Baron Gilbert had not seen the MSS. and thought it would be useful to the World. No considerable Alterations have happened in the Limits of the Ports since that Time, except the Incorporation of Deal.

MAXIMS of Equity, collected from, and proved by Cafes out of the Books of the beft Authority in the High Court of Chancery. To which is added the Cafe of the Lord *Coventry*, concerning the defective Execution of Powers, lately adjudged in the High Court of Chancery. By *Richard Francis* of the *Middle-Temple*, Efq; *Price* 7 s. 6 d. bound.

The Theory and Practice of Gardening; wherein is fully handled all that relates to fine Gardens, commonly called Pleafure Gardens: Confifting of Parterres, Groves, Bowling-Greens, &c. Containing feveral Plans and general Difpofitions of Gardens, new Defigns of Parterres, Groves, Grafs-Plots, Mazes, Banqueting-Rooms, Galleries, Portico's, and Summer-Houfes of Archwork, Terrafes, Stairs, Fountains, Cafcades, and other Ornaments of Ufe in the Decoration and Embellifhments of Gardens, with the Manner of making the Ground, forming Defigns fuitable to the Place, and putting them in Execution, according to the Principles of Geometry. The Method of fetting and raifing, in little Time, all the Plants requifite in fine Gardens; with a new Treatife of Flowers and Orange-Trees: Alfo the Way to find Water to convey it into Gardens, and to make Bafons and Fountains for the fame. Together with Remarks and general Rules in all that concerns the Art of Gardening. By *Le Sieur Alexander le Blond.* Done from the late Edition printed at *Paris*, by *John James* of *Greenwich.* Illuftrated with thirty-eight Copper Plates finely engraven. The Second Edition. *Price* one Guinea bound.

The Inftitute of the Laws of *England:* Or the Laws of *England* in their natural Order, according to common Ufe. Publifhed for the Direction of young Beginners, or Students in the Law; and of others that defire to have a general Knowledge in our Common and Statute Laws. In four Books. By *Thomas Wood*, L. L. D. and Barrifter at Law. The Fourth Edition corrected. *Price* one Guinea bound.

A Law Dictionary: Or the Interpreter of Words and Terms, ufed either in the Common or Statute Laws of *Great Britain*, and in Tenures and jocular Cuftoms: Firft publifhed by the learned Dr. *Cowell*, and in this Edition very much augmented and improv'd, by the Addition of many Thoufand Words, found in our Hiftories, Antiquities, Cartularies, Rolls, Regifters, and other manufcript Records: With an Appendix, containing two Tables: one of the ancient Names of Places in *Great Britain*, and the other of the ancient Surnames; both of them very neceffary for the Ufe of all fuch as converfe with ancient Deeds, Charters, &c. *Price* 16 s. bound.

Inftitutio Legalis: Or an Introduction to the Study and Practice of the Laws of *England*, as now regulated and amended by feveral late Statutes: Divided into Four Parts, viz. 1. The Practice of the Court of *King's-Bench.* 2. The Practice of the Court of *Common-Pleas.* 4. The Nature of all Actions ufually brought in either of the faid Courts. 4. The Order and Method of Pleading; with ufeful Precedents throughout; and a compleat Table to the Whole. The Third Edition, with large Additions. By *William Bohun* of the *Middle-Temple*, Efq; *Price* 6 s.

The Accomplifh'd Conveyancer, Vol. I. Containing the Nature and Kinds of Deeds and Inftruments ufed in Conveyancing; and an Abridgment of the Law relating to all Sorts of Conveyances of Eftates, with every Thing belonging to them, proved by many Law Cafes and Refolutions thereupon: And alfo all Manner of Precedents made Ufe of in Conveyancing, under the Heads of Bargain and Sale, Gifts, Grants, Articles, fpecial Conditions, Covenants, Exchanges, Deeds of Partition, Partnerfhips, fpecial Releafes, Letters of Attorney, Licences, Bills of Sale, Charter-parties of Affreightment, Leafes, Settlements of Leafes, and alfo of perfonal Eftates, Annuities, Money in Funds, &c. inftead of Jointures of Land, &c. Vol. II. Containing Variety of Precedents of fpecial Gifts, Grants, Affignments, Mortgages, and all Kinds of Securities, &c. Vol. III. Containing fpecial Conveyances, Deeds to lead the Ufes of Fines and Recoveries, Settlement, Jointures, Wills, &c. By *Giles Jacob*, Gent. *Price* 18 s.

Where may be had, writ by the fame Author,

I. The Compleat Court-keeper, or Land-Steward's Affiftant: Containing the beft Methods of Court-keeping, and Forms of Grants, Surrenders, Admittances, &c. with the Laws and Cuftoms of Manors, Authority of the Lord, and Privileges of the Tenants, &c. The Third Edition, with Additions. *Price* 6 s.

II. The Modern Juftice: Containing the Bufinefs of a Juftice of Peace in all its Parts, from our Common Law, as well as Statute, with a compleat Charge in the Quarter-Seffions, &c. Improved and continued to this Time. The Third Edition. *Price* 6 s.

III. *Lex Conftitutionis:* Or the Gentleman's Law; being a Compleat Treatife of the Laws and Statutes relating to the King, and Prerogative of the Crown, the Lords, the Commons, all Officers under the Government, &c. *Price* 5 s.

IV. The Laws of Appeals, Murder, Manflaughter, Duelling, &c. with Variety of Pleadings and Proceedings, &c. and three modern Cafes of Convictions on Appeals. *Price* 3 s. 6 d.

V. The Compleat Parifh Officer: Containing, 1. The Authority and Proceedings of High Conftables, Petty Conftables, Headboroughs and Tithingmen, in every Branch of their Duties, purfuant to Acts of Parliament; with the High Conftables Precepts, Prefentments, Warrants, &c. 2. Of Church Wardens, how chofen, their particular Bufinefs in repairing of Churches, Bells, &c. and affigning of Seats, Manner of paffing their Accompts, and the Laws and Statutes concerning the Church in all Cafes; and alfo an Abftract of the Act for building fifty new Churches in *London* and *Weftminfter*, &c. 3. Of Overfeers of the Poor, and their Office; their Power in relieving, employing and fettling poor Perfons; the Laws relating to the Poor, and Settlements, and the Statutes concerning Mafters and Servants. 4. Of Surveyors of Highways and Scavengers, how elected, their Bufinefs in amending the Ways, &c. and the Duty of others; with the Methods of Taxation, Laws of the Highways, &c. To which are added the Statutes relating to Hackney Coaches and Chairs. The Fourth Edition. To which is added, The Office of Conftables, written by Sir *Francis Bacon*, Knt. in the Year 1610. declaring what Power they have, and how they ought to be cherifhed in their Office. *Price* 1 s. 6 d.

A

L I S T

OF THE

Subſcribers NAMES.

A

THE *Rt. Honourable* John *Lord* Aſhburnham
The Rt. Honourable Henry *Lord* Aylmer
Sir William Aſhburnham, *Bart.*
Sir Robert Auſten, *Bart.*
Robert Auſten, *Eſq;*
Edward Auſten, *Eſq;*

B

HEnry Baker, *Eſq;*
Hercules Baker, *Eſq;*
The Honourable George Berkley, *Eſq;*
James Blackmore, *Eſq;*
Raymond Blackmore, *Eſq;*
Capt. Ellis Brand
Thomas Brian, *Eſq;*
Robert Briſtow, *Eſq;*
James Brockman, *Eſq;*
Joſiah Burchet, *Eſq;*
Mr. Richard Butler
Mr. John Button

C

DR. Henry Carleton
Mr. Henry Carleton
Charles Carkeſſe, *Eſq;*
Mr. John Collier, *Solicitor to the* Weſt Ports

Mr. John Collinſon, *Solicitor to the* Eaſt Ports
John Colquit, *Eſq;*
John Crawford, *Eſq;*

D

HIS *Grace the Duke of* Dorſet
Julius Deeds, *Eſq;*
Sir Baſil Dixwell, *Bart.*
George Dodington, *Eſq;*

E

FRancis Eyles, *Eſq;*
George Ellis, *Eſq;*

F

SIR Henry Fermer, *Bart.*
Capt. John Fletcher
Thomas Frewen, *Eſq;*
The Reverend Mr. John Frewen
John Fuller, *Eſq;*
Sir Robert Furneſe, *Bart.*
Henry Furneſe, *Eſq;*

G

SIR William Gage; *Bart. and Knight of the* Bath
James Gambier, *Eſq;*
Capt. Richard Girlington
Maximilian Gott, *Eſq;*

Major

A LIST of the SUBSCRIBERS NAMES.

Major Allen Grebell
Mr. John Grove
Phillips Gybbon, *Efq;*
John Gybbon, *Efq;*

H

HEnry Hare, *Efq;*
Archibald Hutchefon, *Efq;*
Michael Hudfon, *Efq;*

I J

SAmuel Jacomb, *Efq;*
The Honourable Henry Ingram, *Efq;*
The Reverend Mr. Lewis Jones

L

JAmes Lamb, *Efq; Mayor of* Rye
The Honourable Lord Chief Baron Lant

M

CApt. William Mabbot
John Manley, *Efq;*
Richard Manley, *Efq;*
William Manley, *Efq;*
Capt. Charles Martin
Capt. Samuel Mead
Sir Roger Meredith, *Bart.*
George Medcalfe, *Efq;*
The Honourable Samuel Molyneux, *Efq;*

N

HIS Grace the *Duke of* Newcaftle
The Reverend Mr. Richard Nairn
Sir John Norris, *Kt. Admiral of the* Blue
John Norris, *Efq;*

O

SIR George Oxenden, *Bart.*

P

DAvid Papillon, *Efq;*
Capt. Nath. Pigram

The Honourable Hen. Pelham, *Efq;*
Thomas Pelham, *Efq; of* Lewes
James Pelham, *Efq;*
Thomas Pelham, *Efq; of* Stanmere
Thomas Pelham, *jun. of* Lewes, *Efq;*
David Polhill, *Efq;*

S

JOhn Sawbridge, *Efq;*
Exton Sayer, *Efq;* L.L.D.
John Scrope, *Efq;*
Mr. John Slade
Robert Stephens, *Efq;*

T

WIlliam Tempeft, *Efq;*
John Thorpe, Oxon. M. D. .F. R. S.
Mr. William Tournay
Mr. Thomas Tournay
The Honourable Thomas Townfhend, *Efq;*

U

WIlliam Underwood *of* Enfield, *Efq;*
William Underwood *of* Queen's College Cambridge
Thomas Underwood *of* Somerfham, *Efq;*
Mr. Francis Underwood *of* Rye *in* Suffex.
Capt. Philip Vanbrugh

W

THE *Right Honourable* Spencer *Lord* Wilmington
Mr. Walter Waters
The Reverend Mr. Edward Wilfon
Thomas Woodford, *Efq;*

Y

SIR Philip York, *Kt. Attorney General*

CHAR-

CHARTERS

OF THE

Cinque Ports, &c.

CHARTERS.	TRANSLATION.

CArolus secundus, Dei gratia Angliæ, Scotiæ, Franciæ, & Hiberniæ Rex, Fidei defensor, &c. Omnibus ad quos præsentes literæ nostræ patentes pervenerint, salutem. Inspeximus literas patentes inclit. prædecessor. nostræ Dominæ Elizabethæ, nuper Reginæ Angliæ, de confirmatione, in hæc verba, scilicet, Eli-

*C*Harles [a] the Second, by the Grace of God, King of *England* [b], *Scotland,* *France* [c], and *Ireland* [d], Defender of the Faith [e], *&c* [f]. To all to whom our present Letters Patents [g] shall come, Greeting [h]. We have seen [i] the Letters Patents of our famous Predecessor the Lady *Elizabeth* [k], late Queen of *England*, of Confirmation [l], in these Words, that is to say, *Eli-*

ANNOTATIONS.

[a] *Charles,* Son of King *Charles* the First, and Grandson of King *James,* begins his Reign at the Time of his Father's Death, which was *January* 30, 1648. restored by Parliament to the actual Possession of his Kingdoms and Lands at *Dover, May* 25, 1660.

[b] *England, Scotland,* which together make the Isle of *Great Britain*; formerly two Kingdoms, till united by King *James*; whereupon was that Motto on some of his Coin, *Henricus Rosas, Regna Jacobus,* meaning, as King *Henry* VII. had united the Two Houses of *York* and *Lancaster* (that bearing the white Rose, and this the Red, in their Wars) to a firm Peace; so had King *James* the two Kingdoms of *England* and *Scotland* into one Monarchy.

[c] *France* first added in the Title by King *Edward* III. and ever since continuing.

[d] *Ireland.* See afterwards in the Annotations.

[e] *Defender of the Faith.* A Title [*] first given to King *Henry* VIII. by Pope *Leo* X. for writing against *Martin Luther,* in behalf of the Church of *Rome,* as the Bull dated *quinto Idus* confirmed by *Octobr.* 1521. makes appear.   [* *Afterwards by Parliament,* *35 H. 8. c. 3.*]

[f] *Et cetera* signifies the Residue of the Title, as in Queen *Mary* and King *Edward* VI. which afterwards Queen *Mary* did omit, when the Kingdom revolted again to Popery.

[g] *Patents,* from *Pates,* to be open, that they may be read of any one, differencing them from particular Writs, which are closed up in the Wax wherewith they are sealed. But in Letters Patents the Seal is put on a Label, annexed after the Manner of Deeds. *Letters Patents, q. d.* Open Letters.

[h] *Greeting.* Or, Health.

[i] *Seen.* The *Latin* Word, *Inspeximus,* signifies not only a looking upon, but a looking into, and so Inspection implies a curious and serious Perusal.

[k] *Elizabeth,* youngest Daughter of King *Henry* VIII. (by Queen *Anne,* called the Lady *Anne Bollein*) and Sister by the Father to King *Edward* VI. and Queen *Mary,* began her Reign at the Death of Queen *Mary, November* 17, 1558. and died *March* 24, 1602.

[l] *Confirmation.* A Confirmation in Law may be called a Conveyance of an Estate, of Right in *Esse,* whereby a particular Estate is increased, or that which was voidable is made sure, but cannot strengthen a void Estate. Here it is as much as an Approbation and Corroboration of the Privileges and Freedoms the Ports had before, and is used from Queen *Elizabeth* upward to King *Edward* IV. viz. by Queen *Mary,* King *Edward* VI. King *Henry* VIII. and King *Henry* VII. they granting nothing New which the Ports enjoyed not before. It is sometimes used promiscuously for a Charter.

B

[m] *Mary,*

CHARTERS.	TRANSLATION.

Elizabetha Dei gratia Angliæ, Franciæ, & Hiberniæ Regina, Fidei defenſor, *&c.* Omnibus ad quos præſentes literæ pervenerint, ſalutem. Inſpeximus literas patentes Dominæ Mariæ nuper Reginæ Angliæ, ſororis noſtræ præchariſſimæ, de confirmatione, factas in hæc verba: Maria Dei gratia Angliæ, Franciæ, & Hiberniæ Regina, Fidei defenſor, & in terra eccleſiæ Anglicanæ & Hibernicæ ſupremum caput, omnibus ad quos præſentes literæ noſtræ pervenerint, ſalutem. Inſpeximus literas patentes Domini Edvardi nuper Regis Angliæ ſexti, fratris noſtri, de confirmatione, factas in hæc verba: Edvardus ſextus Dei gratia, Angliæ, Franciæ, & Hiberniæ Rex, Fidei defenſor, & in terra eccleſiæ Anglicanæ & Hibernicæ ſupremum caput, omnibus ad quos præſentes literæ pervenerint, ſalutem. Inſpeximus literas patentes Domini Henrici nuper Regis Angliæ octavi, patris noſtri præchariſſimi, de confirmatione, factas in hæc verba: Henricus Dei gratia, Rex Angliæ, & Franciæ, & Dominus Hiberniæ, omnibus ad quos præſentes literæ pervenerint, ſalutem. Inſpeximus literas

Elizabeth, by the Grace of God, Queen of *England*, *France* and *Ireland*, Defender of the Faith, *&c.* To all to whom theſe preſent Letters ſhall come, Greeting. We have ſeen the Letters Patents of the Lady *Mary* [m], late Queen of *England*, our moſt dear Siſter, of Confirmation, made in theſe Words: *Mary*, by the Grace of God Queen of *England*, *France*, and *Ireland*, Defender of the Faith, and in Earth of the Church of *England* and *Ireland* ſupreme Head, To all to whom our preſent Letters ſhall come, Greeting. We have ſeen the Letters Patents of the Lord *Edward* [n], late King of *England*, the Sixth [o], our Brother, of Confirmation, made in theſe Words: *Edward* the Sixth, by the Grace of God King of *England*, *France*, and *Ireland*, Defender of the Faith, and in Earth of the Church of *England* and *Ireland* ſupreme Head, To all to whom theſe preſent Letters ſhall come, Greeting. We have ſeen the Letters Patents of the Lord *Henry* [p], late King of *England*, the Eighth [q], our moſt dear Father, of Confirmation, made in theſe Words: *Henry*, by the Grace of God, King of *England*, and *France*, and Lord of *Ireland*, To all to whom theſe preſent Letters ſhall come, Greeting. We have ſeen the Letters Patents

ANNOTATIONS.

[m] *Mary*, Daughter of King *Henry* VIII. by Queen *Katherine*, who had been before Wife to Prince *Arthur*, his Brother, is reckon'd to begin her Reign at the Death of King *Edward* VI. *July* 6, 1553. and died *November* 17, 1558.
[n] *Edward*, Son of King *Henry* VIII. by Queen *Jane* (called the Lady *Jane Seymour*) began his Reign at the Death of his Father, *January* 28, 1546. and died *July* 6, 1553.
[o] *Sixth*. That is, the Sixth of that Name from the Conqueſt of King *William*, for elſe it muſt be more than the Sixth, ſeeing before there were ſome of the ſame Name.
[p] *Henry*, Son of King *Henry* VII. began his Reign over *England* when his Father died, *April* 22, 1509. In the Thirty Third Year of his Reign he wrote King of *England*, *France*, and *Ireland*, &c. He died *January* 28, 1546.
[q] *Eighth*. That is, the Eighth King of that Name ſince the *Norman* Conqueſt.

CHARTERS.

ras patentes Domini Henrici nuper Regis Angliæ, patris noſtri, de confirmatione, factas in hæc verba: Henricus Dei gratia, Rex Angliæ, & Franciæ, & Dominus Hiberniæ, omnibus ad quos præſentes literæ pervenerint, ſalutem. Inſpeximus cartam Domini Edvardi nuper Regis Angliæ quarti poſt conqueſtum, factam in hæc verba: Edvardus Dei gratia, Rex Angliæ, & Franciæ, & Dominus Hiberniæ, Archiepiſcopis, Epiſcopis, Abbatibus,

TRANSLATION.

tents of the Lord Henry [r], late King of England, our Father, of Confirmation, made in theſe Words: Henry, by the Grace of God, King of England, and France, and Lord of Ireland, To all to whom theſe preſent Letters ſhall come, Greeting. We have ſeen the Charter [ſ] of the Lord Edward [t], late King of England, the Fourth after the Conqueſt, made in theſe Words: Edward by the Grace of God, King of England, and France, and Lord of Ireland, To all Archbiſhops [u], Biſhops [w], Abbots,

ANNOTATIONS.

[r] **Henry**, deſcended by his Mother from the Houſe of *Lancaſter*, being Earl of *Richmond*, invited by the Nobility and Commons, weary of the Tyranny of King *Richard* III. croſſeth the Seas from *Britain* in *France*, landeth in *Wales*, received with good liking of the People, marcheth to *Leiceſterſhire*, and in a Battel at *Boſworth* encountreth with, and killeth King *Richard* III. and in his ſtead is crowned in the Field *, *Auguſt* 22, 1485, and afterward to ſecure his * *As ſome ſay,* Crown, cauſeth innocent *Edward*, Son to *George* Duke of *Clarence* (the only Male Heir of the *Others,*) at the Houſe of *York*) to be killed, and married *Elizabeth*, eldeſt Daughter to King *Edward* IV. *Lord Strange,* reigns till *April* 22, 1509. and then died. Of the aforeſaid King *Richard* III. no mention is *brought* the found to be made in the Charters of the Ports, his Title to the Crown being uſurped, begun *Crown to him to* in the Murder of his Nephews (Sons of King *Edward* IV.) to whom he was Uncle and Pro-*Leiceſter.* tector, to wit, King *Edward* V †. before he was Crowned, and his Brother *Richard*, and ha- † *Who reigned* ving but a ſhort Reign, from the Death of King *Edward* V. *June* 22, 1483. to *Auguſt* 22, *from his Fa-* 1485. I preſume the Ports had neither their old Charters confirmed, nor any new granted *ther's Death,* by him. *Apr. 9, 1483.*

[ſ] **Charter**, in *Latin Carta* and *Charta*, implies here as much as a Gift or Grant, conferring *till he was* ſome Privileges and Freedoms, with Confirmation written and ſealed after the Manner of *murder'd, viz.* Deeds, which in the Law are called Charters. By this Name that of King *Edward* IV. and *June* 22. folthoſe Elder are called, except the Confirmation of King *Richard* II. between whom and King *lowing.* *Edward* IV. is mentioned neither Charter nor Confirmation of the Three King *Henries.* And although of King *Henry* IV. and King *Henry* VI ‖, I will not ſay the Ports had any Grant or Con- ‖ *Since the wri-* firmation, yet am I confident they had of King *Henry* VI. for in a Writ in the Fourteenth Year *ting hereof I* of his Reign, directed to his Uncle, *Humphrey* Duke of *Gloceſter*, then Conſtable of *Dover Caſtle, happened to ſee* and Warden of the *Cinque Ports*, for furniſhing the Shipping, they were bound to provide, by *the Copy of a* their Charters, he adds (*quas confirmavimus*) *which we have confirmed*. And beſides, in the *Writ of K.Hen.* Charter of King *James*, King *Henry* VI. is reckoned up among other Kings, particularly by V. *to his Bro-* Name, for one of them that had confirmed the Ports Privileges. Theſe Three King *Henries, ther Humphrey* were of the *Lancaſtrian* Line, and had reigned de facto Sixty One Years and upwards, for King *D. of Gloceſter,* *Henry* IV. called *Henry Bullingbroke*, began his Reign upon the Depoſition of King *Richard* II. *then Conſtable* which was *September*, 29, 1399. and died *March* 20, 1412. when his Son King *Henry* V. *of Dover Caſtle,* began, and reigned till *Auguſt* 31, 1422. upon whoſe Death King *Henry* VI. (Son *and Warden,* *Henry* V.) began his Reign, and continued till the Depoſition, or rather Diſpoſſeſſion by King *&c. dated* 16 *Edward* IV. *March* 4, 1460. *Apr. 9 Hen. V.*

[t] **Edward**, Earl of *March*, Son of *Richard Plantagenet*, Duke of *York*, after Diſcomfiture *wherein be hath* of the Forces of King *Henry* VI. under Command of the Earls of *Pembroke* and *Wiltſhire*, at *like Words of the* *Mortimer's* Croſs, obtains the Crown, and is reckoned to begin his Reign *March* 4, 1460. *Ports Charters,* aforeſaid. And though ſometime afterward this King *Henry* was reſtored; yet being again *(quas confir-* worſted, the others Reign is counted current from that Time till *April* 9, 1483. when *mavimus, &c.]* he died.

[u] **Archbiſhops**. Of theſe there are but Two in *England*, one of *Canterbury*, intituled Primate and Metropolitan of all *England*; the other of *York*, intituled Primate of *England*, according to the Judgment of *Huyh*, the Pope's Legate, *Anno* 1072. for ending the Contention at *Windſor* between *Lanfranc*, then Archbiſhop of the former, and *Thomas Norman*, Archbiſhop of the latter. The Word *all* is ſupplied in the Tranſlation. *Euphonie gratia.*

[w] **Biſhops**. Within the Province of *Canterbury*, and under the Archbiſhop thereof, are the Biſhops of *London, Wincheſter, Rocheſter, Peterborough, Bath* and *Wells, Coventry* and *Lichfield, Oxford, Ely, Chicheſter, Gloceſter, Exeter, Briſtol, Norwich, Lincoln, Hereford, Worceſter, Saliſbury,* St. *Davids, Aſaph, Bangor,* and *Landaff.* And under the Archbiſhop of *York*, as within his

CHARTERS.

batibus, Prioribus, Ducibus, Comitibus, Baronibus, Jufticiariis,
Vice-comitibus, Præpofitis, Miniftris, & omnibus Ballivis, &
fide-

TRANSLATION.

Abbots[x], Priors[y], Dukes[z],
Earls[a], Barons[b], Juftices[c], Sheriffs[d], Provofts[e], Minifters[f],
and all Bailiffs[g], and faithful
Peo-

ANNOTATIONS.

Its Jona one of gor, and Landaff, the reft in England. As for the Bifhop of *Sodor*[*], he never fat, or had any the Hebrides, Vote in Parliament.

his Province, are only *Durefme, Chefter*, and *Carlifle*. So, as in all, befides the faid Two Archbifhops, are Twenty Four Bifhops, of which Four in *Wales*, viz. St. *Davids, Afaph, Ban-*

and hath Jurif-   [x] *Abbots.* Many of which were formerly in *England*, till the Diffolution of Abbies by King *diction in the Henry* VIII. And fuch of them as were founded to hold of the King *per Baroniam*, and were *muft of his Re-* Ifle of Man, and called by Writ, fat in the Upper Houfe of Parliament among the Lords thereof, and intituled *fidence there,* Lord Abbots, of which there were Twenty Six. The Name, fome fay, came from *Abba*, a *and is under the* Father ; for as Fathers are chief Governors of their Families ; fo had thefe the Rule or Prehemi-*Abp. of York.* nence of thofe Monafteries called Abbies.

[y] *Priors.* Another Sort of Regular Ecclefiafticks, as the Law terms them, with refpect to which, Archbifhops, Bifhops, Deans, &c. are called Seculars, as living under no fuch Rules as the Regulars do. Thefe were Heads, or chief Governors of the Religious Houfes (as commonly termed) called Priories, which, together with the Abbies, fuffered their Diffolution in *England* by King *Henry* VIII. before which, Two of thefe had Place among the Lords of Parliament, as appeareth by the Parliament Rolls.

[z] *Dukes.* Among the Temporal Lords, next the Prince, the Dukes are higheft in Honour and Dignity ; and if they be of the Blood Royal fhould be reputed Arch Dukes. The Name, from *Ducendo*, imports them for Honour and Valour worthy to be Leaders, or Generals, of Imperial or Royal Armies ; wherefore *Dux* is ufed both for a Captain and a Duke.

[a] *Earls.* From the *Saxon* Eorle, equivalent to the old *Roman* Senator, feems with the *Saxons* to be the higheft Title of Noblemen, who for their confiant Attendance on their Sovereigns, in Matters of Counfel and Authority, touching War and Peace, &c. were called in *Latin, Comites*, as much as to fay, The King's Companions. And ftill *Comes* is ufed both for a Companion and an Earl. Thefe, becaufe they had the Government of Caftles, and other Places committed to their Care, gave occafion to their Titles, as Earls of fuch Places, till at laft the Title wrought to a County, called in *Latin Comitatus.*

[b] *Barons.* Sometimes, as here, in the Directions of the Charters of King *Edward* IV. King *Edward* III. King *Edward* II. and King *Edward* I. ufed for the Peers or Noblemen, as well them that hold Baronies, and are called by Writ to the Parliament, as thofe created by Patent. Other where to be taken for the Judges of the *Exchequer*; and oftentimes for Burgeffes or Townfmen, Citizens of *London*, and as afterwards, in the Charters for Freemen of the Ports. The Word *Baron*, in the old *French*, or *Norman* Language, is ufed for an Husband ; and fo a *Feme covert Baron*, is a married Woman.

[c] *Juftices.* Of thefe there have been, and are feveral in *England*, as Juftices in Eyre, or Itinerant ; Juftices of Affize and Gaol Delivery ; Juftices of Oyer and Terminer ; Juftices of the Courts at *Weftminfter*, called the Upper, or *King's Bench*; and Lower, or *Common Bench* ; Juftices of the Peace ; Juftices of Sewers, &c. Importing in general, thofe that have Power and Authority by Law to adminifter Juftice to others.

[d] *Sheriffs.* Sometime wrote *Shrieves*, and rightly *Shireeves*, or the *Reeve* of the Shire, this coming from the *Saxon Shyran*, to cut, part, fhare, or divide into Parts. For all the Shires, or Counties, are but parts of the Kingdom ; and the other Word, *Reeve*, fignifies a Chief Officer or Governor. And now, in ftead of the Earls, who are but Titular as to the Government of the Counties, the Sheriff hath the *Poffe Comitatus*, and is called in *Latin, Vice Comes.*

[e] *Provofts.* Portreeves, or Reeves, by which Name the Head Officer, or Chief Governor of Cities, Towns, and principal Sea Ports, was antiently called. The Word Provoft is yet kept in fome Places in *Scotland*, for which, or Portreeve, the *Latin, Præpofitus*, is proper enough. In the printed Copy, becaufe it begins not with a capital Letter, but joyned with Minifters, it feems to be taken adjectively, for as much as *Chief Minifters*, the Adjective *Præpofitus* fignifying to be fet or put before. But in feveral other, and elder Copies, having feen it with a great P. I take it for a Subftantive, and conceive it ought to be rendered Provofts, or Portreeves, as aforefaid

[f] *Minifters.* Properly Servants, commonly fuch Clergymen as have a Benefice with Cure ; but here it is rather for fuch Serjeants, or Under Officers, as have the ferving of Writs and Procefs, &c.

[g] *Bailiffs.* A Bayliff, or Baily, is fometime taken for one that receiveth his Lord's Rents ; fometime for the Sheriff of the County ; fometime for the Chief Magiftrate in a Corporation ; fometime for a Judge ; but here for fuch Officers as execute the Precepts of the Sheriffs, or fuch Writs as iffue from fome Court of Juftice or other : As well as the Head Officers of fuch Corporations who are fo called.

CHARTERS.

fidelibus, falutem. Infpeximus cartam confirmationis Domini Richardi, nuper Regis Angliæ, fecundi poft conqueftum, factam in hæc verba : Richardus Dei gratia, Rex Angliæ, & Franciæ, & Dominus Hiberniæ, omnibus ad quos præfentes literæ pervenerint, falutem. Infpeximus cartam confirmationis Domini Edvardi, nuper Regis Angliæ, avi noftri, in hæc verba: Edvardus Dei gratia, Rex Angliæ, Dominus Hiberniæ, & Dux Acquitaniæ, Archiepifcopis, Epifcopis, Abbatibus, Prioribus, Ducibus, Comitibus, Baronibus,

TRANSLATION.

People [h], Greeting. We have feen the Charter of Confirmation of the Lord *Richard* [i], late King of *England*, the Second after the Conqueft, made in thefe Words: *Richard*, by the Grace of God, King of *England*, and *France*, and Lord of *Ireland*, to all to whom thefe prefent Letters fhall come, Greeting. We have feen the Charter of Confirmation of the Lord *Edward* [k], late King of *England*, our Grandfather, in thefe Words : *Edward*, by the Grace of God, King of *England*, Lord of *Ireland*, and Duke of *Acquitaine* [l], To all Archbifhops, Bifhops, Abbots, Priors, Dukes, Earls, Barons,

ANNOTATIONS.

[h] *Faithful. People* are here fupplied in the Tranflation, *Fidelibus* being an Adjective ufed for a Subftantive, and afterward, where *fuis* is annexed thereto, is tranflated *Faithful Subjects*; but where *fuis* is wanting, *Faithful People*, the other being fomewhat more reftrictive.

[i] *Richard.* This King *Richard* II. was Grandfon to King *Edward* III. to wit, Son of Prince *Edward*, called the *Black Prince*, who died before his Father, whereupon this King *Richard*, at the Death of his Grandfather, came to the Crown, *June* 21, 1377. and was depofed, *September* 29, 1399.

[k] *Edward.* The Third of that Name King of *England* after the *Norman* Conqueft, Son of King *Edward* II. firft in Arms againft his Father, and before his Death (his Father being depofed) poffeffes the Crown from *January* 25, 1326. to *June* 21, 1377. when he died, and left it to his Grandchild, King *Richard* II. aforefaid. This King *Edward*, in the Fourteenth Year of his Reign, took upon himfelf the Title of King of *France*, which his Succeffors have kept ever fince.

[l] *Acquitaine.* In the printed Copy it is not *Dux Acquitaniæ*, but *Dominus Hiberniæ & Acquitaniæ*, different from what I have feen in Five other feveral Copies, where it is in all *Duke of Acquitaine*, as alfo hereafter, which made me add the Word *Dux* here, and believe it was omitted in the printed Copy by miftake of the Amanuenfis, or Error of the Prefs. This Dukedom is in *France*, and contains Three great Provinces, *viz. Gafcoigne, Guyan* or *Guienne*, and *Xantoigne.* And why fome Tranflations of this, and other Charters, have rendered the *Englifh* only *Guyan*, I fee no reafon. It's true, King *Henry* III. about the Forty Fifth Year of his Reign, by Compofition with *Lewis* VIII. of *France*, agreed to have all *Guyan* beyond the River *Garonne*, all the Country of *Xantoigne* to the River of *Charente*, with the Countries of *Limofin* and *Querry*, for him and his Succeffors, doing their Homage and Fealty to the Crown of *France*, as a Duke of *Acquitaine*, and Peer of that Kingdom. Whereupon afterwards not only he, but King *Edward* I. King *Edward* II. and King *Edward* III. wrote *Dux Acquitaniæ*, till he conquered part of *France*, and altered his Title as King thereof. And it feems at Times afterward, as appeareth by this Charter or Confirmation, bearing Date at *Weftminfter* the firft Day of *July*, in the Thirty Eighth Year of his Reign, which was about Twenty four Years after his writing King of *France*. This I fhould have thought another Error of the Amanuenfis, had not I feen printed in *Weever*'s *Funeral Monuments*, p. 339. a Writ of this King *Edward* III. in the Thirty fifth Year of his Reign, for Reftitution to the Priory of *Montacute*, in the County of *Somerfet*, of the Lands, &c. belonging to that Priory, formerly taken into the King's Hands, with the very fame Title as this Charter in the printed Copy is, *viz. Edward*, by the Grace of God, King of *England*, Lord of *Ireland* and *Acquitaine*. Our *Englifh* Hiftories tell us further, that before this Compofition of King *Henry* III. for part, the Crown of *England* claimed of Right the whole Dutchy of *Acquitaine*. For *Maude*, fole Daughter and Heir of King *Henry* I. married firft to *Henry* the Emperor, and after to *Jeffrey Plantagenet*, by whom fhe had King *Henry* II. he marries *Eleanor*, whereby he had the Dutchy of *Acquitaine*, and Earldom of *Poictiers*; and he had the Earldom of *Anjou, Tournay*, and *Maine*, as Son and Heir to *Jeffrey Plantagenet* his Father.

C

[m] *Edward*,

CHARTERS.

ronibus, Jufticiariis, Vice-comitibus, Præpofitis, Miniftris,
& omnibus Ballivis, & Fidelibus fuis, falutem. Infpeximus
cartam Domini Edvardi, nuper
Regis Angliæ, patris noftri, in
hæc verba: Edvardus Dei gratia, Rex Angliæ, Dominus Hiberniæ, & Dux Acquitaniæ, Archiepifcopis, Epifcopis, Abbatibus, Prioribus, Ducibus, Comitibus, Baronibus, Jufticiariis,
Vice-comitibus, Præpofitis, Miniftris, & omnibus Ballivis, &
Fidelibus fuis, falutem. Infpeximus cartam quam Dominus Edvardus, quondam Rex
Angliæ, pater nofter, fecit Baronibus Quinque Portuum, in hæc
ver-

TRANSLATION.

rons, Juftices, Sheriffs, Provofts,
Minifters, and all his Bailiffs, and
faithful Subjects, Greeting. We
have feen the Charter of the
Lord *Edward* [m], late King of
England, our Father, in thefe
Words: *Edward*, by the
Grace of God, King of *Eng-
land*, Lord of *Ireland*, and
Duke of *Acquitaine*, To all
Archbifhops, Bifhops, Abbots,
Priors, Dukes, Earls, Barons,
Juftices, Sheriffs, Provofts, Mi-
nifters, and all his Bailiffs, and
faithful Subjects, Greeing. We
have feen the Charter which
the Lord *Edward* [n], fometime
King of *England*, our Father,
made to the Barons [o] of the
Cinque [p] *Ports* [q], in thefe
Words:

ANNOTATIONS.

[m] *Edward*, the Second King of *England* of that Name, and Firft after the *Norman* Conqueft, that was depofed. He was Son of King *Edward* I. and at his Death began to Reign, which was *July* 7, 1307. and was depofed *January* 15, 1326.

[n] *Edward*, Son to King *Henry* III. began his Reign *November* 16, 1272. when his Father died, and died himfelf, *July* 7, 1307. He is called King *Edward* I. that is, the Firft of that Name after the Conqueft of King *William* the Conqueror.

[o] *Barons*. Here for Freemen of the Ports, as afore was noted, and in feveral other Places of the Charters, and under the fame often are included Refiants or Inhabitants.

[p] *Cinque*. The Word *Cinque* being *French* for Five, neceffarily denotes, that there are but five Ports, under which Term are underftood here, The Ancient Towns, and the Members annexed to the faid Ports and Towns. But neither of them named in thefe elder Charters, till thofe of Queen *Elizabeth* and King *James*, which latter plainly expreffeth every one. Thofe that pafs by the Name of the *Cinque Ports*, or *Five Ports*, and include the reft that enjoy like Liberties with them, are *Hafting*, *Sandwich*, *Dover*, *New Romney*, and *Hithe*, and fometime καῖ᾽ ἐξοχὴν, are called *The Ports*, there being none other of the Ports of *England*, that have had fuch large Privileges, and can equal the Antiquity of the Grants and Confirmations thereof, or been fo eminent for the Services they are, and ought, to perform, and from Time to Time have performed.

In quo exportantur & importantur merces, à portubus. [q] *Ports*, from the *Latin*, *Portus* [*], implies them all Sea Towns, in whofe Havens and Harbors Ships may fafely arrive and unlade. And no doubt but at firft they were, though now the reftlefs Sea hath fhut it felf off from fome of them, to the fpoiling of their ancient Harbors, as in *Romney* and *Hithe*. And other-where, as at *Hafting*, covered with its Waves the old Town and Port, as fome fay Three Miles, and left this Town, and Port of *Hafting*, only a Scade Place. But whether this or the old Town of *Hafting* be that which was firft enfranchifed and incorporated with the other Ports, I leave as yet uncertain. By the Opinion of Mr. *Lambard*, in his *Perambulation* of Kent, it was old *Romney*, now a Member to *New Romney*, that had the great Privileges before the Conqueft, was the Haven Town, and abounded with Shipping: Though now, and long fince, having loft the Haven, is fubjected to the *New Romney* as the head Port. The other Ports of *Sandwich*, *Dover*, and *Hithe*, feem to enjoy their ancient Situations, and Identical to the Places firft privileged, unlefs, perhaps, *Hithe* hath flept before *Weft Hithe*, now a Member thereto, as *New Romney* hath done to the Old. Yet, as was faid before, *Hithe* is deprived of its old Harbor, and the Harbors of *Sandwich* and *Dover* impaired for that they anciently were reported to be. The Two ancient Towns of *Winchelfea* and *Rye* (of equal Immunities and Privileges with the Ports, and now incorporated with them and their Members) though by a Book (belonging to the Ports, as hereafter mentioned) called *Domefday*, and in an Exemplification of the Services of the *Cinque Ports*, are reckoned up as Members to *Hafting*: Yet was it only in the Accompt there paffed, to fhew they were joined with *Hafting* and its Members, to find fuch a Proportion of the Shipping, which the whole Ports, Towns and Members, were to fit and fet out according to their Charters. Otherwife I find not that they were ever Members to *Hafting*, nor at any

Time

CHARTERS.	TRANSLATION.
verba: Edvardus Dei gratia, Rex Angliæ, Dominus Hiberniæ, & Dux Acquitaniæ, Archiepiscopis, Episcopis, Abbatibus, Prioribus, Comitibus, Baronibus, Justiciariis, Vicecomitibus, Præpositis, Ministris, & omnibus Ballivis, & Fidelibus suis, salutem. *Sciatis*, quod pro fideli servitio quod Barones nostri Quinque Portuum hactenus Prædecessoribus nostris, Regibus Angliæ, & nobis nuper in exercitu nostro Walliæ impenderunt, & pro bono servitio nobis & hæredibus nostris, Regibus Angliæ, fideliter continuand. in futurum, Nos concessisse, & hanc cartam nostram confirmasse, pro nobis & hæredibus nostris, eisdem Baronibus nostris & hæredibus suis, Omnes	Words: *Edward*, by the Grace of God, King of *England*, Lord of *Ireland*, and Duke of *Acquitaine*, To all Archbishops, Bishops, Abbots, Priors, Earls', Barons, Justices, Sheriffs, Provosts, Ministers, and all his Bailiffs, and faithful Subjects, Greeting. *Know ye,* That for the faithful Service which our Barons of the *Cinque Ports* have hitherto done to our Predecessors, Kings of *England*, and to us, in our late Army of *Wales*ᶠ; and for their good Services ˢ to us and our Heirs, Kings of *England*, faithfully to be continued in Time to come, We have granted, and by this our Charter have confirmed, for us and our Heirs, to the same, our Barons and their Heirs ᵘ, All

ANNOTATIONS.

Time paid Contribution thereto, as the Members have done, and yet do to their Head Ports: These two Towns, of *Winchelsea* and *Rye*, in some old Writings, have been called Ports, but though of the same Liberties and Privileges every way, are none of the Five Ports, nor ever were, so as the old Verse,

Dover, Sandwicus, Ry, Rum, Prigmarventus,

mistook to take in *Rye*, and *Prigmarventus* (that is, *Winchelsea*) for Two of the Five, and leave out *Hasting* and *Hithe*, which, with *Dover*, *Sandwich*, and *Rommey*, were the Five Ports, and always have been so accompted by the best Authors, the Ports Men themselves, and by their Charters is sufficiently evident. And that *Rye* and *Winchelsea* pass by the Names of Ancient Towns. Of these *Rye* hath kept its ancient Situation, where it was first enfranchised : But *Winchelsea* hath had the Fate of *Hasting*, for the Sea hath wholly swallowed up the old Town, and above a Mile of Land more to the East of the present ancient Town of *Winchelsea*, and deserted the former Harbor of this, since the Plantation thereof at *Iham*, the Name of the Place before the Inhabitants of Old *Winchelsea* removed, as appears by some Charters of King *Edward* I. about the beginning of whose Reign the Sea prevailed against the old Town, and in the Sixteenth Year thereof was the total Submersion, as may be seen hereafter.

ʳ *Earls.* In this Charter of King *Edward* I. Dukes are omitted, but I reckon it a Failure of the Scribe, for I have seen some old Translations that had Dukes, as in the Charters of King *Edward* II, III, and LV. before mentioned.

ᶠ *Wales.* This was in the Fourth Year of his Reign, *Anno* 1276. For *Lhewellin* or *Leoline*, then Prince of *Wales*, having refused, upon Summons, to come to this King's Coronation (which was solemnized in *September*, 1274.) and after to his first Parliament, holden *April* 25, 1275. gave Occasion to the King (which where a Purpose is to quarrel, is easy to find) to enter *Wales* with a powerful Army, and waste it with Fire and Sword : So that *Leoline* (unable to resist) sues for Peace, which he obtains, but on such Conditions, as made his Principality little different from the Tenure of a Subject. And in his Fall shortly after, about the Eleventh Year of this King's Reign, fell to be united to the Crown of *England*.

ˢ *Service* is here principally to be understood of the Service of Shipping, of which hereafter, but not exclusively, that this is all the Service of the Ports.

ᵘ *Their Heirs.* Instead of, and tantamount to Successors ; for as Heirs, in their personal Capacity, inherit Lands and Possessions of their Ancestors : So Successors in a Body Politick or Corporate, enjoy the Rights and Privileges of their Predecessors.

ᵛ *Liber-*

CHARTERS.

nes libertates & quietancias suas, ita quod quieti sint de omni Theolonio, & de omni consuetudine, videlicet, ab omni Lastagio, Tallagio, Passagio, Carriagio, Rivagio, Aponsagio, & omni Wrec, & de tota venditione, achato, & reachato, suo per

TRANSLATION.

All their Liberties ᵛ and Freedoms ʷ, so that they may be ˣ quit ʸ of all Toll ᶻ, and of all Custom ᵃ; that is to say, of all Lastage ᵇ, Tallage ᶜ, Passage ᵈ, Carriage ᵉ, Rivage ᶠ, from Ponsage ᵍ, and all Wreck ʰ, and of all their Selling, Buying ⁱ, and rebuy-

ANNOTATIONS.

ᵛ *Liberties.* The Laws of *England* are sometime so called, because they make free : But here taken for the particular Liberties or Freedoms in their Corporations or Precincts.

ʷ *Freedoms,* Or Acquirments, for so the *Latin, Quietancias,* may be englished : That is, such Enjoyments as make Men free and quiet.

ˣ *May be,* equivalent in the Sense to *shall be,* here, and generally throughout the Charter of King *Edward* I.

ʸ *Quit,* or quiet and free.

ᶻ *Toll,* from the *Latin, Theolonium,* signifying the Duty or Payment of Monies for Goods, Wares or Merchandizes bought or sold, which have been landed or set upon Wharfs, or common Grounds.

ᵃ *Custom* here is not to be taken for the King's Custom received for Goods imported or exported, but understood here for a Toll, Tax or Charge, usually collected in Cities, Market Towns or Manors, in their Fairs or Markets, or other common selling Places, for the Sale of Goods, Wares or Merchandizes.

ᵇ *Lastage,* says *the Terms of the Law,* is to be quit of a certain Custom exacted in Fairs and Markets, for carrying of Things where a Man will ; paid, it seems, according to the Quantity, that is, by the Last, which is generally accompted two Tons Weight. By the Statute, *Anno* 21 *Richard* II. *cap.* 18. It seems to be used there for the Ballast of a Ship.

ᶜ *Tallage.* Under this Word the Lawyers include the Payments of Taxes, Tenths, Fifteenths, and Subsidies granted in Parliament. Supposed to come from the *French* Word *Tailler,* to cut : Because the Portions to be received are limited, or cut out of the Subjects Estates, and the Prerogative bounded from exacting more.

ᵈ *Passage.* Money required for passing to or fro, of Persons or Goods in common Shores, landing Places, or such like. Or freedom from the Tenants paying Money towards their Lords Passage by Land or Water.

ᵉ *Carriage.* Nothing to be demanded for Carriage of Goods through Forests, or other Ways leading through the King's Grounds. Or the Duty or Service of carrying Corn, Hay, &c. by the Tenure of their Lands, or Money paid in stead thereof. In some Copies it hath been written *Kayage* ; that is, the Duties paid for landing Goods upon, or shipping them off from common Kayes or Wharfs.

ᶠ *Rivage,* or Arrivage, is freedom for Persons with their Ships and Goods to arrive in Harbors, and unlade at common Keys or Wharfs, without payment of Money for their lying there.

ᵍ *Ponsage.* This, in some Translations, I have seen rendred *Poundage,* importing a Duty paid for Goods by the Pound Weight, or Pound Rate, or Poundage for impounding Cattel. But it seems to me to be the same with *Pontage,* afterward in the Charter of King *Edward* IV.

ʰ *Wreck,* is where any Ship or Vessel is driven ashore, and perishes, having no Person, or other Animal alive therein, called in *Latin, Wrecca,* from the *French, Varech.* Anciently the Wreck being made, the Goods that were in any part of the Ship (being brought to Land by the Waves) belonged to the King by his Prerogative, or to whom the King hath granted this Privilege. But if any Person, or Dog or Cat, escape alive out of the Ship, it is no Wreck ; but the Goods are the Owners still, so he claim them within a Year and a Day, as is plain in the Statute of *Westminster,* 1. cap. 4. *Anno* 3 *Edward* I. By *Wreck* in this Place is granted all Goods happening to be wrecked on the Coasts in any of the Precincts of the Ports ; and the rather inserted in this Charter, because the Ports ancient Prescription thereto seems to be barred by that Statute. See more under the Words *Wreck free* and *Warden.*

ⁱ *Selling, Buying.* Hereby is intended the Freedom for Ports Men to buy and sell openly in any Corporation, or privileged Place, without being bound to the Use of Brokers, or other Freemen of that Place. And that Goods so bought or sold shall not be seized as foreign Bought or foreign Sold. Thus I find these Words understood long since in a Case happening to some of *Rye* and *Winchelsea* in *London,* in the Eighth Year of King *Henry* VIII. The Report whereof is thus, according to the Copy I found thereof.

Memorandum, THAT in the Tyme of Sir *William Butler,* Knight, being Maior of *London,* and *Richard Broke,* Recorder, according to the Liberties of the *Cinque Ports,* it fortuned one *William Gaunte,* of the Town of *Winchelsey,* Draper, in *February,* the viith Yere of King *Henry* the viiith, to come unto *Blackwell Hall,* within the Citie of *London* aforesaid, and then

ANNOTATIONS.

then and there bought one Parcel of woollen Cloth, callid [a] Northerne *Carsie*, to the Value of xx *s.* and assone [b] as the said *William* that Cloth had bought, one certaine Officer unto the said Hall apperteining, whose Name is *A. B.* the said Cloth seasid [c], according to their Custome and Charter of *London*, as forren bought and forren sold, forfaited. Whereupon the same *William* approving [d] him to be a Freman of the Five Ports, required the said Cloth to him to be re-delivered, that notwithstanding could not be harde [e], ne of his said Cloth restored, onles [f] he must binde himselfe by his Writing obligatory to one *Nickolas Mattocke*, being Chamberlaine of *London*, in the Some [g] of xxvi *s.* viiid. that to be paid to th'use of the Citie of *London*, by a certaine Day, if he be that Day approved [h] not by the Chartour [i] of the Ports to be free in *London* in bieing [k] and selling. And further, within the said Yere and Time of Mayraltie of the said Sir *William Butler*, that is to wytt, in the Moneth of *Aprill*, into the said Hall, called *Blackwell* Hall, cometh *John Carpinter*, *Thomas Adams*, and *Robert Soggs*, of the Towne and Porte of *Rye* Drapers, and then and there bought they accordinglie to the Liberties of the *Five Ports* ii brod Clothes of the Colour of Vilett [l], to the Value of vj *l.* xiij *s.* iiij *d.* And in like manner, as sone [m] as they those said Clothes had bought, the foresaid supposid [n] Officer theis Clothes seasid [o], as forren bought and forren sold, forfaited. And though they shewid [p] them, not onely by substantial Profe [q], but also by Writing to be Freemen of the said *Cinque Ports*; that notwithstanding in any wise could not be excepted [r], ne taken; but utterly those said Clothes to th'use of the said Citie of *London* as forfaited, observid [s] and kept. Whereupon the said *William Gaunte*, and also the said *John Carpinter*, *Thomas Adams*, and *Robert Soggs*, as Freemen of the Ports, at the next general Court and Assemblie of Brotheryelde at *Romney* holden, that is to say, the *Twesday* [t] next after the Daie of Saint *Margaret*, the viijth Yere of K. *Henry* the viijth came before the honorable Company of Mayers, Bayliffs, and Jurats of the said *Cinque Ports* then and there congregate and assembled, complayning them of the Premisses, and the Circumstances thereof in every Behalfe, as the Matter appeared of trought [u]. Which said Maiors, Bayliffs, and Jurats then and there being present, the said Complaints benyngelie [w] respecting and favouring, for Reformation thereof, considering the Priviledges of the Ports, so by the Citie of *London* injured and wronged, with one Assent and Consent of the hole [x] honourable Court and Assemblie there, did chose and name *John Wastclyfe* of *Sandwich* for the East Ports, and *George Mercer* of *Rye* for the West Ports, Solicitours for the hole [y] Corporation of the *Five Ports*, that they at the next Terme to be holden at *Westminster* should be, for to sue to the Councel for the Reformation for all and singular the Premisses. Which said *John Westclife* and *George Mercer*, according to the Confidence and Trust by the said Corporation put in them, at the foresaid Terme appeared, that is to wytt, *Michaelmas* Terme, *Anno octavo* Henrici *octavi*. After their coming to the said Terme by Councell, first did they make search in the *Chauncerie*, there to have Sight and Knowledge of the Chartour [z] of *London*, to know and understand what Thing it was that made for them to th'use of *London* forren bought and forren sold, forfaited, and there found they theis Words:

- [a] *Called.*
- [b] *As soon.*
- [c] *Seized.*
- [d] *Proving.*
- [e] *Heard.*
- [f] *Unless.*
- [g] *Sum.*
- [h] *Proved.*
- [i] *Charter.*
- [k] *Buying.*
- [l] *Violet.*
- [m] *Soon.*
- [n] *Supposed.*
- [o] *Seized.*
- [p] *Shewed.*
- [q] *Proof.*
- [r] *Accepted.*
- [s] *Reserved.*
- [t] Tuesday.
- [u] *Truth.*
- [w] *Benignly*, or *kindly.*
- [x] *Whole.*
- [y] *Whole.*
- [z] *Charter.*

INspeximus insuper quasdam alias literas patentes ejusdem avi nostri, in hæc verba: Edwardus Dei gratia, Rex Angliæ, & Franciæ, & Dominus Hiberniæ, omnibus ad quos præsentes literæ pervenerint, salutem. Sciatis, &c. nos autem donationes, concessiones, confirmationes, innovocationes, & ordinationes, supradict. necnon omnes articulos & omnia alia & singula in omnibus cartis & literis supradictis content. & explanat. rata habentes & grata ea omnia & singula ad petitionem civium dictæ civitatis nostræ London, & ad instant. nostri Regni Angliæ, de assensu Prælatorum, Dominorum, magnatiæ & proff. [a] ejusdem Regni in præsenti Parliament. nostro nobis assistentium pro nobis & hæredibus nostris, quantum in nobis est, civibus civitat. prædictæ, & eorum hæredibus & successoribus civibus civitatis illius de gratia nostra speciali tenore præsentium concedimus & confirmavimus, sicut cartæ & literæ prædictæ rationabiliter testantur. Propterea volentes civibus civitatis prædictæ gratiam facere uberiorem, ad petitionem & instant. præd. de assensu prædict. concessimus eisdem civibus pro nobis & hæredibus nostris, & hac carta nostra confirmavimus, quod licet ipsi socies eorum prædecessores cives civitatis illius aliqua vel aliquibus libertatum, quietanciarum, concessionum, ordinationum, articulorum seu liberarum consuetudinum, aut aliarum in dictis cartis & literis contentarum aliquo casu emergent. hactenus plene usi non fuerint, ipsi tamen cives & eorum hæredes & successores cives civitatis illius supradictis libertatibus, quietanciis, concessionibus, ordinationibus, articulis & liberis consuetudinibus quibuscunque aliis in cartis & literis illis content. & eorum quibuslibet de cætero plene gaudeant & utantur imperpetuum, sine occasione vel impediment. nostri vel hæredium nostrorum, justic. escaetorum, vice comitum aut aliorum ballivorum seu ministrorum nostrorum quorumcunque. Insuper cum iidem cives per eandem petitionem suam in eodem parliament. nobis supplicaverint, quod licet ipsi, &c ||. eorum liberis consuetudinibus subscriptis hactenus ab antiquo usu fuerint & gavisa, donec paucis rotroact. temporibus inde restricti fuerint [b] minus juste parat. & inquietat. ut evident. petit. apparen. videlicet: Quod nullus extraneus a libertate civitatis prædictæ vendat vel emat ab altero extraneo aliqua Marchandiz. infra libertatem dictæ civitatis, sub forisfactura eorundem. Volumus tamen propter controversias in hac parte de cætero pacificand. parit. & tollendas, hoc ipsis civibus & eorum successoribus cartæ nostræ minime per expressa verba [*] roborare. Nos de assensu præd. volumus & concedimus, & hac carta nostra confirmavimus pro nobis & hæredibus nostris præfatis civibus & eorum successoribus, quod de cætero nullus extraneus mercator a libertate dictæ civitatis vendat aliquas marcandizas infra libertatem dictæ civitati. alteri extraneo mercatori, nec hujusmodi mercatori extraneus ab altero extraneo mercatore marcandizas hujusmodi emat sub forisfactura earundem, privilegiis ligeorum nostrorum acquitan. in omnibus semper salvis, dum tamen emptio & venditio hujusmodi tantum fiat inter mercatorem & mercatorem. Supplicant [c] nobis toti præfati cives per eandem petitionem suam, quod cum ipsi de nobis immediate teneant, & ab antiquo non tenebant, nec solebant intendentes de præceptis seu mandatis alicujus domini, constabularij, senescalli, marescalli, admiralli,

- [a] *I take this Word to be mistaken in the Copy.*
- || *The Clause after this* &c. *not perfect to* videlicet.
- [b] *Fuerant.*
- [*] *If* minime *be not intended* omnino, *this Clause seems imperfect.*
- [c] *Supplicant.*

D

cleric

ANNOTATIONS.

cleric. marcati, nec alterius officiarii seu miniſtri noſui & progenitor. noſtrorum prædictorum de nominibus & titulis noſtris, ſigilliſque noſtris publicis ſeu prænominatis, ſignatis, exceptis mandatis juſtic. juxta formam cartarum noſtrarum, dum ſuper ipſos aſſignand. &c. Volentes inſuper præfatis civibus gratiam facere amplior. conceſſimus pro nobis & hæredibus noſtris eiſdem civibus & eorum ſucceſſoribus, quod ſi forſan aliqua difficultas ſive ambiguitas ſuper aliquo articulo in cartis per nos vel progenitores noſtros eiſdem civibus fact. content. corrigi contigerit, ita quod articul. ille ad adverſos intellectus capi poſſet. Nos ſi & eum pro parte ipſorum civium, ſuper hoc requiſit. fuerimus per aviſament. conſilii noſtri tale inde interpretationem fier. faciemus, qualis fuerit bene fide ac majorum conſanam rationa ^d. Quare volumus & firmiter præcipimus pro nobis & hæredibus noſtris, quantum in nobis eſt, quod præfati cives & eorum ſucceſſores imperpetuum omnibus & ſingulis conceſſionibus prædictis modo & forma ſuperius expreſſat. gaudeant & utant. Nolumus tamen nec intentio noſtra ^e exiſtit, quod colore ſeu virtute alicujus conceſſionis ſeu reſponſionis per nos petitioni ipſorum civium in prædicto parliamento noſtro ut prædict. eſt factur. iidem cives vel eorum ſucceſſores de aliquibus ipſorum libertatibus antiquis approbatis conſuetudinibus civitatis illius aliqualiter reſtringant. Hiis teſtibus venerabilibus, patribus Si. archiepiſcopo Cantuar. totius Angliæ primate, A. archiepiſcopo Ebor. W. London. W. Wynton. D. Meneven. cancellar. noſtro, Tho. Eran. theſaurario noſtro, Tho. Cabill, & Ric. Sar. epiſcopo, Johanne Caſtell, & Legionis Duce Lancaſtri, Edvardo comit. Cantelor. avunculis noſtris chariſſimis, Edvardo de mortuo mari marchionis, Ricardo Arundel, Thoma de Belknapp, Warr. comitibus, Guidon de gran. camerario noſtro, Ricardo le Scroppe ſeneſcall, hoſpitii, Johanne de Prodham clerico privati ſigilli noſtri, & aliis. Dat. per manum noſtram apud Weſtm. quarto die Decembr. Anno R. Rs. primo.

^a *Ratʳri.*

^e *Noſtra.*

^f *Charter.*

That had, and ſeene in the Chartor ^f of the Five Ports, *Quod Barones de Quinque Portuum erunt liberi de tota venditione, achato, & reachato ſuo, per totam terram & poteſtatem Domini Regis.*

^g *Buying.*

Then by Councel was yt knowne and ſeene, that the ſaid Citie of *London* had their firſt Grant of their ſorren byenge ^g and ſellinge of King *Richard* the Second, the firſt Yeare of his Raigne. And the Five Ports had their Grant of the ſaid Words, *De tota venditione*, &c. by King *Edward* the Firſt. This well perceived and knowne, then the ſaid *John* and *George* made not only ſute unto the ſaid Maior of *London*, and Aldermen of the ſame ; but alſo to the Recorder of *London* for the Delivery of the ſaid Goods, ſo by ther ^h ſaid Officers ſeaſed ⁱ, and ſo be ^k ſeveral Times ſute to them made. And alſo the Councell learned of the Five Ports before them had, and not onlie the ſpecial Words of the Chartour ^l of *London*, but alſo the ſpecial Words of the Chartour ^l of the ſaid Five Ports before them diſtinctly redde ^m, and ſeene ; but alſo a certaine Recorde recorded in a Boke lienge ⁿ in the Chamber of *London*, called and named the Boke ^o of ♏, by the Time of one *James Andrew*, Maior of *London*, in the ii Hundreth and eighth Leaſe of the ſame Booke, the xliith. Yere of *Edward* the Third, ther ^p is plainelie reſited ^q, and maketh mention by wryte comaunded to the Maior of *London*, that in ſuch Caſe, upon Diſtreſſions ^r taken in *London* of the Free Barons of the Ports, that the ſaid Free Barons ſhuld ^f be free in bienge ^t and ſellinge in *London*. And that ther ^u Diſtreſſes taken ſhould be againe to them delivered. Which ſayd Wryte and Record folowith ^w in theis Words :

^h *Their.*
ⁱ *Seized.*
^k *By.*
^l *Charter.*
^m *Read.*
ⁿ *Book lying.*
^o *Book.*
^p *There.*
^q *Recited.*
^r *Diſtreſſes.*
^f *Should.*
^t *Buying.*
^u *Their.*
^w *Followeth.*

[*] *Here ſeems to want, &* or *noſtras to be put out.*

[†] *Per to be put out.*

Edwardus Dei gratia, &c. Majori & Vic. London, ſalutem. Cum inter cæteras libertates & quietancias, Baronibus noſtris Quinque Portuum, per cartas noſtras [*] progenitorum noſtrorum quondam Regum Angliæ conceſſas, conceſſum ſic eiſdem : Quod ipſi & eorum hæredes & ſucceſſores ſui ſint quieti de omni Theolonio, & omni conſuetudine, videlicet, ab omni Laſtagio, Kaiagio, Paſſagio, a Ponſagio, & omni Wrecke, & de tota venditione, achato, & reachato ſuo, per totam terram & poteſtatem noſtram, & etiam quod quieti ſint de omnibus rebus ſuis & de toto mercat. ſuo, & nos per † cartas illas per cartam noſtram confirmavimus. Inſuper conceſſimus pro nobis & hæred. noſtris, quod licet iidem Barones vel anteceſſores ſui aliqua vel aliquibus libert. aut quietanciis in dictis cartis content. plene uſi non fuerunt, iidem tamen Barones hæred. & ſucceſſores ſui libertatibus & quietanciis prædictis & eorum quibuſlibet futuris temporibus abſque occaſione vel impedimento noſtro vel hæredium noſtrorum ſeu miniſtrorum noſtrorum quorumcunque plene gaudeant & utant. imperpetuum prout in cartis & confirmatione noſtra prædicta planius continetur. Vobis præcipimus, quod omnes & ſingulos Barones noſtros Portuum prædictorum de hujuſmodi Theolonio, Laſtagio, Paſſagio, Kaiagio, Rivagio, ac de tota venditione, achato, & reachato, & de omnibus bonis & rebus ſuis ad dictam civitatem duct. & adducend. quiet. eſſe permittatis, juxta tenorem cartarum & confirmationum noſtrorum prædict. ipſos contra tenorem earundem non moleſtantes in aliqua ſeu gravantes, & diſtrictionem ſi quam eis ſeu

^{||} *Facias may be left out.*

|| Facias eorum alicui ea occaſione fieri feceritis, ſine dilatione relaxari facias || eiſdem. Teſte me ipſo apud Weſtm. primo die Maii Anno Regni Regis, xlij°.

[*] *Theſe were the Two that proſecuted them.*

Omnibus literis lect. & audit. conſiderat. eſt per præfat. Majorem & Alder. quod omnes Barones de Quinque Portubus ſint quieti de omni Theolonio & omni conſuetudine, &c. prout in dictis literis continetur. Et præfat. Nicholaus & Thomas [*] ulterius monſtraverint præfatis Major. & Aldermannis quod Willielmus Srikeman unus Vic. London recepit. de ipſis xiiii s. ſterl. pro exitu doliorum vini. & etiam quod Johannes de Wirhall, Coll. ipſorum Vic. de Billinſgate, exigit ipſis pro cuſtuma dictorum doliorum vini xiiii d. contra eorum libertates & conſuetudines, &c. Et ſuper hoc præcept. eſt præfato Vic. quod reliberet præfat. Nicholao & Thomæ prædict. xiiii s. quos ab eis ſic recipit ; & etiam quod præmoneant præfat. Johannem de Wirhall Ballivum ſuum prædict. quod nihil capiat ab eis, nec de aliquibus Baronibus Quinque Portuum pro Theolonio ſeu conſuet. ſed ipſos inde omnino quietos eſſe permittant, prout antiquitas ^y fieri conſueverunt, &c. Et memorandum, quod eædem literæ remaneant in ſaga prædicti Jacobi Andrew, Major. inter ſilacia de Anno regni Regis Edwardi tertii poſt conqueſt, xlij°.

^y *Ab ant.quo.*

a

CHARTERS.

per totam terram & potefta-
tom noftram, cum Socoa, &
Sacta, & Thol, & Them. Et
quod habeant Infangtheff. Et
quod fint Wreefree, & Witt-
free, Laftagefree, & Love-
cope-

TRANSLATION.

Rebuyliig, throughout all our
Land and Dominion [k]; with Soc [l],
and Sac [m], and Thol [n], and
Them [o]. And that they may have
Infangtheff [p]. And that they
may be Wreckfree [q], and Witfree [r], Laftagefree [s], and Love-
cope-

ANNOTATIONS.

In Confideration of the faid Writte [a], and alfo confidering, that the faid Grant of the faid [a] *Writ.* Cinque Ports to be elder than the Grant of the Chartour [a] of London, it was ordered by the faids *Charter.* William Baxter, Maior of London, Aldermen, and Recorder, That the faid Diftreffes to the faid John and George fhould be delivered. Upon which Delaie [b] in the Vigil of Al Saints, the viijth [b] *Delay being* of the Raigne of King Henry the Eight, the faid John and George came to the faid Recorder, *made.* then in his Dwelling Place in London being, and then and ther fhewid [c] unto him the faid De- [c] *fhewed.* laies, requiring him that they might be of ther [d] faid Bufynes difpatchid. Which faid Record- [d] *their.* er then wrote unto the faid Mr. Baxter his Letter in this wife, which remayneth of Re- cord, &c.

In this Report there are many literal Imperfections, fome of which are amended in the Mar- gin, which I thought better than to alter the Text it felf. The other Imperfections and Irre- gularities in the Latin Quotations may be alfo paffed over charitably. In Subftance it ferves to fhew, what it is here alledged for. And in effect, in another Place of the Records of the Town of Rye, in a fhort Memorandum, I found the fame obferved thus:

Memorandum, THE Five Ports were infranchefid in the Time of King Edward the Confeffor, before the Conqueft, and in the Time of King Edward the Firft after the Conqueft, the Ports had their Charter of Confirmation, by which they be free, de tota venditiones, achate, & reachate, in the Sixth Year of his Raigne, viz. Anno Dom. 1278. And the Citie of London had their Charter of forrein bought and forrein fold, the Firft Yeare of King Richard the Second, viz. Anno Dom. 1377. And in the Charter of the Ports is elder then the Charter of London, Ninety and Nine Years and more.

[k] *Dominion,* the Word in Latin is Potwr, but ferves well enough in the Senfe tranflated, feeing where the King hath no Power to oblige Obedience, he can expect little Dominion or Lordfhip, or fuch as will be of fhort continuance.

[l] *Soc,* fometime Sock, and Sok, is taken for Suit of Men in their Courts, according to the Cuftom of the Realm; alfo, becaufe Soc in old French for a Plough or the Coulter, or Share thereof, whence came Socage, the Service of the Plough, being an old Tenure of Land held of fome Lord by fervice of Plowing, or fuch like hufbandry Labour, now changed into a certain Rent payable inftead thereof. Some have been ready to think this Word did free whatever Lands within the Ports the Ports Men held of the Crown in Capite, or otherwife, they fhould afterward hold in free and common Socage. But I rather incline to the firft Senfe.

[m] *Sac,* both a Plea and Correction of Trefpafs of Men in their Courts, and all Fines and Forfeitures for the fame. Some fay it is equivalent to the French Achefon, and is ufed for Sick, or Hurt, and fo may be for Power to impote and receive Fines for Fighting, Wounding, fhed- ding of Blood, &c. and to redrefs Affraies and Affaults by punifhing the Offenders.

[n] *Thol.* Some fay, it is to be free of all Homage to any Lord, but to their Sovereign Lord the King; others take it for Toll for Goods bought in a Fair, Market, &c.

[o] *Them.* That is, to have the Generation of all your Villains, or Bond-fervants, with their Suits and Cattle, wherefoever they fhall be found in England. I fuppofe it fhould be wrote Theme, for the Saxon Theme and Theame fignify, The Power Lords have over their Villains or Natives with their Lands and Goods.

[p] *Infangtheff.* To judge in their Courts Thieves or Felons taken within their Precincts, for Fang in the Saxon and Dutch Tongues fignifieth to take or catch.

[q] *Wreckfree.* Whereas by Wreck before, the Ports Men were to have the Benefit of Wrecks happening on their Coafts; by this Word Wreckfree, is intended they fhall lofe nothing as feizable, if their own Goods happen to be wrecked.

[r] *Witfree.* Some have taken this as much as Ideotfree, that none of the Ports fhould be begged for Fools. But I rather conclude Witfree to be Amerciamentfree, that is, being amerced in any Court they fhall pay nothing for it, but have it freely. Wit is frequently ufed in the Saxon Tongue, as Bloodwit, an Amerciament for fhedding Blood. Fledwit, an Amer- ciament paid by an out-lawed Fugitive, when his Outlawry is reverfed on his Return. So Flemefwit, for the Cattel, or Amerciaments of your Man or Fugitive, or the Freedom from fuch Amerciaments. And many fuch others.

[s] *Laftagefree.* See before, Laftage.

CHARTERS.   TRANSLATION.

copefree. Et quod habeant Den, & Strond, apud magnam Jernemouth, secundum quod continetur in ordinatione per nos inde facta & perpetuo observand. Et

copefree [1]. And that they may have Den [2], and Strond [3], at Great *Tarmouth* [4], according to that which *is* contained in the Ordinance [5] thereof by us made, and perpetually to be observed. And

ANNOTATIONS.

[1] *Love-copefree.* The *Saxon* Word *Cope*, in *Low Dutch* still *Kope* or *Koope*, for Trade or Merchandising, makes this as much as to trade freely for Love. So that by no kind of Monopoly, Patent, or Company, or Society of Traders, or Merchants, the Ports Men be hindered from Merchandising : but freely and for Love be permitted to Trade and Traffick, even by such Company of Merchants, whenever it shall happen their Concerns lie together.

[2] *Den.* An old Word used for a Valley or Low Place, and, here, is The Liberty the Ports Fishermen shall have to beet or mend, and to dry their Nets at *Great Tarmouth*, upon Marsh Lands there, yet called *The Dennes*, during all the Herring Season.

[3] *Strond*, used commonly for a Shore or Landing Place, here taken for the Liberty the Fishermen have to come to the Key at *Great Tarmouth*, and deliver their Herrings freely all the fishing Season.

[4] *Great Tarmouth*, a Town in *Norfolk* called *Great*, to difference it from *Tarmouth* in the Isle of Wight. In *Latin*, *Yernmutha*, q. f. The Mouth of the River *Irne*, or *Yerne*, which runs out into the Sea there, beautified with a spacious Church, having an high Spire, built, as *Weever* in his *Funeral Monuments*, p. 862. faith, by *Herbert*, first Bishop of *Norwich*, in the Reign of *William Rufus*, well furnished with goodly Buildings, and so populous in the Time of King *Edward* III. that in the Twenty third Year of his Reign, as this Author tells us (by a Chronological Table hung up in the Church was witnessed) by a grievous Plague there, in the Compass of one Year, were seven Thousand and Fifty two Persons sent to the Grave. Hither resort the Fishermen of the Ports, and other Sea Towns, every Year in the fishing Season, for Herrings, who by a wonderful and rare Providence having their constant Course once a Year round this Island, about the autumnal Equinox begin to keep their Quarters on these Coasts. And to repress and prevent Disorders arising among the Multitude upon the Sale and Delivery of the Herrings brought ashore there, for want of a settled Government in that Town, or, as hereafter noted, for want of a Town built ; the Ports used to send thither yearly certain Men as their Bailiffs, that during the Time of this Herring Fair they might abide there and govern all that fishing Season, which hereafter will more plainly appear. But the fishing Trade continuing and proving profitable, once settled, quickly is supposed to have built a Town there , or, if built before, so to inrich it, as to procure thereto a Government by some Portreeve, or Provost and Bailiffs, which it had in the Time of King *Edward* I. between whom and the Ports Bailiffs Contests did often arise. These endeavouring to keep their ancient Jurisdictions, Rights and Privileges, and the other to wrest them out of their Hands, as more plainly may appear hereafter. So that oftentimes the Ports have complained to their Sovereigns for Redress and Remedy, and yet sometimes been Sufferers by the Outrage and Insolencies of the People and their Head Officers there, so as one of the Ports Bailiffs doing his Office there, was by one of their Bailiffs killed, for which he as deservedly was hanged, and that Town, as a Badge of such an infamous Fact, yet pays a certain Number of Herrings yearly to *Windsor* Castle (as I have heard) or a Sum of Money instead thereof.

[5] *Ordinance.* This Ordinance was made about a Year before this Charter, and is sometime called *The Dite*, from the *French* Word used therein, in which Language it was wrote, signifying as much as *Dictum* in *Latin*, a *Saying* or *Edict* ; and is, as it were, an Award of the King between the Ports and *Tarmouth*, and no more than a Confirmation to the Ports of what they then

* *And also may* claimed as due, and of ancient Right belonging to them long before *, as appeareth by the Ordinance it self.
Charter of K.
John to Hastings, Cart. 7. Joh. *m.* 11. *and Charter of King* Henry III. *to* Romney, *about the Twenty second Year of his Reign.*

Edward,

ANNOTATIONS.

In another Copy.

Edward, *par la grace de Dieu, Roy Denglitere, Seign. Dyrland, & Duk Daquitaigne, a touz* [a] *que ceft* [b] *lettres voiont ou orrount, falutz. Nous fafouns* [c] *affavoir, que come mo' pur bien de peas, & pur amour entr. noz Barons de Portez & mz. gentz de Yernemuth* [d] *noyer* [e], *& meynten, avoun.* [f] *fur plufowrs conteikes, & difcordes, moves* [e] *entre eux, pronouncye noftre dit, noftre volunt. & noftre comaundement, lan de noftre Regn.* V. *en la fourme que enfuyte.*

In *Englifh* thus:
Edward, *by the Grace of God, King of* England, Lord of Ireland, *and Duke of* Acquitaine, To all which thefe Letters fhall fee or heare, Greeting. We give you Knowledge, That *for the good of Peace* [a], *and for Love, between our* [b] *Barons of the Ports, and our People* [c] *of* Yar*mouth to be nourifhed and* [d] *maintained, upon* [e] *Or Men. many Controverfies and Difcords* [f] *moved be-* [e] *tween them, We have pronounced our Dite,* [b] *our Will and our Comandment, in the Fifth Year of our Reigne, in the Forme which followeth.*

[a] *Graut.*
[b] *Prefentz.*
[c] *Fefuns.*
[d] *Gernemewe.*
[e] *Nowrir.*
[f] *Euffions.*
[e] *Mewtz.*

For good & Peace.
For good God, King of Ireland, and Peace.
Difcords.
of Great & Or Men.

[h] *Peet.*
[i] *Suggetz.*

E N le nom del Pier, del Fitz, & del Seint Efpyrit, pur bien du *pece* [h], & pur amour entre noz *fubgetz* [i] meinten. Nous, E. par la grace de Dieu, Roy Denglitere, Seign'. Dyrland, & Duc Daquitaigne, fur toutz trefpaffes & conteikes, mentz entr. noz Barons de Portz, & noz gentz de Graunt Yernemuth [k], pour lours Articles a noz bailles, diouns noftre Dit, en la fourme foutz efcript, ceft aflav.

I N the Name of the Father, the Sonne [d], and [d] *Of the San* the Holy Ghoft, for the good of Peace [e], *and of the Holy* and for Love between our Subjects to be Gloft. maintened: We *Edward*, by the Grace of [e] *For good* God, King of *England*, Lord of *Ireland*, and Peace. Duke of *Acquitaine*, upon all the Trefpaffes [f] *Difcords.* and Controverfies [f] moved between our Ba- rons of the Ports and our People [c] of *Great* [c] *Or Men.* *Tarmouth*, for their Articles to us given, We fay our Dite, in the Forme under written, that is to fay [†], [†] *Or to wit.*

[k] *Gernemewe.*

[l] *En droit du primier article.lez* [m] *Nous.*
[n] *Gernemewe.*
[o] *Ayent leur.*
[p] *Sanfmull.*
[q] *Manner.*
[q] *As above.*
[r] *Reitz.*

Del [l] article de Strande & Den, lez que ux [m] Barons dez Portz demaundent a Yernemuth [n], nous diouns & voillouns qu'ils ayount [o] *lour* eyfements en Strande & Den, faunz [p] appropriement del foil, & nomement en temps de la faire, faunz null. [q] cuftume don. Et auxi voillouns, que ceux de la vile de Yernemuth [q] voydent Den & Strand, des voiles nyefs & de merym, la ou ils deyount aryver & lour *rees* [r] feecher, fo that it be not *ofrive.* fount en fefauntz, & maftes, fur que oy lein poet feecher.

Of [g] the Article of Strand and Den, the [g] *Concerning.* which the Barons of the Ports claime [h] at *Tar-* [h] *Demand.* *mouth*, we fay and will, that they have their Eafements in Strand and Den without Appro- [i] *Or appropria-* prement [i] of Soile; and namely, in Time of the *ting it to other* Faire, without any Cuftome to be given. And alfo We will, That thofe of the Towne *Ufes.* of *Tarmouth* voide Den and Strand of old Ships and Timber, where as they ought [k] to [k] *Should ar-* arrive and dry their Nets, fo that it be not *ofrive.* Ships which are building [l], and Mafts, upon [l] *Making.* which they may dry.

[s] *Here and above volens.*
[t] *Ouftre.*
[v] *Fentures.*
[v] *Ils ont.*
[u] *Ore leues & ceux molins foient leues.*
[w] *Deviont.*
[x] *Reitz.*
[y] *Dions & vo-ftre Provoft.*
[z] *Seifes.*
[a] *Gernemewe.*
[b] *Que.*
[c] *As above.*

Et voillomes [s], que ceux de la vile de Yernemuth ne leveynt *ontre* [t] fink molynes *ventres* [t] fur la Denne, plus. Que *ne* [v] *font oza* [v] *libertes* a meyndar, damages & nunfaunce del Denne, & de ceux que *demont* [w] la lour *rees* [x] feecher. Et *voillomes* & diouns [y], que noz Barons dez Portes eyont & joiffent pefiblement lours rentz dount ils fount *feyfits* [z] en la vile de Yernemuth [a], & fi afcun. ent. lou. deforce par no-ftre Provoft, & noz Baill. de Yernemuth lou. foient en eide, a cett. rent lev folonc droit [b] & ley. Et fi noz Barons des Portes entendent avoir droit [b] en altres lour foit deforces, par noz gentz de Yern. [c] voillomes que ils eyent lou. recoverer par brefz, & par la ley, & lez cuftumes ufes en la ville.

And We will, That thofe of the Towne of *Tarmouth* do not reare more then [†] Five [†] *One Copy hath* Wind Mills upon the Dennes. And thofe *is, Our five* which they have liberty to arreare to be to *Mills more then* the leaft Damage and Annoyance of the Dennes, *they have av-* and of thofe which fhould dry their Nets. *reared to the*
And We will and fay, That our Barons of *leaft, &c.* the Ports have and enjoy peaceably their Rents, of which they be feifed in the Towne of *Tarmouth*. And if any thereof do them de-force, then our Provoft and our Bailiffes of *Tar-mouth* be to them helping, the faid Rents to levy according to Right and Law. And if our Barons of the Ports intend to have Right in others, whereof they may be deforced by our People [m] of *Tarmouth*, we will that they [m] *Men.* have their Recovery by Writs, and by the Law and Cuftomes ufed in the faid Towne.

[d] *As above.*
[e] *Pees.*
[f] *Dions & vo-lons.*
[g] *De Gernem.*
[h] *Fayfant.*

Et de ceo que de noz Barons dez Portes demaundent a Yern. [d] reall juftice, & la garde de noftre *peas* [e], en temps de la faire durant par xl jours, diouns [f] & *voillomes* que ils cient la garde de noftre peas fefauntz, reall ju-ftice, enfemblement ou noftre Provoft [g], en ceft fourm que durant la faire ils eyent quattre ferjan-tes, dount lune port noftre banere, lautie cor-nant un corn, pur la gent affembler pur mientz eftr. oyetz, & lez deux portauntz verges pur noftre pes garder. & ceftes offices *facent* [h] a chivall fils voilent.

And of [n] that which of our Barons of the [n] *Concerning.* Ports is demanded [o] to have at *Tarmouth* Roy- [o] *Claimed.* al Juftice, and the keeping of our Peace, in [p] [p] *This* [and] *is* and [p] during the Time of the Faire by Forty *inferted.* Days, We fay and will, That they have the Keeping of our Peace, [q] and doing Royal Ju- [q] *And is here* ftice, together with our Provoft [†] of *Tarmouth added.* in this Forme, that during the Faire, they [†] *Of Yarmouth* fhall have [q] Foure Serjeants, whereof one to [q] *in another* beare our Banner, another to blow an Horne, *Copy.* for to affemble the People for Proclamation [q] *May have.* to be heard the better; and the other Two 'Proclamation to beare Rods for to keepe our Peace. And *is added, being* thefe Offices they may do on Horfback if they *intended in the* will. *Dite.*

[i] *Volons & di-ons.*
[k] *Oue.*
[l] *As before.*
[n] *Purron.*

Et *voillomes* [i] & diouns, que lour. Barons des Portes od [k] noftre Provoft de Yern. [l] fe-cent lez attachements & pledent lez plees, & trient lez pleintz que ux *purent* [n] eftr. pledz durant la faire, folonc la ley-marchaunde. &

And We will and fay, That the Barons of the Ports, with our Provoft of *Tarmouth*, make [r] the Attachments, and plead the Pleas, [r] *Do.* and determine the Plaints, which may be pleaded during the Faire, according to the

E Law-

ANNOTATIONS.

ⁿ *En la temp de.*

& lez amercymentz & profitz dez gens dez Portz demorgent a noz Barons dez Ports du*rant*ⁿ la faire avauntdit & lez profitz & amercementz de toutz altres que dez Portes demorgent a noz levez par noz Baill. de Yern.

^o *Volont.*
^p *Noz.*
^q *Here Noz is voft omitted.*
^r *Oue.*
^s *De Gernem.*
^t *As before.*
^u *Avienue.*

Et *voillomus*^o, que lez^p Bayliffes de noz^q Barons dez Ports enfemblement od^r noftre Pro-moutb^s durant la faire avaundite. Et fils *avient*^t que afcun. prifon. foit prife por fi grief trefpas, que per eaux ne puiffe en temps de la faire eftr. tries per la ley-marchaunde, ne les prifons delivere demorge en noftre prifon a Yern. jenfqes a la venu de noz juftices.

^t *A.*

Et en droit dez deners queux noz Barons dez Portz demaundont *as*^t fieux fuften. voillomes & dioun. que lez Baill. dez Barons dez Portz referveyvent & eyent lez deux den^{rs}. dez maiftres dez nyefz cuftomes que ux fount appelle fier pens as fieux fuften. a lez lieux accuftomez pur fuerte de lay ryvage dez nyefz, untaunt taunt come ils voldront les fieux fuften. Et fi^v avient que ils defaillent^t lez^u fuftenaunce dez fieux *fufditz.*^w lift. a noftre Provoft de Yar-mouth^x lez ditz den^{rs}.refceyvere & les fieux fu-ften. en la fourme *fufdit*^y.

^v *Sil.*
^u *En la.*
^w *Avauditz.*
^x *Gernemewe.*
^y *Avandit.*

^z *Volons & di-ons.*
^a *Deffore.*
^b *Preignont.*
^c *De Gerne-mewe.*

En droit de ceo que noz Barons dez Portz, dient que eux foleyent prendr. de cheft. nyef. cuftum. quater deners, *voillomus*^z & dioun, pur byen de la pees, que *defore*^a en avaunt ils *prenfuent*^b dan en an. vj l. de fterlyng par la mayne noftre Provoft^c, al parter de la faire, de la cuftum. dez quatre deneres avaunt ditz.

^d *Diftreindre.*
^e *Deners dions & volons.*
^f *Leur.*
^g *As before.*

En droit de ceo que nous Barons dez Portz, dient que ils folient prendr.^d diftr. en mier & deners dions en tere pur lou. *depites*^e, diouns & voillomus que lez^f Baill. nulz diftreffes ne facent faunz noftre Baill. de Yern.^g fil ne foit fur les gentz dez Portz. Et cele diftreffe foit fi refonable, folonc la ley-merchaunde par qui la faire ne fe parde neupaire.

^h *Plaintz.*

En droit de ceo que noz Barons des Portz fe fon *plaines*^h que la faire eft enpaire & lez merchauntz enpoveritz & la commune de la ter-re endamag. par lez gardes que nous gentz de Yernemuthⁱ *mettont*^k fur lez niefs & lez merchauntz & lour merchaundife, *voillomus*^l & dioun que nul tiell. garde foit mys *defore*^m en avaunt par qui lez ditz merchantz ne puiffent fraunchment vendr. lour biens par lour mayns communement la ou ils voldront, paiauntz lez^m cuftumes dues.

ⁱ *Gernemewe.*
^k *Mettont.*
^l *Volons & di-ons.*
^m *Deffore.*

^m *Leur.*

En droit de menftreux & de femmes de vie, *dioune*ⁿ & voillonus, que noz Barons de Portes, ne ceux de Tern.^o ryens ne *prement*^p.

ⁿ *Dions & vo-lons.*
^o *Gernemewe.*
^p *Preignont.*

En droit de Feneftrage & *Stallage*^q, voil-lomes & diomes, que noz Barons des Portes, rien ne *prement*^r *defore*^s en avaunt.

^q *Eftallage vo-lons & dions.*
^r *Preignont.*
^s *Deffore.*
^t *Avant ditz volons.*

Et toutz ceftz chofes *fufditz*^t, voillomes & comaundomus que ils foient ferment tenuz de lune parte & daltr. fur greve forfaiture a noz voluntz. En tefmoigne de quel chofe a ceft. efcript. avoun. mys noftre feall, don. a Weftm. le xxiie. jour de May lan. de noftre Regn. quinte.

Law-Merchant. And the Amerciaments and Profits of the People^u of the Ports, to re-maine^t to our Barons of the Ports, during^t the Faire aforefaid. And the Profits and Amerciaments of all others then || of the Ports || to us, to be levied by our Bai-liffs of *Tarmouth*.

^u *Or Men.*
^t *Si all remain.*
|| *Which are not to remaine.*
^u *Shall remain.*

And We will, That the Bailiffes of the Ports of the Ports, together with our Provoft^u of *Tarmouth*, have the Keeping of our Prifon^u of *Tarmouth* during the Faire aforefaid. And if it fhall happen, that any Perfon^w be taken for fo grievous^x Trefpas, that by them may^x not in the Time of the Faire by Law-Mer-chant be determined, nor the Prifon deliver-ed, he fhall remaine in our Prifon at *Tarmouth* untill the comming of our Juftices.

^u *Of Yarmouth is in another.*
^u *Copy here also.*
^w *Prifoner.*
^x *Great.*

And in right of the Monies^u which our Barons of the Ports demand for fuftaining the Fires, We will and fay, That the Bailiffes of the Barons of the Ports receive, and have the Two Pence of the Mafters of Ships accuftom-ed^y, which are called Fire Pence, for fuftain-ing the Fires at the Places accuftomed, for Se-curitie of the Arrivall of Ships by Night, fo long as they fhall maintaine^z the Fires. And^z if it fhall happen that they fhall faile in the Suftentation of the Fires aforefaid, it fhall^a be^a lawfull to our Provoft of *Tarmouth* to receive the faid Pence^b, and fufteine the Fires in the^b Forme aforefaid.

^u *Or Pence.*
^y *Cuftomable.*
^z *will fuftain.*
^a *It may.*
^b *Monies.*

In right of that which our Barons of the Ports fay, that they were wont to take of every Ship the Cuftome^c of Four Pence, We^c will and fay, for the Good of Peace^d, That from henceforth they take from Yeare to Yeare fix Pounds Sterling, by the Hand of our Provoft^e of *Tarmouth*, at departing of the^e Faire, for the Cuftome of the Foure Pence aforefaid.

^c *Cuftomably.*
^d *For good Peace.*
^e *Of Yarmouth.*
fo in the other Copy.

In right of that which our Barons of the Ports fay, that they were wont to take Di-ftreffe in Sea and Land for their Duties, We fay and will, That the Bailiffes make no Diftreffes without our Bailiffes of *Tarmouth*, if it be not of the People † of the Ports; and † that the Diftreffe be fo reafonable, according to the Law-Merchant, by which the Faire be not deftroyed nor impaired.

† *Or Men.*

In right of that which our Barons of the Ports have complained, that the Faire is im-paired, and the Merchants impoverifhed, and the Commonalty^e of the Land endamaged,^e by the Guards which our People || of *Tarmouth* put upon Ships, and the Merchants and their Merchandife, We will and fay, That no fuch Guarde be put from henceforth, by which the faid Merchants may not freely fell their Goods by their owne Hands commonly where they will, paying the Cuftomes due.

^e *Commons.*
|| *Or Men.*

In right of Minftrells, and Women of Mif-living^f, We fay and will, That our Ba-rons of the Ports, nor thofe of *Tarmouth*, take nothing.

^f *Light Behavi-our.*

In right of Feneftrage and Scallage, We will and fay, That our Barons of the Ports nothing take from henceforth.

And all thefe Things aforefaid, We will and command, That they be firmly holden of the one Part, and the other, upon a grievous Forfeiture at our Will. In witnefs of which Thing^u, to this Writing we have put our^u Seale. Given at *Weftminfter* the Twentie Day of *May*, the Year of our Reign the Fifth.

^u *Or whereof.*

Notwith-

ANNOTATIONS.

Notwithstanding this Ordinance, and after this Charter, whereby it is expressed perpetually to be observed, fresh Differences arise between the Ports Men and People of *Yarmouth*, and Disorders growing high thereupon, both Parts refer themselves to the Arbitrement of this King in the Thirty third Year of his Reign, who thereupon makes another Ordinance, sometime called, Another Composition of their Franchises of the Fair at *Yarmouth*, as followeth, with the Translation

<table>
<tr><td></td><td>In English.</td></tr>
</table>

ET come puis nostre ordinaunce & nostre comaundment susdit, eyent ascunes discordes, riotes, & combatles [a], estee de rechief, moves, & rewes [b] entre noz ditz Barons, & noz gentz Ternemouth [c], dount eux dune parte, & d'altr, pur eux, & pur chest deux, & pur lour heyres, mys haut & bas, en nostre dit & en nostre ordinaunce pur pees faire, & fear ten. entr. eux de toutz lez contakeres [e], riotes, & discordez, suffisit [f] issint que une fokz, & plusoures foitz en puissoms [g] dire, ceo que noz byen [h] sembleroit & resceyoer [i] & dire a nostre volunt. Nous lez ditz surmises d'une parte, & d'autre, reseieux pur bon. accord, & pensible le mientz norir entr. eux assignames certen. gentz de nostre councell, pur tret. ouesque eux amyablement de la pees, & pur eux men. a ceo que bon. accord soit entre eux par assent. Par qui entre [k] ascunes treta. ewes ouesque eux & [l] noz ditz gentz de nostre councell a la syn. noz ditz Barons dez Portz, & noz gentz de Tern. [m] accorderont, sil noz plust & accordes se soverient devaunt noz a ceo que noz ditz Barons eyent ent. ment lours fraunchises en [o] lours droitours en la vile de Tern. [p] solone ceo que il est contenuz en nostre dit, & en nostre ordinaunce de susdit.

[a] *Contekes.*
[b] *Eux.*
[c] *Here and afterward, in nother Copy it is Germemouth.*
[d] *Submiz. haute & base.*
[e] *Contekes.*
[f] *Avauntdit.*
[g] *Empensons.*
[h] *Bon.*
[i] *Reteuir.*
[k] *Apres.*
[l] *Par.*
[m] *Germemeue, se accorderont.*
[n] *Plaist.*
[o] *En toutz. leur.*
[p] *As above.*

AND whereas after our Ordinance and Commandment aforesaid, there have beene certaine Discords, Riots, and Contests [b], revived [c], moved, and had betweene our said Barons, and our People [l] of *Yarmouth*, whereof they of the one part, and of the other for them, and for either of them, and for their Heires, have submitted [f] High and Low, to our Saying and [f] Ordinance, for Peace to be made [h], and being made, to be held [i] betweene them, of all the Contests [k], Riots, and Discords aforesaid, so that one Time, and many Times, we may say that [p] which shall seem [l] good to us, and to accept and say what we will: We the said Surmises of the one Part and of the other having received [n] for good Accord and Peace [o], the better to nourish betweene [p] them, have assigned certain Men of our Councel for to treat with them amicably [f] for Peace, and to move them, that good Accord may be betweene them by their [f] Assent. By which, after certaine Treaties had with them, and our said Men of our Councel, to that end [t], our said Barons of the Ports, and our People [u] of *Yarmouth* did accord, if it pleased us, and accorded [w] they be before us, so that our said Barons [x] shall have entirely their Franchises and their Rights in the Towne of *Yarmouth*, according to that which is conteined in our Dite, and in our Ordinance aforesaid.

[a / ?] *Our Commaundment.*
[b] *Controversies.*
[c] *Grown to Head.*
[l] *Men.*
[f] *Put themselves.*
[l] *And to one.*
[h] *To make.*
[i] *To hold.*
[p] *Controversies.*
[l] *Pleaseth us.*
[m] *Reserve and say at our will.*
[n] *Heard.*
[o] *Peaceability.*
[o] *Among.*
[f] *Friendly concerning Peace.*
[f] *Their is added.*
[t] *At the End, of Men.*
[w] *Agreed.*
[x] *May have wholly.*

Et que ceo que serra trove purpris sur la Strand & Denne, en la dit vill. de Yern. a nusfance dez ditz Barons dez Portz, soient vewes par gens que ux noz envoirons & pleigement redresses & remys en estate du [r], solone la fourme de nostre ordynaunce suisdit. Et que toutz maneres de trespas, outrages, injuries, & damages que els ou que ils soient, en personez, ou en biens, en que cunq; [f] man. & en quel lieu qu'ils ount esces [f] faitz. entr. eux tanque a tierce jour de cest mois de Marz proch. passe, soient de tout au tout remys, relesses & pardonesses d'une parte & d'altre taunt come en eux est. Et que desore [s] soit entr. eux bones amours, & bone pees, ferme & estable, perpetuelment a durer.

[q] *As above.*
[r] *Deuot.*
[f] *Queque.*
[f] *Estre.*
[x] *Defore.*

And that of that which shall be found purpresture upon the Strand and Denne in the said Towne of *Yarmouth*, to the Nusance [y] of the said Barons of the Ports, there may be View by Men which we shall send, and fully redressed and remitted in Estate [a], according to the Forme of our Ordinance aforesaid. And that all Manner of Trespasse, Outrages, Injuries, and Dammages whatsoever, it, or they be, in Persons or in Goods, in whatsoever Manner, and in what Place soever they have beene done betweene them, untill the third Day of the Month of *March* last past, be in all, and to [‡] all, remised, released, [‡] and pardoned, of the one Part and of the other, as much as in them is. And that after this there be betweene them good Love and good Peace firm and stable perpetually to endure.

[y] *Annoyance.*
[a] *Estate thereto. of, or due Sort.*
[‡] *In all Things for ever.*

Et pur ceo que ils noz ount pries, que il noz pleza le maner & la seurte ordyner, nous iour ditz accordes & assentz acceptaunz & agreantz, Si [t] voillomes [u] dioums & comaundomes que bon amour, & ferme pees, soit desore [v] entre eux, & chest deux, & lo[n]. heyres, entier & en mier, perpetuelment a dure. Et que nostre dit, & nostre ordeignaunce suisdit soient, tenutz, meintenutz, & gardes desore [w], en avaunt en sez [x] pointz, d'une partie, & d'autr. saunz countrevein.

[t] *Si is not in the other Copy.*
[u] *Volons dions.*
[v] *Defore.*
[w] *Defore.*
[x] *Toutz sez.*

And forasmuch as they have prayed us, that it may please us to ordaine the Manner and Suretie [a], We their said Accords and Assents accepting and agreeing to, We will, say, and command, That good Love and firm Peace be from henceforth betweene them and every [u] of them, and their Heires, on Land and Sea perpetually to endure. And that our Dite and Ordinance aforesaid be holden, maintened, and kept from henceforth, in the Points thereof, of the one Part, and of the other, without contradiction [b].

[a] *Assurance thereof.*
[u] *Or each of them.*
[b] *Opposition.*

Et sil adveygne qu'eux ount la real justice, la gard de nostre pees en la vile de Tern. [y] all suite dez pleintyfs de trespas faite par qui sil soit, & envers qui quil soit, en temps du faire, ou en altre, la quel faire, soit a la Graunt

[y] *As above.*

And if it happen that they that have Royal Justice, and the keeping of our Peace in the Town of *Yarmouth*, at the Suite of the Plaintiffs, of Trespas done, by whom, and against whom it be, in the Time of the Faire, or other-

ANNOTATIONS.

Graunt Yern.[a] entirement & nemy aillours ‡ facent dues amendes & *haſtynes*[a] juſtice, ſolonc la ley, & lez uſages de cell. parties. Et ſi pleint a noz veigne, eient lez parties brefs de noſtre Chauncellerye a faire ven. lez Baill. en qui la defaute ſerra aſſign. a reſpoundr. ſur ceo devaunt noz & noz heyres Roys Dengl. & ſi de ceo ſoient attaintz pardront la fraunchiſe de *la*[b] juſtice.

[a] *Gernemewe.*
‡ *Ne.*
[a] *Haſtyf.*
[b] *La dit.*

/

Et quaunt a la fraunchiſe de fier pens, pur le fieux ſuſten. pur perill & damager de Straungers en temps obſſr're de la *faire*, [c] voilloms & dioms que ſi nul damage en le dit *faire*[d] pur defaute dez ditz fewes ſuſten. a veign. as nyefs ou as autres choſes ſur mier par defaute dez ditz Barons que lez ditz deners reſceyvent, & de ceo ſerront attaintz, lez ditz Barons ſerrount tenutz lez ditz damages, a lez ditz endamages pleignement reſtorer. Et a donques noſtre Provoſt *de*[e] Yernem. lez ditz fier pens reſceve & pregne pur lez detz feux ſuſten. en temps du faire ſur meſme la perill tanque lez ditz Barons, lez ditz pardez & dam. eyent pleignement reſtorer as ditz endamages.

[c] *Eſch. volons & dions.*
[d] *Temps.*
[e] *La dit ville de Gernemewe.*

Et pur le pees meintz meinten. & garder, *voillonis*[f] & dioms, que le meſter & deux dez plus *prodeſſe*[g] homes de cheſt. nyefs, *qui quel*[h] *ſoit*, ſi bien dez *villes*[i] Portez, & de lours membres come de la vill. de Yern.[k] facent corporell ſerement devaunt Meire, Barons, & Baill. & Provoſt dez lieux ſuiſditz, eiux que lez ditz nyefs iſſent dez havenes, que eux noſtr. pees[l] tendront & de lours compaignons, & de lours ſubgets *ferront*[m] garder enſy qui ſi & null deſtourbe[u], noſtre pees, meſfeſour, felony ou treſpas feſſauntz, entre eux ſoient troves, meſm. ceux treſpaſſours *od*[n] toutz lou. chatells haſtynement areſtont, & lez meſuent. al plus procheyn lieu ou ils arriverent en noſtre royalme & al Baill. de meſm. le lieu lez liveront a garder & a Juſtice, ſolonc la ley & lez uſages *en*[o] cette. partiez. Et que dez ditz Baill. lez chatelx de meſm. *cett.*[p] gentz par eſcript entre eux endente *reſceyvent*[q] & a noz *entre*[r] ſpoignent ſi de felonie[ſ] atteintz. Et ſi aſcu. deux dautres treſpas ſoient atteintz eux enſemblement od lou. biens[s] demoergente areſlutz tanque as pleintifs ſoyent reſonable amendez faitz. Et *voilloms*[t] & dioms pur noſtre pees *diſtreines*[v] entre eux plus ferment garder & meinten. que ſi lez meſters dez nyefs tiels maneres des felons ou meſfeſours concelont dareſt. ou liverer ne voillent a Gardeyn. *ou*[u] as Baill. come de ſuis e dit, eyent meſme la juſtice, que a tiels manere de melfeſſours appent. Eiltre ceo *voillons*[w] & dioms que ſi lez Seignurs a qui lez nyefs ſount reſceyvont les meſtres dez dits nyefs qui *cettez*[x] man'z des felons & treſp[s] concelont, ſachantz lour concelment, ſaunz eux areſt. ou faire aſſavoir al Gardein. ou as Baill. ſuiſditz, & de ceo ſoient atteintz ſoient lez chattelx dez tielx reſceytours a noz forfaitz.

[f] *Volons & dions.*
[g] *Prude.*
[h] *A qui que elle ſoit auxi.*
[i] *Dez.*
[k] *As above.*
[l] *Fermement.*
[m] *Seront.*
[n] *Cue.*
[o] *De.*
[p] *Ceſtye.*
[q] *Releignent.*
[r] *Enriſpoygnent*
[ſ] *Soit.*
[s] *Et leur chatealx.*
[t] *Volons & dions.*
[v] *Deſormes.*
[u] *Et.*
[w] *Volons & dions.*
[x] *Teux.*

Et voloms & dioms, que lez ditz Gardeins, Baill. & Provoſts, facent quat. foitz par lan enqueſts en la meillours man's quils ſaueront, une en temps dez vendages, un. altre en temps

otherwiſe[c], which Faire is at *Great Yarmouth*, wholly[d], and no where elſe, do not † due Amends, and ſpeedy Juſtice, according to the Law, and the Uſages of thoſe Partes. And if Plaint come to us, the Parties having Writs of our *Chancery* to make to come the Bailiffes in whom the Default ſhall be aſſigned, to anſwer thereupon before us and our Heires, Kings of *England*; and if thereof they be attainted, they ſhall looſe the Franchiſe ‖ of Juſtice.

[c] *In other Time.*
[d] *Entirely.*
† Not *is added, being omitted in the* French *in this Copy, but* Ne *is in the other.*
‖ *That Franchiſe.*

And as to the Franchiſe of the Fire Pence, for the Suſteining the Fires for avoiding[e] the Perill and Dammage of Strangers in the Time of the Faire, we will and ſay, That if any Dammage in the ſaid Faire[f], by Default of ſuſteining the ſaid Fires, come to Ships, or to other Things on the Sea[g], by Default of the ſaid Barons which the ſaid Pence receive, and of the ſame * ſhall be attaint, the ſaid Barons ſhall be holden[h], the ſaid Dammages to the ſaid endammaged fully to reſtore, and then our Provoſt of *Yarmouth* to receive and take the ſaid Fire Pence for ſuſteining the ſaid Fires, in time of the Faire, upon the ſame Perill, untill the ſaid Barons, the ſaid Loſſes and Dammages have fully reſtored to the ſaid endammaged.

[e] *Eſchewing, or preventing.*
[f] *For Default.*
[g] *Or Sea Side.*
* *Thereof.*
[h] *Bound.*

And for Peace † the better to be maintained and kept, We will and ſay, That the Maſter, and Two of the moſt proved[i] Men of every Ship, whoſoever it be, aſwell of the Port Townes and their Members, as of the Towne of *Yarmouth*, make their corporal Oath before the Maior, Barons, and Bailiffs, and Provoſt of the Places aforeſaid, ere that the ſaid Ships go out of the Havens, that they our Peace keepe ‡, and of their Company and Subjects ſhall make to be kept, ſo that there be no Diſturbance of our Peace, Miſ-doing †, Felony or Treſpas done, among them may be found: But thoſe Treſpaſſors, with all their Chattels, haſtily * they arreſt, and the ſame, at the next Place where they ſhall arrive in our Realme, and to the Bailliffe of the ſame Place them to deliver, to be kept and adjudged according to the Law, and the Uſages in thoſe Parts. And that the ſaid Bailliffes, the Chattells of the ſame Men receive by writing betweene them indented, and anſwere to us thereof, if of the Felony they be attaint. And if any of them of other Treſpas be attaint, they together with their Goods ſhall remaine arreſted untill to the Plaintiffes there be reaſonable Amends made. And we will and ſay, for our Peace to be betweene them more firmly kept and maintained, That if the Maſters of Ships ſuch Manner of Felons or Miſdoers ‡ conceale from arreſt, or will not deliver to the Warden *, or to the Bailliffe, as aforeſaid, they ſhall have the ſame Juſtice, which to ſuch Manner of Malefactors appertaine. Alſo We will and ſay, That if the Owners[k], of whom the Ships are, receive the Maſters of the ſaid Ships, which theſe Manners † of Felons and Treſpas do conceale, knowing their concealment, without arreſting them, or making it knowne to the Warden ‖, or to the Bailliffes aforeſaid, and thereof be attaint, be[l] the Chattells of ſuch Receivers forfeited to us.

† *Better Peace.*
[i] *Honeſt Men.*
‡ *Or hold.*
† *Miſdeeds, or Miſdoers.*
* *Speedily.*
‡ *Malefactors.*
* *Or Keeper.*
[k] *Lords.*
† *Or Manner.*
‖ *Or Keeper.*
[l] *Let be, or they may be, or ſhall be.*

And We will and ſay, That the ſaid Wardens[m], Bayliffes, and Provoſts, do foure Times in the Yeare make Enqueſts in the beſt manners * they may: One in time of the Vintage;

[m] *Or Keepers.*
* *Or Manner.*

ANNOTATIONS.

[*] *Saleyson.* temps de Reke, la tierce en temps de *Salison* [*], la quarte en temps de Harengeson, dez feloniez
[*] *Aux avoinz.* & trespas faitz [*] entre eux, *en* [b] *quels* partie
[b] *Quelque.* que ceo foit par tout lan. & ceux que lez ditz Gardeins, Baill. ou Provoft troveront enditus, facent attacher, & jufticer, folonc la ley, & lez ufages de cett. parties en la fourme fufdit.

[c] *Elles.* Nemye pur ceo noz voloms que null encourge lez peynes fufdditz, ne null de *eles* [c],
[d] *Avenir et.* jofques a xii[me]. jo[n]. Daverill procheyn [d], de cell. jou. en avaunt.

[e] *Queux.* En tefmoyn. de *quel* [e] chofe noz avoms fait faire ceft. efcript. endente enfeall. de noftre feall. dont la une partie eft Baill. as ditz Barons dez Portes, & lautre as avaundirz gentz de Yern. Don. a Weftm. la darr. jo[n]. de Mars, lan. de noftre reign. trentifme & tierce.

tage; another in time of Reke; the Third in time of Salt Seafon; the Fourth in time of Herring Seafon, of the Felonies and Trefpas done among them, in Whar part fo ever it be throughout ‡ the Yeare: And thofe which the ‡ *By the Whole,* faid Wardens [*], Bayliffes or Provoft, fhall *or by all the* find indicted, fhall make to be attached and *Tear.* jufticed, according to the Law, and the Ufa-[*] *Keepers and* ges of thofe Parts, in the Forme aforefaid. *Bailiffs, fo in*

Notwithftanding we will, That none in- *one Copy, where* curre the Paines aforefaid, nor any of them, *Provoft is left* untill the Twelfth Day of *April* next, from *but.* this Day [n] forward. [n] *That Day.*

In witnefs of which Thing †, We have † *Whereof.* made this Writing indented to be enfealed with our Seale, whereof the one Part is given to the faid Barons of the Ports, and the other to the aforefaid People [o] of *Yarmouth.* Given [o] *Men.* at *Weftminfter* the laft Day of *March,* the Yeare of Our Reign the Thirty third.

Neither did this quiet and compofe the former Difcords fo, but that the Ports had caufe to complain to King *Edward* III. in the Thirty firft Year of his Reign; whereupon he not only in anfwer, befides particular Orders of his own to their Petition, granted the Confirmation of his Grandfathers Ordinances (which are before recited) but alfo took Order, in the Parliament then fitting, for Reformation of fome Abufes, and Regulation of the Fair there, according to the Compofition aforefaid. This Ordinance of Parliament is to be feen in the printed *Statutes* of *Pulton's* Collection, p. 177, 178. The former, as I find them in a Manufcript, are thus:

Petitions of the Barons of the Cinque Ports ‡, *holden at* Weftminfter *in* Eafter Term, *the* xxxi ‡ *I fuppofe the*
Year of King Edward *the Third.* *Copy intended*
to the King and

Inprimis, LOWLY complaineth, and humbly befeecheth our Lord King, and his Counfel, *Parliament,* your poore Orators, the Barons of the *Cinque Ports,* that where in an Ordinance *but the Anfwers* late made in the Time of your gracious and good Grandfire, betweene the late Barons, and the *are only from* People of *Great Yarmouth,* therein is conteined as followeth: *the King here.*

That the Barons of the Ports have their Eafements in Strand and Denne, without any Im- *Pet.* provement of Soile, and without any Cuftome giving, and that the People of *Yarmouth* voide Strand and Den of old Ships and Timber, whereas they fhould arrive and dry their Nets. And the People of *Yarmouth* not having regard to thefe Words, nor will fuffer the Barons to have their Eafements in Strand and Den abovefaid, ne will avoide in Manner as they fhould, according to the Ordinance therein taken, to the great Dammage of the Barons, whereof they befeechen Remedy.

I will and command, That the Barons have their Writ upon our Dite and Ordinance, to the Bay- Anfw. *liffs and Commonalty of the Towne of* Yarmouth. *And in cafe they will not fo do as above is faid, that Proceffe be done againft them by Attachment and Diftreffe.*

And further, in the fame Ordinance of your gracious Grandfire, That the Barons fhould *Pet.* have and enjoy peaceably all fuch Rents as they have, or ever had in the faid Towne; and if the faid Barons intend to have Right in any other Rents, whereof they fhould be deforced by the People of *Yarmouth,* that then they fhould recover it by Writ, Law and Ufage of the faid Towne: The faid People of *Yarmouth* have detained their faid Rents from the Barons of the Five Ports, and will not do them right, according to the Ordinance aforefaid, whereof they pray Remedy.

I will and command, That the Barons have their Writ, upon this Article, unto the Bayliffs of the Anfw. *faid Towne, willing them, that they be helping and aiding to the Barons to levy their Rents, after the Purport and Effect of the faid Ordinance.*

And whereas the Barons of the Five Ports have the Keeping of the Peace, and to do Royal *Pet.* Juftice, with the Provoft of the Towne of *Yarmouth;* and that the faid Bayliffs of the Ports make with the faid Provoft all Attachments, and plead all Pleas, and determine the Plaints that may be determined during the Faire, after Law-Merchant; and that the Amerciaments and Profits of the People of the Ports fhall be unto the Barons during the Faire; and that the faid Barons with the Provoft have the Keeping of the King's Prifon in *Yarmouth,* during the Faire there: But the People of *Yarmouth* incroached to themfelves Royal Juftice, and the Garde abovefaid, and will not fuffer the Bayliffs of the Ports nothing to meddle, ne of the Plaints, Attachments and Amerciaments, with other Profits aforefaid to have Knowledge, whereof they pray Remedy.

I will and command, There be a Writ made and directed to the Bayliffs of Yarmouth *upon this* Anfw. *Article, that in cafe they will not obey the Order, there be Proceffe againft them by Attachment and Diftreffe.*

And alfo it was in that Ordinance, by your gracious Grandfire, that no Guard fhould be *Pet.* upon any Ship-Merchant, with their Merchandife, by the which the Merchants, to whom the faid

F

ANNOTATIONS.

said Ships and Merchandise do belong, may sell freely their Goods, commonly by their owne Hands, to whomsoever they will, paying their Customes thereof due : The People of *Tarmouth* will not suffer the Merchants comming to the Towne to sell their Goods and Merchandise to their most Profit, but only put them therefro, and sell it at their Will, to what Value the Merchants are thereof ignorant, to the great Dammage and Impoverishing of the common People, and against the Ordinance of your gracious and good Grandsire, whereof they do pray Remedy.

Answ. *Upon this Article also I will, and straightly command, A Writ to be directed to the Bayliffs of Yarmouth, to cease off from these Enormities upon a grievous Paine.*

Pet. And over this the said Barons beseech the King and his Counsel, to do convenable and hastie Remedy of these said Griefes ; and over this to see and examine all the Articles comprised in the said Ordinance, and then to declare and inlarge that shall be to the Profit of the King and of the Barons, and of other the Kings liege People, as well to the Merchants and Fishers, as all others comming to the Faire for the Traffique of Merchandise.

Answ. *This Article shall be answered.*

And afterwards, in the Thirty third and Forty seventh Years of his Reign, issues forth other Orders, the last of which is all in *Latin,* but the other in *French,* from the Word [*Eorasmuch*] to the Words [*And therefore*] and the rest in *Latin* ; this I have inserted only in the Translation, finding the other Copy imperfect : But the other, both Copy and Translation, shall follow.

Edward, by the Grace of God King of England, and France, and Lord of Ireland, To our Bailiffs
* Or Wardens. *of the Cinque Ports, and Bailiffs of the Towne of Great Yarmouth, Keepers* * *of the Faire of*
‡ Or Concord. *the same Towne, Greeting. We send a certaine Agreement ‡ made by us and our Councell, which we will to be holden and executed in the present Faire of the Towne aforesaid, the Tenor whereof followeth in these Words :*

FOrasmuch as the Price of Herring in the Faire of *Yarmouth* is greatly indearthed, more then it hath beene before these daies, to great Dammage unto the common People of all the Realme ; and it is to be doubted, that more greater Dammage there will come after this, if Remedy be not had : It is ordained by our Lord King, and his Councell, by assent of the Merchants Fishers of *London,* and of *Yarmouth,* for such Dammages to eschew, That the Fishers that come with their Herring into the Haven of *Great Yarmouth* in the Time of the Paire, that they sell no Herring before that they come to land in the same Haven, and fasten their Moaring upon the Land ; and then they to sell upon the Land openly to whom it pleaseth them. And that the Merchants repairing thither be also free to buy Herring of the Fishers, as the Hosts, without Disturbance or Impeachment of any. And that none remove, ne go against the said Fishers by Sea, ne by Land, to buy Herring by the Way of Forestalling, ne in such other Manner, upon paine of Imprisonment, and to yeeld the Value to the King. And that the Fishers, nor their Hosts, absent themselves not by Covin, ne by other Means, but to be at the Tide when the Ships come to the Land within the Haven, and have fastened their Moaring Rope ; but that they there be ready to sell their Herring, aswell to Merchants that be Strangers, as Privie, that will them buy, under the same Paine. And that Herring be delivered out of the Ship before that it be sold. And that the Sale be made by Day-light ; so that after the Sale be made the Fishers may deliver their Herring, and discharge them, aswell by Night as by Day. And that those Vessels called Pycardes buy no Herring in the Sea, ne in none other Place upon the Coasts of the Sea, but only in the said Haven, and in the Road of *Kyrkelye,* so that at all Times the Price of Herring at the Faire, ne in the Road of *Kyrkelye,* be the dearer, upon the Paine aforesaid. And in case that any will complaine against any that hath trespassed against these Points aforesaid, let the Trespasser be attached, by the Wardens of the Faire, by his Goods, and if he have not whereof sufficient, he be attached by his Body, for to answere to the Partie Plaintiffe ; and have they their Day in Court after Law-Merchant. And if it be pleaded to an issue of the Country ; that the one halfe of the Quefte be of Neighbours, and the other halfe of Forreiners, if the Plea touch Neighbour and Forreiner. And the Wardens of the Faire be attendant at every Tide of the Sea to governe duly and truly all these Points abovesaid, rightfully, and hasty Execution unto every Person that will plaine in this Part, under the same Paine. And that none go by Boat, ne in no point into the Sea, ne into the Road of *Kyrkelye,* to meet with the Fishers to constraine them, or procure them, to sell their Herring in the said Road, or in the Sea, in Disturbance of the said Faire, under the same Paine. But if the Fishers be in free will to sell their Herring in the said Road, after that they be anchored there, it shall be lawfull unto the Merchants of *Layftoffe* and *Winterton* to buy Herring of the Fishers as free as the Pycards, to serve the Carts and the Horses that come thither from divers Countreys, and to hang there ; so that all Times they sell no fresh Herring against the Tide under the Paine afore rehearsed. And in case if any Fisher charged with one Laste of Herring and an Halfe, or beneath, in the Road of Saint *Nicholas,* and lift not to come into the Haven for so little a Thing, and would sell that Herring there in the Road, it shall be lawfull to him to set up his Signe there, and to sell his Herring to the Merchants that will come.

And therefore we command you, That the Agreement aforesaid, and every the Articles contained in the same, be publiquely proclaimed in the present Faire as long as the same shall last, firmly and inviolably, under the Penalties aforesaid, to be kept, and made to be holden. And all, and singuler those, which you shall find contrary, or rebellious, by their Bodies ye take and arrest, and in our Prison safely ye cause to be kept, untill of their Punishment otherwise we have made to be ordained. We of the Names of them arrested, and for what Causes they have

ANNOTATIONS.

have beene arrested, under your Seales distinctly and plainly being certified. Witnes My Selfe, at *Westminster*, the Five and Twentieth Day of *September*, in the Yeare of our Reigne of *England*, the Three and Thirtieth, but of our Reigne of *France* the Twentieth.

By the King Himselfe and His Councell.

EDwardus, Dei gratia, Rex Angliæ, & Franciæ, & Dominus Hiberniæ, Præposito ac probis hominibus, ac toti communitati villæ magnæ Yermouthæ, salutem. Cum inter cætera in literis patentibus Domini Edwardi, quondam Regis Angliæ, avi nostri, content. quam nos per literas nostras confirmavimus, super quandam compositionem inter Barones Quinque Portuum, & gentes de Yermouthæ, pro placitis, contentionibus, & discordiis, hinc & inde dudum motis sedandis & pacificandis fact. contineatur : Quod idem avus noster dixit & voluit, quod Barones dictorum Portuum, tempore feriæ de villa Yermouthæ, durant. quadraginta diebus, habeant custodiam pacis nostra, & faciant justiciam, una cum Præposito dictæ villæ Yermouthæ, in hac forma : Quod durant. dict. feria ipsi Barones habeant quatuor servientes, unus vexillum Regni portet, & alter unum cornu cornotet pro gente congregand. & pro meliore audita faciend. & habend. & alii duo servientes corni virgas portent pro pace ibidem custodiend. & hoc officium faciant equitand. si voluerint : Ac quædam alia in dictis literis content, faciant & exequantur : Vobis mandamus firmiter injungent. quod Barones, libertatibus & officiis prædictis, & omnibus aliis libertatibus & quietanciis in dictis literis, & confirmatione nostra contentis, quatenus dictam feriam concernent, in eadem feria ipsa durant. absque impedimento uti & gaudere. Necnon ipsos Barones proclamationes suas de pace nostra, infra dictam villam, durante dicta feria, per ipsos conservand. libere facere, & officium suum prædictum ibidem debit. exequi permittatis, juxta tenorem, vim & effectum literarum confirmationis nostræ prædictarum, ne propter vestri defect. & molest. oportet nos ad hoc extendere manum nostram. Teste me ipso apud Westmonasterium quinto decimo die Octobris, Anno Regni nostri Angliæ quadragesimo septimo, Regni vero nostri Franciæ tricesimo tercio.

EDward, by the Grace of God, King of *England* and *France*, and Lord of *Ireland*, To the Provost and good Men, and to all the Commonalty of the Towne of *Great Yarmouth*, Greeting. Whereas among other Things, in the Letters Patents of the Lord *Edward*, sometime King of *England*, our Grandfather, is conteined, that which we by our Letters have confirmed, upon a certaine Composition betweene the Barons of the *Cinque Ports*, and the People of the said Towne of *Yarmouth*, for settling and pacifying the Pleas, Contentions, and Discords, late made and moved thereof: That the same our Grandfather said and would, that the Barons of the said Ports, the Time of the Faire of the Towne of *Yarmouth*, during Forty Daies, might have the Keeping of our Peace, and might do Justice, together with the Provost of the said Towne of *Yarmouth*, in this Forme, That during the said Faire, the Barons might have Foure Serjeants, one whereof should beare the Banner of the Kingdom; and another one Horne should sound for gathering together the People, and for the better Hearing to be made and had; and the other two Serjeants should bear horne * Rods for the Peace, there to be * Horn *here it kept, and this* Office they might do riding if *corruptly inserted they would.* And certain other Things in the *ed (I suppose) in* said Letters conteined they might do and *exe- the English, and cute.* To you we command, firmly injoyn- Corn. *in the* ing, that the Barons, the Liberties and Offi- Latin, *for it is in* ces aforesaid, and all other Liberties and *not in the Dito* Freedomes in the said Letters and our Con- *of K. Ed. I, not firmation conteined, so much as concerneth did the. Serje- the said Faire, in the same Faire, during the ants bear horn* same, without Impediment, to use and enjoy. *Rods, but white Also that ye permit the same Barons, freely Rods in their* to make their Proclamations concerning our *Hands, when Peace within the said Towne, during the said they attended Faire by them to be kept, and their Office the Bailiffs to aforesaid there duly to execute, according to had from the* the Tenor, Force, and Effect, of the Letters *Court, &c.* of our Confirmation aforesaid, lest for your Default and Molestation, we must to this extend our Hand. Witnes My Selfe at *Westminster*, the Fifteenth Day of *October*, in the Yeare of our Reigne of *England* the seven and Fortieth, but of our Reigne of *France* the ‡ *By the Rethirtie and Thirtieth. cords in the Tower, a like*

Order to this forms to be made in the Fortieth Yeare of this King Edward III. Memb. 4. in Dorso Rotuli.

Yet after all this, (to omit many Things) *Yarmouth*, unwilling to remember their first Rise, puffed up with Riches, and scorning their old Check Mates, cannot forget to stir up and foment Contentions, on purpose to shake off their Competitors in Administration of Justice, though but for a Season of the Year, takes Advantages to quarrell with the Ports Bailiffs, not only about those Things so often and long before confirmed to the Ports, and upon their Complaints always adjudged rather for them then against them, by the supremest Arbitrator of the Nation ; but also for Trifles and Puntilloes, such as the Stile of the Court there kept, in naming the Ports Bailiffs before theirs, the Sitting of the Bailiffs at Court, and several such others, not worth the mentioning ; so that in the Eighteenth Year of the Reign of Queen *Elizabeth*, certain Articles, Orders and Resolutions, were agreed upon by several of the Judges, learned Lawyers, and others Referees in the Case, to be observed by both Parties. The Copy whereof ensueth, *viz.*

ANNOTATIONS.

Articles, Orders and Resolutions, indented, set downe by Roger Manwood, *one of the Queenes Majesties Justices of the* Common Plees, John Jeffereis, *one of her Majesties Serjeants at Law,* Wilyam Lovelace, *Serjeant at Law,* John Boyse, *Esquyer,* Edward Peeke, *Maior of the Towne of* Sandwich, Thomas Lake *and* Robert Boncham, *Commissioners and Arbitrators assigned for the Barons of the* Cinque Ports, *on the one Parte; and* Thomas Gawdye, *one of her Majesties Justices of her Bench;* Robert Bell, Francis Wyndham, Edward Flowerdewe, Charles Calthorpe, *and* Wilyam le Gryse, *Esquyers,* Wilyam Harborne, *and* Thomas Dammett, *Commissioners and Arbitrators assigned for the Baylyffs of* Great Yarmouth, *on the other Parte, as followeth, viz'.*

I.   *First,* THAT the Baylifs of the Barons of the *Cinque Ports,* during the free Faire at *Great Yarmouth,* shall there have the Administration of Royal Justice, and the Keeping of the Peace, together with the Baylifs of *Great Yarmouth,* as hath bin continued and used.

II.   *Item,* That the Baylifs of the said Barons of the *Cinque Ports* shall then and there, together with the Baylifs of *Great Yarmouth,* have the holding and determining of all Plees moved, or depending, and determinable during the free Faire there, according to the Law-Merchant.

III.   *Item,* That the Prison there shall be kept joyntly together, by the Baylifs of the said Barons of the *Cinque Ports,* and the said Baylifs of *Yarmouth,* for all Prisoners committed, or remaining there, during the said free Faire, and at their first coming to peruse, and have a View of the Prisoners, and to know for what Cause they be imprisoned.

IV.   *Item,* That the Prenomination of the Stile of the said Court to be (*alternis vicibus*) one Yeere to the Baylifs of the said Towne of *Great Yarmouth,* and another Yeare to the Baylifs of the Barons of the said *Cinque Ports.* And the Prenomination for the next free Faire to come, concerning the said Court, to be to such of the Baylifs of *Yarmouth,* or the said Baylifs of the *Cinque Ports,* as the said *Roger Manwood* and *Thomas Gawdy* shall name in the Indorsement hereof, and subscribe with their Hands.

V.   *Item,* That the Proclamation of the said free Faire shal be in this Manner and Forme, that is to say, That the Baylifs of the said Barons of the *Cinque Ports,* with all their usual Officers and Ornaments, shall at the usual Place assemble together, and that it shall be lawfull to the said Baylifs of *Yarmouth,* with their usual Officers and Maces, to be then and there present, if they will, and in the Name of all the Queenes Majesties Baylifs there present, without particular Nomination, or Prenomination of the said Baylifs of the said Barons, or Baylifs of *Great Yarmouth,* make their usual Proclamation of the Articles of the said free Faire.

VI.   *Item,* That the Bayliffes of the Barons of the said free Ports shal by all Means and Waies, that they conveniently may, cause aswell their owne Fishers and People, as all other Fishers and People, not to discharge any Herrings or other Merchandise, during the Time of the free Faire, at any Place within seaven Miles of *Great Yarmouth,* but only at the Towne of *Great Yarmouth,* according to the Edict made betweene the said Barons and the Baylifs, and Burgesses of the Towne of *Great Yarmouth.*

VII.   *Item,* Where it hath beene used that a Partie Inquest should be impannelled, whereof some to be of the Ports, and a like Number of the said Towne of *Great Yarmouth,* to enquire of the Mysdemeanors and Offences committed during the said free Faire, and the same to present before the Baylifs of *Great Yarmouth,* and the Baylifs of the said Barons: The said Inquirie shall from henceforth continewe as it hath bin used and accustomed.

VIII.   *Item,* Where of every Fisher Vessel comming to the said free Faire in ancient Time, Foure Pence for Toll or Custome, was paid to the Baylifs of the *Cinque Ports,* which afterwards by Composition was reduced to a Summe certeine of Six Pounds yearly: Now for good and quiet Accord it is agreed, that the said Baylifs of *Great Yarmouth* shall from henceforth yearly pay to the said Baylifs of the Barons of the *Cinque Ports,* at their Departure from *Great Yarmouth,* Three Pounds and Tenn Shillings, for, and in Recompense and Satisfaction of the said Toll or Custome of Foure Pence, for such Fisher Vessel, not charging in any wise any of the Boats or Shippes of any of the Inhabitants of the *Cinque Ports.* And in Consideration thereof, the said Baylifs of *Yarmouth* to be discharged of all Arrerages to be demanded for any Time past.

IX.   *Item,* That all the Inhabitants of the said Ports, and their Members, together with their Shippes and Merchandizes, shall be free of Deane and Strand, and of all Taxes, Charges and Burdens unaccustomed whatsoever, and have and enjoy all other their Priviledges, Liberties and Commodities whatsoever, heretofore used, not repugnant to these Articles and Orders. And that they, and every one of them, shall and may francklye sell his or their Herring to whom it shall please them, without let or interruption of the said Baylifs of *Yarmouth.*

X.   *Item,* That no Superfedeas shall be awarded, or made by the Baylifs of the Barons of the *Cinque Ports,* of themselves, for discharge, or setting at Liberty, any arrested or bound for the Peace, or good Behaviour, by warrant of the said Baylifs of *Great Yarmouth,* without the Consent of both, or one of the same Baylifs of *Yarmouth.* And *è converso,* that no Superfedeas shall be awarded, or made by any of the Baylifs of *Yarmouth,* of themselves, for discharge, or setting at Liberty, any arrested or bound for the Peace; or good Behaviour, by warrant of the said Baylifs, of the said Barons of the *Cinque Ports,* without consent of one, or both the same Baylifs. But that every such Superfedeas, or other Discharge, shal be made by consent of both, or one of those Baylifs, which granted the said Warrant during the said free Faire.

In witnes whereof, aswell the said Commissioners and Arbitrators assigned for the Barons of the *Cinque Ports,* as the said Commissioners and Arbitrators assigned for the Baylifs and Towne of *Great Yarmouth,* to these *Articles, Orders* and *Resolutions,* indented, their Seales interchangably have set. Dated the last Day of *May,* in the Eighteenth Yeare of the Raigne of our Soveraigne Lady *Elizabeth,* by the Grace of God, Queene of *England, France* and *Ireland,* Defendor of the Faith, &c. 1576.

                                     Touch-

CHARTERS.

Et etiam quod quieti de Shires & Hundreds, ita quod si quis versus illos placitare voluerit, ipsi non respondeant, nequo placitent, aliter quam placitare solebant tempore Domini Henrici Regis, proavi nostri. Et quod habeant inventiones suas in mari & in terra. Et quod quieti sint de omnibus rebus suis, & toto mercato suo, sicut nostri liberi homines. Et quod habeant honores suos in curia nostra, &'libertates

TRANSLATION.

And also that they may be quit of Shires [r] and Hundreds [s], so that if any will plead against them, they shall not [a] answer nor plead, otherwise than they were wont [b] to plead in the Time of the Lord King *Henry* [c], our great Grandfather. And that they may have their Findals [d] in Sea and in Land. And that they be quiet [e] of all their Goods [f], and all their Merchandize [g], as our Freemen. And that they have their Honours [h] in our Court, and their Liberties

ANNOTATIONS.

Touching the Ports Bayliffs to *Yarmouth*, further may be seen in their Customals, and especially among the Records of their Court of *Brotherhood*.

[r] *Shires*, from the *Saxon Shyran*, q. f. a Part or Share of the Kingdom, all one with a County, a Division said to be made by King *Alfred*; and here intends not only a Separation from the Counties in which the Ports lie; so that though it may be said they are in the Counties, yet not of the Counties; but also an Exemption from Attendance at the Shire or County Court, called the Sheriffs Turn, and other Courts holden for the County.

[s] *Hundreds*. These are lesser Divisions of the Shire agreed on by the aforesaid King *Alfred*, and took the Name from the Number, because it contained Ten Tithings, and every Tithing Ten Persons. These Hundred Men dwelling near together (though in divers Parishes) had then the Administration of Justice among themselves, and were Pledges one for another, Tithing within Tithing, and Hundred within Hundred; out of which Limit they were not to remove without Security, and if any of them were accused of a Crime, he was to produce some of that Precinct to be Sureties for his Behaviour, or else to endure the Punishment of the Law. And if any Malefactor, before or after such Sureties found, escaped, all the Tithing or Hundred were fined to the King. These Hundreds still continue, though not altogether to the same Purpose whereto at first they were appointed. And by this Charter the Ports Men claim to be freed, as well from Attendance at the Hundred Courts, and serving of Offices, by Election of those Courts, as Constables, Headboroughs, and Tithing Men; as also, to be quit of Money to be paid, or Customs to be done to the Hundredors, or the Chief of them.

[a] *Shall not*, or, may not.

[b] *Were wont*. Hereby is more evident the Exemption of Ports Men from being sued, or forced to answer Suits in any other Court, than where, long before the making of this Charter, they had used to do, that is, as afterward is expressed, at *Shepway*.

[c] *King Henry*, that is, King *Henry* II. who was Great Grandfather to this King *Edward*, viz. Father of King *John*, the Father of King *Henry* III. who was the Father of King *Edward* the First.

[d] *Findals*. Before the making of this Charter it is a Question, whether the Ports Men claimed, or had all their *Findals*, seeing Treasure trove (that is, found) was one of the principal Articles inquirable in the Court of *Shepway*, as may be seen hereafter.

[e] *Quiet*. Quit or Free, as before noted.

[f] *Goods*. *Res* in the *Latin* being often used for the Substance whereof a Man is possessed, which is commonly called his Goods.

[g] *Merchandize*. The *Latin* Word *Mercatum* is more commonly used for a Market in which Merchandises are sold, than for the Merchandizes sold there.

[h] *Honours*. This is construed to intend the honourable Service the Barons of the Ports perform, in bearing the Canopy over the Kings and Queens at their Coronations, for which they have the further Honour of dining with them that Day. These Honours I look not upon as conferred on the Ports by this Charter of King *Edward* I. but only confirmed; for by the before mentioned Exemplification of the Services of the *Cinque Ports* (hereafter copied upon the Service of Shipping) it appeareth, That when Queen *Elianor*, Daughter of *Hugh*, Earl of Provence, Wife to King *Henry* III. in the Twentieth Year of his Reign, was crowned, the Barons of the Ports did bear the Canopy then, of purple Silke, by four Staves silvered over, with four little Bells silver and gilt; and did claim and obtain the same as their ancient Right and Privilege, and to have the said Canopy parted among them, although the Marquisses of the Marches of *Wales* opposed the Barons of the Ports, and challenged the same, as belonging to them. And it is further evident by the said Exemplification, that the said Barons then claimed the

G   Privi-

CHARTERS.   TRANSLATION.

bertates fuas per totam terram noftram, quocunque venerint. Et quod ipfi de omnibus terris fuis, quas tempore Domini Henrici Regis, patris noftri, videlicet, anno regni fui quadragefimo quarto poffider. quieti fint imperpetuum de communibus fummonitionibus coram jufticiariis noftris, ad quæcunque placita itinerantibus, in quibufcunque comitatibus hujufmodi terræ fuæ exiftunt, ita quod ipfi non teneantur venire coram jufticiariis prædictis, nifi aliquis ipforum Baronum aliquem implacitet, vel ab aliquo implacitetur. Et quod non placitentur alibi nifi ubi debuerunt, & ubi folebant, fcilicet, apud Shepweiam. Et quod habeant libertates & quietancias fuas de cætero, ficut ipfi & Anteceffores fui eas unquam melius, plenius, & honorificentius habuerunt

ties throughout all our Land, wherefoever they fhall come. And that they of all their Lands, which in the Time of the Lord King *Henry* [i], our Father, that is to fay, in the Forty fourth Year [j] of his Reign, they poffeffed, may be free for ever of common Summons, [k] before our Juftices for all manner of Pleas [ll] itinerant [l], in whatfoever Counties fuch their Lands be, fo that they be not bound to come before the Juftices aforefaid, except any of the fame Barons implead any, or of any be impleaded. And that they fhall not be impleaded other where but where they ought, and where they were wont, that is to fay, at *Shepway* [m]. And that they may have their Liberties and Freedoms from henceforth, as they and their Anceftors [n] them at any Time better, more fully, and more honourably have

ANNOTATIONS.

Privilege of Sitting at the King's Tables that Day, at the right Hand of the King, and did fo fit.

[i] *King Henry*, that is, King *Henry* III. (laft above mentioned) who reigned Fifty fix Years and upwards; the longeft of any of the *Norman* Race that ever wore the Crown of *England*.

[j] *Forty Fourth Year*, that is, about Eighteen Years before the Date of this Charter.

[k] *Summons*, from *Sub* and *Moneo*, is a Notice or Warning. By this it appeareth that the Ports Men, though they had Lands that lay out of the Precincts of the Ports, fhould not be fummoned againft their Wills, upon thofe Lands, at the Suit of any Party, to appear out of the

* *Alfo before* Ports before the King's Juftices *.

this were the [l] *Itinerant*, that is, Journeying, from *Iter*, a *Journey*; and fo Juftices Itinerant, or, as com-

Ports free of monly in the Law, Juftices in Eyre, are fuch as travelled from Place to Place to adminifter Ju-

thefe Summons, ftice: Thefe were fomewhat like the Juftices of Affize, but are now worn out. With refpect to

for K. Henry thefe itinerant Juftices, the Juftices refiding at *Weftminfter* are called *Jufticarii refidentes*.

III. *about the* [m] *Shepway*, fometime *Shipway*, a Place lying near *Hithe*, in the County of *Kent* (giving

11th *Year of his* Name to one of the Five Divifions of the County, called *Lathes*) fo called, as *Talbot* in his Com-

Reign writes mentary on the Itinerary of *Antonius Auguftus* thinks, becaufe it lay in the Way to the Haven

to the Sheriff of where Ships were wont to ride, which Haven he taketh to be *Lymene*, or *Lymne*. This *Shep*-

Kent *to ftop the way* was famous, in old Time, for the Court where the Pleas of the Ports were heard and de-

levying of 100 termined before their Lord Warden, who, at his Entrance into his Office of the Wardenfhip,

Marks on Sand- did ufe here to take his *Serement* or *Oath*, for the Prefervation of their Liberties: And here

wich, *which* did this King *Edward*, before he came to the Crown, *Anno* 1265. when he was Lord Warden,

was amerced exact of the Barons of the Ports their Oath of Fidelity to his Father, King *Henry* III. againft the

on them for de- Maintainers of the Barons Wars. Neverthelefs this Court, though anciently here held, and re-

fault of fuch taining ftill the Name of *Shepway*, is not reftrained to be kept there, but may be held elfewhere,

Summons, as within the Ports or Members, at the Pleafure of the Lord Warden, as well for fwearing him, as

contrary to for other Occafions; for I find this Court, *Anno* 1597. held at *Beakiborn* in *Kent*, upon the Admi-

their Charters. niftration of the *Oath* or *Serement* to Sir *Henry Brooke*, Lord *Cobham*, and fometimes fince at other

Places. Of this Court of *Shepway*, and the Proceedings therein, more may be feen in the Cuftomals and Records of the *Ports*, and *Dover* Caftle.

[n] *Anceftors*. Anceftor is properly applied to a natural Perfon, as Predeceffor to a Perfon in a politick or corporate Capacity, yet here taken fynonymically for Predeceffors.

CHARTERS.

buerunt temporibus Regum Angliæ Edvardi, Willielmi primi &
fecundi, Henrici Regis, proavi noftri, & temporibus Regis Richardi, & Regis Johannis, avi noftri,
& Domini Henrici Regis, patris
noftri, per cartas eorundem, ficut cartæ illæ, quas iidem Barones noftri inde habent, & quas
infpeximus, rationabiliter teftantur. Et prohibemus ne quis
eos injufte difturbet neque mercatum eorum, fuper forisfacturam noftram decem librarum, ita
ta-

TRANSLATION.

have had in the Times of *Edward* °, *William* the Firft *·* and
Second *ᴼ*, King *Henry* ʳ our
great Grandfather, and in the
Times of King *Richard* ᶠ and
King *John* ᶿ, our Grandfather ;ᵗ
and of the Lord King *Henry* ᵗ
our Father, Kings of *England*,
by their Charters ᵘ, as the fame
Charters ᵛ, which the fame our
Barons thereof have, and we
have feen ᵂ, do reafonably teftify. And we forbid, left any ˣ
unjuftly difturb ʸ them or their
Merchandize ᶻ, upon our Forfeiture ᵃ of Ten Pounds ᵇ, fo
never-

ANNOTATIONS.

° *Edward,* that is, *Edward,* the Confeffor, Son of King *Ethelred,* fometime called St. *Edward,* who ruled before the Conqueft of King *William,* and began his Reign, *Anno* 1043. and died *Anno* 1066.

ᴾ *William the Firft.* This is *William* the Conqueror, the Baftard Duke of *Normandy,* who is reckoned to begin his Reign *October* 14, 1066. the Day of his Battle fought with King *Harold* at *Battel* in *Suffex,* who being flain in the Field, and his Army overcome, King *William* purfues the Victory, and obtains the Government of the whole Kingdom, which he holds till his Death, that was *September* 9, 1087.

ᑫ *And fecond,* that is, *William Rufus,* fecond Son to *William* the Conqueror, who, after his Father's Death, fteps before his elder Brother *Robert,* and feats himfelf in the Throne ; he reigned till *Auguft* 1, 1100. when he was killed in *New Foreft* in *Hampfhire* ; after whofe Death fucceeds his younger Brother *Henry,* called King *Henry* I. (though the elder Brother *Robert* was yet living) and continues his Reign till *December* 2, 1135. when dying, *Stephen,* Earl of *Bologne* and *Mortagne,* Son of *Stephen* Earl of *Blois,* and *Adela,* the Daughter of *William* the Conqueror, poffeffed himfelf of the Crown, that belonged to *Maude* the Emprefs, the only furviving Heir of King *Henry* I. and holds it till he dies, *October* 25, 1154. Of him, nor King *Henry* I. (as of fome other Kings is before noted) no mention is here made : Though it is not probable that the Ports, if they got nothing new, would neglect to fecure their old Rights and Privileges, by the Confirmation of thefe Kings, at leaft to prevent the feizing or invading their Liberties, fometimes ufual with them who ftick not to invade Crowns.

ʳ *Henry.* This great Grandfather of King *Edward* I. was King *Henry* II. as before obferved, Son of *Jeffrey Plantagenet,* and *Maude* the Emprefs, Daughter and Heir of King *Henry* I. This King *Henry* II. begins his Reign at King *Stephen's* Death, and continues in the Government till his own Death, which was *July* 6, 1189.

ᶠ *Richard* is King *Richard* I. Son of King *Henry* II. at his Father's Death poffeffes the Throne, and reigns till *April* 6, 1199. when he yielded to Death, occafioned by a Shot of an Arrow he received from a Caftle he befieged in *France.*

ᶿ *John,* youngeft Son of King *Henry* II. then living, at the Death of his Brother, King *Richard* I. gets Poffeffion of the Crown from *Arthur,* Son of *Jeffrey,* another of his elder Brothers, and enjoys it with Trouble till he died, as fome fay, by Poifon, *October* 19, 1216.

ᵗ *Henry,* he was Son of King *John,* and called King *Henry* III. He had a long but troublefome Reign, from the Time of his Father's Deceafe, to *November* 16, 1272.

ᵘ *Their Charters,* or, the *Charters of them* ; that is, the Charters of the fame Kings afore-named.

ᵛ *Same Charters,* or, thofe Charters.

ᵂ *We have feen.* Whatever became of thefe old Charters here mentioned I cannot fay, but it feems they were extant at the Time King *Edward* I. granted this Charter, and produced before him by the Barons of the Ports, as this Paffage plainly implies. It is likely length and tract of Time hath worn them out, or they are otherwife perifhed or loft, as is hinted in the Charter of Queen *Elizabeth* afterward.

ˣ *Left any,* or we forbid that none, or not any difturb them.

ʸ *Difturb.* An unjuft Moleftation or Stop. For to difturb Judgment in the Law, is to arreft or ftay Judgment.

ᶻ *Merchandize. Mercatum* ufed here in the *Latin,* as before, for Merchandize.

ᵃ *Our Forfeiture,* for Forfeiture to us.

ᵇ *Ten Pounds.* Since the making of this Charter Money being advanced to the treble Value of what it then was, the Forfeiture, according to this Rate, would be 30 *l.* yet if any Suit fhould be

CHARTERS.   TRANSLATION.

tamen quod cum ipfi Barones in juſticia faciend. & recipiend. defuerint, cuſtos noſter, {& hæredum noſtrorum Quinque Portuum, qui pro tempore fuerit, Portus & libertates ſuas in defectu eorundum ingrediatur ad plenam juſticiam ibidem faciend. ita, etiam quod dicti Barones & hæredes ſui faciant nobis & hæred. noſtris, Regibus Angliæ, per annum, plenarium ſervitium ſuum quin-

nevertheleſs, that when the ſaid Barons ſhall fail in Juſtice to be done^c, and to be received, the Warden ^d of us, and of our Heirs of the *Cinque Ports*, which for the Time ſhall be ^e, the Ports and their Liberties ^f, in default ^g of the ſame, may, enter ^h, to do there full Juſtice, ſo, alſo that the ſaid Barons and their Heirs ⁱ do ^j to us and our Heirs, Kings of *England*, yearly ^k, their full Service of

ANNOTATIONS.

be (of which I never had yet any Acquaintance) for this Forfeiture, I take it no more than 10 *l*. could be recovered.

^c *Juſtice to be done.* Hereby evidently appeareth that the Barons of the Ports, at the Time this Charter of King *Edward* I. was granted, and before, had within, and amongſt themſelves reſpectively, Power to adminiſter Juſtice according to Law, and the Cuſtom of the Ports, and ſo conſequently had Courts of Record in which the ſame was adminiſtred ; for if they had nothing to do in the Adminiſtration of Juſtice, the Proviſion following for the Entrance of the Warden to remedy their Failure, or rectify their Male-Adminiſtration thereof, had been altogether needleſs.

^d *Warden,* now commonly ſtiled, The *Lord Warden,* becauſe oftentimes the Wardens have been of the Nobility, and ſometimes Princes of the Blood Royal. It is an Office none leſs than a Knight ought to occupy. This great Officer, or *Limenarcha,* as *Camdden* obſerves, was an

* *At leaſt under* Imitation of the ſame Officer, which the *Romans* * eſtabliſhed for Defence of our Coaſts, and
Conſtantine called *Littoris Saxonici,* or *Tractui maritimi Comes,* who had the Charge of Nine Sea Ports,
the Great, who And it is no doubt but theſe *Cinque Ports* and *Towns,* were under ſome ſpecial Government, and as
did, amongſt the Time of the *Saxons,* Neceſſity ſo requiring, though *Guardians,* from whence *Barons,* in
others, appoint plain *Engliſh, Keeper,* and in *Latin Cuſtos,* imports the Name impoſed by King *William* the Con-
ſuch Officers, queror : Yet may it not thence be concluded, that the Office was born with him, ſeeing his
and ſome ſay, Deſign was to have altered the whole Language he found here, by injoyning the Teaching
the Office was here of his own *French* Tongue to Children, the Grammar in Schools, the Laws and Plea-
executed under ings thereof in this Tongue, ſhortly after his Settlement in the Throne. Theſe Wardens
Valentinian therefore being ſet for the Defence of the Ports, and Coaſts on which they are, and as the chief
by Nectaridius. Commanders of their Ships they were to furniſh to Sea, gave them as well the Name of Admi-
vid. Selden's ral, in reſpect of their Office as to the Sea ; as Wardens, with reference to their Care in Keep-
MareClauſum. ing and preſerving the Liberties of the Ports at Land, both as Mediators between their Sove-
reigns and them, if Differences ſhould ariſe there ; and as Judges among them, and between them and others, to guard and defend them againſt the unjuſt Encroachments of Foreigners upon their Rights and Juriſdictions, and to determine ſuch Differences as might grow irreconcilable (without an interpoſing Power) and correct the Errors and Irregularities in Judgment as might happen among themſelves ; for as to the former, he is the immediate Officer of the King to the Ports, and hath the Return of his Writs that run there, they being directed to him ; and as to the latter, the Cauſes were heard, and Judgment concerning them given in the old Court of *Shepway,* and Courts of *Chancery* and *Admiralty,* which ſince frequented have withdrawn to the latter moſt of the Matters determinable in the former, and drawn too much Obſcurity thereon. That the Warden of the Ports might have a Place of Reſidence near the Ports, and a Seat ſuitable to his Quality, is the Caſtle of *Dover* committed to his Charge and Cuſtody, of which he is alſo entituled the *Conſtable,* as hereafter doth appear. And though I will not, ſay, but anciently they might ſerve for Titles of Honour and Office, to ſeveral Perſons, yet long ſince the Conſtableſhip of *Dover* Caſtle, and Wardenſhip of the *Cinque Ports,* have both been conjoined in one Perſon. See more under the Words *Conſtable* and *Caſtle,* and the Cuſtomals of the Ports.

^e *Which for the Time ſhall be* ; or, for the Time being.

^f *Liberties.* For the Precincts of the Ports, the ancient Towns, and their Members of the ſame Liberties, with the Ports, and the Precincts of every of them, that ſhall be ſo defective in Juſtice.

^g *Default* ; or, for Defect or Failing of Juſtice doing.

^h *Enter.* See hereafter, the Annotations upon the Charter of King *Edward* IV.

ⁱ *Heirs,* as before, uſed for Succeſſors.

^j *Do,* or, Make.

^k *Yearly,* or, Year by Year, in the *Latin, per Annum* for *Annuatim.*

CHARTERS.

TRANSLATION.

quinquaginta & septem navium, ad custum suum per quindecem dies,

of Fifty and seven Ships[1], at their Cost, for Fifteen Days, at

ANNOTATIONS.

[1] *Fifty Seven Ships.* The whole Number of Ships to be furnished to Sea by the whole Ports Towns and Members. These were sometime, after the first Charge thereof, and general Union and Association of the Ports Towns and Members into one Society, divided to every one a Proportion, as is recorded in the Ports *Domesday* [*] Book, before mentioned, which I so call, to [*] *That there* difference it from that other in the *Tower of London,* also so called, made by Order of the Con- *was such a* queror, and finished in the Twentieth Year of his Reign, which was not later than *Anno* 1086. *Book, and so* in imitation of the Roll of *Winchester,* which contained the Accompt only of King *Alfred's* Lands *called, appears* and Revenues, as this Book of King *William,* the Survey of the whole Kingdom, in imitation of *plainly, Patent* which, as that of the former, this latter Domesday seems to be made, containing, besides the 34 Ed. III. whole Tenures and Orders of the Castle of *Dover,* the Names of the *Cinque Ports,* two ancient *Part* 1. Mem. Towns, and their Members of old, with the Services they were to perform; and the Authority 45. *in the* and Custom of the Court of *Shepway,* with the Articles inquirable there; which Book was kept Tower, *where* with the Records of the Castle till the late Times, though now, as I have heard, removed *and the King hav-* missing. In this Book, as aforesaid, the several Proportions of the Shipping respectively to be *ing granted to* found by the Ports and Members is set down, as by the Memorandum thereof among the Records John de Bello of the Town of *Rye,* Fol. 55. of their old Custumal, and specified as an Ordinance of the King, *campo, the* touching the Service of Shipping, *Anno Domini* 1229. (which was about the Fourteenth Year of *Constableship* King *Henry* III.) appeareth thus, with the Translation. *and Wardenship, commands* Guy de Seinctclere

Domesday.

Isti sunt Portus Regis Anglie, *habentes libertates quas* ubi *Portus non habent, viz[t]. prout plenius patet in cartis inde factis.*

These are the Ports of the King of England hav- to deliver to the ing Liberties which other Ports have not, said John *the that is to say, as more fully appeareth in the Castle and Seal Charters thereof made.* *of the Office of the Constable- ship aforesaid, and the Book*

Hastyng.

[*] *Town, Street, or Village.* AD quam pertinent tanquam membra unus vicus [*] litus maris in Seford, Pewymse, Bulwarheth, Hydonaye, Iham, Bekysborn, Greneche, & Northye. Servicia inde debita [||] *Here is added* Domino Regi, xxi naves[||], & in qualibet nave *in the Copy,* xxi homines, cum uno gartione, qui dicitur *Modo xx na-* gromet [†]. *ves, modo u-*

Hastyng.

TO which pertaineth as Members one *and the Book* Town on the Sea Shore, in *Seaford, Pe- called Domes- called Domes- venfea, Bulvarbithe, Hydney, Iham, Beaksborn,* day, *&c.* *Grench,* and *Northye.* The Services thereof due to our Lord the King 21 Ships, and in every Ship 21 Men with one Boy, which is called a *Gromet.*

nam, which Words seem to be inserted by the Scribe, wherefore I omitted them.

Wynchelsey & Rye tanquam membra, Viz[t]. Wynchelsey xi naves, & Rye quinque naves cum hominibus & gartionibus, ut supra.

Winchelsea and *Rye* as Members, That is to say, *Winchelsea* 10 Ships, and *Rye* 5 Ships, with Men and Boys as above.

[†] *Grom. Dutch* vetus Romone, *for a Stripling, from whence our Word Groom.*

Romone ad quam pertinent, Prombell, Lyde, Oswarstone, Dengemarsh & quinque naves cum hominibus & gartionibus, ut supra.

Romney, to which pertaineth, *Prombill, Lyd, Oswardstone, Dengemarsh,* and old *Romney,* five Ships, with Men and Boys as above.

[‡] *Non de solo,* Hethe ad quam pertinet, Westhethe, quinque naves cum hominibus & gartionibus, ut supra.

Hithe, to which pertaineth, *Westhithe,* five Ships, with Men and Boys as above.

[‡] *Non de solo, sed in catallo, both in Dover and Sandwich, folo, I found not in some other Co- pies. It seems to note as much as that their Lands then were not charg-*

Doverr. ad quam pertinent, Folkston, Feverysham & Mergate, non [‡] de solo, sed de catallo, xxi naves ut Hastyng cum hominibus & gartionibus, ut supra.

Dover, to which pertaineth, *Folkstone, Feversham* and *Margate,* not of Soil, but of Cattle, 21 Ships, as *Hasting,* with Men and Boys as above.

Sandwich ad quam pertinent, Fordwych, Recolver, Sarre, Storey & Dale, non de solo, sed de catallo quinque naves cum hominibus & gartionibus, ut supra.

Sandwich, to which pertaineth, *Fordwich, Recolver, Sarre, Storrey* and *Deale,* not of Soil, but of Cattle, five Ships, with Men and Boys as above.

ed to the Ship- ping in those Members, but their Chattels only. [*] *The Sum of the Persons I found false, and have altered here.*

Sum. navium lvii naves. Sum. [*] hominum in eisdem. M.Cxl. homines except. gartionibus. Sum. gartionum lvii. Sum. to[lis] personarum, M.Cxcvii. personæ.

Sum of the Ships, 57 Ships. Sum of the Men in them, 1140 Men, except Boys. Sum of the Boyes 57. Sum total of the Persons, 1197 Persons.

Servicium quod Barones quinque Portuum recognoscunt facere Regi ad summon. servicii per xl dies ante exit. scil. per annum, con-

The Service which the Barons of the *Cinque Ports* acknowledge to do to the King, at the Summons of the Service by 40 Daies, before H the

I

ANNOTATIONS.

contigerit, est per xv dies ad custum eorum proprium ita quod primus dies computetur à die quo vela navium erexerint ad sigland. ad partes ad quas tendere debent, & ulterius, quam diu Rex voluerit, ad custodiend. Regis ordinat. Anᵒ. Domini M.CCᵒ. xxixᵒ.

the going out, *viz.* yearly, if it shall happen ; for 15 Daies, at their own Cost, so that the first Day be reckoned from the Day in which they shal hoist up the Sails of the Ships to saile to the Parts to which they ought to go, and further, as long as the King will, to be kept by Ordinance of the King, *Anᵒ. Domini* 1229.

Here the Ten Ships found by *Winchelsea*, and the Five by *Rye*, are to be taken inclusively for part of the Twenty one to be found by *Hasting* and its Members, because otherwise the Total of the Ships will be Seventy two, that is, Fifteen more than they were to find ; so as besides *Winchelsea* and *Rye*, *Hasting* and her Members were to find only Six Ships. Herewith also agreeth the Exemplification of the Services of the *Cinque Ports* before mentioned *, as I find the Transcript thereof remaining with the Records of the said Town of *Rye*.

* Page 6.

Edwardus, Dei gratia, &c. salutem. Inspeximus quandam certificationem coram nobis, in Canc. nuper per Thes. & Baron. de Scaccario nostro ad mandat. nostrum missam, servicia regalia annuatim debita de Quinque Portubus, cum eorum membr. si necesse fuerit, inter alia specificantem in hæc verba : Scrutatis rotulis & memorandis scaccarii pretextu brevis Regii huic schedulæ confisti, compertum est in rubreo libro in eodem scaccario residente contineri sic, Quinque Portus & eorum membra cum serviciis Regi debitis de *Portubus* prædictis annuatim cumᵃ necesse fuerit. Memorand. quod in oct. sancti Hill. Anno R. Rᵉ. E. fil. Reg. Henr. xxx primo Steph. de *Pencester*,ᵇ tunc Const. Castri Dovorr. & Custos Quinque Portuum existen. in scaccario super composito suo Baillie sua predicte, coram magistro Willielmo de March, tunc Thes. scaccarii & Baronum ejusdem, ipsoque Stephano plenius allocuto de predictis Quinque Portubus, videlicet, qui fuerint Portus, & quæ eorum Membra, & quæ servicia ipsi Portus Regi debeant, & qualit.* quomodo, idem Stephanus predictos Thes. & Baron. de premissis certificabat in hunc modum, Sussex & Kanc. Hastyng est capitalis portus, cujus membra sunt, videlicet, Wynchelfte, Rie, Leucata de Pevensæ & Bulvarheth, in Com. Sussex, Bekesborne & Greneche, in Com. Kanc. quod Portus cum suis membris predictis *debent* ᶜ invenire. ad scm. Regis viginti & unam naves, & in qualibet nave *debens* ᵈ else viginti & i homines, fortes, apti, bene armati, & apparati ad servicia Rs. ita tamen quod somon. inde fiat ex parte Rs. per xl. dies ante. Et cum predict. naves & homines in ill. existentes ad illum locum venerint, ad quem fuer. sommoniti, morabunt. ibidem in servicio Domini Rs. per xv dies ad custus suos proprios. Et si Rex servicio illorum post predictos iv dies indiguerit, seu ipsos ibidem amplius morari voluerit, erunt naves illæ cum hominibus in illis existentibus in servicio Rs. morantes ad custus Rs. quamdiu Regi placuerit, videlicet, magister capiet sex denarios per diem, & constabular. sex denar. per diem, & quilibet aliorum capiet tres denar. per diem. Kanc. Romenall Portus capit. vetus Romenall & Lyde membr. ejusdem, qui Portus cum suis membris inveniet Regi quinque naves in forma predicta. Portus de Heth debet Regi quinque naves in forma

ᵃ Si.
ᵇ Pinchester.
* Et.
ᶜ Debet.
ᵈ Debet.

In English thus :

Edward *, by the Grace of God, &c. Greeting. We have seen a certain Certificate before us, into the *Chancery*, by the Treasurer and Barons of our *Exchequer*, at our Command late sent, specifying the Royal Services yearly due from the *Cinque Ports*, with their Members, if need be, among other Things, in these Words : The Rolls and Remembrances of the *Exchequer* being searched, by pretext of the King's Writ to this Schedule fixed together, it is found in the red Book remaining in the said *Exchequer* so to be contained ; *The Cinque Ports, and their Members, with the Services to the King due from the Ports aforesaid, yearly, when need shall be*. Be it remember'd, that in the Eighth of St. *Hillary*, in the 31 Yeare of the Reigne of King *Edward*, Son of King *Henry*, *Stephen de Pencester*, then Constable of *Dover* Castle, and Warden of the *Cinque Ports*, being in the *Exchequer*, upon his Accompt of his Bayliwick aforesaid, before Mr. *William de March*, then Treasurer of the *Exchequer*, and the Barons of the same, and to him the said *Stephen* fully allowed of the *Cinque Ports*, vizᵗ. which were the Ports, and which their Members, and what Services the said Ports owe to the King, and how, and in what manner, the said *Stephen* did certify the aforesaid Treasurer and Barons of the Premises, on this wise : *Sussex* and *Kent*, *Hasting* is an Head ‡ Port, whose Members are, *viz. Winchelsea*, *Rye*, the *Lowey or capital Port*, of *Pevensey*, and *Bulvarbithe*, in the County of *Sussex*, *Beaksborne* and *Grenche*, in the County of *Kent*, which Port, with its Members aforesaid, ought to find at the Summons of the King Twenty and one Ships, and in every Ship there ought to be Twenty and one Men, strong, apt, well armed, and prepared || for the Services of the King ; so that the || Summons thereof be made of the Part of the King by 40 Days before : And when the said Ships, and Men in them being, shall come to that Place to which they were summoned, they shall tarry there in the Service of our Lord the King by 15 Daies, at their own Costs ; and if the King shall need their Service after the aforesaid 15 Daies, or will them there longer to tarry, the Ships, with the Men in them, being in the Service of the King, shall be abiding at the Costs of the King, as long as it shall please the King, *viz.* the Master shall take Six Pence per Day, and the Constable * Six Pence *per* Day, and every one of the others shall take Three Pence *per* Day. *Kent*, *Romney* the Head † Port, old *Romney is used for a* and *Lydde*, Members of the same, which Port and *Lydde*, shall find to the King Five † Ships in Form aforesaid. The Port of *Hithe* ought

* That is K. Ed. III. as appeareth by the Records of the Tower. Pa-tents 33 Ed. III. Part 3. Memb. 6.

‡ A chief Port, and so again of Suffex afterward.

|| Furnished or ready.

* Constable of a Ship in Dutch Kent, Gunner.

† Or a chief it capital Port.

ought

ɪ

ANNOTATIONS.

Serre.

Vicesimo.

Serica.

Per.

Pinchester.

formâ predicta. Dovorr. est Portus capitalis, cujus membr. sunt, videlicet, Feversham, Folstan. & Mergate, & debet Portus ille cum membris suis predictis viginti & unam naves in formâ predicta. Sandwyche est Portus captalis, cujus membra sunt Potdwych, Stonore & Sorre*, qui Portus cum suis membris debet Regi quinque naves in formâ predicta. Sum. servicii, Quinque Portuum, lvii. naves. Et quoad servicia in coronatione, &c. continentur in eodem libro sic: A° vicesimo* Rs. Henrici fil. Ra. Johannis coronata Regina Alianora, filia Hugonis, com. Provinciæ, apud Westm. dominica ante prr. beate Marie, int. alia invenitur sic: Primum vero de cerico* quadratum purpureum quatuor hastis de argentatis, sustentatum cum quatuor campanellis argentes & deauratis ultra Regem incedentem quocunque incederet, gestabant Barones Quinque Portuum, assign. ad quamlibet hastam quatuor pro diversitate Portuum ne videretur Portus Portuum præfari. Consimiliter sidem pannum sericum supra Regiam post Regem incedentem. Quos quidem pannos suos esse de jure vendicant, & illos optinuerunt in Cur. licet Marchiones de Marchia Waliæ, viz. Johannes fil. Alani, Radulphus de Mortuo mari, Johannes de Monemne, & Walterus de Clysford, nomine Marchiæ use dicerent hastias inveniend. & illas deferend. Sed quodammodo frivolum reputabatur. Asserebant autem Barones de Quinque Portubus jus suum sedendi in mensis Regis eadem die a dextris Domini Regis, & ita sederunt. Compertum est etiam in quodam quaterno libro ad scacc. An° xxx primo dicti Regis E. fil. Henrici. Et* predictum Stephanum de Pencestr.* de serviciis quæ predicti Quinque Portus Regi debent sic:

ought to find to the King Five Ships in Portsé aforesaid. *Dover* is an Head Port, whose Members are, viz. *Feversham, Folstone* and *Margate,* and this Port, with its Members aforesaid, ought to find Twenty and one Ships in Form aforesaid. *Sandwich* is an Head Port, whose Members are *Fordwich, Stonore* and *Sarre,* which Port, with its Members, ought to find to the King Five Ships in Form aforesaid. The Sum of the Service of the *Cinque Ports,* 57 Ships. And as to the Service in the Coronation, &c. it is contained in the same Booke thus: In the 20 Yeare of King *Henry,* the Son of King *John,* Queen *Elianor,* the Daughter of *Hugh,* Earl of *Provence,* being crowned at *Westminster* on *Sunday* before the Purification of the blessed *Marie,* among other Things it is found thus: And a Cloth foure Square of purple Silke by four Staves silvered over, borne up with Foure [Or Spears, little Bells silver and gilt, over the King, going and so afterward whither he would, did the Barons of the Cinque Ports assigned beare, at every beam. Foure, according to the Diversity of the Ports, lest Port should seeme to be preferred to Port. That is, one Likewise the same, a silke Cloth over the with another, Queene going after the King*, which said the Barons at Clothes they did claime to be theirs of Right, the Staves, and obtained them in Court, although the to that respect Marquesses of the Marches of Wales, viz. to wit of the *John Fitz Alan, Ralfe de Mortimer, John de Ports they did Monemne,* and *Walter de Chfford,* in the Name belong. of the Marquissate, said it to be the Right of By that is to be the Marquisate to find and bear those Staves, as devised, that but it was reputed in a sort frivolous. And the the Barons of the Barons of the *Cinque Ports* did affirm their Ports did bear Right of sitting at the King's Table the same the Canopy over Day, at the right Hand of our Lord the King, the Queen as and so they sate. It is found also, in a cer-well as over the taine Foure Square Booke at the Exchequer, King. in the 31 Yeare of the said King *Edward,* Or Marqui-Sonne of *Henry.* And the aforesaid *Stephen de* sate, and so af-*Pencester,* of the Services which the aforesaid terward, viz. *Cinque Ports* owe to the King, thus: These Lords that were Governors of the Marches of Wales, by the Force of the Latin Word, are here rendered Marquisses, and Wales a Marquisate, otherwise none in England, till K. R. II.

Serront le maryners.

La en.

La venue.

CES sount lez services que lez Barons des Sink Portés deynent a nostre seigneur le Roy dan en an per mier, si niest est, cest afsav*. la vill. de Hastynges trois niefs, la Lewe de Pevense une nyef, Balvarhyeh & petit Ihame une nyef, Bekesborne en Kent une nyef, Greneche en Rent deux hommes, one deux auyroun oue lez nyefs de Hastyng, la vill. de Rie sink nyefs, la vill. de Wynchelsea dice nyefs, la port de Romenall, & viell. Romenall quatre nyefs, Lyde une nyef, le Port de Hethe sink nyefs, la port de Dovorr. dice & noef niefs, Folstan. une nyef, la vill. de Feversham une nyef, le port de Sandwich, Stonore, Fordwich, Dale & Serr. sink nyefs. la somme totall lvii nyefes. Et cestassavoir, que quant le Roy vodra av*. son service des avantditz nyefs, ils averont xl jours de somonce & troveront al Roy en chescune nyef xx hommes & le mastr. *Et sont lez mar*.* de chescune nyef armie, & en. atire pur faire la service le Roy, & erount les nyefs al propers costages de Sink Portz *lou*' ils serount somonce. Et quant les nyefs serount* demorrount

THESE are the Services which the Barons of the *Cinque Ports* owe to our Lord the King from Yeare to Yeare by Sea, if need be, that is to wit, The Towne of *Hasting* Three Ships, the Lowey of *Pevensey* One ship, *Balwarhithe* and *Petit Iham* One Ship, *Bexborne in Kent* One Ship, *Grenehe in Kent* Two Men with Two Anchors, with the Ships of *Blurred in the Hasting,* the Towne of *Rye* Five Ships, the Copy, that with Towne of *Winchelsea* Tenne Ships, the Port ther is to with of *Romney* and old *Romney* Foure Ships, *Lydde* Anchors or no One Ship, the Port of *Hithe* Five Ships, the *I am not cer-*Port of *Dover* Nineteene Ships, *Folstan.* one sail, but rather Ship, the Towne of *Feversham* One Ship, take it for a the Port of *Sandwich, Stonor, Fordwich, Dale* Hand Irons, the and *Sarre* Five Ships; the Summe Totall 57 old Saxon Ships. And it is to wit, that when the King Word for Dag-will have his Service of the aforesaid Ships, gers or spers they shall have 40 Daies of Summons, and Swords. shall find to the King in every Ship 20 Men and the Master, and the Manner* of every* Mariners of Ship is to be armed and furnished for to do every Ship shall the Service of the King. And the Ships shall be armed, and be fitted at the proper Costs of the *Cinque* well attired. Ports when they shall be summoned. And Or Charges. when the Ships shall have tarried 15 Daies in the

ANNOTATIONS.

rount xv jours en ſervice le Roy ac propres coſtages dez Sink Ports, & apres lez xv jours paſſes, neſt demorrount ac coſtages le Roy ſil ad faire, ceſt aſſav. le meſtr. del nyef prendra del jour vi *d.* le coneſtable vi *d.* & cheſcune dez autres trois deneres. La court de Shypwey avera xl jours de ſomonce, & eſt tenuz pur Sink Poynts, ou pur une des ſink, ceſtaſſavoir pur faux jugement, pur ſervice le Roy ſuſtet. pur treſoure trove deſouz ter. pur fauſſeio de money, pur treſon pur parle entre le Roy, & ſa pees trubler. Aliud vero non comperimus ſuper contentis in brevi prædicto. Nos autem tenorem certificationis prædictæ ad requiſitionem dilecti nobis Nicholai Aſpilon, uni. Baron. dicti Portus de Sandwico, & nunc Major. vill. de Sandwico ad majorem noticiam premiſſorum duximus exemplificand. per preſentes. In cujus rei teſtimonium, &c. has literas fieri fecimus patentes, &c.

the Service of the King, at the proper Coſts of the *Cinque Ports*, and after the 15 Days paſt they tarry not, but at the Coſts of the King, if he have to do, that is to wit, The Maſter of the Ship ſhall take for a Day 6 Pence, the Conſtable 6 Pence, and every of the others Three Pence. The Court of *Shipwey* ſhall have 40 Daies of Summons, and is holden for Five Points, or for One of theſe Five, that is to wit, for falſe Judgment, for the Service of the King to be ſuſteined, for Treaſure found under the Earth, for falſifying of Money, for Treaſon ſpoken ‡ againſt the King, and the Diſturbers || of his Peace. But other Thing we found not upon the Contents in the Writ aforeſaid. And we the Tenor of the Certificate aforeſaid, at the Requeſt of our beloved *Nicholas Aſpilon*, one of the Barons of the ſaid Port of *Sandwich*, and now Maior of the Towne of *Sandwich*, for greater Knowledge of the Premiſſes, have cauſed to be exemplified by theſe Preſents. In witneſs whereof, *&c.* We have made theſe our Letters Patents, *&c* *.

> ‡ *Or for ſpeaking.*
> || *Or Troublers.*
> * *By the Records in the Tower this Exemplification bears Teſte at* Reading 29 *Day of* November, 33 Ed. III.

Nevertheleſs, as Occaſion required, ſome Alterations have been made in theſe Proportions, and Allotments, of more and leſs to ſome Towns, by Order and Decree of the Ports Men amongſt themſelves, in their Courts of Brotherhood and Gueſtling, charging and eaſing one another, and ſometime one and the ſame Town, according to Conſent or Complaint. And having formerly, upon Complaint of *Sandwich*, conſented to a Surpluſage of Five Ships and an half, to make them Allowance proportional to other Towns, in their Billets at the Tenths and Fifteenths. By the laſt Accompt that I have ſeen, as I remember, every of the Ports Towns and Members ſtand charged to find as followeth:

	Ships		Ships
Haſting	3 $\frac{1}{4}$	*Seaford*	1 $\frac{1}{4}$
Winchelſea	5	*Pevenſea*	1 $\frac{1}{4}$
Rye	4	*Tenterden*	3
Romney	3 $\frac{1}{4}$	*Lydde*	3
Hithe	5	*Folkſtone*	0 [illegible]
Dover	20	*Feverſham*	1
Sandwich	10 $\frac{1}{2}$	*Fordwich*	0 $\frac{1}{4}$
	51 $\frac{1}{4}$		10 $\frac{1}{4}$

That is together 62 $\frac{1}{2}$, *viz.* the former 57, and 5 $\frac{1}{2}$ Surpluſage.

And it may further be noted, that ſince the Nation hath increaſed the Royal Navy in the Number of great and warlike Ships; theſe being ſmall, (ſufficient, as appeareth, to be manned with Twenty Men and a Boy) this Number of Fifty ſeven Ships hath not been exacted, but ſometimes Two or Three, or more, which notwithſtanding to equip, hath been equivalent in the Charge to the fitting out of the old Total, conſidering their Burden. And moreover, how chargeable ſoever this Service hath been to the Ports, they, from Time to Time, have faithfully performed it, as ſeveral Records will teſtify for them. For not only upon all Occaſions have the Navy of the Ports been ready, to guard the Narrow Seas from Pirates infeſting the Coaſts (by which, as ſome ſay, and firmly believe, from Tradition of their Anceſtors, they firſt obtained their Privileges) but imployed in frequent Tranſportations of the King's Forces, if not Perſon and Family, during the long Differences and Wars between *England* and *France*; ſo as it ſeems to be the chief of the Royal Navy, till the State provided a bigger and better, and that wherein the Kings of old did much confide for Aſſiſtance, as our Hiſtories intimate. King *John*, in his Retirement in the Iſle of *Wight* *, was almoſt forſaken of all his Kingdom, ſave the Ships and Mariners of the *Cinque Ports*, with which he ſecured himſelf till he recovered all again. In the beginning of the Reigne of King *Henry* III. *Anno* 1217. the Ports armed Forty tall Ships, and put them to Sea under the Command of *Hubert de Burgo* (then Warden of the *Cinque Ports*, and Commander of *Dover* Caſtle) who meeting with Eighty Sail of *French* Ships coming to aid *Lewis*, the *French* King's eldeſt Son, gave them a moſt couragious Encounter, wherein he took ſome, ſunk others, and diſcomfited the reſt. And at other Times ‡ this King *Henry* had great Benefit by the Shipping of the Ports. About 1293, or 1294. in the Reign of King *Edward* I. an Hundred Sail of the Ports Navy fought at Sea with a great Fleet of *French* Ships, of whom (notwithſtanding great odds) they ſlew, took, and ſunk ſo many, that *France* was thereby for a long Seaſon after in a manner deſtitute, both of Seamen and Shipping. *Rot. Scotiæ*, 10 Edward III. *Memb.* 16. The Navy of the Ports, together with other Veſſels taken up

> * *In the 17th Year of his Reign.*
> ‡ *As the* 8, 10, *and* 11 *Years of his Reign, wherein he writes to have the Ports ſet out double their Number of Ships this Time, with Promiſe it ſhould be no Preſident,* 13 Febr. *Pat.* 11 Hen. III. Mem. 8.

CHARTERS.　　TRANSLATION.

dies, ad noſtram vel hæred. noſtrorum ſummonitionem. Conceſſimus etiam	at the Summons ᵐ of us, or of our Heirs. We have alſo grant-

ANNOTATIONS.

up for that Service, under the Command of *Geffrey de Say*, Admiral of the Sea from the Mouth of the *Thames* to the ſouthern and weſtern Parts, defended the Seas, and hindered the bringing of Succors from foreign Parts to the King's Enemies in *Scotland*. Under † King *Henry* IV. † *Before this,* *Anno* 1406. the Navy of the *Cinque Ports*, conducted by *Henry Paye*, ſurprized One Hundred *in the* 10ᵗʰ and Twenty *French* Ships, all laden with no worſe Merchandiſe than Salt, Iron and Oil. In *and* 11ᵗʰ *Tears* the Fourteenth Year of King *Henry* VI. the Navy had ſummons to fit out their whole Number *of* K. R. II. *the* of Ships, to be ready at *Winchelſea* by the Feaſt of St. *George*, which was *Anno* 1436. *June* 15, *Ports Navy both* *Anno* 23 *Henry* VI. the Town of *Sandwich* ſet out Five Ships to fetch Queen *Margaret* out of *Times were or* *France*. *May* 23, *Anno* 27 *Henry* VI. the Town of *Sandwich*, by command from the King, ſent *dered to be rea-* out One Ship for Four Months Service. *July* 18, *Anno* 27 *Henry* VI. the ſame Town, by like *dy at Sand-* command, ſet out another Ship for Four Months Service. Hen. VI. 49. *& receptionis regia poteſtatis prima*, the Navy of the Ports were ſet out to fetch *terwards the* Queen *Margaret* and the Prince out of *France*. *March* 31, *Anno* 15 *Edward* IV. the King com- *like in the* 9 H. manded the Navy of the Ports to be ready in the *Downs*, *May* 16. then next to come, for V. Tranſportation of the King and his Army, and the King and his Army came to *Sandwich*. *Anno* 7 *Henry* VII. in *May*, the Ports Navy tranſported the King's Army from *Sandwich* into *France*. *Anno* 8 *Henry* VII. in *November*, the Ports Navy brought back the King's Army from *Calais*. *Anno* 10 *Henry* VII. in *July*, the Trained Bands of *Sandwich* beat back the King's Enemies landing in the *Downs*. *Anno* 5 *Henry* VIII. in *May*, Preparation for the King's Army was made at *Sandwich*, and the Ports Navy tranſported his Army from thence and *Dover* into *France*. *Anno* 34 *Henry* VIII. in *Auguſt*, at the King's Command, the Navy of the Ports was prepared, and ready, the Tenth of *October*, at *Sandwich* and *Dover*, to tranſport his Horſes and Army into *France*, and did tranſport them. *Anno* 35 *Henry* VIII. in *April*, the King commanded the Ports Navy to be in readineſs in the *Downs* the Twenty ſixth of *May*, to do their Service, which they did. *Anno* 30 *Elizabeth*, 1588. in *April*, the Ports, at the Queen's Command, ſet out Five ſerviceable Ships, and a Pinace for her Majeſty's Service, for two Months, but they ſerved four Months at their own Coſts. *Anno* 38 *Elizabeth*, 1595. in *January*, the Ports, at the Queen's Command, ſet out Five ſerviceable Ships, of One Hundred and ſixty Tons a piece, for five Months, at their own Charges. *Anno* 2 *Charles* I. in *July*, 1626. at the King's Command, the Ports ſet out Two ſerviceable Ships for three Months, which coſt them 1825l. 8s. One Paper I have ſeen mentioned ſomewhat leſs.

ᵐ *Summons.* This is the Writ directed to the Lord Warden, to warn the Ports to provide and make ready the Ships required to be imployed in the King's Service. A Copy of one of which, found among the Records of the Town of *Winchelſea*, by which the reſt may be judged, here followeth, repeated *verbatim* in the Letter of Attendance, or Writ of the then Lord Warden ſent in to the Ports thereupon.

HUmfridus, Dei gratia, Regum filius, frater, & patruus, dux Glouceſtr. &c. Conſtabular. Caſtri Dovorr. & Cuſtos Quinque Portuum, Omnibus & ſingulis Majoribus, Ballivis, Juratis, & Baronibus, dictorum Quinque Portuum, & eorum Membrorum, ſalutem. Breve Domini noſtri Regis nobis direct. recepimus in hæc verba: Henricus, Dei gratia, Rex Angliæ, & Franciæ, & Dominus Hiberniæ, cariſſimo avunculo ſuo Humfrido, Duci Glouceſtr. Conſtabular. Caſtri ſui Dovorr. & Cuſtodi Quinque Portuum ſuorum, vel ejus locuntenenti ibidem, ſalutem. Cum Barones noſtri Quinque Portuum prædictorum, de an.° in annum debent nobis certa ſervicia per mare, ſi neceſſe fuerit, videlicet, Quinque Portus prædicti, cum membris, invenient quinquaginta & ſeptem naves ſuper mare, ad ſummonitionem noſtram quadraginta dier. & in qualibet navi viginti homines & magiſtrum, armatos bene, arriatos ad faciend. ſervicium noſtrum. Quæ quidem naves, ad proprios cuſtos dictorum Quinque Portuum, ubi ſummonitæ fuerint proficiſcend. & quando dictæ naves ibidem venerint, quindecim diebus in ſervicio noſtro ad proprios cuſtos Quinque Portuum prædictorum morabuntur, & quindecim diebus elapſis, naves illæ cum hominibus in

HUmfrey, by the Grace of God, Son, Brother and Uncle of Kings, Duke of Gloceſter *, &c., Conſtable of the Caſtle of Dover, * *This Duke* and Warden of the *Cinque Ports*, To all and *was Son to K.* ſingular Mayors, Bailiffs, Jurats and Barons H. IV. *Brother* of the ſaid *Cinque Ports*, and their Members, *to K. H. V.* Greeting. We have received a Writ of our *Uncle to K. H.* Lord the King, to us directed, in theſe VI. Words: *Henry*, by the Grace of God, King *of England*, and *France*, and Lord of *Ireland*, to his moſt dear Uncle *Humfrey*, Duke of *Gloceſter*, Conſtable of his Caſtle of *Dover*, and Warden of the † *Cinque Ports*, or his Lieute- † *Or his* nant there, Greeting. Whereas our Barons Cinque Ports. of the *Cinque Ports* aforeſaid, from Year to Year, owe to us certain Services by Sea, if need ſhall be, *viz.* the *Cinque Ports* aforeſaid, with their Members, finding Fifty and ſeven Ships upon the Sea, at our Summons of Forty Days, and in every Ship Twenty Men and the Maſter, well armed, and arrayed to do our Service. Which ſaid Ships, at the proper Coſts of the ſaid *Cinque Ports*, where they ſhall be ſummoned, are to go, and when the ſaid Ships ſhall come there, ſhall tarry Fifteen Days in our Service, at the proper Coſts of the *Cinque Ports* aforeſaid, and the Fifteen Days being elapſed ‡, the Ships with the Men ‡ *Or paſt.* in

CHARTERS.

etiam eifdem de gratia noftra, fpeciali, quod habeant Ut-fangtheff, in terris fuis infra Portus

TRANSLATION.

granted to them of our fpecial grace [a] that they may have Ut-fangtheff [o], in their Lands with-in

ANNOTATIONS.

in illis exiftentibus morabuntur ad cuftos noftros, fi de fervicio illo indiguerimus, quamdiu nobis placerit, videlicet, magifter navis percipiet per diem fex denarios, conftabular. fex denarios, & quilibet aliorum tres denarios, ficut per tenorem cartar. de libertatibus dictis Baronibus Quinque Portuum per progenitores noftros conceffis, quas confirmavimus, in rotulis Cancellar. noftræ irrotulatarum nobis conftat. Et quia nos jam certis de caufis nos & concilium noftr. fpecialiter moventibus firmum propofit. ad quofdam magnates cum poteftate congrua ad partes regni noftri Franciæ, fuper falva cuftodia earundem moratur. Deo duce in proximo æft. deftinand. volumus ut dicti Barones fervicium fuum navium prædictarum in fortificationem armat. perfonarum in hac parte fiend. faciant in forma prædicta. Et ideo vobis mandamus, quod Barones fingulorum Portuum prædictorum ac membrorum eorundam ex parte noftra fine dilatione fummoniri faciat. quod ipfi cum navibus & marinariis hujufmodi fufficient. arraiat. prompti fint apud Portum villæ noftræ de Wynchelfe in fefto fancti Georgii prox. fatur. ad proficifcend. fuper mare cum armata noftra fupradicta, & fervicium fuum fub pœna & periculo incumbentibus in forma predicta fidelit. faciant ut tenentur. Et nos de fummonitione illa, cum fic facta fuerit, nobis in Cancellar. noftra fub figillo veftro diftincte & aperte certificet.T. me ipfo apud Weftm. xiiii° die Februarii A° R. noftri quartodecimo. Quare vobis & cuilibet veftrum ex parte dicti Domini noftri Regis mandamus, firmiter injungentes, quod dictum breve juxta vim, formam, & effectum ejufdem in omnibus & fingulis ex parte veftra diligent. exequamini, & hoc nullatenus omittatis, nec aliquis veftrum ullatenus omittat. Data apud Caftrum predictum fub figillo officii noftri ibidem xii° die Martii, Anno regni Regis Henrici fexti xiiii°.

in them being, fhall tarry at our Cofts, if we fhall have need of that Service, as long as it fhall pleafe us, *viz.* the Mafter of the Ship fhall receive Six Pence by the Day, the Conftable Six Pence, and every one of the others Three Pence, as by the Tenor of the Charters of the Liberties to the faid Barons of the *Cinque Ports* by our Progenitors granted, which we have confirmed, in the Rolls of our *Chancery* inrolled, to us appeareth. And becaufe we now for certain Caufes us and our Council efpecially moving, have taken a firm Purpofe * to defign certain Nobles, with a * *Or Refoluti-fuitable* Power to the Parts of our Kingdom of *on.* *France,* for the fafe Keeping thereof, there to abide, God guiding †, in the next Summer : † *Or God being* We will that the faid Barons their Service of *Guide.* the aforefaid Ships, for Fortification of the armed Perfons in this Part to be done, make in Form aforefaid. And therefore to you we command, that the Barons of all the Ports aforefaid, and their Members, on our Part, without delay, you make to be fummoned, that they with their Ships and Mariners of this fort fufficiently arrayed, be ready, at the Port of our Town of *Winchelfea,* on the Feaft of St. *George* next to come, to go upon the Sea with our Forces ‡ abovefaid, and that ‡ *Or Army,* they faithfully do their Service in form aforefaid, under the Penalty and Peril incumbent, as they are bound. And that you diftinctly and plainly certify us of that Summons, when fo the fame fhall be made in our *Chancery,* under your Seal. Witnefs My Self at *Weftminfter* the Fourteenth Day of *February,* in the Year of our Reign the Fourteenth. Wherefore to you, and every of you, on the Part of our faid Lord the King, We command, firmly injoyning, that the faid Writ, according to the Force, Form, and Effect thereof, in all Things ‖, on your part you diligently execute, ‖ *Or in all and* and this by no means you omit, nor any of *every Thing.* you by any means omit. Dated at the Caftle aforefaid, under the Seal of our Office there, the Twelfth Day of *March,* in the Fourteenth Year of the Reign of King *Henry* the Sixth.

[a] *Grace,* here, and in feveral other Places, for Favour.

[o] *Utfangtheff,* or, *Outfangthiefe,* that is, Thieves or Felons of the Precincts of the Ports taken out of them, fhall be brought back and there tried and judged. And thus I find the Ports Men well underftood it in the Cafe of *John Burrell,* in the Reign of King *Henry* VIII. thus reported :

FOrafmuch as it is granted by Chartours unto the Ports, by the noble Progenitors of our Soveraigne Lord the King that now is, and by his Highnes the fame Chartour ratified, approbat. and confirmed, *Infangthefe* and *Outfangthefe,* which not onlie by the faid Chartour fo appeareth, but alfo by auncient Rules and Cuftomals of divers of the Towns of the faid Ports it is recited, and fo maketh mention, That if any Manner of Perfon or Perfons, Straungers or Indwellers, do within the Precinct and Jurifdiction of any Port, or Member of the fame, commic Felony, and thereupon fuch Felony committed do fle *, and avoid from thence ; that then it * *Flee.* fhall be lawfull to the Maior, or Baylye of fuch Towne and Member, to fend for fuch Perfon or Perfons fo the Felony committing, to any Place within the King's Realme, as well franchifed as other (holy Sanctuary only excepted) and that not onlie fuch Perfon or Perfons to be reftored to fuch Towne or Townes, and Port, but alfo Goods and Cattalles as the faid Perfon or Perfons have felonioufly taken away, as Time without minde hitherto peaceably hath beene ufed. So it is, that the xxiith Day of *Aprill,* the viiith Yere of the Raigne of King *Henry* the viiith, within the

ANNOTATIONS.

the Jurisdiction and Liberties of the auncient Towne and Port of *Rye*, which is one of the auncient Townes of the *Five Ports*, one *John Burrell*, late of the Towne of *Lidd*, in the Countie of
Kent, Painter, committed Felony, in the Stealing of an Horse, the Colour Graye, the Price of
xxx *s*. and so sone **b** as the said *John* the said Horse had stolen, fled and avoided from thence, **b** *Soon.*
and the xxiii^th Day of the said Moneth of *April* then next ensuing, at a Place called *Alfreston*, in
the said County of *Suffex*, and within the Jurisdiction and Liberties of the Abbot and Convent
of *Battell*, the same *John* upon the same Felony was taken, and so not onlie the said *John*, but
also the said Horse, together were brought to Ward into the Porter's keping **c** of the Monastery **c** *Keeping.*
of th'Abbot of *Battell* aforesaid. And sone **d** after, that is to say, the last Day of the said **d** *Soon.*
Moneth of *April* theis Premisses to the Maior and Jurats of the Towne and Port of *Rye* knowen,
the same Maior and Jurats, by their Writing, under their Seale of Office of Mairalty of the said
Towne, according to the said Liberties of the *Five Ports* written and asselid **e**, made Request to **e** *Seale.!.*
Lawrance, then, and yet being, Abbot of the said Monastery of *Battell*, for Restitution and
Delivery, not only of the said *John*, but also of the said Horse, to th'intent that the King's
Lawes might proceed **f**, and have Plea againe the same *John Burrell*, according his Demeritts, **f** *Proceed.*
after Law within the said Towne and Port used, which said Abbot utterlie denied the same
John Burrell Prisoner, and right so the said Horse to the said Towne and Port of *Rie* to be restored and delivered ; but incontinentlie the same Abbot the same *John Burrell*, for the said Felony
committed, and done by Warrant made from Mr. *William Ashburnham*, then being Sheriffe of
Suffex and *Surrey*, contrary to the Liberties of the Ports, by the proper Servant of the said Abbot, did so send to the Prison and Gaill of the King's *Bench* in *Southwarke*, next unto the Citie
of *London*, which Premisses thus used and done, the said Maior and Jurats of the said Towne
and Port of *Rie* that considering, that the Liberties of the said Ports then should **g** be usurped, **g** *Should.*
injured and wronged, if that so should **g** be suffered, thought it necessary to call a Commen **gh** *Common.*
Councell of the Three West Ports for especiall Purpose and Reformation of the same. Wherefore they, by one Assent, sent the brotherlie Letters of Monytion unto the Townes of *Hasting*
and *Winchelsey*, to pray the Maior and Bayliffes of the same, at a Day appointed, to be and have
Assemblie at the Towne of *Winchelsey*, and a Court called a *Gestillinge*, to be holden ther, according to the old Usages of the said Three Townes as of old Time used. At which Day and Assembly, that is to say, the xii^th Day of *May*, *Anno predicti Regis now*, ther appeared for *Hasting*,
Henry Crowher, Bayliffe, *Richard Rogerson* and *Thomas Goddard*, Jurats ; for *Winchelsey*, *Robert
Sparrow*, Maior, *John Kirkely*, *James Marshall* and *Moyse Pette*, Jurats ; for *Rye*, *Nicholas Sut-
ton*, Maior, *George Mercer*, *Gabriel Wayte*, Jurats. At which said Assemblie and Court the said
Injuries, and other the Premisses, before the said Maiors, Baylif and Jurats, shewed and al-
legid **i**, it was at the said Court condiscended and agreed, that the said *George Mercer* and **i** *Alledged.*
Richard Rogerson, Men ther named, shuld **k** be Sollicitours at the next Terme, for, and in the **k** *Should.*
Name of the hole **l** Corporation of the Ports, ther to sue in Councel for Reformation of the said **l** *Whole.*
Usurpation and Injury done, and to have for ther Expences and Costs such as they shall di-
spend for the same. Whereupon, at the next Terme, that is to say, *Easter* Terme, *Anno pre-
dicti Domini Regis now*, the said *George Mercer* and *Richard Rogerson* being at *Westminster*, by
Processe of Time in there Suite had, it was there condiscended by Counsel, that the said *John
Burrell* shuld **m** with spede be indytid **n** within the Towne of *Rye*, of, and for the said Felony **m** *Should.*
committed, and that Inditement to be asseald **o** aswell with the general Seales of the Jurors, as **n** *Indicted.*
with the Seale of Office of Mairalty of the said Towne of *Rye*. Which Indytement, for suffici- **o** *Sealed.*
ent Instruction to be had of all the Ports, in such case wher such Things shall fortune, which
was noted, and made by substantiall learned Counsel, followeth in theis Words :

INquisitione indentat. capt. apud villam de Ria, una antiquarum villarum Quinque Portuum, &
de libertate eorundem Quinque Portuum, vicesimo sexto die Maii, Anno regni Regis Henrici
octavi nono, in Hundred. ejusdem villæ, ad tunc ibidem infra eandem libertatem, tam juxta usum &
consuetudinem ejusdem ville de Ria, & aliarum villarum Quinque Portuum, & eorum membrorum
a tempore cujus contrar. memoria hominum non exist. quam juxta libertatem & privilegium, Majoribus, Ballivis, & Juratis, & aliis Inhabitantibus prædictorum Quinque Portuum, per cartas diversorum Regum Angliæ Progenitor. Domini Regis, nunc concessas ac per ipm. Dominum Regem nunc
per literas suas patentes concessas, confirmat, & ratificat. coram Nicholao Sutton, Majore ejusdem
villæ de Ria, Clemente Adam, Georgio Mercer & Johanne Carpinter, Jurat. ejusdem villæ, Jurat. ejusdem villæ ac custodibus pacis ipsius Domini Regis nunc infra villam de Ria predicta, ac
ad omnia & singula felon. transigr. & alia malefacta infra villam illam perpetrat. audiend. &
determinand. assign. per sacram. Roberti Soggs, Roberti Gervis, Richardi Broke, Thomæ Tew-
mell, Alex. Shalforde, Roberti Bennet, Johannis Russell, Haukyn Barrett, Roberti White,
Thomæ Webb, Thomæ Heseman, & Simonis Clifforde, proborum & legalium hominum de villa
& libertate predictis, qui dicunt & present. pro Domino Rege, quod quidam Johannes Burrell,
nuper de Lidd, in com. Kanc. paynter, vicesimo die Aprilis, Anno Regni Domini Regis, nunc
octavo, vi & armis, viz. baculis & cultellis unum equum coloris de gray, precii trigint. solido-
rum cujusdam Thomæ Adam apud Ria predictam infra libertatem ac prædict. pred. ad tunc in-
vent. felonice cepit & abduxit contra pacem Domini Regis nunc, &c. In cujus rei testimonium
tam pred. Major. & Jurati villæ predictæ sigillum officii prædicti Major. quam pred. Jur. per quos
præsent. inquisitio capt. exist sigilla sua utrumque part. present. inquisitioni indent. apposuerunt. Dat. apud villam de Ria pred. xxi die Aprilis, A°. viii°. suprad.

And that Indytement so indented, and asselid **a**, not onlie in the next Terme, before the **a** *Sealed.*
King's Justices in the King's Bench, but also at that Time to bring and present iiii sufficient
Persons to take to Bayle the said *John Burrell* Prisoner to a Day. And the aforesaid Inditement, according as Councell advised in every Thing, spedd at the next Terme, that is to
say, in *Trinitie* Terme next ensuing, not only the said *George Mercer* bringing with him Two
suffi-

ANNOTATIONS.

sufficient Men from *Rie*, but alfo the faid *Richard Rogerfon*, the xxii^th Day of *June, Anno nono prediɛto*, perfonally appeared before the faid Juftices in the King's *Bench*, then and ther perfonally prefent the faid *John Burrell* Prifoner, which *John* at that Time then ftanding only as Prifoner to the faid Sheriffe of *Suffex*, and not Prifoner recorded to the faid Juftices in the King's *Bench*, wherefore the faid *George Mercer* and *Richard Rogerfon*, by th'Advice of ther Councell incontinentlie, the fame *John Burrell* Prifoner being at Barre, fued a Writ, called an *Habeas Corpus*, to remove the faid *John* to ftand and be as Prifoner only to the faid King's Juftices in his Bench. That Writ done and fped, the fame *John Burrell* then on-

b *Stood.*   ly ftanding, and being Prifoner to the faid Juftices, the faid *George Mercer* and *Richard Rogerfon* fhewed forth the faid Inditement, whereby the fame *John Burrell* ftode **b** indyted of Felony before the Maior and Jurats of the Towne and Port of *Rie*, which is one of the auncient Townes of the Liberties of the *Five Ports*, requiring the fame *John Burrell* to them to be

c *Read.*   delivered to Bayle to a certaine Day in them to be limitted. The faid Juftices taking unto them the faid Indytement, that well perceiving, redd **c** and underftanding, granted to the faid *George Mercer* and *Richard Rogerfon* the fame *John Burrell* to them to be delivered, according to a Copie of a Bill of the Record of Bayle taking ther entred appeareth, to th'intent that

d *I take it to be miftaken for Octabis Martini, as afterward.*   the faid Mayneprifoners, at the faid Day of *October* **d**, the fame *John Burrell* ther againe tô deliver, and els him in the meane Time to commit to the Order of the King's Lawes according to his Demerits, and as fhall be in the mean Time with the faid *John Burrell* Prifoner ufed and done, thereof to the faid IJuftices at the faid Day of *Octab. Martini* duly to certifie. And anon, after the Delivery of the faid Prifoner, requeft was made to the faid Abbot for the faid Horfe, and upon fuch Requeft made, without Delay, the Horfe was delivered, and fo was reftored to the faid Towne and Port of *Rye*. The Copy of the faid Bill of Bayle followeth, in thefe Words :

Johannes Burrell, capt. pro fufpicion. felon. tradit. in baillium Georg. Mercer, de Ria, in Com. Suffex, gentelman, Ricardo Rogerfon, de Haftinge, in Com. Suffex, gent. & Thomæ Adam, de Ria, in Com. Suffex, drap. Octab. Martini ubicunque, &c.

Afterwards, that is to fay, the vi^th Day of *July, Anno prediɛts Domini Regis nono*, then next enfuing, the faid *John Burrell* Prifoner, before the faid Maior and Jurats of *Rye* upon

e *Verdict.*   the faid Indytement arrayned, and of the Felony aforefaid, by Verdytt **e** of xii Men condempned ; which faid *John Burrell*, after Time of Condempnation, pretending to be a Clerke,

f *Reprieved.*   was repryved **f** over to a further Day, that is to fay, the xvith of *July* then next enfuing, for the Appearance of an Ordynarye, at which fayd Day the fame *John Burrell*, Prifoner at the Barre, before the faid Maior and Jurats of *Rye*, fitting in *Platea Hundred*, in the King's Court, ther an Ordynarye appeared, the fame *John Burrell* examined, Clerke or no Clerke, the the fame Ordynary him admitted as Clerke and Member of Church, the faid *John Burrell* then and there, according to the Lawes of the Land, with the Letter of *T.* was brent in the Brawne of the left Hand, and then to the faid Ordynarye ther was delivered *ad falvo cuftodiend. juxta legem & confuetudin. Regni Angliæ*, &c. And after that Time appointed, the faid *George Mercer* and *Thomas Adam*, by Councel, put into the Court of the King's Bench before the King's Juftices, ther Plee of Certificate made touching the final End and Conclufion of all the Premiffes : Which Plee, and Conclufion of the faid hole Matter, followeth, as hereafter fpecified and written.

Johannes Burrell, nuper de Lidd, in Com. Kanc. painter, per Willielmum Afhburnham, Vic. Com. Suffex, virtute literarum Domini Regis, de Habeas Corpus, ad fectam ipfius Regis ad ftand. reɛt. &c. ei inde direɛt. & coram Domino Rege duɛt, cum caufa, viz¹. quod prediɛtus Johannes capt. fuit apud Battell in Com. pred. pro fufpicione felon. apud Ria in Com. pred. perpetrat. qui comittitur Majori, &c. poftea ift. termino tradit. in ballivum Georg. Mercer de Riæ, in Com. Suffex, gentelman, Ricardo Rogerfon, de Hafting, in Com. Suffex, gent. & Thomæ Adam, de Ria, in Com. Suffex, drap. ufque Octab. Martini ubicunque, &c. Ad quas quidem Octab. fanɛti Martini loquela pred. adjornat. fuit per literas Domini Regis de ce. adjournament. coram Domino Rege ufque in Octab. fanɛti Hilarii, ex tunc prox. fequen. ubicunque, &c. Ad quem diem coram Domino Rege apud Weftm. pred. pred. Johannes Burrell, folempnit. exaɛt. non venit, fuper quo prediɛti Georgius Mercer & Thomas Adam duo pleg. prediɛti Johannis Burrell, in hac parte in Cur. Domini Regis hic perfonaliter comparentes dicunt ipfi nendum Johannem Burrell, coram Domino Rege hic ad præfat. Octab. fanɛti Hilarii habere non poffunt. Et inde idem diɛtus Johannes Burrell poft terminum pred. quo recogn. pred. capt. fuit & ante pred. Octab. fanɛti Hillarii, fcilicet, fexto decimo die Julii, Anno regni diɛti Domini Regis nunc nono, coram Nicholao Sutton, Majore villæ de Ria, in Com. Suffex, quæ eft·una antiquarum villarum Quinque Portuum & de libertate eorund. Quinque Portuum in Hundred. ejufd. villæ ad tunc & ibidem infra eandem libertatem tam juxta ufum & confuetud. ejufd. villæ de Ria, & aliarum villarum Quinque Portuum, & eorum membrorum a tempore cujus memoria hominum non exiftit quam juxta libertates & privilegia Majoribus, Ballivis & Juratis, & aliis Inhabitantibus prediɛtorum Quinque Portuum, & Cart. diverforum Regum Angliæ progenitor. Domini Regis nunc conceffas & per ipfum Dominum Regem nunc per literas fuas patentes conceffas confirmat. & ratificat. ac coram Clemente Adam, Johanne Carpinter, & aliis Jurat. ejufd. villæ ac cuftodibus pacis ipfius Domini Regis nunc infra villam prediɛtam fic ad omnia & fingula felon. tranfgreffiones & alia malefaɛta infra villam illam ·perpetrat. audiend. & terminand. affign. apud eandem villam de Ria, in Com. Suffex, idem Johannes Burrell, coram præfat. Majore & Jurat. perfonaliter adduɛt. fuit & comparuit. Nec non ibidem termino in pred. Cur. Hundred. villæ prediɛtæ de quibufdem felon. per ipfum Johannem infra villam de Ria, pred. & libertatem ejufd. perpetrat. & unde idem Johannes coram prediɛtis Majore & Juratis ante indiɛt. fuit & tunc exiftebat

          2   de

CHARTERS.

Portus prædictos eodem modo quo Archiepiscopi, Episcopi, Abbates, Comites, & Barones, habeant in maneriis suis in comitat. Kanciæ. Et quod non ponantur in Assisis, Juratis, vel Recognitionibus aliquibus, ratione forin-

TRANSLATION.

in the Ports aforesaid, in the same manner which the Archbishops, Bishops, Abbots, Earls, and Barons, have in their Manors [p] in the County of *Kent* [q]. And that they be not put in any Assizes [r], Juries [s], or Recognitions [t], by Reason of their fo-

ANNOTATIONS.

de feloniis illis ibidem fuit arrenat. qui dixit quod ipse in nullo fuit inde culpabilis, & inde de bono & malo posuit se super patriam, per quam quidem patriam inter alia compertum fuit, quod dictus Johannes Burrell fuit culpabilis de feloniis predictis, prout per indictamentum pred. supponebat. ac idem Johannes Burrell coram prefatis Majore & Jurat. tunc dixit, quod ipse clericus fuit, & petiit beneficium Ecclesiæ sibi in hac parte allocari; super quo quidem Johannes Prediam clericus Commissar. Roberti Cicestren. Episc. infra Archidiacon. Lewes, loci illius ordinarii gerens que vices ipsius Epis. ad quoscunque clericos de quocunque conduct. per literas patentes. ipsius Epis. coram prefatis Majore & Juratis in Cur. predicta tunc probat. petend. calumniand. recipiend. & ad carceras dicti Epis. speciales conducend. tunc ibidem personaliter comparens, petiit prefat. Johannem Burrell legent. ut clericum prefat. ordinario liberare ‡ ob quod idem Johannes ‡ *For* Liberari.
Burrell prius ut clericus in Cur. predicta legens in manu sua leva * caudrizat. juxta formam statu- * *For* Sinistra.
ti inde nuper edit. & provisi ad tunc & ibidem per prefatum Majorem & Jurat. deliberat. fuit prefato ordinario, ut clericus convict. occasione premissorum salvo custodiend. quousque, &c. Qui quidem Johannes Burrell in prisona pred. Epis. apud. Cicestren. in dicto Com. Sussex, ad huc remanet, quo minus predicti Georgius Mercer & Thomas Adam ipsum Johannem coram dicto Domino Rege ad prefat. Octab. sancti Hillarii habere non possunt, & hoc parat. sunt verificare, prout Cur. &c. Unde petunt judicium, & quod processus versus ipsos cessat in hac parte, & quod ipsi a Cur. Domini Regis hic de recogn. predict. quiet. dimittant, &c. Et Johannes Ornely, general. Attorn. Domini Regis, qui pro ipso Rege in hac parte sequit. pro eo quod ipse per Johannem Hales, gentelman, Nicholaum Sutton, gentelman, & alios fide dignos credibilit. informat. existit. quod placitum predictum per predictum Georgium Mercer & Thomam Adam, superius placitatum pro dicto Domino Rege cogn. fore verum; super quo vic. ‖ tam placit. predictorum Georgii ‖ *For* Visis.
Mercer & Thomæ Adam quam cogn. predicti Regis Attorn. conc. † quod pleg. predicti Johannis † *For* Consideratum est.
Burrell de premissis eant inde sine die, &c.

[p] *Manors.* A Manor, from *Maneo*, is as much as a fixed State, *Secundum excellentiam, sedes magna fixa & stabilis dicitur.* A Manor may be, *per se*, of many Edifices coadjuvat, or *Villes* and *Hamlets* adjacent. Also *per se & cum pluribus Villis & Hamlettis adjacentibus*, as the Lord *Coke* saith.

[q] *Kent*, a Kingdom in the Heptarchy of the *Saxons*, now a County, retaining yet its old Customs. Some of which, in the Towns equally privileged with the *Kentish* Ports, are kept, as well as this of *Utfangthiefe*, though in the County of *Sussex*, as in their Customals may further appear.

[r] *Assises*, or Assizes, in *Latin Assisa*, or *Assiza*, accordingly, from *Assideo*; or from the *French Asseoire*, to associate or set together; a Name now used for the Court held twice a Year in every County, for Trial of Malefactors, and Causes between Party and Party, by the Judges thereto appointed: Of old used for the Writ of Assize now triable before these Justices, and from thence they are called Judges or Justices of Assize. Sometime for a Jury that tries a Cause in question, the Sense most proper in this Place; and sometime for an Ordinance to dispose or order a Matter, as the *Assiza* of Bread, Ale, &c.

[s] *Juries*, so called from *Juro*, to swear, because every Man of the Jury or Inquest, that is to inquire and try the Cause or Matter of Fact in question (of which they are Judges) is sworn to try the Issue joined between Party and Party, according to their Evidence. The same *Latin* Word here used for Juries is elsewhere used for Jurats, who are Assistants to the Head Officer, or Chief Magistrate in the Corporations of the Ports Towns and Members, in the Administration of Justice.

[t] *Recognitions.* The *Latin* Word, in several Translations of the old Charters I have seen rendered *Recognisances*, which are Bonds upon Record, testifying the Recognisor to owe to the Recognisee a Sum of Money acknowledged in some Court of Record, or before some Judge, Justice, or other Officer that hath Authority to take the same. But because no Man can be forced by Law, against his Will, to enter into such Recognisance, therefore it must not be so taken here; but seeing every Verdict of a Jury is taken in Law for a serious Acknowledgment of the Truth (for which *Recognitio* is *Latin* as well as for Recognisance) and in some Jury Writs, these Words, *to Recognise* (that is) acknowledge, I have seen used: It can be but explanatory to Juries, as Juries to Assizes, and so plainly expresses, that Ports Men should not be enforced to serve in any of them, out of the Ports, against their Wills.

[t] *Foreign*

CHARTERS.

forinfecæ tenuræ fuæ, contra voluntatem fuam. Et quod de propriis vinis fuis de quibus negotiantur, quieti fint de recta
prifa noftra (videlicet) de uno
dolio vini ante malum, & alio
poft malum. Conceffimus infuper eifdem Baronibus, pro nobis & hæredibus noftris, quod
ipfi imperpetuum hanc habeant
libertatem (videlicet) quod nos
vel hæredes noftri non habeamus cuftodias vel maritagia
hæredum fuorum, ratione terrarum fuarum quas tenent infra
libertates & Portus prædictos,
de quibus faciunt fervitium fuum
ante-

TRANSLATION.

reign Tenure[t], againft their
Will. And that of their proper Wines for which[v] they
Trade[u], they be quit of our
right Prife[w] (that is to fay)
of one Ton[x] of Wine before
the Maft[y], and another after
the Maft. We have granted,
moreover, to the faid Barons,
for us and our Heirs, that they
for ever may have this Liberty;
(that is to fay) that we or
our Heirs may not have the
Wardfhips[z] or Marriages[a] of
their Heirs, by reafon of their
Lands which they hold within the
Liberties[b] and Ports aforefaid,
of which they do their Service[c]
afore-

ANNOTATIONS.

[t] *Foreign Tenure.* Tenure, from *Teneo*, to hold, is as much here, as the Service which he that holdeth Lands or Tenements, is bound, or ought to do, for the Hold or Tenure thereof. So that if a Man, free of the Ports, have Lands in the Foreign, (that is, out of the Ports) yet becaufe of thofe he fhall not be compelled, or drawn out of the Ports, to ferve in Juries in the Country.

[v] *For which,* or, of which.

[u] *Trade.* The Word *Negotiantur* fignifies fo much. Some Tranflations have it *Travel,* becaufe Wines are fetched from beyond Sea, and not of the ordinary Growth of this Country, but pro-cured by Travel.

[w] *Right Prife* ‡. Prifage of Wines, or Butlerage, is mentioned in the Statute *Anno* 1 *Henry* VIII. *cap.* 5. and was a Cuftom whereby the King challenged out of every Bark laden with Wine, lefs then Forty Tons, two Tons of Wine at his own Price. This Claufe, therefore, in the Charter, is a Remiffion of that Claim out of the Wine any Ports Man fhall adventure for upon his own Account. Butlerage is fometime taken for two Shillings upon every Ton of Wine imported.

‡ Recta Prifa *is alfo called* Regia Prifa, *becaufe taken for the King;* and Butlerage, *becaufe received by his Butler.*

[x] *Ton.* The *Latin, Dolium,* is fometime ufed for an Hogfhead, or other large Cask, lefs than a Ton, but in feveral Tranflations, fome of which are very ancient, it is rendered a *Ton,* and muft be fo, that it may agree with the King's Right of Prifage, or taking (as the Word *Prife* fignifies) which is not lefs than Tons.

[y] *Maft,* meaning the Main Maft, or Middle Maft of the Ship, in which the Wine is brought, if the Ship have more Mafts than one. From which Main Maft to the Head of the Ship which fails foremoft, is the Fore-Part of the Ship, and the other Part, to the Stern of the Ship, which follows after, is the Aft-Part of the Ship; whence the Sea Phrafe Afore and Abaft, or Abach, for both Parts, or all the Length of the Ship.

[z] *Wardfhips.* The *Latin, Cuftodia,* is fometime ufed for Imprifonment, and the Wardfhip of an Heir is a kind of Reftraint; for the Lord, of whom his Lands were holden, whilft he or fhe was within the Age limited by the Law in fuch cafe, had both the keeping and firft marry-ing of the Heir (only without Difparagement) and the Profits of his or her Lands, if held by Chivalry or Knight's Service. And if fuch Ward or Heir refufe to be married, the Lord fhould have the Value of the Marriage, and if within the Age of Twenty one he marry himfelf, againft the Will of the Lord, the Lord fhould have double the Value of the Marriage by the Statute of *Merton, cap.* 6. So this Paffage in the Charter is the Exemption of Orphans, that are Heirs of any Lands within the Ports, charged to the Maintenance of their Shipping aforefaid, from the Wardfhip and Marriage of the King, and other Lords, of whom their Lands were holden.

[a] *Marriages. Maritagium,* the *Latin* Word, fometime of old was taken for Dower, fometime for the Tenure of Fee tail, as the Lord *Coke* faith.

[b] *Liberties,* for Precincts.

[c] *Service,* that is, the Service of their Fifty feven Ships before mentioned, fo as though the Heir had other Lands befides thefe charged by Contribution towards the Shipping, yet thofe other Lands could not make him a Ward; for the Exemption and Liberty followed the Perfon, and being freed by the one, he could not be in Cuftody by the other, as it feemeth.

[d] *Ance-*

CHARTERS.

antedictum, & de quibus nos vel antecessores nostri custodias & maritagia non habuimus temporibus retroactis. Prædictam autem confirmationem nostram de libertatibus & quietanciis prædictis, & alias concessiones nostras sequentes, eis de gratia nostra speciali de novo fieri fecimus; salva semper in omnibus regia dignitate, & salvis nobis & hæredibus nostris, placitis coronæ nostræ, vitæ & membrorum. Quare volumus &

TRANSLATION.

aforesaid, and of which we or our Ancestors[d] have not had the Wardships and Marriages in Times past[e]. And our aforesaid Confirmation of the Liberties and Freedoms aforesaid, and other our Grants following, to them, of our special Grace, We of new have made[f]; saved[g], always, in all Things, our kingly Dignity[h], and saved to us and our Heirs, Pleas of our Crown[i], Life and Members[k]. Wherefore we will and

ANNOTATIONS.

[d] *Ancestors* includes Predecessors also in this Place.

[e] *Times past.* It seems by this, that the Ports before the Grant of this Charter, enjoyed this Freedom from Wardships.

[f] *Made,* or, caused to be made.

[g] *Saved,* or, saving.

[h] *Kingly Dignity,* or, Royal Dignity, including Pardon of capital Offenders, Coinage and Value of Monies, Arraying of Men in Arms, and such others, by the *Salva* here are reserved from the Ports.

[i] *Pleas of our Crown,* as Treasons, and such others as were triable at the Court of Shepway.

[k] *Life and Members.* Some, because of these Words, have questioned the Power of the Ports before the Charter of King *Edward* IV. to hear and determine Felonies or Pleas that touched the Life or Member of the Subject; but these Pleas of Life and Member here mentioned, seem those which were before this Charter of King *Edward* I. determinable at the Court of *Shepway* and no other; for it is evident by the Custumal of *Hasting,* penned in the Thirtieth Year of King *Edward* III. and by the Custumal of *Winchelsea,* penned in the Tenth Year of King *Henry* IV. the latter about Fifty five, and the former above One Hundred and eight Years before the Charter of King *Edward* IV. they both express their Customs for the Trial of Felons to be then, at the penning of their Custumals, Time out of mind used within their Franchises. And by the Records of *Winchelsea,* yet extant, have I seen, in the Twelfth Year of King *Henry* VI. in the Return of a Writ in nature of a *Certiorari,* to remove an Indictment thence to *Dover,* the Mayor, King's Bailiff and Jurats there certify, That Time out of mind they had used and accustomed to take and determine Inquisitions taken on the Part of the King, and all Pleas, according to their Tenures, &c. which yet was above Thirty one Years before the Charter of King *Edward* IV. The Copy of this Writ, and Return, as I found them, followeth, with the Translation I have bestowed thereon.

HUmfridus, Dei gratia, Regum filius, frater, & patruus, Dux Gloucestr. &c. Constabular. Castri Dovorr. & Custos Quinque Portuum, Majori, Ballivo & Juratis de Winchelsee, salutem. Ex certis causis Dominum nostrum Regem, necnon officium nostrum Custodiæ Quinque Portuum prædictorum tangentibus, nos de tenore recordi & processus cujusdam indictamenti coram vobis versus Willielmum Morfot, Willielmum Tilly, & Ricardum Snaylham, ut dicitur capti cerciorari volentes, vobis ex parte dicti Domini nostri Regis ac authoritate officii nostri Custodiæ Quinque Portuum prædictorum firmit. injungentes mandamus, quod tenorem recordi & processus indictamenti prædicti habeatis coram nobis seu locum nostrum tenentem apud ecclesiam sancti Jacobi Dovorr. tertio die Julii prox. futur. sub sigillis vestris, & hoc mandatum, & hujusmod penh censum-mercer. nullatenus omittetis.

HUmfrey, by the Grace of God, Son, Brother, and Uncle of Kings, Duke of *Glocester,* &c. Constable of the Castle of *Dover,* and Warden of the *Cinque Ports,* To the Mayor, Bailiff and Jurats of *Winchelsea,* Greeting. For certain Causes* touching our Lord [* Or, of certain Causes.] the King, also our Office of Wardenship of the *Cinque Ports* aforesaid, we willing to be certified of the Tenor of the Record and Process of a certain Indictment before you, against *William Morfot, William Tilly,* and *Richard Snaylham,* taken, as it is said, to you on † the [† Or, of the Part of our, &c.] Part of our said Lord the King, and by Authority of our Office of Wardenship of the *Cinque Ports* aforesaid, firmly enjoining, we command, that the Tenor of the Record, and Process of the Indictment aforesaid you have before us, or our Lieutenant, at the Church of St. *James* in *Dover,* the Third Day of *July* next to come, under your Seals, and this Mandate, and this by no means that you omit, under the Penalty of One Hundred Marks. Dated

CHARTERS.   TRANSLATION.

& firmiter præcipimus pro nobis & hæredibus noftris, quod prædicti Barones & hæredes fui imperpetuum, habeant omnes libertates & quietancias prædictas, ficut cartæ prædictæ rationabiliter teftantur. Et quod de gratia noftra fpeciali habeant Utfangtheff in terris fuis infra Portus prædictos, eodem modo quo Archiepifcopi *, & Abbates, Comites, & Barones, habeant in Maneriis fuis in Comitat. Kanciæ. Et quod non ponantur in Affifis, Juratis vel Recognitionibus aliquibus, ratione forinfecæ tenuræ fuæ, contra voluntatem fuam. Et quod de propriis vinis fuis de quibus

*In the old Copies, next to Archbishops, instead of and was Bishops, in the Latin Episcopi to be inserted l. 11. of this Page in the Charter, and l. 12. of the Translation; and so before, p. 2. l. 33.

and firmly command, for us and our Heirs, that the aforesaid Barons and their Heirs, for ever, may have all the Liberties and Freedoms aforesaid, as the Charters aforesaid do reasonably teftify. And that of our fpecial Grace they have Utfangtheff in their Lands within the Ports aforefaid, in the fame Manner which the Archbishops *, and Abbots, Earls, and Barons, have in their Manors in the County of *Kent*. And that they be not put in any Affizes, Juries, or Recognitions, by reafon of their foreign Tenure, againft their Will. And that of their proper Wines for which they

ANNOTATIONS.

tatis. Data apud Caftrum predictum fub figillo officii noftri ibidem quinto die Junii, Anno R. Rs. Henr. fexti duodecimo.

Dated at the Cafle aforefaid, under the Seal of our Office there, the Fifth Day of *June*, in the Twelfth Year of the Reign of King *Henry* VI.

SEreniffimo Principi & Domino, Domino Humfrido, Duci Glouceftr. Cuftodi Quinque Portuum, feu eju locumtenenti, nos Major. Ballivus & Jurati Domini Regia Angliæ, villæ fuæ de Winchelfe, fignificamus, quod cum inter cetera libertates & liberas confuetudines per cartas noftras per dictum Dominum Regem & fuos nobiliffimos progenitores, dudum Angliæ Reges, Baronibus villæ predictæ conceffas, & per eofdem Barones, anteceffores & predeceffores fuos a tempore immemorato, cujus contrarii memoria non exiftit, ufitatas, ufi fuerunt, debuerunt & confueverunt, inquifitiones ex parte dicti Domini Regi, placitaque omnia de tenuris fuis infra eandem villam ac de omnibus contractibus perfonalibus emergentibus infra libertatem ejufdem villæ coram Majore, Ballivo & Juratis ejufdem villæ, capere, placitare & finalit. determinare finefque concordias recordare fine intromiffione cujufcunque perfonæ, nifi pro defectu ipforum Majoris, Ballivi & Juratorum in juftitia faciend. Cuftos Quinque Portuum qui pro tempore fuerit ingrediat. villam predictam ad plenam jufticlam ibidem facien. & non alibi, prout cartæ & confirmationes earundem rationabiliter teftantur. Quapropter tenorem recordi & proceffus indictamenti infra memorati coram vobis ad diem & locum infra limitatos habere non debemus, nec tenemur, contra tenorem cartarum predictarum & enervationem libertatum & liberarum confuetudinum noftrarum predictarum, quod abfit.

TO the moft excellent Prince and Lord, the Lord *Humfrey*, Duke of *Glocester*, Warden of the *Cinque Ports*, or his Lieutenant, We the Mayor, Bailiff and Jurats of our Lord the King of *England*, of his Town of *Winchelfea*, fignify, That among other Liberties, and free Cuftoms, by our Charters, by our faid Lord the King, and his moft noble Progenitors, late Kings of *England*, granted to the Barons of the Town aforefaid, and by the fame Barons, their Anceftors and Predeceffors, Time out of mind, (the contrary whereof Memory is not ufed) they have ufed, ought and accuftomed, Inquifitions of the Part of our faid Lord the King, and all Pleas after their Tenures within the fame Town, and of all perfonal Contracts arifing within the Liberty of the faid Town, before the Mayor, Bailiff and Jurats of the faid Town, to take, plead, and determine, Fines and Concords to record, without intermiffion of any Perfon whatfoever, unlefs for Default of the faid Mayor, Bailiff and Jurats, in doing Juftice. The Warden of the *Cinque Ports*, for the Time being, may enter the Town aforefaid, to do full Juftice there, and not elfewhere, as the Charters and Confirmations hereof do reafonably teftify. Wherefore the Tenor of the Record, and Procefs of the Indictment within remembred before you, at the Day and Place within limited ‡, we ought not, nor are bound to ‡ *Or, within* have, againft the Tenor of the Charters afore-*mentioned.* faid, and to the Enervation of our Liberties, and free Cuftoms aforefaid, which God forbid,

¹ *Venerable,*

CHARTERS.

bus negotiantur, quieti fint de recta prifa noftra (videlicet) de uno dolio vini ante malum, & alio poft malum. Et quod fimiliter imperpetuum habeant libertatem prædictam (videlicet) quod nos, vel hæredes noftri, non habeamus cuftodias vel maritagia hæredum fuorum, ratione terrarum fuarum quas tenent infra libertates & Portus prædictos, de quibus faciunt fervitium fuum antedictum, & de quibus nos, vel antecefiores noftri, cuftodias & maritagia non habuimus temporibus retroactis. Prædictam autem confirmationem noftram de libertatibus & quietanciis prædictis, & alias conceffiones noftras fequentes, eis de gratia noftra fpeciali de novo heri fecimus; falva femper in omnibus Regia dignitate, & falvis nobis & hæredibus noftris, placitis coronæ noftræ, vitæ & membrorum, ficut prædictum eft. Hiis teftibus venerabili patre Roberto Portuenfe Epifcopo, facro fanctæ Romanæ ecclefiæ Cardinale, fratre Gulielmo de South, priore provincial. fratrum prædicatorum

TRANSLATION.

they trade, they be quit of our Right Prife (that is to fay) of One Ton of Wine before the Maft, and another after the Maft. And that likewife, for ever, they have the Liberty aforefaid (that is to fay) that we or our Heirs may not have the Wardfhips or Marriages of their Heirs, by reafon of their Lands which they hold within the Liberties and Ports aforefaid, of which they do their Service aforefaid, and of which we or our Anceftors have not had the Wardfhips and Marriages in Time paft. And our aforefaid Confirmation of the Liberties and Freedoms aforefaid, and other our Grants following, to them, of our fpecial Grace, we of new have made; faved always, in all Things, our kingly Dignity, and faved to us and our Heirs, Pleas of our Crown, Life and Members, as is aforefaid. Witneffes to thefe Prefents, the Venerable[1] Father *Robert Portuenfis*[m], Bifhop, Cardinal[n] of the moft Holy[o] Church of *Rome*, Frier *William*[p] of *South*, Prior Provincial[q] of the Friers Preachers

L   *Priers*

CHARTERS.

dicatorum in Anglia, Gulielmo de Valentia avunculo noftro, Rogero de Mortuo mari, Rogero de Clifford, magiftro Waltero Stamell, decano Sarum, magiftro Roberto de Scardeburgh, archidiac. Eftridings, magiftro Roberto de Sexton, Bartholomeo de Southley, Thoma de Wayland, Waltero de Hopton, Thoma de Normannel, Stephano de Penceftre, Francifco de Bonona, Johanne de Levetot, Johanne de Metingham, & aliis. Dat. per manum noftram apud Weftmonafter. decimo feptimo die Junii, Anno Regni noftri fexto. Ifta carta Rege præcipiente, ante confignationem ejufdem, recitata fuit in præfentia teftium & aliorum de concilio noftro tunc ibidem præfentium, & audita, examinata, & concordat in forma fupradicta. Infpeximus etiam literas patentes, quas idem pater nofter fecit prædictis Baronibus, in hæc verba: Edvardus, Dei gratia, Rex Angliæ, Dominus Hiberniæ, & Dux Acquitaniæ, Omnibus Ballivis,

TRANSLATION.

ers [r] in *England*, *William* of *Valence*, our Uncle [f], *Roger* of *Mortimer* [s], *Roger* of *Clifford*, Mafter *Walter Stamell*, (Dean of *Salisbury* [t],) Mafter *Robert* of *Scardeburgh* [u], (Archdeacon of the Eaft Ridings [v],) Mafter *Robert* of *Sexton*, *Bartholomew* of *Southley*, *Thomas* of *Wayland*, *Walter* of *Hopton*, *Thomas* of *Normannel*, *Stephen* of *Penceſter* [w], *Francis* of *Bonona*, *John* of *Levetot*, *John* of *Metingham*, and others. Dated by our Hand at *Weftminfter* [x], the Seventeenth Day of *June*, in the Sixth Year [y] of our Reign. This Charter, at the King's Commandment, before the enfealing of the fame, was recited in the Preface of the faid Witnefles, and others of our Council [z] then there prefent, and heard, examined, and agreeth in Form aforefaid. We have feen [a] alfo the Letters Patents which the fame our Father made to the aforefaid Barons, in thefe Words: *Edward* [b], by the Grace of God, King of *England*, Lord of *Ireland*, and Duke of *Acquitaine*, To all his Bailiffs and

ANNOTATIONS.

[r] *Priers Preachers*, called alfo *Black Friers*, or *Dominicans*.

[f] *Our Uncle*. He was one of the Sons of King *John*'s Wife by another Husband.

[s] *Mortimer*, or Dead Sea.

[t] *Salisbury*, or *Sarisbury*, a City, and Epifcopal See, in the County of *Wilts*.

[u] *Scardeburgh*, now called *Scarborough*, a Town in *Yorkfhire*.

[v] *Eaft Ridings*. A part of *Yorkfhire*, which County is divided into Three Ridings, the Eaft, Weft, and North, in the Eaft Riding whereof the Town of *Scarborough* lies.

[w] *Stephen of Pencefter*, or, *Stephen of Pencefire*; he was afterward Warden of the *Cinque Ports*.

[x] *Weftminfter*, before called *Thorn*, or the Ifle of *Thorns*, and *Weftminfter*, with refpect to the *Eaftminfter*, or *Monafery* in *London*, before the Diffolution thereof by King *Henry* VIII. a City honoured with the Royal Palace, Parliament Houfes, High Courts of Chancery, both the Benches, and Exchequer, the Sepulture of many of the Kings and Queens of *England*, &c.

[y] *Sixth Year*. The Date of this Charter, of King *Edward* I. being *June* 17. in the Sixth Year of his Reign, was in the Year of our Lord, 1278.

[z] *Our Council*. This Charter had not only Allowance of the King's Privy Council, but Approbation afterwards, if not Confirmation of his Common Council, to wit, the Parliament, in the Twenty Eighth Year of his Reign, as appeareth by the Statute called, *Articuli fuper Chartas*, cap. 7.

[a] *We have feen*. This *Infpeximus* is of King *Edward* II. Son of King *Edward* I.

[b] *Edward*. Here beginneth another Charter of King *Edward* I.

Good

CHARTERS.

livis, & fidelibus suis, ad quos
præsentes literæ pervenerint, salutem. Sciatis quod pro bono
& fideli servitio quod dilecti
& fideles Barones, & probi
homines nostri Quinque Portuum, nobis & progenitoribus nostris, quondam Regibus Angliæ,
impenderunt & in futurum impendent, concessimus eis pro
nobis & hæredibus nostris, quod
ipsi & eorum hæredes, Barones
eorundem Portuum, de cætero
imperpetuum, sint quieti de omnibus Tallagiis & Auxiliis nobis
& hæredibus nostris de corporibus propriarum navium suarum, & earum *articulo* † præ-
stand. Concessimus etiam eisdem Baronibus & hominibus
pro nobis & hæred. nostris
quod de legalibus rebus & mercimoniis quæ ipsos infra terram
nostram Hiberniæ, debito modo
emere contigerit, nullus de rebus
& mercimoniis * sit eorum par-
ticeps, nec cum illis contra voluntatem eorundem Baronum &
hominum inde participet quoquomodo. Concessimus insuper

† *In the Ma-*
nuscript of
Mr. Francis
Thynn, Lan-
caster Herald,
where this
Charter is
transcribed, it
is Artilio for
Articulo.

* *Here is the*
Word illis *in the*
same Manu-
script.

TRANSLATION.

and faithful Subjects, to whom
these present Letters shall come,
Greeting. Know ye, that for
the good and faithful Service
which our beloved and faithful
Barons, and good ᶜ Men of our
Cinque Ports, to us and our
Progenitors, sometime Kings of
England, have done ᵈ, and in
Time to come may do, We
have granted to them, for us
and our Heirs, that they and
their Heirs ᵉ, Barons of the said
Ports, from henceforth ᶠ for
ever, may be quit of all Tallages ᵍ, and Aids ʰ to us and our
Heirs, of the Bodies of their
proper Ships and Tackling
thereof to be done. We have
granted also to the said Barons
and Men, for us and our Heirs,
that of their lawful Goods ⁱ
and Merchandises which in due
Manner they shall buy within
our Land of *Ire-*
land ʲ, no Man be Partner of
those Goods and Merchandises,
not with them, against the Will
of the said Barons and Men,
shall partake thereof in any wise.
We have granted, moreover,
for

ANNOTATIONS.

ᶜ *Good.* Sometimes the Word is rendered *Honest*, sometimes *Worthy*, sometimes *Good*; it properly signifies proved or approved Men.

ᵈ *Have done. Impendo* implies the Service of the Ports costly, in which they had expended or
laid out great Sums of Money.

ᵉ *Their Heirs*, used again for Successors.

ᶠ *From henceforth*, or for the Time to come.

ᵍ *Tallages.* See the Annotations upon the former Charter.

ʰ *Aids.* The *Latin*, *Auxilium*, in *English*, *Help*, in *French*, *Aid*, is, in the Sense of the Law,
the Assistance given to the King from the People in Money, generally to the Carrying on of his
publick Affairs, especially to the making of his eldest Son a Knight, and the Marriage of his
eldest Daughter. Some understand it here in both Senses, but others in the latter. And so the
following Passage about Shipping hath been liable to a double Construction, which those that
take the latter Sense construe thus : That the Ports, in Consideration of their Ships found and
fitted according to their Charters, shall be freed for ever of all those Allowances toward
Knighthood and Marriage of any the King's Children. But those that follow the former Sense
construe, That the Ports should not in any wise, for those Ships with which they serve the
King, be taxed or assessed to any Tallage or Aid granted by Parliament to the King.

ⁱ *Lawful Goods. Res, Things*, is often used, especially in the Civil Law, for *Goods*. And
by *lawful* here is intended such Goods as were not prohibited for Merchants to import or
export.

ʲ *Ireland.* Then, and from the Time of King *Henry* II. a Lordship to *England*, and therefore called here, *Our Land*, and not our Kingdom; but afterward King *Henry* VIII. about the
Thirty third Year of his Reign, wrote King of *Ireland*, ever since which his Successors have
kept the Title and Possession also of that Kingdom.

2

Born,

CHARTERS.

per pro nobis & hæredibus noftris, quantum in nobis eft, Baronibus & probis hominibus fu-
pradictis, quod omnes illi infra
prædictos Quinque Portus oriun-
di, licet ipfi terras vel tenementa extra libertatem eorundem
Portuum tenuerint per tale fervitium, quod maritagia eorum ratione minoris ætatis ipforum ad
nos vel hæredes noftros pertinere deberent, fecundum legem
& confuetudinem Regni noftri;
nihilominus juxta libertatem
Portuum fe maritare poffunt fine
occafione vel impedimento noftri vel hæredum noftrorum imperpetuum, falvo jure alterius
cujufcunque. Et ideo vobis mandamus, quod prædictos Barones
& homines contra has conceffiones noftras non moleftis in aliquo feu gravetis. In cujus rei
teftimonium has literas noftras
fieri fecimus patentes. Tefte
me ipfo apud fanctum Albanum
vicefimo octavo die Aprilis, Anno Regni noftri vicefimo fexto.

TRANSLATION.

for us and our Heirs, as much
as in us is, to the Barons and
good Men abovefaid, that all
they have born [k] within the aforefaid *Cinque Ports*, although they
fhall hold Lands or Tenements
without [l] the Liberties [m] of the
faid Ports, by fuch Service, that
the Marriage of them, by reafon
of their Nonage [n], to us or our
Heirs ought to pertain [o], according to the Law and Cuftom of our Kingdom; neverthelefs, according to the Liberty of the Ports, they may marry themfelves without Occafion [p] or Impediment of us or
our Heirs for ever, faved [q] the
Right of every other whatfoever. And therefore to you
we command, that you do not
moleft [r] in any Thing, or grieve [s]
the aforefaid Barons and Men,
againft thefe our Grants. In
witnefs whereof we have made
thefe our Letters Patents. Witnefs My Self at Saint *Albans* [s],
the Twenty eight Day of *April*,
in the Twenty fixth [t] Year of our
Reign.

ANNOTATIONS.

[k] *Born,* or to be born ; or that fhall be born.

[l] *Without,* or out of.

[m] *Liberties,* for Precincts.

[n] *Nonage,* or Minority. Full Age, in the Common Law, is Twenty one Years, within which it is called Nonage, and the Child faid to be a Minor, or in his Minority, *viz.* in his leffer, younger, or fmaller Eftate ; yet Fourteen Years is called the Age of Difcretion, and at that Age he may be depofed as a Witnefs. A Woman hath fix Ages, *Firft,* At Seven Years old the Lord her Father may diftrain his Tenants for Aid to marry her, and fhe may confent to Matrimony. *Second,* At the Age of Nine Years fhe is Dowable. *Third,* At Twelve Years fhe is able to confirm her former Confent given to Matrimony *Fourth,* At Fourteen Years fhe is enabled to receive her Land into her own Hands, and fhall be out of Ward if fhe be of this Age at the Death of her Anceftor. *Fifth,* At Sixteen Years fhe fhall be out of Ward, though at the Death of her Anceftor fhe was within the Age of Fourteen Years. *Sixth,* At Twenty one Years fhe is able to alienate her Lands and Tenements.

[o] *Pertain,* appertain or belong.

[p] *Occafion,* that is, without Let or *Hindrance,* or taking occafion thereby to fue, vex, or trouble them.

[q] *Saved,* or faving, as before ; that is, if a Ports Man hold fuch Lands or Tenements as are here mentioned, and fome of thefe, or other Lands, alfo of other mean Lords, the Rents or Rights of thefe are fecured to them by this Salvo.

[r] *Moleft,* or trouble.

[s] *Grieve,* or burden.

[s] *Saint Albans,* a Town in *Hartfordfhire,* famed to be built about the Time *Offa,* King of the *Mercians,* built the Monaftery here, in Memory of the famous Proto Martyr of *England,* Saint *Alban,* who, for his Conftancy to the Truth of Chrift, is faid to fuffer Death under *Dioclefian,* near to this Place.

[t] *Twenty fixth.* The Date of this other Charter of King *Edward* I. was *April* 28. *Anno Domini* 1298.

CHARTERS.

 to. Infpeximus etiam quafdam
alias literas patentes, quas idem
pater nofter fecit præfatis Baronibus, in hæc verba: Evardus,
Dei gratia, Rex Angliæ, Dominus Hiberniæ, & Dux Acquitaniæ, omnibus ad quos præfentes literæ pervenerint, falutem.
Confiderantes, quod navigium
noftrum, Quinque Portuum, non
abfque magnis fumptibus & expenfis poterit fuftentari, ne navigium illud deficiat vel pereat in
futurum, conceffimus, pro nobis
& hæredibus noftris, quod omnes illi de Quinque Portubus
prædictis, & alii quicunque advocantes fe de libertate eorundem, & inde gaudere volentes,
contribuant (videlicet) quilibet
eorum juxta facultates fuas, ad
faciend. fervitium noftrum & hæredum noftrorum, de navibus
fuis, cum a nobis *ac* * hæredibus
noftris hoc habuerint in mandatis.
In cujus rei teftimonium has literas noftras fieri fecimus patentes.
Tefte me ipfo apud fanctum Albanum.

* *This* Ac *in*
Mr. Thynn's
Manufcript is
vel.

TRANSLATION.

Reign. We have feen [u] alfo
certain other Letters Patents,
which the fame our Father made
to the aforefaid Barons, in thefe
Words: *Edward* [v], by the Grace
of God, King of *England*, Lord
of *Ireland*, and Duke of *Acquitaine*, To all to whom thefe
prefent Letters fhall come, Greeting. Confidering that our Shipping [w] of the *Cinque Ports*, not
without great Cofts and Expences can be maintained [x], left that
Shipping fhould fail or perifh for
the future [y], We have granted
for us and our Heirs, that all
they of the *Cinque Ports* aforefaid, and others whofoever, calling themfelves [z] of their Liberty, and willing to enjoy the
fame [a], fhall contribute [b] (that
is to fay) every of them, according to their Faculties [c], to do
the Service of us and our Heirs,
with their Ships [d], when this
from us and our Heirs they fhall
have in Commandment. In
witnefs whereof thefe our Letters we have made Patents.
Witnefs My Self, at Saint *Albans*,

ANNOTATIONS.

[u] *We have feen.* This *Infpeximus* is alfo of King *Edward* II. as was the laft before.

[v] *Edward.* Here begins another Charter of King *Edward* I. fo as here are Three of his Charters confirmed by his Son King *Edward* II.

[w] *Shipping.* The before mentioned Service of Fifty feven Ships. Some Tranflations have rendered it *Navy*.

[x] *Maintained,* upheld or fuftained.

[y] *Future,* or Time to come.

[z] *Calling themfelves.* Thefe were Men that did not inhabit in the Ports, but dwelt elfewhere in the Foreign, and contributed to the Maintenance of the Ports Shipping, whereupon, by con-fent of the Ports, they enjoyed with the Ports Men feveral Privileges and Freedoms, as to their Perfons, Lands and Goods. They agreed with fuch Port or ancient Town as they lived neareft to, or liked beft, what particular Sums of Money, yearly, or otherwife, to contribute, and fo called themfelves of the Liberties of the Ports, and from thence afterward were called *Advocants*. Of thefe, *Rye*, in the Twenty feventh Year of King *Henry* VI. had no lefs than Thirty five, fome of which paid yearly Six Shillings and Eight Pence, fome others Three Shillings and Four Pence, and fome but Two Shillings. Afterwards, in the declining State of the Ports, they fell off, when the ancient Liberties and Enjoyments of either, or both, were curtailed, or more chargeable to keep than let go, whereas before, fo many were defirous to be Advocants, that in the Thirteenth Year of King *Henry* VI. by Decree of Brotherhood, each Port was reftrained to make no more Advocants than they then had, without Licenfe of that Court of Brother-hood.

[a] *The fame,* or thereof.

[b] *Shall contribute,* or may contribute ; and fo afterward.

[c] *Faculties,* a Word of different Interpretations, here to be taken for Subftance or Eftate : Some have rendered it, *after their Faculties or Degrees* ; others, *according to their Qualities or Abilities.*

[d] *With their Ships,* or of their Ships.

M

Twenty

CHARTERS.   TRANSLATION.

banum, vicefimo octavo die Aprilis, anno Regni noftri vicefimo fexto. Nos autem conceffiones & confirmationes prædictas ratas habentes, & gratas eas, pro nobis & hæredibus noftris, quantum in nobis eft, præfatis Baronibus Quinque Portuum, & hæredibus & fucceffibus fuis, pro bono & fideli fervitio fuo, quod nobis hactenus impenderunt, & impendent in futurum, concedimus & confirmamus, ficut cartæ & literæ prædictæ rationabiliter teftantur. Præterea volentes eifdem Baronibus gratiam facere uberiorem, conceffimus eis, pro nobis & hæredibus noftris, quod licet ipfi aliqua vel aliquibus libertatum vel quietanciarum in dictis cartis & literis content. hactenus plene ufi non fuerint, ipfi tamen Barones, hæredes & fucceffores fui, libertatibus & quietanciis prædictis, & earum qualibet futuris temporibus, abfque impedimento noftri vel hæredum noftrorum, feu miniftrorum noftrorum quorumcunque, gaudeant & utantur. Hiis teftibus, venerabilibus patribus, W. Wigorn. J. Bathon. & Wellen. & W. Exon. epifcopis, Gilberto de Clare, comit. Glouc. &

baus, the Twenty eighth Day of *April*, in the Twenty fixth Year of our Reign. We alfo the Grants and Confirmations aforefaid having ratified, and freely them, for us and our Heirs, as much as in us is, to the aforefaid Barons of the *Cinque Ports*, and their Heirs and Succeffors, for their good and faithful Service which to us hitherto they have done, and in Time to come fhall do, do grant and confirm, as the Charters and Letters aforefaid do reafonably teftify. Furthermore, willing to gratify the faid Barons more largely, We have granted to them, for us and our Heirs, that although they hitherto have not fully ufed any of the Liberties or Freedoms in the faid Charters and Letters contained, notwithftanding the fame Barons, their Heirs and Succeffors, the aforefaid Liberties and Freedoms, and every of them, in future Times, without Impediment of us or our Heirs, or Minifters whatfoever, may enjoy and ufe. Witneffes to thefe Prefents, the venerable Fathers, *W.* of *Worcefter*, *J.* of *Bath* and *Wells*, and *W.* of *Exeter*, Bifhops; *Gilbert* of *Clare* Earl of *Gloucefter* and

ANNOTATIONS.

Twenty fixth. The Date of this Charter is the fame with the laft before recited.

We alfo. Here followeth the Confirmation of King *Edward* II. of the aforefaid Charters of King *Edward* I. his Father. It may be tranflated, *And we.*

Heirs may here be taken ftrictly (being joined with Succeffors) for the Heirs of the Ports Men who are exempted from Wards, &c. as before, though not Freemen, and derive their Privileges from their Fathers.

Furthermore. Here begins the additional Grant of King *Edward* II. to the Charters of his Father.

Gratify, or fhew more plentiful or abundant Favour.

Ufed. By this Grant of King *Edward* II. the Ports neglect, non-ufe, or defuetude of their Liberties, fhall be no Impediment to their Enjoyment and Ufe thereof, when they have occafion.

Future Times, or Times to come.

Worcefter, a City in the County of the fame Name.

Bath and *Wells,* Cities in the County of *Somerfet,* both under one Epifcopal See.

Exeter, a City in *Devonfhire* ; the Epifcopal See whereof takes in alfo the County of *Cornwal.*

Gloucefter, a City in the Shire of the fame Name.

CHARTERS.

& Herteford, Johanne de Brittan. comite de Richmond, Adamaro de Valentia, comite Pembroche, Hugone de le Spencer, Roberto filio Pagani, Edmundo de Malo Lacu, fenefcallo hofpitii noftri, & aliis. Dat. per manum noftram, apud Weftm. vicefimo fexto die Julii, anno Regni noftri feptimo. Nos conceffiones & confirmationes prædictas, ratas habentes, & gratas eas, pro nobis & hæredibus noftris, quantum in nobis eft, præfatis Baronibus Quinque Portuum, hæredibus & fucceffor. fuis, pro bono & fideli fervitio fuo nobis & progenitoribus noftris hactenus impenfis, & nobis & hæredibus noftris in futurum impendend. ratificamus, & tenore præfentium confirmamus, ficut cartæ & literæ prædictæ rationabiliter teftantur. Et infuper volentes præfatis Baronibus Quinque Portuum gratiam facere ampliorem, conceffimus, pro nobis & hæredibus noftris, eifdem Baronibus Quinque Portuum, quod licet ipfi vel anteceffores fui aliqua vel aliquibus libertatum aut quietanciarum in dictis cartis & literis contentarum hactenus plene ufi non fuerint, ipfi tamen Barones, hæredes & fucceffores fui

TRANSLATION.

and *Hartford* [p], *John* of *Britany* Earl of *Richmond* [q], *Adamar* of *Valence* Earl of *Pembroke* [r], *Hugh* de le *Spencer*, *Robert fitz Pagan*, *Edmund* of *Evil Lake*, Steward [f] of our Houfhold [s], and others. Dated by our Hand, at *Weftminfter*, the Twenty fixth Day of *July*, in the Seventh Year [t] of our Reign. We the Grants [v] and Confirmations aforefaid having ratified, and freely them, for us and our Heirs, as much as in us is, to the aforefaid Barons of the *Cinque Ports*, their Heirs and Succeffors, for their good and faithful Service to us and our Progenitors hitherto done, and to us and our Heirs hereafter [u] to be done, do ratify, and by the Tenor of thefe Prefents confirm, as the Charters and Letters aforefaid do reafonably teftify. And moreover [w], willing to gratify the aforefaid Barons of the *Cinque Ports* more largely, we have granted, for us and our Heirs, to the fame Barons of the *Cinque Ports*, that although they or their Anceftors, any of the Liberties or Freedoms in the faid Charters and Letters contained hitherto fully have not ufed, notwithftanding the fame Barons, their Heirs and Succeffors, the

ANNOTATIONS.

[p] *Herteford*, or *Hartford*, a County in *England*.
[q] *Richmond*, an Honour, part of *Torkfhire*, and the Name of one of the King's Palaces in *Surry*.
[r] *Pembroke*, a County in *Wales*.
[f] *Steward*. The *Latin* is a Word made from *Sein* *, an Houfe or Place, and *Schalc*, another * Sen taken for *Saxon* Word for an Officer, Governer or Mafter. Juftice, makes
[s] *Houfhold*. *Hofpitium* is ufed for a great Houfe, as the Royal Palace, Inns of Court, *fome others take* &c. the Word Senef-
[t] *Seventh Year*. The Date of this Confirmation, with the fhort Addition of King *Edward* II. challus for an being *July* 26. in the Seventh Year of his Reign, was *Anno Domini* 1313. Officer of Ju-
[v] *We the Grants*. Here followeth the Confirmation of King *Edward* III. of what his Father ftice. and Grandfather had before granted and confirmed.
[u] *Hereafter*, or in Time to come.
[w] *And moreover*. Here begins the fhort additional Grant of King *Edward* III. as his Father had done before, concerning the Non-ufe of their Liberties.

Ely,

CHARTERS.

fui, libertatibus & quietanciis prædictis, & earum qualibet, futuris
temporibus abfque occafione vel
impedimento noftri vel hæredum
noftrorum, feu miniftrorum noftrorum quorumcunque, plene
gaudeant & utantur imperpetuum. Hiis teftibus, venerabilibus
patribus S. Elien. cancellario,
J. Bathon. & Wellen. thefaurar. noftro, epifcopis; Lyonel-
lo Clarenciæ, Johanne Lancafter. ducibus; Edmundo comite
Cant. filiis noftris cariffimis; Edvardo de le Spencer, Guidone
Bryan, Johanne Atley, fene-
fchallo hofpitii noftri, & aliis.
Dat. per manum noftram, apud
Weftm. primo die Julii, anno
Regni noftri tricefimo octavo.
Infpeximus etiam literas patentes ejufdem, avi noftri, in hæc
verba: Edvardus, Dei gratia,
Rex Angliæ, Dominus Hiberniæ, & Dux Acquitaniæ, omnibus ad quos præfentes literæ,
pervenerint, falutem. Infpeximus cartam noftram confirmationis, quam nuper fub figillo quo
tunc utebamur, fecimus, Baronibus Quinque Portuum noftrorum,
in hæc verba: Edvardus, Dei
gratia, Rex Angliæ, Dominus
Hiberniæ, & Dux Acquitaniæ,
omnibus ad quos præfentes literæ,

TRANSLATION.

the aforefaid Liberties and Freedoms, and every of them, in
future Times, without Occafion
or Impediment of us or our
Heirs, or Minifters whatfoever,
may fully enjoy and ufe for
ever. Witneffes to thefe Prefents, the venerable Fathers, *S.*
of *Ely* ˣ, Chancellor ʸ, *J.* of
Bath and *Wells,* our Treafurer ᵃ, Bifhops; *Lionel* of *Clarence, John* of *Lancafter* ᵃ,
Dukes; *Edmund* Earl of *Cambridge,* our moft dear Sons; *Edward de le Spencer, Guy
Bryan, John Atley,* Steward
of our Houfhold, and others.
Dated by our Hand, at *Weftminfter,* the Firft Day of *July,*
in the Thirty eighth ᵇ Year of
our Reign. We have feen ᶜ alfo
the Letters Patents of the
fame, our Grandfather, in thefe
Words: *Edward,* by the Grace
of God, King of *England,* Lord
of *Ireland,* and Duke of *Acquitaine,* To all to whom thefe
prefent Letters fhall come,
Greeting. We have feen our
Charter of Confirmation which
we have late made, under the
Seal which then we did ufe, to
the Barons of our *Cinque Ports,*
in thefe Words: *Edward,* by
the Grace of God, King of
England, Lord of *Ireland,* and
Duke of *Acquitaine,* To all
to whom thefe prefent Letters
fhall

ANNOTATIONS.

ˣ *Ely,* a City in the Ifland of the fame Name, the Epifcopal See whereof was tranflated from *Cambridge.*
ʸ *Chancellor,* the fupreme Judge of the High Court of *Chancery* at *Weftminfter.*
ᵃ *Treafurer,* an Officer of the *Exchequer* for the King's Treafure.
ᵃ *John of,* &c. commonly called *John of Gaunt,* becaufe he was born there.
ᵇ *Thirty Eighth.* The Date of the Confirmation, and fhort Addition of King *Edward* III. being *July* the Firft, in the Thirty eighth Year of his Reign, was *Anno Domini* 1364.
ᶜ *We have feen.* At this *Infpeximus* begins the Confirmation, and additional Grant thereupon, of King *Edward* III. of one of thofe Charters of his Grandfather King *Edward* I. concerning
Advocants, which this King *Edward* III. before the former recited Confirmation (as appeareth
by the Dates of both) it feems had not only confirmed in the Firft Year of his Reign, with En-
largement, under the Seal he then ufed, but under his new Seal again, in the Second Year of
his Reign. In the Recital whereof may be obferved, in his Title, Duke of *Acquitaine,* as was
before noted, *p.* 5.

And

CHARTERS.

teræ pervenerint, falutem. Infpeximus literas patentes, quas
celebris memoriæ Dominus Edvardus, quondam Rex Angliæ,
avus nofter, fecit in hæc verba:
Edvardus, Dei gratia, Rex Angliæ, Dominus Hiberniæ, & Dux
Acquitaniæ, omnibus ad quos
præfentes literæ pervenerint, falutem. Confiderantes quod navigium noftrum Quinque Portuum, non abfque magnis fumptibus & expenfis poterit fuftentari,
ne navigium illud deficiat vel pereat in futuro, conceffimus pro
nobis & hæredibus noftris, quod
omnes illi de Quinque Portubus
prædictis, & alii quicunque advocantes fe de libertate eorundem,
& inde gaudere volentes, contribuant (videlicet) quilibet eorum,
juxta facultates fuas, ad faciend.
fervitium noftrum & hæredum
noftrorum, de navibus fuis, cum
a nobis vel hæredibus noftris hoc
habuerint in mandatis. In cujus
rei teftimonium has literas noftras fieri fecimus patentes. Tefte me ipfo, apud fanctum Albanum, vicefimo octavo die Aprilis, anno Regni noftri vicefimo
fexto. Nos autem conceffionem
prædictam ratam habentes, &
gratas eam, pro nobis & hæredibus noftris, concedimus & confirmamus, ficut literæ prædictæ
rationaliter teftantur. Et quia
fuper verbis generalibus in prædictis literis contentis (videlicet)
*quod quilibet contribuant, juxta
facultates fuas,* ante hæc tempora diffentiones variæ funt fubor-
tæ,

TRANSLATION.

fhall come, Greeting. We have
feen the Letters Patents, which
the Lord *Edward,* of famous
Memory, fome Time King of
England, our Grandfather, made
in thefe Words: *Edward,* by
the Grace of God, King of *England,* Lord of *Ireland,* and
Duke of *Acquitaine,* To all to
whom thefe prefent Letters fhall
come, Greeting. Confidering
that our Shipping of the *Cinque
Ports,* not without great Cofts
and Expences can be maintained, left that Shipping fhould fail
or perifh for the future, we
have granted, for us and our
Heirs, that all they of the
Cinque Ports aforefaid, and
others whofoever, calling themfelves of their Liberty, and willing to enjoy the fame, fhall
contribute (that is to fay) every of them, according to their
Faculties, to do the Service of us
and our Heirs, with their Ships,
when this from us or our Heirs
they fhall have in Commandment.
In witnefs whereof thefe our
Letters we have made Patents.
Witnefs My Self, at Saint *Albans* the Twenty eighth Day of
April, in the Twenty fixth Year
of our Reign. And we [d] the
Grant aforefaid having ratified,
and freely the fame, for us and
our Heirs, do grant and confirm,
as the Letters aforefaid do reafonably teftify. And becaufe [e],
upon the general Words in the a-
forefaid Letters contained (that is
to fay) *that every of them fhould
contribute, according to their
Faculties,* before thefe Times [f]
have arifen various [g] Diffentions,
We,

ANNOTATIONS.

[d] *And we.* Here the Charter of King *Edward* I. dated at Saint *Albans,* is ratified by King *Edward* III.

[e] *And becaufe.* Here begins the Addition, enlarging and explaining that Charter.

[f] *Thefe Times,* or this Time, the Plural being put for the Singular.

[g] *Arifen various,* grown or fprung up divers Diffentions, or Diverfities of Seafes, or Con-
ftructions of the Words there mentioned.

N

CHARTERS.

tæ, Nos, ut Barones Portuum prædictorum, servitium prædictum nobis & hæredibus nostris commodiùs facere valeant temporibus opportunis, de consilio Prelatorum, Comitum, & Baronum nostrorum, ac communitatum Regni nostri in præsenti Parliamento nostro convocat, concessimus, pro nobis & hæredibus nostris, eisdem Baronibus Quinque Portuum, quod omnes illi de Portubus illis, & alii quicunque advocantes se de libertate eorum, & inde gaudere volentes, contribuant ad navigium & servitium prædictum manutenend. & faciend. de omnibus bonis & catallis suis, tam extra libertatem Quinque Portuum, quam infra existentibus; & ad hoc per Majores & Juratores Por-

TRANSLATION.

We, that the Barons of the Ports aforesaid may be able more commodiously to do the Service aforesaid, to us and our Heirs, in Times convenient [b], of the Counsel [i] of our Prelates [j], Earls and Barons, and of the Commonalties [k] of our Kingdom in our present Parliament [l] called together, Have granted, for us and our Heirs, to the same Barons of the *Cinque Ports*, that all they of those Ports, and others whosoever, calling themselves of their Liberty, and willing to enjoy the same, shall contribute to maintain, and do the Shipping and Service aforesaid, of all their Goods and Chattels [m], as well without the Liberty of the *Cinque Ports*, as within being; and to this, by the Mayors [n] and Jurats [o] of the

ANNOTATIONS.

[b] *Convenient*, opportune or fit Times.

[i] *Of the Counsel*, or by the Counsel.

[j] *Prelates*, from *Præfero*; and in the Preterperfect Tense, *Prælati*, for the Spiritual Lords, as termed in Distinction from the Temporal Lords, these having their Honours descending to their Heirs; the other by Preferment are raised to their high Places or Dignities, neither of which descend to their Issue.

[k] *Commonalties*, or Commons of our Realm, signifying those Knights, Citizens, and Burgesses, that sit in the lower House of Parliament, often called, The House of Commons.

[l] *Parliament*. By this it appears, this Charter hath Authority of Parliament, though no express mention be made in the Statute Books; and whether or no in the Parliament Rolls there be any Thing thereof to be found, I know not *, but believe such a Patent as this would never have passed the Broad Seal with so manifest an Error therein, if it had not so been. Indeed, in this very Parliament it was enacted, That all Cities, Boroughs, and franchised Towns, should enjoy their Franchises and Liberties, as they ought, and were wont to do. But this, though a Confirmation of the Ports old Privileges, as *Magna Charta* before was, is no more particular to this about *Advocants* than to others. So as it appears not, this general Confirmation of Liberties was that the Charter here refers to, but somewhat more specifical of the Parliament in this case.

* *Since this was wrote I have seen the Manuscript of Mr. Francis Thynn, Lancaster Herald, penn'd July 29,* 1604. *wherein are Copies of two Writs of K. R.* II. *to the Collectors of his* 10ths *and* 15ths, *and in both it is asserted that this Charter was discussed and agreed in Parliament,* 1 Ed. III. *and* 15 Ed. III. *These Writs are to be seen in the Tower, Clauf.* 6 R. II. Part 1. Mem. 1. Clauf. 9. R. III. Mem. 23.

[m] *Chattels*, or Cattels, which are Goods real or personal: Real, as Terms for Years of Lands or Tenements, Wardships, the Interest of Tenants by Statute Staple, Statute Merchant, Elegit, &c. Personal, as Cattel, Houshold Stuff, Money, Plate, &c.

[n] *Mayors*, a Maior, sometime writ Mayor, is the Head Officer, or Chief Magistrate, of a City or Town corporate. And hence may be noted, that at the making of this Charter (though those before this mention nothing thereof) there were Mayors and Jurats (who are assistant with them in Administration of Justice) within the Ports. (I mean in some of them, for some had a Bailiff for the Head Officer, and others only Jurats, where the eldest of them was President.) But this Charter doth not mention any Thing of their Election, or by whom, or when, or any new Grant to them; but only points out the Power they had to compel by due course of Law, such as should refuse to pay their Contribution to the Service aforesaid when Occasion required.

[o] *Jurats*, from *Juro*, to swear, because these take an Oath to assist the Head Officer of the Place, whether Mayor or Bailiff, in administring Justice to poor and rich righteously. The same Word in *Latin* here used is elsewhere taken for Jury Men. Of these Jurats, by the Customs

CHARTERS.	TRANSLATION.
Portuum prædictorum, & etiam per Conftabular. Caftri noftri Do-	the Ports aforefaid, and alfo by the Conftable **ᵖ** of our Caftle **ᑫ** of

ANNOTATIONS.

ftoms of the Ports, in every Corporation fhould be Twelve, befides the Head Officer ; as it were a Jury of Juftices.

ᵖ *Conftable,* a Word derived, as moft think, from *Cunning,* whence afterward, *King,* and *Stable,* q. f. a Stay or Support to the Chief Governor and Government of the Kingdom ; or an Helper in the Confervation of the publick Peace of the Nation ; from whofe ancient Authority and Office much hath been detracted and drawn into the Juftices of the Peace fince their Inftitution. Here it is all one with *Caftellanus,* one that hath the Command and Keeping of a Caftle ; and befides that of the Caftle of *Dover,* the Wardenfhip of the Ports and their Members, as was before noted.

ᑫ *Caftle,* a Caftell (or Caftell, in *Latin Caftellaria, Caftellatus, Caftellum,* and *Caftrum*) includes one or more Manors. This Caftle of *Dover* is fituate on the Top of an Hill on the north Side of the Town, and very near thereto, and in the Profpect thereof was built, as both *Lydgate* and *Roffe* fay, by *Julius Cæfar* the *Roman* Emperor, in Memory of whom they of the Caftle kept, as *Lambard* faith (till his Time) certain Veffels of old Wine and Salt, as part of the Provifion he brought into it ; though he thinketh the Foundation of the Caftle may be better afcribed to *Arviragus,* a King of the *Britains,* that married the Daughter of *Claudius* the Emperor ; and that old Provifion (if natural, and not fophifticate) to be part of the Store laid in there by *Hubert de Burgh* in the Reign of King *John.* That it muft be of greater Antiquity than King *Lucius,* the firft Chriftian King of the *Britains,* (who was converted to the Faith of Chrift about the Year One Hundred and Eighty) is evident, becaufe he built a Church within the Caftle to the Name and Service of Chrift, and endowed it with the Toll and Cuftom of the Haven of *Dover.* Famous it was in former Times for the Report it had, and ftill kept, for one of the ftrongeft Bulwarks of the Nation, fo as *Matthew Parife* writeth, that in his Time (which was under the Reign of King *Henry* III.) it was reckoned *Clavis & Repagulum totius Regni,* The very Lock and Key of the whole Kingdom. And before it feems to have been no lefs, for it is faid, that *William* the Conqueror, when *Harold* was in *Normandy* with him, in the Reign of *Edward* the Confeffor *, and made Oath to *William* to put him into the Poffeffion of the Crown after the Death of King *Edward,* it was part of the Oath to deliver him this Caftle, and the *Some part of bis Reign* God-Well within it. It was held to be of the greateft Importance by other Nations, for when *Lewis,* wine, *Earl of* Son of King *Philip* of *France,* inftigated by the Pope, and invited by the Nobility of *England,* Kent, *was Con-*invaded King *John,* and had gained feveral Caftles and ftrong Holds lying in the fouth Part *ftable of Dover* of this Realm, but wanted Poffeffion of *Dover* Caftle, his Father, King *Philip,* fwore by Saint *Caftle, and af-**James*'s Arm (his accuftomed Oath) that he had not gained one Foot in England. *William the terwards bis* Conqueror had no fooner overthrown *Harold* in the Field, and reduced the *Londoners* to Obedi-*Son Harold,* ence, but forthwith he marched his Army towards this Caftle, as a Place of great Importance ; *who was King* and meeting at *Swanfcombe* with *Stiganda,* Archbifhop of *Canterbury,* at the Head of the *Kentifh after the Death* Men in Arms for their Liberties, and they capitulating for the Commons of *Kent,* upon Agreement *of Edward, and* that they fhould enjoy their ancient Liberties, and free Cuftoms, he received this Caftle of *Dover killed by* Will. into his Poffeffion, and committed the Charge thereof to *Odo,* Bifhop of *Bajeux,* his Baftard *the Conqueror.* Brother, whom alfo he made Earl of *Kent* ; but afterward offended with him, and willing to difplace and imprifon him, but queftioning whether, becaufe he was a Bifhop, it would not be an Offence to the Ecclefiaftical State, he confulted with *Lanfranc,* then Archbifhop of *Canterbury,* and Enemy to *Odo* ; *Lanfranc* counfels the King to commit *Odo* to fafe Cuftody, and for his Defence arms him with this Shift, That if it were laid to his Charge he had laid violent Hands upon a facred Bifhop, he fhould fay, that he imprifoned not the Bifhop of *Bajeux,* but the Earl of *Kent.* Whereupon having apprehended him and caft him in Prifon, he feized the Caftle into his own Hands, fortified it, and chofe out a Noble Man called *John Pynes* (of whofe Prowefs and Fidelity he had good Experience) and committed the Cuftody thereof, with the Government of the Ports, to him, and by gift of Inheritance created him Conftable of *Dover* Caftle, and Warden of the *Cinque Ports.* And for the better enabling him to the Difcharge of his Office, and Defence of the Caftle, gave him Fifty fix Knights Fees † of † *Some fay* 66 ½ Lands and Poffeffions, willing him to impart fome Portions thereof to fuch other valiant and *Knights Fees.* trufty Perfons as he fhould like beft, for the more fure Confervation of this Caftle. According-ly this *Pynes* calling to him Eight other worthy Knights, imparted to them liberally of the King's free Gift to him, and bound them, by the Tenure of their Land received, to maintain One Hundred and Twelve Soldiers, which Number he divided by the Months of the Year, and ordered Twenty five to watch and ward continually within the Caftle, in their appointed Times, and the others to be ready at Commandment whenfoever Neceffity required : Thefe Eight, named *William of Albrance, Eulbert* ‡ of *Dover, William Arficke, Galfride Peverell, William* ‡ *Another Maynemouth, Robert Porthe, Hugh Crevequer* (or after the Latin, *Decrepito corde,* that is, *Crack'd writes him Heart*) and *Adam Fitz Williams,* had each their feveral Charges in fundry Towers, Turrets, Fulbert. and Bulwarks of the Caftle, and were contented, at their own Charge, to maintain and repair them, whereupon divers of them bore the Names and Titles of thefe new created Captains. After this *John Pynes,* his Son *James Pynes* had the Office and Honour of Conftablefhip and Wardenfhip aforefaid, according to the Conqueror's Grant ; and after deceafe of the faid *James,* who died at *Folkftone* (as *Lambard* faith) it defcended to *John Pynes,* Son of the faid *James.* Some fay *Euftace,* Earl

a   of

ANNOTATIONS.

of *Boloigne*, had the Office in the Reign of King *Henry* I. In the Time of King *Stephen* one

‖ Or Walche- Walkelin ‖, having delivered the Castle up to the King, had the Government thereof till the
line Maymey- King's Death, and then abandoned the Charge and fled into *Normandy*. King *Henry* II. restored
not, *as one calls* Allen Pynes, the Heir of the said *John Fynes*, put out by King *Stephen*, after whom *James Fynes*,
him, and some eldest Son of the said *Allen*, possessed it, and some say *Hugh de Essex*. In the Time of King
say that Eu- *Richard* I. *Matthew Clere* was Constable of this Castle, when he imprisoned therein *Godfrey*,
stace, Son of Archbishop of *York*. After him was *William* of *Wrotham*, but the certain Time I have not yet
K. Stephen, seen. After whom, in the Time of King *John*, was *John Pynes*, the last of that Family, Con-
had the Office stable of the Castle, as some affirm. *Thomas Basset, Anno* 3 King *John*, had the Custody of the
sometime, du- Castle without any mention of the Ports. *Hubert de Burgh*, the King's Chamberlain, *May* 3,
ring his Fa- *Anno* 3 King *John*, had this Honour conferred on him. Also *William de Huntingfield, Anno* 5
ther's Reign. King *John*; and *William de Sarum*, 9 *Sept. Anno* 6 King *John*; and *May* 25, *Anno* 8 King *John*,
the Castle, without mention of the Ports, was committed to the Custody of *Geofry Fitz-Peter*,
Earl of *Essex*; but how long he held it I dare not be confident, sometimes questioning whether
William de Wrotham, before mentioned, did not succeed him. And afterwards, as the next I
have observed, *Hubert de Burgh* (suppos'd to be the same before, though after advanced to be
Lord Chief Justice of *England*, and Earl of *Kent*) *June* 27, *Anno* 17 King *John*, obtained the
Office, and out-lived the King, and in the beginning of the Reign of King *Henry* III. this *Hubert
de Burgh* defended the Castle so valiantly against the *French*, that (although otherwise not without spot) the Nation owes Honour to his Memory; but afterward growing out of Favour and
laid by, several others succeeded, as *Robert Nereford, Anno* 5 *Henry* III. and *October* 31, 8 *Henry*
III. *Hugh de Windsor*, or *Windlesore, April* 13, 9 *Henry* III. *Geofry de Serland. August* 16,
9 *Henry* III. was Constable of the Castle only. About *March* 14, 10 *Henry* III. the King grants
to *William de Autrenches* (who was then Constable of the Castle) and to *Tergusius*, then Provost
or Mayor of *Dover*, the Custody of the Ports. In 16 *Henry* III. mention is made of *Symon Hoese*.
From the Feast of St. *Michael* 16 *Henry* III. to the same Feast 17 *Henry* III. *Bertram de Cryoll* had
the Office. And *Hubert de Husato* in 18 *Henry* III. The former *Bertram de Cryoll* was put in again
Dec. 15. 21 *Henry* III. and once more, *July* 25, 25 *Henry* III. *Peter de Subaudia, Anno* 16 *Henry* III.
And in the same Year *Humphry Bohune*, Earl of *Hereford* and *Essex*, is found in the same Office.
In the 35th and 39th Years of King *Henry* III. is *Bertram de Cryoll* in the Office again,
or another of that Name; but *July* 13, 39 *Henry* III. *Reginald de Cobham* is made Custos of
Dover Castle, and of the *Cinque Ports*. *June* 9, *Roger Northwood*, and *June* 10, *Nicholas Moeles*,
are both in Office in the Forty second Year of this King. Then by the Barons that warred
against him was *Richard Gray* appointed, *July* 28, 42 *Henry* III. and afterwards, *September* 8,
43 *Henry* III. deprived by *Hugh Bigot*, Chief Justice of *England*, because he let in the Pope's Legate, by the King's Licence, against the Mind of the Barons. After which *Hugh* were *Henry
Braybrooke, Henry Mountsforde*, and *Roger Leyborne*, in the Time of this King *Henry*, as Mr. *Lambard* reckons them up, but omits several others; and it is hard, indeed, to keep pace in un-
settled Times; for sometimes by the King, other while by the Barons, and anon by the whole
Parliament, are Officers placed and displaced. In the Forty fifth Year of this King's Reign he
took into his Hands, from *Hugh Bigot*, the Constableship of the Castle, Chamberlainship of *Sandwich*, and Wardenship of the Ports, and *May* 3. granted them to one *Robert de Walerond*. And
July 18, *Anno* 47, he orders *Edmund* and *Robert de Gascoyn* Constables of the Castle, to deliver
the same to *H.* the Bishop of *London*, to whom he had committed it *July* 10. And Two Days
after commits the Wardenship of the Ports to *Walter de Bersted*. But neither of these kept it
long, for in the same Forty seventh Year *Richard de Grey* is mentioned to be Constable, and *Nicholas Cryoll* Warden. And *May* 25, 48 *Henry* III. both Offices were committed to *Henry Montfort*, Son of *Symon*, Earl of *Leicester*, and Nephew of the Sister of King *Henry* III. In *Dec.* 5.
48 *Henry* III. the Wardenship passed by Patent to *Roger de Leyborne*. And 49 *Henry* III.
Richard Grey received command to deliver both Castle and Ports to *Henry de Montfort*, dated
March 25. About the Fiftieth Year of this King he granted the Offices to his eldest Son, Prince
Edward, who was afterwards King *Edward* I. under whom is found to officiate the aforesaid
Roger de Leyborne, and *July* 26, 51 *Henry* III. *Matthew Belers*, or *Besils*, as some call him,
who upon command, *December* 5, 52 *Henry* III. surrendered to the before mentioned *Stephen de
Penceftre*, or *Pinchester*, as some write him, who acted under the said Prince till he came to the
Crown, and afterwards was both Constable and Warden himself; for in the first Year of the
Reign of King *Edward* I. is to be seen, by the Records in the *Tower* of *London*, as followeth.

REX scripsit Stephano de Penceftre, Constabulario Castri de Dovor. & Custodi Quinque Portuum, providere naves & galeas sufficientes contra Regis adventum in Angliam, & meli-
ores & fideliores Regis amicos Portuum prædictorum secretius premuniat. Ut ipsi causæ & sine
strepitu præparent se ad veniend. in obviam Regis in adventu suo supradicto, &c. Dat. apud
Westm. &c. Julii 4, Clauf. An° 1. Ed. primi, cedul. pendent.

This *Stephen de Penceftre* held this Office of both Constable and Warden till toward the latter
End of this King *Edward* I. for in the Twenty second Year of this King he is expressed to be
Warden of the *Cinque Ports, Rot. Vascon. in dorso Mem.* 7. And *Anno* 31 *Edward* I. he passed
his Account in the *Exchequer* as Constable and Warden, mentioned before *p.* 38. yet nevertheless
some mention the Office to be held *Anno* 6 *Edward* I. by *Ralph de Sandwich*, and after by one
Simon de Grey about Two Years; and *Anno* 19 *Edward* I. by *Robert de Burgers*, he who was
put again in Office *July* 10, 27 *Edward* I. and 30 *Edward* I. a Writ is directed to him for the
Ports to fit out Twenty five Ships. Near the End, *viz. Anno* Thirty four of this King's Reign,
was the Lord *Henry Cobham*, the first Baron of *Cobham*, Warden of the *Cinque Ports*, and continued so till *December* 16, 1 *Edward* II. The Son and Heir of this *Henry, Anno* 36 *Edward* III.
founded *Cobham* College. This *Henry* Lord of *Cobham*, by the Leiger Book of *Feversham*, is said

ANNOTATIONS.

to flourish in the Reigns of King *Edward* I. and King *Edward* II. and also to marry *York*, the Daughter of the aforesaid *Stephen de Penceftre*. *December* 16, 1 *Edward* II. *Robert de Kendall* is made Constable of *Dover* Castle, and Warden of the *Cinque Ports*; and after him *Bartholomew Badlefmere*, *Anno* 15 and 16 *Edward* II. *Edmund de Woodflock*, Earl of *Kent*, the King's Brother, is Constable. And *Hugh Peecho*, *alias Peccanon*, Constable and Warden, *Anno* 18 *Edward* II. *Ralph Baffet* of *Dray* on likewise, *Anno* 19 *Edward* II. And so was *Hugh Spencer* (or *Spenfer*) the younger, Son of *Hugh Spencer* Earl of *Winton*, *Anno* 20 *Edward* II. In the Sixth Year of King *Edward* III. *William Clynton*, afterward Earl of *Huntingdon*, was Constable and Warden. Who next succeeded him I well know not, but *Bartholomew de Burghersh*, one of the first Companions of the Order of the Garter, was Constable, *Anno* 19 *Edward* III. And *Stephen de Burgherfh*, *Anno* 22 *Edward* III. *Otto de Grandifome*, *August* 4, *Anno* 29 *Edward* III. was made Custos of *Dover* Castle, without any mention of the Ports. *February* 16, 31 *Edward* III. *Roger de Mortuo mari* (commonly called *Mortimer*) Earl of *March*, was made Constable and Warden. And a while after *Guy Saint Clere*. But after Sir *John Beauchampe* (in *Latin Johannes de Bellocampo*) Brother to the Earl of *Warwick*, in the Thirty fourth Year of this King, was made both Constable and Warden; we find no severance of the said Offices. This Sir *John* dying the same Year, *viz.* 1360. *Reginald de Cobham* occupies the Place, and dies *Anno Domini* 1361. *Anno* 35 and 37 of *Edward* III. Sir *Robert Herle*, Knight, is in Occupancy of this Office now omitted. And *Anno* 39 *Edward* III. Sir *Ralph Spignorel* (whom others write *Spigurnel*). He surrenders to Sir *Richard Penbrugge*, *June* 21, *Anno* 44 *Edward* III. and him the King outs about Two Years after, because he refused to undertake the Lieutenancy of *Ireland*. *Anno* 49 *Edward* III. you may find in Office *William* Lord *Latimer*, who next Year, *viz. Anno* 50 *Edward* III. gives Place to *Edmund* Earl of *Cambridge*, one of the Sons of King *Edward* III. and he surviving his Father, had the Office re-granted by other Letters Patents, *June* 19, 1 *Richard* II. *February* 1, 4 *Richard* II. the Patent passed to Sir *Robert Afheton*, who died, as some say, *January* 9, 7 *Richard* II. and then the King granted the Office to Sir *Simon Burley*, Knight, his Sub-Chamberlain, and delivered the Keys of the Castle to him in sign of Possession. This Sir *Simon*, by Sentence of Parliament, *Anno* 11 *Richard* II. was condemned of Treason, and beheaded on *Tower* Hill, but before his Death is commanded to surrender to Sir *John Devereux*, Knight, *Jan.* 3, 11 *Richard* II. After him, as I take it, comes the Lord *Henry Cobham*, Son of the aforesaid *Reginald*. This Lord *Henry Cobham* died 1392. and in the same Year, being 16 *Richard* II. is Sir *John Beaumont* in place. Mr. *Lambard* mentions next Sir *John Ewes*, and Sir *Thomas Beaumont* (which was first, and the certainty of the Name may be further inquired.) *Anno* 22 *Richard* II. the Office was bestowed on *Edward Plantagenet* (or *Plantagenift*) Duke of *York* and *Aumerle*, which Duke the succeeding King removed, and substituted in his Place, *Anno* 5 *Henry* IV. Sir *Thomas Erpingham*, Knight; after whom some place *John Beauford*, Marquiss of *Dorfet*, and Earl of *Somerfet*; but afterward the King added it to the Honours of his Son *Henry*, Prince of *Wales*, *Anno* 12 *Henry* IV. who, when he was King *de fafto*, first gave it to *Thomas* Earl of *Arundel* and *Surrey*, *Anno* 2 *Henry* V. but afterward to his Brother *Humphry*, Duke of *Gloucefter* (whom I have mentioned before) for in the Ninth Year of his Reign I find his Titles accordingly. This good Duke *Humphry*, after the Death of his Brother King *Henry* V. and so long under the Reign of King *Henry* VI. almost, held this Honour and Office as he held his Life; though some mention *John Reynsford* to be in the Office, *Anno* 4 *Henry* VI. Afterwards a large Patent, with great Privileges, passed to *James Pynes*, Lord *Say* of *Seale*, *February* 14, 25 *Henry* VI. who unhappily was beheaded by *Jack Cade*; whereupon one mentions *Henry* Duke of *Buckingham*, *Anno* 27 *Henry* VI. to supply the Place; and others, *Edmund* Duke of *Somerfet*, *Humphry* Duke of *Buckingham*, *Anno* 36 *Henry* VI. And *Simon Montfort* afterwards under this King. But *Anno* 1 *Edward* IV. *Richard Nevill*, the Earl of *Warwick*, is seated therein. And *April* 4, 10 *Edward* IV. *John Scot*. And *Anno* 19 *Edward* IV. *William Fitz Alen*, Earl of *Arundel*. After whom *Richard* Duke of *Gloucefter*, Brother of King *Edward* IV. that after usurping the Crown, was called King *Richard* III. He kept the Office during the short Reign of King *Edward* V. but after he himself had got the Crown, *viz. Anno* 1 *Richard* III. *Henry Stafford*, Duke of *Buckingham*, enjoyed it; as did *William*, Earl of *Arundel*, *Anno* 1 *Henry* VII. Next him Mr. *Lambard* places Sir *William Scot*, and then *Henry* Duke of *York*, that is to say, the King's second Son, afterward King *Henry* VIII. for *Anno* 8 *Henry* VII. he had the Gift to be Constable of *Dover* Castle during Life, and Warden of the *Cinque Ports* during Pleasure; whereby the King reserved Liberty to dispose the Wardenship, when, and to whom, he pleased; and so to sever it from the Constableship, as he saw cause. But *Anno* 10 *Henry* VII. the King renewed the Grant, and gave to his Son the said Offices with Castle Guard, and many other Benefits. Afterwards I find some mention of *James Pines*, Lord *Say*, and *Arthur Plantagenet*, Viscount *Lifle*, Bastard Son of King *Edward* IV. But *Anno* 1 *Henry* VIII. Sir *Edward Poynings* hath the Office, and is sworn at *Shepway*. Next whom some place the aforesaid *Arthur*, but others (to which I rather incline) *Henry Fitz Roy*, Duke of *Richmond*, natural Son of King *Henry* VIII. In the Twentieth of *April*, *Anno* 13 *Henry* VIII. the Office is granted to Sir *Edward Guldeford*, Knight; and *Anno* 26 *Henry* VIII. to *George Boleyne*, Viscount *Rocheford*; and *Anno* 34 *Henry* VIII. to Sir *Thomas Cheyne*, Knight, Treasurer of the King's Houshold, who held it during the rest of this King's Life, and throughout the Reigns of King *Edward* VI. and Queen *Mary*, and died *Anno* 1559. in the beginning of Queen *Elizabeth's* Reign, who preferred thereto Sir *William Brooke*, Lord *Cobham*, and Lord Chamberlain of her Majesty's Houshold, *Anno* 1 *Elizabeth*. He continuing therein till towards the latter end of her Reign, left it to his Son Sir *Henry Brooke*, Lord *Cobham*, about 1597. who held the Office till the coming of King *James*. He gave it, *January* 2, 1 King *James*, *Anno Domini* 1603. to *Henry Howard*, second Son of *Henry*, Earl of *Surrey*, who was afterwards created Baron *Howard of Marnehill*, and Earl of *Northampton*. Then about the Tenth of King *James*, *Anno Domini* 1613. *Edward* Lord *Zouch* had the Honour thereof, and was sworn about Two Years after at *Shepway*, with whom it lasted till the beginning of King

O   *Charles*

CHARTERS.

Dovor, fi neceffe fuerit, debite compellantur. Et quod bona & catalla dictorum Baronum & aliorum, five extra dictam libertatem fuerint, five infra, quæ pro navigio & fervitio manutenend. & faciend. taxantur, ad tallagia, feu alia onera quæcunque, cum bonis & catallis hominum forinfecorum, nullatenus taxentur. In cujus rei teftimonium has literas noftras fieri fecimus patentes. Tefte meipfo apud Weftm. vicefimo quinto die Februarii, anno Regni noftri primo. Nos autem cartam noftram prædictam fub figillo quo nunc utimur, ad requifitionem ipforum duximus exemplificand. In cujus rei teftimonium has literas noftras fieri fecimus patentes. Tefte me ipfo apud Ebor. vicefimo fexto die Febru-

TRANSLATION.

of *Dover* [r], if need fhall be [s]; they may be duly compelled. And that the Goods and Chattels of the faid Barons, and others, whether they fhall be without the faid Liberty [t] or within, which are taxed for to maintain [u] and do the Shipping and Service, in no wife [w] fhall be taxed to the Tallages, or other Charges whatfoever, with the Goods and Chattels of foreign Men. In witnefs whereof thefe our Letters we have made Patents. Witnefs My Self at *Weftminfter*, the Twenty fifth Day of *February*, in the Firft Year [y] of our Reign. We alfo [w] our Charter aforefaid, under the Seal which we now ufe, at their Requeft have caufed to be exemplified. In witnefs whereof thefe our Letters we have made Patents. Witnefs My Self at *York* [x] the Twenty fixth Day of *February*,

ANNOTATIONS.

Charles I. when *George Villiers*, Duke, Marquifs, and Earl of *Buckingham*, was entituled thereto; and after his Death *Theophilus Howard*, Earl of *Suffolk*, who was fworn *Auguft* 20, 1629. and after him *James Steward*, Duke of *Richmond* and *Lenox*, was made Conftable and Warden, *Anno* 17 *Charles* I. *Anno* 1640. but never fworn that I find. And after him, during the Differences that continued between the King and Parliament, and until the Reftoration of King *Charles* II. the Officer of the Army that commanded the Caftle officiated in the Office as Warden, but were none of them fworn, till the Patent was granted to his Royal Highnefs, *James*, Duke of *York* and *Albany*, &c. who took the Oath in a Court of *Shepway*, holden at *Dover*, yet not till the Year 1668. feveral Years after the Grant of the Conftablefhip and Wardenfhip aforefaid to him.

[r] *Dover*. See afterward.

[s] *If need fhall be*, that is, if towards the Service the Ports were to perform, the Advocants that dwelt out of the Ports fhould refufe or neglect to pay their Contributions or Taxations, the Conftable of *Dover* Caftle fhould be helpful to the Ports to enforce the Payment thereof by due Courfe of Law, or the Cuftoms of the Ports.

[t] *Liberty*. Meaning the Precincts of the Ports-Towns and Members.

[u] *To maintain*, or for the Maintenance and making of the faid Service.

[w] *In no wife*, or by no means, or in no fort. The Advocants and others, whofe Eftates were taxed, and did contribute to the Suftentation of the Ports Services, were not to be taxed with the Goods and Chattels of Foreigners (that is, fuch not Advocants as lived out of the Ports) to fuch Tallages and Affeffments as the Ports were free of, and were paid only by others, not Ports Men; for if thefe Advocants had been taxed, or fcotted with Foreigners, and the Ports Men too, they had been doubly charged above the Example of other Subjects, or Reafon it felf they fhould be.

[y] *Firft Year*. This additional Grant of King *Edward* III. bearing date *February* 25, in the Firft Year of his Reign, muft be prefently after his coming to the Crown, for that was *Jan.* 25, but a Month before, *Anno Domini* 1326.

[w] *We alfo*. Here is fubjoined the Exemplification of his former Confirmation of his Grandfather's Charter at St. *Alban*'s aforementioned, and his own additional Grant together, under his new Seal.

[x] *York*, the fecond City in *England* for Bignefs (*London* the firft) and the fecond for Primacy (*Canterbury* the firft) a provincial City, and fo the Bifhop's See is an Archbifhoprick. The City gives Name to the whole Shire, which is the greateft in *England*, and bigger than Two or Three of fome of the reft.

[y] *Second*

CHARTERS.

Februarii, anno Regni noftri fecundo. Nos autem conceffiones & confirmationes prædictas ratas habentes, & gratas eas, pro nobis & hæredibus noftris, quantum in nobis eft, præfatis Baronibus Quinque Portuum, hæredibus & fucceforibus fuis, Baronibus Portuum prædictorum, pro bono & fideli fervitio fuo nobis & progenitoribus noftris hactenus impenfo, ac nobis & hæredibus noftris impofterum impendend. concedimus & confirmamus, ficut cartæ & literæ prædictæ rationabiliter teftantur, & prout iidem Barones & anteceffores fui, Barones Portuum prædictorum, libertatibus & quietanciis prædictis huc ufque rationabiliter ufi funt & gavifi. In cujus rei teftimonium has literas noftras fieri fecimus patentes. Tefte me ipfo apud Weftmon. vicefimo fecundo die Januarii, anno Regni hoftri primo. Nos ex humili infinuatione dictorum Baronum & proborum hominum Quinque Portuum prædictorum, & Membrorum fuorum, accipientes, quod licet in Magna Carta de libertatibus Angliæ, inter alia continetur,

TRANSLATION.

bruary, in the Second Year [y] of our Reign. And we [z] the aforefaid Grants and Confirmations having ratified, and freely them, for us and our Heirs, as much as in us is, to the aforefaid Barons of the *Cinque Ports*, their Heirs and Succeffors, Barons of the Ports aforefaid, for their good and faithful Service to us and our Progenitors hitherto done; and to us and our Heirs hereafter [a] to be done, do grant and confirm, as the aforefaid Charters and Letters do reafonably teftify, and as the faid Barons and their Anceftors, Barons of the Ports aforefaid, hitherto have ufed and enjoyed the Liberties and Freedoms aforefaid reafonably. In witnefs whereof thefe our Letters we have made Patents. Witnefs My Self at *Weftminfter*, the Twenty fecond Day of *January*, in the Firft Year [b] of our Reign. We, by [c] the humble Information [d] of the faid Barons and good Men of the aforefaid *Cinque Ports*, and their Members [e], underftanding [f], that although in the great Charter [g] of the Liberties of *England*, among other things it is contained;

ANNOTATIONS.

[y] *Second Year.* The Exemplification of this King *Edward* III. juft a Year and a Day after his former Confirmation, and additional Charter added thereto, that is *February* 26, *Anno Domini* 1327.

[z] *And we.* At this Place beginneth the Confirmation of King *Richard* II. including all the former Charters and Confirmations before recited.

[a] *Hereafter*, or in Time to come.

[b] *Firft Year.* This Confirmation of King *Richard* II. bearing Date *January* 22, in the firft Year of his Reign, muft be *Anno Domini* 1377.

[c] *We by.* Here beginneth the Charter of King *Edward* IV.

[d] *Information*, Infinuation, according to the *Latin* ; but it is often taken in the Law for Information, according to the Tranflation thereof here.

[e] *Their Members.* Of the Members of the Ports fee afterwards : This is the firft Place they are mentioned in the Charters.

[f] *Underftanding.* The *Latin*, *Accipientes*, in this Place, will bear fuch a Conftruction.

[g] *Great Charter*, commonly called by the *Latin* Name, *Magna Charta*, was made *February* 10, *Anno* 9 *Henry* III. *Anno Domini* 1214. and afterwards confirmed by his Son, King *Edward* I. in the Twenty eighth Year of his Reign, *Anno Domini* 1299. and by divers other Kings and Parliaments; and is called the great *Charter* of *England*, as the Lord *Coke* faith, not from the Largenefs thereof, but from the Weighty Matters contained therein.

i

CHARTERS.

tur, quod Barones de Quinque Portubus habeant omnes libertates suas & liberas confuetudines fuas, ipfi tamen de nonnullis libertatibus & liberis confuetudinibus, necnon quietanciis & privilegiis, quibus ipfi in Portubus & Membris prædiétis, à tempore confeétionis cartarum, literarum, & confirmationum prædiétarum, libere, pacifice, & quiete uti & gaudere confueverunt, occafione quarundam ambiguitatum, obfcuritat. & dubitationum, ac finiftrarum interpretationum quorundam verborum & terminorum generalium in cartis, literis, & confirmationibus prædiétis contentorum, impediti fuerunt & exiftunt, in ipforum Baronum & probo rum hominum depreffionem & depauperationem, necnon in fervitii navigii noftri ibidem deteriorationem, & deperditum verifimiliter manifeftum, nos igitur nedum præmiffa, verum etiam bona, prona, & gratuita fervitia, quæ prædiéti Barones & probi homines Quinque Portuum & Membrorum prædiétorum, omnibus progenitoribus noftris, & præfertim nobis, in juris Regni noftri reduétione impenderunt in-time

TRANSLATION.

ed [h], that the Barons of the *Cinque Ports* fhall have all their Liberties and free Cuftoms [i], notwithftanding they of fome Liberties and free Cuftoms, Freedoms alfo and Privileges [j], which they in the Ports and Members aforefaid, from the Time of the making of the Charters, Letters, and Confirmations aforefaid, freely, peaceably, and quietly, were wont [k] to ufe and enjoy, by occafion [l] of certain Ambiguities, Obfcurities, and Doubts, and of finifter [m] Interpretations of certain Words, and general Terms [n], in the aforefaid Charters, Letters, and Confirmations, contained, have been, and yet are hindered [o], to the depreffing and impoverifhing [p] of the faid Barons and good Men, alfo to the Hurt [q], and manifeft Lofs, very likely, of our Service of Shipping there. We therefore not only the Premifes, but alfo the good, ready, and grateful Services [r], which the aforefaid Barons, and good Men of the *Cinque Ports*, and Members aforefaid, to all our Progenitors, and chiefly to us [s], have done in the Reduétion of the Right of our Kingdom fe-

ANNOTATIONS.

[h] *Is contained*, that is, in the Ninth Chapter thereof, as it is printed among the Statutes at large.

[i] *Free Cuftoms*, thefe are equivalent to Ufages, fuch as the Ports had long, continually, and peaceably enjoyed, and fhould or ought ftill to have or enjoy.

[j] *Privileges* are Liberties and Franchifes granted to their Ports by their Charters, or by Aét of Parliament, including alfo fuch for which they can prefcribe.

[k] *Were wont*, or have accuftomed to enjoy and ufe.

[l] *By Occafion*, or by Reafon of.

[m] *Sinifter*, or wrong Interpretations, becaufe the left Hand, in *Latin*, *Sinifter*, is counted the wrong Hand.

[n] *Terms*. Expreffions or Phrafes not plain to be underftood, or particularly explained. *Terms* are fometimes taken for Limits or Bounds, and for Days or fet Times, but not fo here.

[o] *Hindered*, Impedited.

[p] *Impoverifhing*, or Impoverifhment.

[q] *Hurt*, Impairing or worfing.

[r] *Grateful Services*, that is, free, thankful or acceptable; and here *Services* is ufed not for the Service of Shipping only, but for others, as their Service at the Coronation, and Affiftance with Men and Arms in the Wars, &c.

[s] *To us*, or efpecially to us, by which it feems the Ports took part with King *Edward* IV. againft King *Henry* VI.

[s] *Serioufly,*

CHARTERS.

time confiderantes, & ipforum quieti & tranquillitati; necnon bono publico in hac parte perfpicere volentes; Omnes donationes & conceffiones prædictas, necnon omnia & fingula in cartis, literis, & confirmationibus prædictis contenta & fpecificatà, & omnia & fingula libertates, quietancias, privilegia, & liberas confuetudines, quæ ipfi ac anteceffores & prædeceffores fui progenitorum noftrorum temporibus habuerunt & exercuerunt, ac quibus uti & gaudere confueverunt, rata habentes, & grata ea, pro nobis & hæredibus noftris, quantum in nobis eft, acceptamus, approbamus, ratificamus, & præfatis nunc Baronibus Portuum & Membrorum prædictorum, & eorum hæredibus & fucceforibus, tenore præfentium adeo plene, plane, & integre, ac fi verbatim in præfentibus expreffa, declarata, & manifeftata fuiffent, damus, concedimus, & confirmamus; volentes infuper, & concedentes pro nobis & hæredibus noftris prædictis, quod prædicti Barones, & eorum hæredes & fucceffores, Portuum & Membrorum prædictorum, omnia, libertates, quietancias, privilegia, & liberas confuetudines, fua adeo integre, & plene reftituantur, ficut ipfi, anteceffores aut prædeceffores fui, ea, tempore fancti Edwardi confefforis, & Willielmi conqueftoris, nuper Regum Angliæ, aut aliquorum aliorum progenitorum noftrorum, liberius, plenius, & honorificentius habuerunt. Ac licet iidem Barones & probi homi-

TRANSLATION.

ferioufly ' confidering, and their Peace ᵗ and Tranquility; alfo willing to refpect the publick Good in this Behalf ᵘ; All the aforefaid Gifts and Grants, alfo all and fingular the Things in the aforefaid Charters, Letters, and Confirmations contained and fpecified, and all and every the Liberties, Freedoms, Privileges and free Cuftoms, which they and their Anceftors and Predeceffors ᵛ have had and exercifed in the Times of our Progenitors, and which they were wont to ufe and enjoy, having ratified, and freely them, for us and our Heirs, as much as in us is, we do accept, approve ᵂ, ratify, and to the aforefaid now Barons of the Ports, and Members aforefaid, and their Heirs and Succeffors, by the Tenor of thefe Prefents, fo fully, plainly, and perfectly ˣ, as if Word by Word they had been expreffed, declared, and manifefted in thefe Prefents, we do give, grant, and confirm; willing moreover, and granting, for us and our Heirs, that the aforefaid Barons, and their Heirs and Succeffors, of the Ports and Members aforefaid, may have all their Liberties, Freedoms, Privileges and free Cuftoms, fo perfectly, and fully reftored, as they, their Anceftors or Predeceffors, the fame, in the Time of Saint *Edward* the Confeffor, and *William* the Conqueror, late Kings of *England*, or any other of our Progenitors, more freely, more fully, and more honourably have had. And although the faid Barons and good

ʸ *Hap-*

CHARTERS.

homines, aut antecessores vel prædecessores sui, Barones & probi
homines Portuum & Membrorum
prædictorum, seu alicujus eorundem, aliqua, vel aliquibus libertatum, quietanciarum & privile-
giorum in dictis cartis & literis
content. aut liberarum consuetud.
suarum aliquo casu emergente,
hactenus plene usi non fuerint,
seu forsan abusi fuerint; ipsi tamen Barones & probi homines,
eorum hæredes & successores, libertatibus & quietanciis, privilegiis, & liberis consuetudinibus
suis quibuscunque, taliter non usis
vel abusis, & eorum qualibet,
de cætero plene gaudeant & utantur, sine occasione vel impedimento nostri vel hæredum nostrorum,
Justic. Vicecomit. Coronatorum,
Escæatorum, aut aliorum Ballivorum seu Ministrorum nostrorum, vel hæredum nostrorum
quorumcunque (aliqua interrup-
tione quocunque tempore 'retro-
acto in contrarium habita 'sive
facta non obstante.) Concessimus etiam, pro nobis & hæredibus nostris, & hac carta nostra
confirmavimus, Majoribus, Ballivis & Juratis, cujuslibet Portus,
& Membri Portuum, & Mem-
brorum prædictorum, in Portubus & Membris prædictis, per
com-

TRANSLATION.

good Men, or their Ancestors
or Predecessors, Barons and good
Men of the Ports and Members
aforesaid, or of any of them, any
of the Liberties, Freedoms and
Privileges in the said Charters
and Letters contained, or of
their free Customs in any case
happening[r], hitherto fully have
not used, or perhaps have abused[s]; notwithstanding the same
Barons and good Men, their
Heirs and Successors, their Liberties and Freedoms, Privileges and free Customs whatsoever, in such wise not used or
abused, and every of them, from
henceforth fully may enjoy and
use, without Occasion or Impediment of us or our Heirs, or of
the Justices, Sheriffs, Coroners[a], Escheators[b], or other the
Bailiffs or Ministers of us or our
Heirs[c], whosoever (any Interruption in Time past whatsoever to the contrary had or
made notwithstanding.) We
have granted also, for us and
our Heirs, and by this our Charter have confirmed, to the
Mayors, Bailiffs[d], and Jurats
of every Port, and Member
of the 'Ports, and Mem-
bers aforesaid, in the aforesaid
Ports and Members, by the
Com-

ANNOTATIONS.

[r] *Happening*, arising or emergent.

[s] *Abused*, the Abuse or Misuse of any or many of the Liberties and Privileges of the Ports
by Ports Men were hereby pardoned, and the same Liberties and Privileges to be used and enjoyed notwithstanding, without any Seizure thereof into the King's Hands, or Impediment of
his Officers, by *Quo Warranto*, or Forfeitures thereof, or Fines to be paid for the same.

[a] *Coroners*, are ancient Officers of the Land, so called, because they deal wholly for the King
and Crown. There be Four commonly in every County, and they are chosen by the Freehold-
ers of the same upon Writ, and not by Letters Patents.

[b] *Escheators*, these were Officers of the King that inquired after Land escheated, that is fallen into the King's Hands for default of an Heir casually, and after Enquiry certified them into
the *Exchequer*: He continues in his Office but one Year, nor can be an Escheator but once in
Three Years.

[c] *Our Heirs*, including the Successors of the King.

[d] *Bailiffs*, the Chief Magistrates or Head Officers of some of the Ports and Members were so
called, but differed nothing in Power or Authority from the Title of Mayors, only in Name,
though when they come to be repeated together, the Mayors are commonly first mentioned; nevertheless Bailiffs seem to be the most ancient Title, and some that were Bailiff Towns at first
have since obtained Charters for their Head Officer to be called Mayor, as hereafter upon the
particular Towns shall be noted.

[e] *Com-*

CHARTERS.

communes eorundem electis, quod
fi aliquæ confuetudines in Portubus & Membris illis, feu aliquo eorundem hactenus obtentæ
& ufitatæ, in aliqua parte diffici-
les feu defectivæ exiftant, aut
aliqua in eifdem Portubus &
Membris feu eorum aliquo de
novo emergent, ubi remedium
prius non extitit, ordinatione &
emendatione indigeant, iidem
Majores, Ballivi & Jurati, cujuflibet Portus, & Membri Portuum, & Membrorum prædictorum, & eorum hæredes & fucceffores, de affenfu communitatis illius Portus, five Membri
Portuum, & Membrorum præ-
dictorum, ubi hujufmodi emen-
dationem, defectum, five difficul-
tatem fieri feu habere contigerit,
remedium congruum bonæ fidei
& rationi confonum pro communi utilitate Baronum & proborum hominum, & inhabitantium
ejufdem Portus five Membri,
necnon aliorum fidelium noftrorum illuc confluentium, apponere
poffint, & ordinare, quoties &
quando eis videbitur expedire.
Dum tamen ordinatio hujufmodi
nobis & populo noftro utilis, ac
bonæ

TRANSLATION.

Commons[e] of the fame elected,
that if any Cuftoms[f] in the faid
Ports and Members, or in any
of them hitherto obtained[g] and
ufed, in any part be difficult or
defective[h], or any Thing in the
faid Ports and Members, or in
any of them happening[i] of new,
where before Remedy was not
ordained, and fhall lack[j] A-
mendment, the fame Mayors,
Bailiffs, and Jurats of every
Port, and Member of the Ports,
and Members aforefaid, and
their Heirs and Succeffors, with
the Affent[k] of the Commonalty[l] of that Port, or Member of
the Ports, and Members aforefaid, where fuch Amendment,
Defect or Difficulty fhall happen
to be made or had, may appoint[m] and ordain meet Remedy[n], according to good Faith
and Reafon, for the common
Profit[o] of the Barons and good
Men, and Inhabitants.[p] of the
fame Port or Member, alfo of
other our Leige People[q] thither
reforting, fo often[r], and when to
them it fhall feem expedient; fo
that, notwithstanding[s] fuch Ordinance be to us and our People profitable, and agreeable to
good

ANNOTATIONS.

[e] *Commons,* that is, the Freemen, often called Commoners, who elect their Head Officers, as
by their Cuftomals may appear.
[f] *Cuftoms,* that is, fuch Ufages as have been accuftomed in any of the Corporations of the Ports
Towns and Members.
[g] *Obtained,* practifed or had.
[h] *Defective,* or faulty.
[i] *Happening,* arifing or emergent, as before, *p.* 54.
[j] *Shall lack,* or may want Amendment.
[k] *With the Affent,* or of the Affent.
[l] *Commonalty.* That is, alfo the Freemen or Commoners affembled together with their Mayor
and Jurats, or Bailiff and Jurats refpectively.
[m] *Appoint,* or put.
[n] *Meet Remedy.* By making at fuch Affemblies good and wholfome Orders and Decrees, according to the Law and Cuftoms of the Ports.
[o] *Common Profit.* Thefe are the right Directions according to which every Law, Ordinance
and Decree ought to be made, both in the higher and lower Courts or Affemblies, *viz.* the
Truft repofed, right Reafon, and the publick Good.
[p] *Inhabitants,* fuch as are not Freemen but refide within their Precincts.
[q] *Leige People,* or faithful Subjects.
[r] *So often,* or as often.
[s] *Notwithstanding.* A kind of Provifion or Limitation, that none of thofe Decrees be againft
the Weal publick, but for the Profit and Benefit thereof.

[t] *Record,*

CHARTERS.	TRANSLATION.
bonæ fidei & confona fit rationi, ficut prædictum eft; & quod libertates & liberas confuetudines fuas recordare poffint coram nobis, jufticiariis, & aliis miniftris noftris quibufcunq; Et ulterius, ut iidem Barones talia fervitia, qualia præfatis progenitor. noftris, & nobis ante hæc tempora impenderunt, aut, pro poffe fuo, meliora, nobis & hæred. noftris impendere animari poterunt in futurum, alias libertates, & quietancias planas, & expreffas eifdem Baronibus & probis hominibus de novo dignum duximus concedend. Ac de uberiori gratia noftra, necnon ex mero motu, & certa fcientia noftris, conceffimus, & per præfentes concedimus, pro nobis & hæredibus noftris, quantum in nobis eft, eifdem Baronibus & probis hominibus Quinque Portuum prædictorum, ac Baronibus & probis hominibus omnium & fingulorum Portuum & Villarum Membrorum eifdem Quinque Portuum, feu eorum alicui annex. unit. & pertinent. quod ipfi, eorum hæredes & fucceffores, ac quicunque refidentes infra Portus & Membra prædicta, aut infra aliquos eorundem,	good Faith and Reafon as is aforefaid; and that they may record[1] their Liberties and free Cuftoms before us, our Juftices, and other Minifters whatfoever. And furthermore, that the fame Barons may be encouraged[t] in Time to come to do to us and our Heirs fuch Services, as to our aforefaid Progenitors, and to us, before thefe Times they have done, or better, according to their Power, we have thought fit[u] to grant of new[v] to the fame Barons and good Men other Liberties and Freedoms plain and expreffed[w]. And of our more plentiful Grace, alfo of our meer Motion[x] and certain Knowledge, have granted, and by thefe Prefents do grant, for us and our Heirs, as much as in us is, to the fame Barons and good Men of the *Cinque Ports* aforefaid, and to the Barons and good Men of all and fingular the Ports and Towns[y] of the Members to the faid *Cinque Ports*, or to any of them annexed, united and appertaining, that they, their Heirs and Succeffors, and whofoever are Refident[z] within the Ports and Members aforefaid, or within any of them, contributing to the

ANNOTATIONS.

[1] *Record*, enter upon Record, or make to be remembred.

[t] *Encouraged*, put in Heart or animated.

[u] *Thought fit*, meet or worthy.

[v] *Of new*, yet all that follows in this Charter of King *Edward* IV. was not firft granted by him to the Ports, but many Particulars thereof, as by Examination plainly will appear, the Ports had long before.

[w] *Expreffed*, or exprefs, to wit, by exprefs Words after fpecified in the Charter.

[x] *Meer Motion*, as proceeding of the King's own Inclination, fpontaneous, and of himfelf, voluntarily.

[y] *Towns*. Becaufe Ports and Members befides Towns are here expreffed, the Towns are taken by fome to intend the Towns of *Rye* and *Winchelfea*, and accordingly this Paffage hath been conftrued, *Ports Towns and Members*, which the Senfe will bear well enough; for if thefe Towns be not particularly intended in the Words & *villarum membrorum*, yet were they included, as both they and the Members were under the Word *Ports* only, in the foregoing Charters. *Villa*, in the *French Ville*, is ordinarily rendered a *Town*, though the Word imports, and is alfo taken for, fome other Things; from *Villa* comes the Word *Village*, a little Country Town: It is called *Villa*, faith the Lord *Coke*, *Quafi vebilla, quod in eam convehantur fruttus*.

[z] *Refident*, Refidents or Refciants, which are thofe that inhabit or dwell there, though not Freemen.

    [a] *Toll*,

CHARTERS.	TRANSLATION.
dem fervitio & navigio prædictis contribuentes, quieti fint imperpetuum de Theolonio, Panagio, Pontagio, Kiagio, Muragio, Paffagio, Laftagio, Stallagio, Tallagio, Carriagio, Peifagio, Picagio, Terragio, & Scoto,	the Service and Shipping aforesaid, may be quit for ever of Toll [a], Panage [b], Pontage [c], Kaiage [d], Murage [e], Paffage, Laftage, Stallage [f], Tallage, Carriage, Peifage [g], Picage [h], Terrage [i], and Scot,

ANNOTATIONS.

[a] *Toll*, this, as alfo *Paffage, Laftage, Tallage,* and *Carriage,* are before mentioned in the other *Charters,* to which the Reader is therefore referred for their Explanation ; fo, as I faid before, all granted here is not new.

[b] *Panage,* or *Pannage* *, the running of Hogs in Forefts, Woods, &c. in Acorn Time ; fo as * *wrote alfo* the Lands in the Ports are freed thereof ; and the Ports Mens Lands held of the King by fuch Service, or Money paid inftead thereof, though out of the Ports, are difcharged thereof. —— *Pawnage.*

[c] *Pontage,* a Toll paid, or Labour to the Repair of any Bridge ; from *Pons,* a Bridge. Thus taken, *Weftm.* 1. *cap.* 25. *Anno* 13 *Edward* I. It may be alfo a Toll taken to this Purpofe for paffing over Bridges, *Stat.* 1 *Henry* VIII. *cap.* 9, and 22 *Henry* VIII. *cap.* 5. and 39 *Elizabeth, cap.* 14.

[d] *Kaiage,* or *Keyage,* a Toll or Duty paid to the Maintenance of a common Kay or Wharf for the Landing or Shipping off of Goods.

[e] *Murage,* a Toll paid towards the Walling of a Town ; from *Murus,* a Wall. By *Fitz Herberts's Nat. Bre.* fol. 227. it feems to extend to the Repairing of publick Edifices ; and by the Stat. *Anno* 3 *Edward* I. *cap.* 30. to be a Liberty granted by the King to gather Money towards the Walling of a Town ; of which Payment the Ports are hereby free.

[f] *Stallage,* Money paid for pitching or fetting up Stalls in Fairs or Markets.

[g] *Peifage,* from *Pois,* a Weight in *French.* The Ports are to weigh freely at the King's Weigh-houfe or common Beam.

[h] *Picage,* Money exacted in Fairs for picking or breaking up the Ground to fet up Booths or Standings.

[i] *Terrage,* or *Groundage,* nothing to be paid for their Ships lying a Ground, or at Anchor in any of the King's Havens or Harbours. Thus I find the Ports Men, who beft know their own Privileges, underftood the Word in a Letter wrote from the Mayor and Jurats of *Rye* to the Mayor and Aldermen of *Hull,* almoft One Hundred Years fince, upon requeft of one *Edward Beale,* a Freeman of *Rye* going to buy Corn in *Hull,* where he was demanded certain Duties or Exactions which he ought not to pay ; and thereupon having by former Letters cleared up fome Scruples, in another Letter, the Tenor whereof followeth, this of Terrage is alfo cleared, and he was accordingly difcharged, as I conceive, for that I find no more queftion thereof.

To the Right Worfhipfull, our Loving Friends, the Maior and Aldermen of Hull.

Right Worfhipfull,

WITH our due and hearty Commendations we falute you. Whereas of late we wrote our Letters to you in the Behalfe of our honeft Neighbour and Combaron *Edward Beale,* touching certain Duties ye required of him, which he denies to pay, being a Freeman of the Ports ; he hath made Relation unto us of your courteous Ufage of him, for which we thanke you, being ready to requit it to any of your People, as Occafion fhall ferve : But yet he advertifeth us, that ye ftand in doubt, that we be not free of Anchorage and Juttage, and hath prayed us to certify you therein. Thefe are therefore to fignify to you for Truth, that neither we, nor any our Aunceftors, have ever paid any Anchorage within this Realme, for it is one of the chiefeft Things whereof we are, and alwaies have beene free. And for Juttage, we never heard that it hath beene demanded of any of the Ports untill now. For whereas we are by our Charter free of *Terrage,* if we pay *Anchorage,* we cannot be *Terrage* free ; for *Groundage* and *Anchorage* is within the Compafs of that Word *Terrage* ; for there is feldom Anchor-hold without Ground. And for *Juttage,* we cannot be free of *Ryeage,* if we be compelled to pay *Juttage* ; for to be free of *Ryeage* is to arrive freely and depart freely without any Exaction. Befides, the general Words of our Charter is, that we fhall have all our Liberties and Quietances throughout the Realme of *England,* &c. and our Liberties are fuch, as we are free of all Taxes, Exactions and Demands whatfoever, except any Act of Parliament bind us thereunto. Thus having briefly certified you in what fort we have ever hitherto beene free from fuch Duties paying, as you now demand of the faid *Edward Beale,* and praying you to deal fo friendly with him, as he may enjoy the Liberties of a Freeman of the Ports, as his Aunceftors before him have done, We commit you, &c.

June 20, 1580.

Your Worfhip's loving Friends,

The Maior and Jurats of *Rye.*

CHARTERS.	TRANSLATION.
Scoto, & Gildo, Hidagio, Scutagio, necnon feĉt. Comitat. & Hundred. (ne Laſtis Hundred.) viſibus franci-pleg. & de denariis ad viſ. franci-pleg. pertinent. necnon quibuſcunque denariorum ſummis, reditibus, ſeu præſtationibus pro aliquo præmiſſorum nobis, hæredibus, vel ſucceſſoribus noſtris ſolvendis : Ac de finibus pro	Scot', and Gild ᵏ, Hidage ', Scutage ᵐ ; alſo of Suits of Counties and Hundreds ⁿ (and Lathes ° of Hundreds) Views of frank Pledge ᵖ, and of Monies ᵠ appertaining to the Views of frank Pledge ; alſo of whatſoever Sums of Money, Rents ʳ or Payments ˢ for any of the Premiſſes to us, our Heirs or Succeſſors, to be paid : And of Fines ᵗ for

ANNOTATIONS.

ᶤ *Scot*, from the *French Eſcot*, as ſome ſay, by the Statute *Anno* 33 *Henry* VIII. *cap.* 19. imports a cuſtomary Contribution laid upon all Subjects after their Ability. *Raſtal* ſaith, it is a Cuſtom, or common Tallage made to the Uſe of the Sheriff or his Bailiff. *Camden*, It is called that which of divers Things is gathered into one Heap. And in this Senſe it is uſed in a Company to pay a Reckoning, where he that pays nothing is ſaid to go *Scotfree*.

* Geld *in* Domeſday Book *is often taken for* Scot. ᵏ *Gild*, or *Geld*, a Tribute paid for ſervile Cuſtoms, as *Hornegeld*, to pay for every horned Beaſt. *Damgeld*, the Money levied on the People by or for the *Danes*, or after the Manner that was levied, and ſuch others ; *Gelt* in the Low Dutch being yet uſed for Money. And the Word *Gildable* is as much as *Taxable*. *Gilda* is alſo taken for a Fraternity or Company combined together by Orders and Laws made amongſt themſelves, by the Prince's Licence, and the Place where ſuch meet is hence conceived to be called a *Gildhall* or *Guildhall*. I have ſeen *Guilda* uſed for an Aſſembly, or Meeting of ſuch a Fraternity, but here take it in the former Senſe.

ᶩ *Hidage*, or *Hydage*, the Tax laid upon every Hide of Land, which ſeveral expound a *Plough Land*, a Kind of Taxing uſed much before the Conqueſt, and ſometime afterwards, as well for Proviſion of Armour, as Payments of Money, as appears by King *Ethelred*, who *Anno* 1006. when the *Danes* landed at *Sandwich*, taxed all his Land by Hides thus, that every Three Hundred and Ten Hides ſhould find one Ship furniſhed, and every Eight Hides ſhould find one Jack and one Sallet, for the Defence of the Realm.

ᵐ *Scutage*, from the *Latin*, *Scutum*, a Shield or Buckler, is the Service of the Shield uſed ſometime for Knight's Service, being a Kind thereof, called *Eſcuage* in the *French*, of the ſame Signification with *Scutage*. A Service whereby a Tenant ſo holding is bound to follow his Lord into the *Scotiſh* or *Welſh* Wars at his own Charge. *Eſcuage* uncertain is Knights Service, Certain is *Socage*. Thoſe holding of ſuch Tenures refuſing to go to thoſe Wars where the *Eſcuage* is uncertain, ſhall pay a certain Sum to their Lords as ſhall be aſſeſſed upon them, according to the Quantity of his Tenure in Parliament. The Lord *Coke* ſaith, no Eſcuage hath been aſſeſſed ſince the Eighth Year of King *Edward* II. Of this *Eſcuage* the Ports are freed.

ⁿ *Counties and Hundreds*, the ſame as Shires and Hundreds before, in the Charter of King *Edward* I.

° *Lathes*, thus the Latin *Laſtis* by ſome Tranſlations hath been rendered, and by others *Leibes*, as if for the Court Leets holden therein : But ſeeing *Leta* is uſed afterwards in this Charter for a Court Leet, it cannot be reſtrained to the Court Leet holden within and for the Hundred, for then it would be a Tautology, being included before in the Suit of the Hundred. Wherefore *Laſtis* muſt imply either Parts of an Hundred where any ſuch were divided, and had more Courts than one holden therein ; or more Hundreds than one included in the Word *Leaſh*, by which Name every of the Five great Diviſions of the County of *Kent* is yet called, and ſo had one Court for ſeveral Hundreds, to which latter I rather incline.

ᵖ *Views of frank Pledge*, ſo the Court Leet is commonly called, and entered in the Rolls. Frank Pledge is as much as a free Pledge or Surety ; or a Pledge or Surety for Freemen.

ᵠ *Monies* due for Fines, Amerciaments, &c. in the Court Leet.

ʳ *Rents*, from *Reddo*, to render, becauſe for many of the former Services, after the Time of their firſt Uſage, were required Sums of Money, aſcertained after the Manner of Rents, and at ſet Times to be paid or rendered.

ˢ *Payments*, the Latin, *Præſtatio*, ſignifieth properly Performance, whether of the Labour or Service to be done, or Money paid in lieu or ſtead thereof.

ᵗ *Fines*. A Fine is ſo called from the *Latin*, becauſe it maketh an End of the Difference, Offence, or Matter in Controverſy. Sometime it is taken for a friendly Compoſition, or Sum given by the Tenant to the Lord for Concord and Admittance to his Lands ; alſo for a final Concord by Licence of the King or his Juſtices to aliene Lands, &c. one of the higheſt and beſt Aſſurances thereof the Alienee can have. And ſometime, as here, it is taken for ſome pecuniary Mulĉt, Penalty, &c. impoſed for ſome Offence, or Contempt againſt the King, and regularly to this Impriſonment belongeth to enforce the Payment thereof upon neglect or refuſal.

ᵗ *Murr-*

CHARTERS.

pro murdr. & de communi mise-
recordia, quando contigerit comitat. five villæ. coram nobis
vel hæredibus noftris, feu coram
nobis aut quibufcunque jufticiariis, officiariis, feu miniftris noftris,
hæredum feu fucceflorum noftrorum, in manum noftram feu hæredum noftrorum incidere; ab omni
hujufmodi confuetud. per totum
regnum & poteftatem noftram.
Et etiam conceffimus præfatis
Baronibus & probis hominibus,
hæredibus & fucceffor. fuis, quod
lpfi imperpetuum habeant omnia
bona & catalla waviat. vel quæ
dicuntur Waife, & etiam omnia
bona & catalla quæ vocantur
Eftray,

TRANSLATION.

for Murder [t], and of common
Amerciament [u] when it fhall
happen [v]; the County or Townfhip [w] before us or our Heirs, or
before us, or whatfoever our
Juftices, Officers, or Minifters of
us, our Heirs or Succeffors, to
fall into the Hand of us or our
Heirs; from all Cuftom of this
fort [x] throughout our whole
Realm and Dominion [y]. And
alfo we have granted to the
aforefaid Barons and good Men,
their Heirs and Succeffors, that
they for ever may have all the
Goods and Chattels waived [z],
or which are called Waife,
and alfo all the Goods and
Chattels which are called
Stray;

ANNOTATIONS.

[t] *Murder*; a Word derived from the *Saxon Morthen*, or *Mordren*, as little differing as our *Mur-der* and *Murther*, fignifying, in the Common Law, *one that wilfully, with Malice, Forethought, kills another Perfon*. The Words for *Murder* here muft, as I conceive, be taken as touching or con-cerning Murder. Not that the Ports fhould be freed by Fines for committing Murder, or that Murder is finable; for it is punifhable with Death in the Ports, as well by their Cuftoms as by the Common Laws of the Land. But it feems to be Fines for Efcapes of Murderers out of their Franchifes, if accidently it fo happen againft the Will of the Ports Men, or that fome Negligence fhould be proved in not levying Hue and Cry after them, or not apprehending fuch as flee out of the Foreign into the Ports, or the like; for which fome Fine may be impofed.

[u] *Amerciament*, from the *French Mercie*, in Latin *Mifericordia*, becaufe it ought to be affeffed mercifully. It is commonly taken for a Sum of Money affeffed in a Court for the Nonfuit of a Plaintiff, or fome Delay or Default in a Defendant. Here it feems equivalent to a Fine impofed for fome Offence committed, whereby their Liberties might be feized or fall into the King's Hands. Some make this Difference between Fines and Amerciaments, that Fines are certain, but Amerciaments arbitrary.

[v] *When it fhall*, &c. It may be read thus, *When the County or Townfhip fhall happen before us or our Heirs, or before us, or whatfoever Juftices, Officers or Minifters of us, our Heirs or Succeffors, to fall into the Hand of us or our Heirs.*

[w] *Townfhip*, including both Lands and Inhabitants within the Limits thereof, upon whom a Fine or Penalty may be levied, or the Franchifes and Liberties of fuch Town that may be feized or taken from them that inhabit or dwell there.

[x] *This fort*, or from all fuch Cuftoms, or the Cuftom of this kind.

[y] *Dominion*, the Latin Word *Power*, as before, p 11. *Annot.*

[z] *Waived*: A Woman being fued in Law, and contempuoufly refufeth to appear, is called *Waviata* in the Latin, and *Waive, Waife, Weife*, in the French, q. f. one wavad, left out, or not regarded by the Law; that is, a Woman in the Condition of one Out-lawed, for Women cannot be Out-lawed, becaufe they are not fworn in Leets to the King, nor to the Law, as Men are; fo that a Man is faid to be Out-lawed, or without the Law to which he was fworn, and a Woman waived: And the Goods, not only of fuch a Woman, are called *waved*, but alfo fuch Goods as are left or forfaken of their Owners, fo as the true Proprietor thereof can-not be known; the Civilians call them *Dereliffs*: Both thefe belong to the Ports by this Charter, the latter Sort efpecially in this Place, becaufe the other is mentioned afterward; and thefe may be challenged by the Owner in a Year and a Day, fo that when they are found they muft be cried or publifhed in Markets and Churches near about, or elfe the Year and Day runs not to the Prejudice of him that loft them. *Waife* alfo is taken by fome to include *Eftrays*, and Goods of Felons left by them when they are purfued, whether their own or ftolen; but thefe latter, if the Owner make frefh purfuit after the Felon, and fue an Appeal, or give in Evidence againft him at his Arraignment upon the Indiffment, and the Felon be attaint thereof, the Owner fhall have the Reftitution of his Goods fo ftolen and waived.

[a] *Stray,*

CHARTERS.

Eſtray; necnon theſaurum inventum ſive inveniend. infra Portus prædictos, vel infra aliquod Membrum eorund. ac bona & catalla vocat. Manu opera, capt. ſeu capiend. cum aliqua perſona ubicunque infra Portus & Membra prædicta, coram quocunque judice, per eandem perſonam deadvocata. Et quod iidem Barones & probi homines, hæredes & ſucceſſores ſui, Barones & probi homines Portuum & Membrorum prædictorum, habeant catalla felonum qualitercunque dampnat. ſeu convictorum, dampnandorum ſeu convincendorum felonum, & de eſcapia felonum, ac

TRANSLATION.

Stray[a]; alſo Treaſure[b] found or to be found within the Ports aforeſaid, or within any Member of the ſame, and the Goods and Chattels called Maynour[c], taken, or to be taken, with any Perſon whereſoever within the Ports and Members aforeſaid, before whatſoever Judge, by the ſame Perſon diſowned[d]. And that they the ſaid Barons and good Men, their Heirs and Succeſſors, Barons and good Men of the Ports and Members aforeſaid, may have the Chattels of Felons[e], howſoever[f] condemned or convict, to be condemned[g] or convicted[h] of Felons[i], and of Eſcape[j] of Felons, and

ANNOTATIONS.

[a] *Stray* or *Eſtraye*, properly Cattle, or ſuch Animals that wander and ſtray from the known Maſter; theſe, when taken up, ought alſo to be proclaimed in ſundry Markets and Pariſh Churches, as was above ſaid of *Waifes*, *Derelict*, or otherwiſe the Detainer may be accuſed of Theft.

[b] *Treaſure*. Though after the making of this Charter *Treaſure trove* was inquirable at *Shepway*, yet was the Judgment thereof to paſs for the Ports Men, and not for the King or Lord Warden to have the ſame.

[c] *Maynour*, the *Latin*, *Manu opera*, is ſometime uſed for the Baſe Services by the Tenure of ſome Lands the Tenant is to do for the Lord; but here it is when a Thief is purſued with Hue and Cry, and taken with the Goods he hath ſtolen about him: Theſe Goods are called *Maynour*, as the Terms of the Law expound it.

[d] *Diſowned* or diſavowed. If one be indicted for the felonious Stealing the Goods of another, whereas in truth thoſe Goods are his own, and they are brought into the Court as a Maynour, and he is demanded what he ſaith to thoſe Goods, and he denieth them to be his, now by this denying them he ſhall loſe thoſe Goods, although afterward he be acquitted of the Felony.

[e] *Felons*, Felony, from the *Latin*, *Fel*, i. e. *Gall*, or the old *Engliſh*, *Fell*, i. e. *Fierce* or *Cruel*, is every capital Crime done *Felleo animo*, or an Heart imbittered with Malice, Miſchief and Cruelty. Of theſe Offences there are ſeveral Sorts, ſome by the Common Law, and ſome Felonies by Statute. The Perſons acting ſuch heinous Evils, and found guilty, are called Felons.

[f] *Howſoever*, or in what manner ſoever.

[g] *Condemned*, all one with *Damnatus* in the *Latin*. A Felon is ſaid to be condemned, when the Judgment of the Law due for the Offence, whereof he is found guilty, is pronounced againſt him by the Judge of the Court where he had his Trial, openly in the ſame Court.

[h] *Convict* or convicted. Conviction (from *Convinco*) goes before Condemnation. It is a proving guilty of the Party accuſed, either by his own Confeſſion, or by Verdict of a Jury or Recreancy, where Battaile is allowed for Trial. Here Convict is ſet after Condemn, becauſe a Felon upon Conviction forfeits all his Goods and Chattels, though he ſhould never be condemned.

[i] *Felons*. Several old Tranſlations of this Charter have it *Felons of themſelves*, but finding not *de ſe* in the printed Copy, and having ſeen only Copies and not the Original of this Charter of King *Edward* IV. I thought it better to go as it is, than alter the *Latin* by inſerting *de ſe* therein; nevertheleſs it ſeems to be intended ſo, becauſe the Chattels forfeited by other Sorts of Felons are granted in the foregoing Words; and the Word *Felons* here, unleſs *de ſe*, were a vain Repetition.

[j] *Eſcape*. If any Perſon be arreſted and committed to Cuſtody, and afterward go at liberty, without being delivered by Award of any Juſtice, or by due Order of Law, this is an Eſcape. And it ſeems before the Statute *Anno* 1 *Edward* II. every Priſoner ſo eſcaping was adjudged a Felon, and forfeited his Goods and Chattels; but now Breach of Priſon is but Treſpaſs, except the Cauſe for which the Priſoner is taken and impriſoned be Treaſon or Felony, and then the Priſon Breach is Felony, and his Goods forfeited thereby as by this Clauſe in the Charter given to the Ports.

I

[k] *Fines*.

CHARTERS.

ae fines quofcunque pro eifdem efcapiis, in quibufcunque curiis noftris, hæredum feu fucceflorum noftrorum, coram nobis vel hæredibus noftris, jufticiariis & judicibus noftris vel hæredum noftrorum, quibufcunque adjudicat. feu adjudicand. ac etiam catalla quarumcunque perfonarum in exigend. pro prodictione vel felonia pofit. vel ponend. Necnon catalla utlagat. & waviat. utlagand. & waviand. ac catalla qualitercunque confifcata omnium

TRANSLATION.

and Fines ᵏ whatfoever for the fame Efcapes, in whatfoever Courts ¹ of us, our Heirs or Succeffors, before us or our Heirs, the Juftices and Judges of us or of our Heirs, whatfoever adjudged or to be adjudged, and alfo the Chattels of whatfoever Perfons put or to be put in Exigent ᵐ for Treafon ⁿ or Felony. Alfo the Chattels of Outlawed ° and Waived Perfons, and to be Outlawed and Waived ; and the Chattels, by what Means foever ᵖ confifcate ᑫ, of all

ANNOTATIONS.

ᵏ *Fines.* Efcapes of Prifoners, whether Felons or others, are fineable in the Gaolers or Keepers of fuch Prifons, whether the Efcapes be voluntary or negligent. If the Gaoler wilfully let his Prifoner go at liberty, then, if the Arreft of him that efcaped were for Treafon, it is Treafon in the Gaoler ; and fo, if for Felony, Felony ; and if for Trefpafs, Trefpafs ; for which latter the Gaoler fhall be fined. If the Efcape were through Negligence, yet is it fineable ; and the Fines or Amerciaments for both thefe Efcapes are thofe here mentioned. Sometime an Efcape may be where there is no Arreft, as if Murder be committed in the Day time, and the Murderer be not taken, this is an Efcape, for which the Town where the Murder was done fhall be amerced.

¹ *Courts.* A Court is a Place where Juftice is judicially adminiftred. *Curia,* the *Latin* Word, is derived from *Cura, Care,* becaufe in *Curiis publicis curas gerebant.* This fame *Latin* Word is ufed for a *Clofe* or *Court* before or befide an Houfe.

ᵐ *Exigent* is a Writ, and it lieth where a Man fueth an Action perfonal, and the Defendant cannot be found, and hath nothing within the County whereby he may be attached or diftrained ; then this Writ fhall go forth to the Sheriff to make Proclamation in five Counties, every one after another, that he appear, or elfe that he fhall be outlawed ; and if he be outlawed, all his Goods and Chattels be forfeit. Alfo in Indictment of Felony the *Exigent* fhall go forth after the firft *Capias,* and in feveral other Cafes : Of fuch *Exigents* fpeaks the Charter.

ⁿ *Treafon.* The higheft Offence againft the Law, and punifhed with the fevereft Judgment, triable in the Court of *Shepway,* where more may be feen thereof.

° *Outlawed,* for a Man put out of the Protection of the Law, as fome phrafe it ; as *Waived* for a Woman fo left, as before noted. The Perfons of both are not without all Protection of the Law ; for if any fuch Perfon be wilfully and malicioufly flain, the Murderer fhall fuffer Death ; but the Goods of both are forfeit. And I have known the Mayor and Jurats of *Rye,* by Authority of this Charter, feize and take the Goods of Outlaws after the *Capias* hath been in the Hands of the Officers of *Dover* Caftle to execute. And long before my Time, viz. Anno 1577. I find *Richard Streat* of *London,* Gent. upon the Original, fued *John Stonne* of *Rye* in an Action of Debt to the Outlawry, and upon the *Capias Utlagatum* Notice was given to the Mayor and Jurats of *Rye,* that *John Stonne* was outlawed ; whereupon they feized his Goods. Before the Seizure thereof *John Stonne* obtains the Queen's Majefty's Pardon, and thereupon alledgeth that his Goods were pardoned alfo, and ought to be reftored him. Neverthelefs it was refolved, that after Forfeiture, and the Intereft of the Town vefted, the Queen, by her Pardon, could not give away the Goods, but by her Pardon the Contempt of the outlawed Perfon was pardoned, and he received to his Allegiance again. And thus was the Opinion of Councellor *Aleocks* in the Cafe, fo as the faid *John Stonne* was forced to agree with the faid Mayor and Jurats before he could have his Goods again.

ᵖ *What Means foever.* Howfoever, or in what manner foever ; and the like may be underftood in other Places, where the Word *qualitercunque* is ufed in the Charters.

ᑫ *Confifcate.* Some fay from *Fifcus,* an Hamper, Pannier, Basket or Frail, fuch as the Emperors Treafure was anciently kept in, and fo Metonymically for the Treafure it felf ; which Goods forfeited to the King, faid to be confifcate (and not granted away, as thefe by Charter here are) come to the King's Exchequer as if it were into his *Hamper.* Confifcate moft take like to forfeit, and fo fome Tranflations have rendered it ; but it feems here to be fuch Goods or Chattels whofe Confifcation came by fome Attainder or Outlawry of the Perfon, and not fuch Goods which are feized as forfeited * to the King, and condemned in the *Exchequer* for being * *Confifcare* uncuftomed or uncuftomable ; becaufe the Ufage in fuch Cafes (the beft Expofition of the Char- *and Forisfacere*) declares they were never intended to the Ports, nor did I ever hear the Ports claimed *re are* fynony-them ma.

R

CHARTERS.

niúm & fingulorum Baronum, &
aliórum refidentium quorumcún-
que infra Portus & Membra prædict. ubicunque bona & catalla
illa inveniri contigerint infra Portus vel Membra prædicta, vel
extra in comitatibus Kanciæ &
Suffex, feu corum altero, licet
ipfi Officiarii feu Miniftri noftri vel
hæredum noftrorum exiftant, feu
aliquis corum exiftat. Et quod
dicti Barones & probi homines,
& fucceffores fui, habeant imperpetuum Wreccam maris in quibufcunque cofteris & brachiis
maris Portubus & Membris prædictis adjacentibus qualitercunque contingent. ac omnia & fingula ad hujufmodi Wrec. pertinent. five fpectant. Et quod ipfi hæred. & fucceffor. fui per fe
vel per Miniftros fuos hujufmodi
catalla vocata Waife, Stray, thefaurum inventum, catalla vocáta
manu opera, catalla felonum,
qualitercunque dampnatorum &
dampnandorum, convictorum &
convincendorum, catalla quarumcunque perfonarum in exigend. pro prodictione feu pro felonia pofitarum feu ponendarum,
catalla utlagat. & utlagand.
waviat. & waviand. & catalla
qua-

TRANSLATION.

all and fingular the Barons, and
other Refidents whofoever,
within the Ports and Members
aforefaid, wherefoever thofe
Goods and Chattels fhall happen to be found within the Ports
or Members aforefaid, or without, in the Counties of *Kent* and
Suffex, or either of them, although they, or any of them,
be Officers or Minifters of us or
our Heirs. And that the faid
Barons and good Men, and
their Succeffors, may for ever
have Wreck of the Sea, howfoever happening, in whatfoever
Coafts and Arms of the Sea adjacent to the Ports and Members
aforefaid, and all and fingular
Things to fuch Wreck appertaining or belonging. And
that they, their Heirs and Succeffors, by themfelves, or by
their Minifters, fuch Chattels
called Waife, Stray, Treafure
found, Chattels called Maynour,
Chattels of Felons, howfoever
condemned and to be condemned, convicted and to be convicted, Chattels of whatfoever Perfons put or to be put in Exigent
for Treafon or Felony; Chattels of them Outlawed and to
be Outlawed, Waived and to be
Waived, and the Chattels by
what

ANNOTATIONS.

them by virtue of thefe general Words in the Charter, *And the Chattels by what Means foever
confifcate.*

Refidents, Refciants or Inhabitants ; and fo in feveral other Places.

Whofoever or whatfoever.

Suffex, a County in which one of the Ports and feveral of the Towns privileged with
them lie, called in *Domefday* Book *Sudfex*, and before *Southfex*, from the South *Saxons*, who
held it for one of the Seven Kingdoms of their Heptarchy.

Wreck appertaining. Of Wreck fomewhat was faid before, on the Charter of King *Edward* I.
Here the Grant is enlarged in Words that take in the Coafts and Arms of the Sea adjacent, or
near adjoining to the Ports and Members, and all Things appertaining to fuch Wreck, whereby are included Flotfon, Jetfon, Lagon and Shares. Flotfon or Flotzam fignifieth any Goods
wrecked that are taken up as they lie floting or fwimming upon the Water. Jetfon is a Thing
caft out of a Ship in danger to be wrecked, and beaten by the Waters to the Shore, or caft on
the Shore by the Mariners, and there taken up : It comes of the French jetter, to caft out. Lagon, Lagam or Lagan, is that which lieth in the Bottom of the Sea, of the Dutch Liggben, to lie.
Shares from Shyren, the Saxon Word to divide, imports Goods due to feveral by Proportion ; as
in Salvage of Goods wrecked the King's Share or Part is to come to the Ports according to this
Charter.

Of them, or of Perfons, neceffarily fupplied in the Tranflation, as fome other little Words
elfewhere.

CHARTERS.

qualitercunque confiscat. ac hujusmodi Wreccam, ac omnia ad hujusmodi Wreccum pertinent. five spectant, seisire & capere possint ad opus eorum, absque perturbatione, molestatione seu impedimento nostri vel hæred. nostrorum, Justiciariorum, Escaetorum, Vicecomitum, Coronatorum, seu aliorum Ballivorum nostrorum vel hæredum nostrorum, aut aliorum quorumcunque, licet ea antea per nos vel hæredes nostros, aut aliquos Ballivos, Officiarios seu Ministros nostros vel hæredum nostrorum seisit. fuerunt. Concessimus etiam pro nobis & hæredibus nostris, præfatis Baronibus & probis hominibus hæred. & successoribus suis in sustentationem navigii & servitii prædictorum, quod quilibet Major & Jurat. in quolibet Portu & Membro Portuum, & Membrorum prædictorum, ubi Major & Jurat. existunt, ac quilibet Ballivus & Jurat. in quolibet Portu & Membro eorundem Portuum, ubi talis Ballivus per Communes hujusmodi Portus five Membri Portuum, & Membrorum prædictorum est electus; ac etiam Jurati in quolibet Portu & Membro, prædictorum Portuum & Membrorum, ubi nec Major nec Ballivus per Communes hujusmodi Portus five Membri, est electus, & eorum successor. imperpetuum, habeant omnes & omnimod.

TRANSLATION.

what Means soever confiscated, and such Wreck, and all Things to such Wreck appertaining or belonging, may seise, and take to their Use, without Disturbance, Molestation or Impediment of us or our Heirs, or the Justices, Escheators, Sheriffs, Coroners, or other the Bailiffs of us or of our Heirs, or others whosoever, although the same were before seized by us or our Heirs, or by any Bailiffs, Officers or Ministers of us or our Heirs. We have also granted for us and our Heirs, to the aforesaid Barons and good Men, their Heirs and Successors, for the Maintenance of the Shipping and Service aforesaid, that every Mayor and Jurats in every Port and Member of the Ports, and Members aforesaid, where a Mayor and Jurats are; and every Bailiff and Jurats in every Port and Member, of the same Ports and Members, where such Bailiff, by the Commons of such Port, or Member of the Ports and Members aforesaid is elected; and also the Jurats in every Port and Member, of the aforesaid Ports and Members, where neither Mayor nor Bailiff, by the Commons of such Port or Member, is elected, and their Successors for ever, may have all and all manner of

ANNOTATIONS.

᾿ *Seise* denotes as much as to take into Possession; and sometime *Seisin* is used synonymically for Possession: Though properly *Seisin* is applied to Possession of a Freehold, and Possession to Goods and Chattels.

ᵂ *Disturbance*, Trouble or Perturbation.

ˣ *Whosoever* or whatsoever; and the like in other Places.

ʸ *Neither Mayor.* At the Making of this Charter of King *Edward* IV. the Head Officer in *Hasting* was a Bailiff, and not a Mayor, and the like was then in *Tenterden*; but some of the Ports, as *New Romney* and *Hithe*, had neither Mayor nor Bailiff, but only Jurats and Commonalty, amongst whom the eldest Jurat on the Bench was as President. And this was the Occasion of these and some of the foregoing Passages in this Charter.

I

ᵃ *Pisces*

CHARTERS.

nimod. fines pro transgr. offensis, misprisionibus, extortionibus, negligentiis, ignorantiis, conspirationibus, concelamentis, regratariis, forstallariis, manutenentiis, ambidexteris, cambypertiis, falsitatibus, deceptionibus, contemptibus, & aliis delictis quibuscunque.

TRANSLATION.

of Fines [a] for Trespasses [a], Offences [b], Misprisions [c], Extortions [d], Negligences [e], Ignorances [f], Conspiracies [g], Concealments [h], Regratings [i], Forestallings [j], Maintenances [k], Ambidextries [l], Champerties [m], Falsities [n], Deceipts [o], Contempts [p], and other Offences [q] whatsoever.

ANNOTATIONS.

[a] *Fines* here are Sums of Money imposed for the Offences after mentioned.

[a] *Trespasses* or Transgressions. To pass that which is right, or not to keep the Manner and Measure, that is, the Boundaries the Law hath set, is to transgress or trespass.

[b] *Offences,* equivalent to Trespasses.

[c] *Misprisions,* from the French *Mespris,* in the Common Law, a *Negligence, Oversight, Mistake, Contempt* or *Despising.* So *Misprision* of Treason or Felony, is a Neglect or light Account shewed thereof, by not revealing it when we know it to be committed.

[d] *Extortions.* Largely taken are all Oppressions by any extort Power, or by colour or pretence of Right, from *Extorqueo;* called *Crimen Expilationis,* or *Concussionis:* But properly it is a great Misprision by unlawful or violent wresting or wringing Money or Money's worth by any Officer, by colour of his Office, of or from any Person, either not due, or more than is due, or before it be due. Millers taking excessive Tolls, and some other such like Offences, may be referred hither.

[e] *Negligences* principally in Officers, as Bailiffs, Serjeants, Constables, &c. that neglect the Execution of their Offices.

[f] *Ignorances. Ignorantia juris non excusat,* is a Maxim of the Law; so as an Offence done through Ignorance is nevertheless fineable and punishable.

[g] *Conspiracies.* Where Two or more by Oath, Covenant, or other Manner of Alliance, knit or combine themselves together to help each other to indite or appeal a Person of Felony, or do some unlawful Act, this is a Conspiracy; and where the Writ lieth the Party found guilty is fineable.

[h] *Concealments.* To keep Possessions unjustly of Lands belonging to the Crown, though by pretence of some other Title thereto. Or rather here, Concealments of Jurors. *Stat.* 3 *Henry* VII. *cap.* 1.

[i] *Regratings.* Regrators strictly (from the *French* Word) are Hucksters that trim up old Wares for Sale; anciently, in the Common Law, such as bought by the *Gross,* and sold by *Retail,* that is by small Parcels, *Anno* 27 *Edward* III. *Stat.* 1. *cap.* 3. But now, since the Statute *Anno* 5 *Edward* VI. *cap.* 14. they are taken for such as buy and sell again any Wares or Victuals in the same Market or Fair, or within five Miles thereof.

[j] *Forestallings.* Forestallers are they that buy Corn, Cattle or other Merchandise by the Way, as it comes towards the Fair or Market to be sold, to the Intent to sell the same again at a more high and dear Price. *Forstallamentum,* now used for Forestalling, is as much as to prevent, or as to say, they set up their Stalls or Standings before they come to the appointed Place of Sale, whereby the Buyers resorting to such usual Place are prevented.

[k] *Maintenances.* Where any giveth to another, that is Plaintiff or Defendant in any Action, any Sum of Money, or other Thing to maintain his Plea, or else extremely laboureth for him, when he hath nothing to do therewith: This is Maintenance, and a Writ thereupon lieth against such Party for maintaining such Suit. The Lord *Coke* briefly defineth it to be, *The taking in Hand, bearing up or upholding of Quarrels and Sides, to the Disturbance or Hindrance of common Right in Court or Country.*

[l] *Ambidextries.* In the Law *Ambidexters* signify such Jurors or Embraceors as take of both Parties for the giving of their Verdict; the Forfeit thereof is ten Times as much as was taken. *Stat. Anno* 38 *Edward* III. *cap.* 12.

[m] *Champerties* or Champarties, in our Common Law, is a Maintenance of any one in a Suit depending, upon Condition to have part of the Thing (be it Lands or Goods) when it is recovered. For this the *Champertor* is to be fined by the Statute *Anno* 33 *Edward* I.

[n] *Falsities,* in Weights, Measures, corrupt and adulterate Wares, fraudulent Bargains, forging Deeds, &c.

[o] *Deceipts,* as before in *Falsities,* so also in selling Lands or Goods, wherein the Vendor hath no Title or Property, whereby the Purchaser is deceived; and all Cheating and Cousenage whatsoever.

[p] *Contempts.* Wilful Refusals to abide a lawful Trial, or to appear when duly summoned in order thereto.

[q] *Offences,* Faults or Delinquencies.

CHARTERS.

bufcunque. Ac ctiam fines pro licentia concordandi, ac omnia amerciamenta, redemptiones, exitus, & poenas forisfact. & forisfaciend. annum, diem, vaftum, ftrepum, & omnia quæ ad nos feu hæredes noftros pertinere poterunt de hujufmodi anno, die, vafto, & ftrepo, de omnibus & fingulis Baronibus, & aliis refidentibus prædictis, hæredibus & fuccefforibus fuis ubicunque, tam infra Portus & Membra prædicta, quam extra, ipfos Barones, & alios refidentes, hujufmodi, in quibufcunque curiis noftris & hæredum noftrorum, fines facere, & amerciare exitus, & poenas, forisfacere, annum, diem, vaftum, ftrepum. & forisfactur. hujufmodi adjudicari contigerit; quæ fines, amerciamenta, redemptiones, exitus, poenæ, annus, dies, vaftum, ftrepum,

TRANSLATION.

ever. And alfo Fines ʳ for Licenfe of Concords, and all Amerciaments, Redemptions ˢ, Iffues ᵗ, and Penalties ᵗ forfeited ᵘ and to be forfeited, Year, Day ᵛ, Wafte, Strepe ʷ, and all Things which to us or our Heirs may appertain of fuch Year, Day, Wafte and Strepe, of all and every the Barons, and other the Refciants ˣ aforefaid, their Heirs and Succeffors wherefoever, as well within the Ports and Members aforefaid, as without, in whatfoever Courts of us and our Heirs the fame Barons, and other Refciants ˣ, fhall happen to be adjudged to make fuch Fines, and to be amerced ˣ and forfeit ˣ *This Tranflation renders it,* And to be amerced and forfeit fuch Iffues, Penalties, &c. *but verba*tim *after the Latin it is,* And to amerce the Iffues and forfeit the Penalties, &c. fuch Iffues, Penalties, Year, Day, Wafte, Strepe and Forfeitures ʸ; which Fines, Amerciaments, Redemptions, Iffues, Penalties, Year, Day, Wafte, Strepe,

ANNOTATIONS.

ʳ *Fines* here are fuch Sums of Money as are to be paid for Licenfe to aliene or fell Lands or Tenements; when a Fine in Court is levied thereupon, and the Agreement between the Parties is commonly called a Concord or the final Agreement.

ˢ *Redemptions* or Ranfoms, which legally are great Sums of Money paid for redeeming of great Delinquents from fome heinous Crime, who are to be capivate in Prifon till they pay them. It comes from *re* and *emo*, and is all one with a Fine; and fome fay it is a Fine of the whole Eftate, others a treble Fine; all conclude it great.

ᵗ *Iffues.* Iffue is commonly underftood for the Effect of fomething precedent, applied in the Law to feveral Things; to Children, as the Iffue of the Body; to the particular Point in any Caufe depending for Trial, affirmed of the one part and denied of the other, which is faid to be the Iffue for the Jury to try. But Iffues in the Plural are generally taken for the Sums of Money returned by the Sheriff or other legal Officer (having the Return of Writs) upon the Jury Men impannelled in the Caufe, warned to try the Iffue joined between Party and Party, or to ferve in Inqueft for the King. And thus Iffues are here to be underftood.

ᵗ *Penalties,* Pains or Punifhments, efpecially here thofe of the Purfe or Pecuniary, incurred or run into by Difobedience, either in doing fomething forbidden, or not doing fomething required by the Law.

ᵘ *Forfeited,* from *foris* and *facio*, a doing without or againft Law or Cuftom, for which fuch Fines are to be paid or Penalties fuffered.

ᵛ *Day, Day,* &c. In cafe of Murder, and fome other Felonies at the Common Law, if a Tenant in Fee Simple of Lands in Gavel Kind, held of the King in free *Socage*, for fuch Felony committed fuffer Judgment of Death, the Lands defcend to the Heir, and not to the King; yet he fhall have for the Space of a Year and a Day the Profits of the Lands and Tenements of fuch Felon, and may commit what Wafte and Strepe he will within that Time thereupon, in the Buildings and Timber: So by this Grant of the Charter, where the King had the Year, Day, and Wafte within the Ports, the Ports now have the fame, and before the making of this Charter fo had, as their Cuftomals make appear.

ʷ *Wafte, Strepe.* Wafte, in *Latin Vaftum* from *Vaftando*; and *Strepe* from the old Word *Strip*, to leave bare or naked; both implying as much as *Ruin, Spoil, Depopulation, Deftroying, Taking away, and bereaving the Lands and Tenements of what can be taken therefrom to make Advantage thereof.*

ˣ *Refciants,* Refidents or Inhabitants, as before and after in the Charter.

ʸ *Forfeitures.* Here and p. 66. l. 1. whether the Word fhould be fingular or plural is uncertain, becaufe *Forisfactur.* the *Latin* anfwering thereto, is abbreviated: The like in fome other Places.

S

ᶻ *Might*

CHARTERS.

ftrepum, & forisfactur. ad nos & hæredes noftros pertinere poterunt, fi ea præfatis Baronibus & probis hominibus & fucceſſoribus fuis conceſſa non fuiſſent: ita quod dicti Major & Jurati, Ballivus & Jurati, ac etiam Jurati in quolibet Portu & Membro Portuum & Membrorum prædictorum, ut prædictum eſt, electi per ſe vel per miniſtros ſuos, hujuſmodi fines, amerciamenta, redemptiones, exitus, pœnas & forisfactur. & omnia quæ ad nos, hæredes & fucceſſor. noftros poterunt pertinere de anno, die, vaſto, ftrepo, & forisfactur. prædict. levare, percipere & habere poffunt ad commune proficuum & ufum dictorum Baronum, hæredum & fucceſſorum ſuorum, fine impedimento noftri vel hæredum noftrorum, Jufticiar. aut ſuorum Ballivorum feu Miniſtrorum noftrorum quorumcunque. Et quod iidem Barones & probi homines, hæredes & fucceſſores fui, infra quemlibet Portum & Membrum, Portuum & Membrorum prædictorum, prout fibi placuerit, habere poffint thewe, pilſorum atque

TRANSLATION.

Strepe and Forfeitures, might appertain [a] to us and our Heirs, if the fame had not been granted to the aforefaid Barons and good Men, and their Succeſſors: So that the faid Mayor [a] and Jurats, Bayliff and Jurats; and alſo Jurats in every Port and Member of the Ports, and Members aforefaid, as is aforefaid, choſen [b] by themſelves or their Miniſters, ſuch Fines, Amerciaments, Redemptions, Iſſues, Penalties and Forfeitures, and all Things which to us, our Heirs and Succeſſors, may [c] appertain of the Year, Day, Waſte, Strepe and Forfeitures aforefaid, may levy [d], perceive and have to the common Profit [e] and Uſe [f] of the faid Barons, their Heirs and Succeſſors, without Impediment of us or our Heirs, our Juſtices or their Bailiffs [g], or our Miniſters whatſoever. And that the fame Barons and good Men, their Heirs and Succeſſors, within every Port and Member of the Ports, and Members aforefaid, as it ſhall pleaſe them, may have Thewe [h], Pillory [i] and

ANNOTATIONS.

[a] *Might appertain*, or might have appertained.

[a] *Mayor.* Here and in ſeveral other Places ſingular, though Plural in the printed Copy only here.

[b] *As is aforefaid, choſen,* or elected as aforefaid.

[c] *May* or might appertain.

[d] *Levy*, from whence the Writ called a *Levari facias*, the ſame with a *fieri facias*, and both judicial Writs to take the Goods and Chattels of the Party condemned to ſatisfy the Judgment, or raiſe the Sum to be paid for the Fines, &c. here before mentioned.

[e] *Common Profit,* that is, for the Uſe of the reſpective Corporations of the Ports Towns and Members where it happeneth, and not for the Mayors and Jurats, Bailiffs and Jurats, or any of them particularly, nor to be converted to any private Uſe.

[f] *Uſe.* To be brought to the Chamber of the Town, and employed as Monies that come to the Common Purſe for the Service of the Corporation.

[g] *Their Bailiffs.* In the printed Charter it is in the Latin, *ſuorum Ballivorum,* as here; but in an old Copy of this Charter it is, *aliorum Ballivorum,* which I take to be right, and ſhould be rendered in the Engliſh, *Or other our Bailiffs or Miniſters whatſoever.*

[h] *Thewe.* Stocks, ſo have I ſeen it tranſlated; but whether from the Saxon Word *Then* or *Theu* for a *Servant* or *Bondman,* becauſe one in the Stocks is in a Sort bound, I cannot affirm.

[i] *Pillory*, a kind of Stocks for the Head and Hands, as the common Stocks for the Feet; and perhaps ſo called from *Pilus,* Hair, becauſe the Head or moſt hairy Part of Man is faſtened thereby [*].

[*] *Some derive it from the French Pilaſtre, a Pillar, the Pillory being a kind of Pillar of Wood.*

CHARTERS.

atque tumbrellum pro punitione
malefactorum ibidem. Ac etiam
quod ipfi & fucceffores fui imperpetuum habeant Letas & Lawdaies, cum omnibus proficuis ad
Letas & Lawdaies qualitercunque
pertinent. five fpectant, de quibufcunque refidentibus infra libertatem prædictam. Et quod
prædicti Barones & probi homines ac eorum hæredes & fucceffores fui ex nunc habeant, & quilibet eorum habeat, omnes inventiones fuas in terra & in mari, libere, pacifice & quiete, abfque
aliquo impedimento feu grava-
mine noftri aut hæredum noftrorum, vel Conftabularii noftri aut
hæredum noftrorum caftri noftri
Dover, Cuftodis Quinque Portuum prædictorum, vel Admiralli
infra Portus & Membra prædicta,
abfque aliqua noftra partitione
inde facienda, aut aliqua parte
nobis aut hæred. noftris aut ali-
... ... cui

TRANSLATION.

and Tumbrel [i], for the Punifhment [k] of Malefactors [l] there.
And alfo that they and their
Succeffors for ever may have
Leets [m] and Lawdays, with all
Profits [n] to the Leets and Lawdays in any wife appertaining or
belonging, of whatfoever Refidents within the Liberty alore-
faid. And that the aforefaid
Barons and good Men, and their
Heirs and Succeffors, from henceforth may have and every of
them may have all their Findals [o] by Land and Sea freely,
peaceably and quietly, without
any Impediment or Grievance [p]
of us or of our Heirs, or of the
Conftable of us [q] or of our Heirs
of our Caftle of Dover, Warden of the Cinque Ports aforefaid, or of the Admiral [r] within
the Ports and Members aforefaid, without Partition [s] thereof
to be made for us, or any part
thereof to be rendered, to us or
to

ANNOTATIONS.

[i] *Tumbrel*, a Dung Cart, or Court, wherein the Party worthy of this Punifhment is carried about, and Dirt thrown upon him by any of the People that will. Some have taken it for a Ducking Stool or Cucking Stool, wherein the Offender being fet, the fame is dip'd under Water; but the beft Expofitors take the former.

[k] *Punifhment*, or punifhing, that is corporally, by their Bodies.

[l] *Malefactors*, or Evil-Doers, intended here to be thofe againft whom an Indictment would lie.

[m] *Leets*. A Leet or Court-Leet is all one with a Law-Day. This Court, in whofe Manor *Leet or Leth*, foever it is kept, is accounted the King's Court, and is commonly held but twice in the Year, and the Latin *fciliet*, betwixt the Month of *Michaelmas* and *Eafter*, *Magna Charta, cap.* 35. At this Court Leta, *from the* feveral Offences are ftill inquirable and prefentable, but before the Seffions of the Peace were Saxon Zelethi-appointed was in much greater Efteem than now." ... ... *an or Zelathi-*
[n] *Profits*, by Fines, Amerciaments, &c. ... ... *an, that is, To*
[o] *Findals*. Thefe the Ports had before, as appears by the former Charter of King *Edward I.* *affemble toge-* ... ... *ther.*
[p] *Grievance*. Notwithftanding thefe and feveral other Paffages in the Charters fometimes exprefs, and fometimes tantamount to ftrict Prohibitions, that the Ports Men fhould not be mo-lefted or grieved in the Enjoyment of their Privileges, the Ports have not been without their Grievances, and that fometimes by their Lord Wardens themfelves, and by his Officers of Dover Caftle; as, if it were convenient, I could fufficiently demonftrate.

[q] *Conftable of us*. Thus it is in all the old Copies I have feen. In the printed Copy it is *Con-ftabulorum noftrorum*, intending it plural; but feeing then it fhould have been *Conftabulariorum noftrorum*, I followed the old Copies: The Senfe is one and the fame.

[r] *Admiral*, from the *Saxon Aen mere al*, that is, *Over all the Sea*. An Officer that commandeth on the Sea. Now, as to all the Sea Coafts along which the Ports lie, the Admiralty thereof is common to the Warden of the Ports; and he is called *Warden, Chancellor,* and *Admiral* of the *Cinque Ports*; the Two antient Towns and their Members; according to which Titles are the Courts held before him, viz. as he is Warden, the Court of *Shipway*; as Chancellor, a Court of *Chan-cery* or Equity; and as Admiral, a Court of *Admiralty*; both which latter are ufually kept at the Church of St. *James* the Apoftle in *Dover*.

[s] *Partition*. The King to have no part of the *Findals*, nor the Warden or any of his Officers.

[t] *Galloweis*,

CHARTERS.

cui alio inde reddend. Ac infuper conceffimus pro nobis &
hæredibus noftris, quántum in
nobis eft, prædictis Baronibus &
probis hominibus ac eorum hæredibus & fucceffor. quod ipfi fur-
cas infra quemlibet Portum &
Membrum Portuum, & Mem-
brorum prædictorum erigi; & judicium de malefactoribus, quos
ibidem capi & deprehendi contigerit, juxta dictam libertatem de
Infangtheff & Utfangtheff, ac
juxta confuetudinem in Portubus
& Membris prædictis ab antiquo ufitat. facere poffint, fine occafione, impetitione vel impedimento noftri vel hæred. noftrorum, Jufticiar. Coronatorum, Ef-
ceatorum, Vicecomitum, aut aliorum Ballivorum feu Miniftrorum noftrorum quorumcunque.
Et quod prædicti Major & Jurati, Ballivus & Jurati, & etiam
Jurati in quolibet Portu & Membro Portuum, & Membrorum
prædictorum, prout fuperius limitantur, ex nunc imperpetuum
habeant & teneant, & habere &
tenere poffint, coram eifdem Majore & Juratis, Ballivo & Juratis,
     ac

TRANSLATION.

to our Heirs, or to any other.
And moreover, we have granted for us and our Heirs, as much
as in us is, to the aforefaid Barons and good Men, and their
Heirs and Succeffors, that they
may erect Gallows [1] within every Port and Member [t] of the
Ports, and Members aforefaid,
and Judgment [u] caufe to be done
of Malefactors, which there fhall
happen to be taken and apprehended, according to the faid
liberty of Infangtheff and Ut-
fangtheff, and according to the
Cuftom [v] in the Ports and Members aforefaid of ancient Time [w]
ufed, without Occafion, Let [x] or
Impediment of us or our Heirs,
or the Juftices, Coroners, Ef-
cheators, Sheriffs, or other our
Bailiffs or Minifters whatfoever [y].
And that the aforefaid Mayor
and Jurats, Bailiff and Jurats,
and alfo Jurats in every Port
and Member of the Ports, and
Members aforefaid, as above are
limited [z], from henceforth for
ever may have and hold,
before them the faid Mayor
and Jurats, Bailiff and Jurats,
     and

ANNOTATIONS.

[1] *Gallows*, upon which, or Gibbets, Felons condemned are to be hanged.

[t] *Member*, that is, Member corporate, not others, who have no Court of Judicature wherein to try and condemn a Malefactor.

[u] *Judgment*, or make or give Judgment, or make Execution of Judgment given. Judgment is the pronouncing by the Judge in open Court againft the guilty Perfon convicted the Sentence of the Law in the cafe, declaring the Punifhment to be executed upon him for the Offence done. *Judicium*, faith the Lord *Coke*, is *quafi juris dictum*. In other Cafes, not of Life and Member, Judgment is the Confideration, Order or Award of the Court, what Land fhall be recovered, Fine fhall be made, Debt or Damages recovered, Money paid for Satisfaction, or the like, as the Cafe in juftice requireth.

[v] *Cuftom*, the Ufage in the Ports and their Members corporate before the making of this Charter.

[w] *Ancient Time.* The Liberty of *Infangtheff* and *Outfangtheff*, at the Granting of this Char-ter, was efteemed an ancient Cuftom in the Ports and Members, as that which they had had long before.

[x] *Let* or Impeachment, for fo *Impetitio* properly fignifies, derived from *in* and *peto*.

[y] *Whatfoever* or whofoever.

[z] *Limited.* That is, only fuch Jurats in the Port or Member where they had no Head Officer; as fome before noted had not when this Charter was granted; for if there were a Mayor or Bailiff, the Jurats could not keep Court without him or his Deputy. Such Jurats were mention-ed before, and therefore faid, *as above limited*, which fome Tranflations have rendered, *as are above affigned.*

     2   [a] *Plaint.*

CHARTERS.

ac etiam Juratis, per querelam, coram eis levand. in curia cujuslibet Portus, five Membri Portuum, & Membrorum prædictorum, in loco infra quemlibet hujufmodi Portum five Membrum magis convenient. diebus & temporibus ibidem confuet. tenend. omnia & omnimoda placita de & fuper omnimod. actionibus, realibus, perfonalibus & mixtis, infra quemlibet hujufmodi Portum vel Membrum, per terras vel per mare emergent. Ac perfonas verfus quas hujufmodi actiones perfonales in dictis curiis profequi & moveri contingent, per eorum copora attachiare & pri-

TRANSLATION.

and alfo Jurats, by plaint [a], before them to be levied [b] in the Court [c] of every Port, or Member of the Ports, and Members aforefaid, in the Place within every fuch Port or Member moft convenient, in the Days [d] and Times [e] there accuftomed [f] to be holden, all and all manner of Pleas [g], of and upon all manner of Actions [h], real, perfonal and mixt, within every fuch Port or Member by Land [i] or by Sea [k] arifing [l]. And the Perfons againft whom fuch perfonal Actions in the faid Courts [m] fhall happen to be profecuted and moved, to attach [n] by their Bo-

ANNOTATIONS.

[a] *Plaint.* Some Copies have it in the Plural, but the Senfe is the fame. Here *Querela* is a *Complaint* or *Suit*; otherwife it might have been conftrued a *Quarrel.*

[b] *Levied,* Raifed, ftirred, properly commenced, brought or entred upon Record.

[c] *Court,* in the old Copies fingular, in the printed Copy abbreviated. This Court of Record for determining of Pleas the Commoners or Freemen cannot hold, but only the Mayor, Bailiff and Jurats, in each Corporation refpectively.

[d] *Days.* The Court-Days are different in feveral Towns; as, *Saturday* at *Hafting*; *Tuefday* at *Winchelfea*; *Wednefday* at *Rye*; *Monday* at *Romney*; *Friday* at *Dover*, &c.

[e] *Times,* according to the Times ufual between Court and Court; for in moft it is a Fortnight, that is, from fifteen Days to fifteen Days inclufive, and, as I take it in all, both Ports and Members, except *Dover* and *Sandwich*, which keep Court every Week.

[f] *Accuftomed,* becaufe this Charter refers the Ports to their ufual and accuftomed Days and Times to keep their Courts: It is plain enough, that they held Plea before the making of this Charter; and do generally, *Tenterden* excepted, prefcribe for their Courts; and not only for thefe conftant and ufual Courts, but for their Courts for Strangers, held, when Occafion ferves, from Day to Day, as is to be feen in the Cuftomals, which have alfo Allowance by thefe Words in the Charter.

[g] *Pleas* or *Pleos, Placitum* (from *placendo*) moft proper for the Defendant, and other Allegations of the Plaintiff after the Declaration, and not the Declaration it felf.

[h] *Actions,* real, are fuch as touch the Freehold or real Eftate; perfonal, fuch as reach the Perfon or his moveable (called perfonal) Eftate; and mixt are fuch Actions as are partly real and partly perfonal.

[i] *Land. Terras* in the printed Copy; the old Copy had it *Terr.* abbreviated.

[k] *Sea.* Not *altum mare,* the deep *Sea,* for there the Admiral hath Jurifdiction, but in the Havens, Creeks and Arms of the Sea, fo far as can be judged in the County, where the Land is on both fides: The Admiral, as Admiral, can have no Jurifdiction nor claim any Felons Goods there happening, though it be full Sea [*]; more efpecially upon any Place within the Compafs of Low Water Mark, the Admiral or his Officers can have no Power; but fuch Piere, Creek, Haven, &c. fhall be taken for parcel of the County: fo was it adjudged in the Cafe of *Lacy,* and thus was the Opinion of Mr. *Thomas Harris* and Mr. *Richard Hutton,* Serjeants at Law, in anfwer to certain Queries propounded to them, *Anno* 1609. whereunto agreed Councellor *Finch* and Baron *Bemden, Anno* 1611. in the Cafe of one *Peter Bowenfon,* who in a Creek within the Harbor of *Rye* had his Bark robbed, and Monies ftolen out thereof, whereupon the Felons were tried as for a Felony upon the Land, and not for a Piracy, nor by any Commiffion on the Statute of 28 *Henry* VIII. *cap.* 15.
    [*] *See* Coke 4 part. Inftit. chap. 22.

[l] *Arifing,* happening or iffuing, for fo the Word *Emergent.* may be rendered here, and in other Places.

[m] *Courts,* plural according to the printed Copy; in the old Copies abbreviated, and fo uncertain whether Court or Courts.

[n] *Attach,* arreft, apprehend, take or lay hold of. The Defendants may be, and ufually by the Cuftoms of the Ports are, attached by their Goods as well as by their Bodies.

T   *Com.*

CHARTERS.	TRANSLATION.

prisonæ committere, & prædicta omnia & singula placita audire & terminare, & processus & executiones judicialiter juxta consuetudinem Portuum prædictorum fiend. inde facere: Ita quod nec Coństabularius noster & hæred. nostrorum prædicti Castri Dover. nec Custos Quinque Portuum prædictorum, nec Admirallus eorundem, nec aliquis eorum locum tenens, nec deputatus ab eo, de seu super aliquo hujusmodi placito infra Portus & Membra prædicta, aut de aliquo alio placito, seu de aliqua re seu materia infra fines & limites eorundem Portuum & Membrorum per terras, nec per mare, nec per aquam dulcem, seu limites vel ripas alti maris fact. sive emergent. aut faciend. sive emergend. aliqualiter se intromittat, nec hujusmodi Portum sive Membrum ea de causa quovis modo ingrediatur, nisi

Bodies and commit [o] to Prison, and to hear and determine [p] all and singular the aforesaid Pleas, and to make Process [q] and Executions [r] judicially, according to the Custom of the Ports aforesaid thereupon to be made: So that neither the Constable [s] of us and our Heirs of the aforesaid [h] Castle of *Dover*, nor the Warden of the *Cinque Ports* aforesaid, nor the Admiral of the same, nor any Lieutenant [t] of them, nor Deputy [u] from him, of or upon any such Pleas within the Ports and Members aforesaid, or of any other Plea [w], or of any Thing or Matter done, or happening to be done or happen within the Bounds and Limits of the same Ports and Members by Land [w], nor by Sea, nor by fresh Water [x], or the Limits or Shores [y] of the deep Sea [z], may, intermeddle [a] in any wise, nor such Port or Member for that Cause in any wise may enter [b], except

ANNOTATIONS.

[o] *Commit to Prison*, that is, for want of Bail; otherwise upon the mean Process no *Committitur*: But upon Execution there is no Bail to be given, but the Party taken is to be committed to Prison irrepleadgable.

[p] *Hear and determine*, try and judge.

[q] *Process*. To issue out of the Court for the Arrest of the Party, and trial of the Cause after the manner of original Writs.

[r] *Executions*, Writs judicial upon the Judgments given in the same Court.

[s] *Neither the Constable, nor the Warden, nor the Admiral*, do not imply the Offices in several Persons, but that he enter not as Warden or Admiral, or in any other Capacity, to hold Cognizance of any the Plea before mentioned, but only for Failure of Justice, as after mentioned.

[h] *Of the aforesaid*, this after the old Copies; the printed Copy hath it, *hæred. nostrorum prædictorum*, and then *aforesaid* must refer to Heirs, and not to the Castle.

[t] *Lieutenant*, the Chief Commander of *Dover* Castle under the Constable or Warden himself, holding his Place in his Absence, as the Name imports, and acting in his stead.

[u] *Deputy*, one that in stead of the Lieutenant acteth for him in his Absence, as he for the Warden.

[w] *Other Plea*, as upon penal Statutes, for transporting of prohibited Goods, or the like.

[w] *Land*, according to the old Copies; plural in the *Latin*, after the printed Copy.

[x] *Fresh Water*, upon any River or Stream.

[y] *Shores* or *Banks*, commonly called the Water side.

[z] *Deep Sea*, or high Sea, *Altum* being rendered *Deep* by an Antiphrasis.

[a] *Intermeddle*. To hold Cognizance of the Plea in the Common Law, and so oust the Court held before the Justices in such Port or Member of their Jurisdiction.

[b] *Enter*. In defect of Justice at the Common Law, the Parties were not to be called out of the Place, but the Warden, upon Complaint to him made, may enter, &c. as in the Charter. This Case seems special only in the Failure, not Doing, or Neglect to do Justice, by the Magistrates in the Ports, and impeaches not the Authority of the Court of *Shipway* to correct false and erroneous Judgments, nor the Courts of *Chancery* and *Admiralty*; this in Causes Civil and Marine, and that in the Equity of Common Law Causes, to abate the Rigor thereof.

[c] *Default*,

CHARTERS.

nisi in defectu justitiæ hujusmodi
Majoris, Ballivi & Jurat. & si
hujusmodi defectum evenire contigerit, tunc volumus tantummodo prædictum Custodem prædictorum Quinque Portuum, pro
tempore existent. per loquelam
sive petitionem sibi per partem
sentientem se fore gravatam inde
faciend. hujusmodi Portum sive
Membrum de tempore in tempus ingredi, & placitum hujusmodi defectum tangens coram
eo infra eundem Portum sive
Membrum, in præsentia hujusmodi Majoris, Balivi & Jurat.
venire facere, & ibidem placitum
prædictum examinare, & hujusmodi defectum, si quis fuerit, cor-
rigere & emendare, ac omnibus
& singulis quibuscunque inde in-
teresse habentibus justitiæ com-
plement. cum celeritate juxta legem & consuetudines ibidem
ministrare. Et quod prædicti
Major & Jurat. Balivus & Jurat.
ac etiam Jurati cujuslibet Portus,
& Membri Portuum, & Mem-
brorum prædictorum, modo &
forma supradictis electi, imperpetuum habeant cognitiones, tam
omnimod. placitorum in actionibus supradictis, quam omnimod.
placitorum coronæ infra quom-
libet hujusmodi Portum sive
Membrum quovis modo emer-
gent. ac potestatem audiendi &
terminandi omnia placita coronæ

TRANSLATION.

except in default of Justice of
such Mayor, Bailiff and Jurats,
and if such Default shall happen, then we will only the aforesaid Warden of the aforesaid
Cinque Ports, for the Time being, upon Complaint or Petition to him thereof to be made
by the Party thinking himself
grieved, such Port or Member
from Time to Time to enter, and
the Plea touching such Default
before him, within the same
Port or Member, in the Presence
of such Mayor, Bailiff and Jurats, to cause to come, and
there the Plea aforesaid to examine, and such Default, if any
shall be, to correct and amend,
and to all and singular whosoever Interested therein fulnefs
of Justice with speed to mini-
ster, according to the Law and
Customs there. And that the
aforesaid Mayor and Jurats, Bailiff and Jurats, and also Jurats of
every Port, and Member of the
Ports, and Members aforesaid,
in Manner and Form abovesaid
elected, for ever may have Cognisance, as well of all manner
of Pleas in the Actions abovesaid, as of all manner of Pleas of
the Crown, within every such
Port or Member in any wise happening, and Power of hearing
and determining all Pleas of the
Crown

ANNOTATIONS.

e *Default,* Defect or Neglect to do Justice.

d *Complaint.* *Loquela* is sometime used for an Action, because every Action implies a Complaint in the Party bringing it; from whence he is called the Plaintiff.

f *Thinking himself,* feeling, finding or perceiving himself to be grieved.

f *Interessed,* or having Interest or Concern therein.

g *Fulness of Justice,* or full Justice speedily.

h *Cognisance,* denotes not only Knowledge or Skill, but Authority to judge and determine.

i *Crown.* These Pleas of the Crown, by this Grant of the Charter, may be determined
within the Ports and Members where they shall arise, except Pleas of Treason, which still are
reserved for the Court of *Shepway.*

j *Hearing,* or to hear and determine; in the old Copies it was, *Audiendi & terminandi,* as
it is here.

CHARTERS.

ronæ noftræ & hæredum noftrorum, tam ad fectam noftram five
hæredum noftrorum, quam ad
fectam aliorum conquerentium;
Placitis de omnimodis prodit-
ionibus omnino duntaxat exceptis,
quæ coram Cuftode Quinque
Portuum prædictorum, pro tempore exiftente, vocat. fibi Majoribus, Ballivis & Juratis, eorundem Portuum, juxta confuetud.
in eifdem Portubus ufitat. apud
Shepweyam, pro nobis & hæred.
noftris, quantum in nobis eft, ibidem audiri & terminari volumus, fecundum legem & confuetud. curiæ prædictæ. Et
quod

TRANSLATION.

Crown of us and of our Heirs,
as well at the Suit [k] of us or of
our Heirs, as at the Suit of other
Complainants; Pleas of all manner of Treafons altogether only
excepted, which before the Warden of the *Cinque Ports* aforefaid, for the Time being, calling
to him [l] the Mayors, Bailiffs and
Jurats [m], of the fame Ports, according to the Cuftom in the
fame Ports ufed, at *Shepway*,
for us and our Heirs, as much as
in us is, we will there to be
heard and determined, ac-
cording to the law and Cuftom
of the Court aforefaid [n]. And
that

ANNOTATIONS.

[k] *Suit. Secta*, the *Latin* from *sequor*, to follow or purfue.

[l] *Calling to him*, or having called to himfelf, that is, by Writ or Summons, as the Cuftom is.

[m] *Mayors, Bailiffs, and Jurats*. The Mayors and Bailiffs to fit with the Warden in Judicature, as the Juftices of the Peace in the County fit on the Bench with the Judge of Affize at the
Affizes: The Jurats to ferve as Jury Men for the Trial of Caufes depending in that Court. How
many of the Jurats were to be returned to the Court of *Shepway* the Charter mentions not, but
I find, in the Twenty Ninth Year of King *Henry* VI. a Decree of Brotherhood, That no Mayor
nor Bailiff fhould return to any Court of *Shepway*, befides themfelves, more than fix Barons,
upon pain of One Hundred Shillings.

[n] *Court aforefaid*, that is, the Court of *Shepway*, the Cuftom and Ufage whereof I may not
undertake to fhew, wanting the Perufal of the Records of *Dover* Caftle; but fo much as I have
found in two ancient Records, is here inferted, by which fomething of the Practice and Proceedings of that Court may be underftood.

*Copy of that concerning the Court of Shepway, recorded in the Cuftumal of Winchelfea, Fol. 37, 38,
and in the old Cuftomal Book of Rye, Fol. 50, 51.*

CUM vero contigerit officium Cuftod.
Quinque Portuum, per obitum vel mu-
tationem, vacari, folet Dominus Rex per literas
fuas patentes alterum committere Cuftodem,
qui fic commiffus cum opportunum viderit, literas fuas cuilibet villæ Quinque Portuum &
eorum Membris, in quibus fuerit Major vel Ballivus, folet tranfmittere, ut certo die fint coram ipfo ad curiam de Shipweya: Ita tum
quod illæ literæ liberenter Majori, vel Ballivo
ubi Major non fuerit, cujuflibet villæ dictorum
Quinque Portuum vel fuorum Membrorum per
xl⁴. dies ante diem de Shipweya.

Acceptis vero literis de fummonit. de Shipweya, habet Major vel Ballivus per fervientem
communem præmunire omnes juratos villæ,
per unum diem vel duos dies poft receptionem
dictarum literarum, & affenfu eorum aliquid
fonar. ad totam communitatem congregand. &
eifdem etiam dicend. ad elfpend. fex probos
homines fimul cum Majore & Ballivo ad com-
parend. coram Cuftode Quinque Portuum tali
die ad curiam de Shipweya, quibus electis
& cum coram dicto Cuftode cum cæteris Baronibus

BUT when it fhall happen the Wardenfhip of the *Cinque Ports*, by Death or
Alteration, to be vacant, our Lord the King
is wont by his Letters Patents to commit [a] ano-   [a] *Appoint.*
ther Warden, who fo committed, when he
fhall fee fit, is wont to fend his Letters to
every Town of the *Cinque Ports* and their
Members, in which there fhall be a Mayor or
Bailiff, that at a certain [b] Day they may be [b]   [b] *In fuch a Day,*
before him at the Court of *Shepway*: So al-   *one Book hath*
ways [c] that thofe Letters be delivered to the *it*, talio,   *and*
Mayor, or to the Bailiff where a Mayor fhall *the other certo;*
not be, of every Town of the faid *Cinque* [c]   *So then.*
Ports or their Members, by forty Days before
the Day of *Shepway*.

And the Letters of Summons of *Shepway* being received, the Mayor or Bailiff by the
common Serjeant is to warn all the Jurats of the Town, by one Day or two Days
after the Receipt of the faid Letters, and by
their Affent to found fomething [d] to gather to-   [d] *Either their*
gether the whole Commonalty, and to fpeak Horn *or a*
to them alfo to choofe fix good Men, together Bell, *one of*
with the Mayor and Bailiff to appear before *which was an-*
the Warden of the *Cinque Ports*, fuch a Day at *ciently ufed to*
the Court of *Shepway*, who being chofen, and *affemble the*
when before the faid Warden with the other *Freemen.*
Barons

ANNOTATIONS.

ronibus Quinque Portuum comparuerint, habent audire a dicto Custode causam congregationis suæ ibidem ; quam etiam cum idem Custos eis demonstraverit, & commissionem de officio Custodiæ suæ eisdem declaraverit, prout decet, unus de Baronibus prædictis ex consensu omnium Baronum ibidem interessentium electus dicet sibi, Mos & consuetudo hujus curiæ est, ut quicunque venerit acceptor. pro Custode sacramentum suum super sacrosanctum Evangelium præstet, tangendo librum, quod libertates, usus & consuetudines Quinque Portuum pro posse suo inviolatas conservabit & manutenebit ; & est sacramentum suum in hunc modum :

EGO N. per sacramentum meum Domino Regi Angliæ præstitum, & per militiam meam, omnes libertates, usus & consuetudines Quinque Portuum pro posse meo inviolatas servabo & manutenebo.

Et sciendum est, quod ab antiquo hucusque usitatum est, quod quicunque fuerit Custos Quinque Portuum miles erit, & de concilio Regis ; qui Custos si hujusmodi sacramentum facere recusaverit, non admittatur pro Custode quousque fecerit. Et quo sacramento facto, solent Majores & Ballivi, & alii qui ex parte communitat. ibidem assignati fuerint, conjunctim dare eidem Custodi sic recepto aliquod donum vel promissum solempne, prout viderint faciendum ; & illo die nihil ulterius fiat ibidem.

Cum autem Custos Quinque Portuum, postquam receptus fuerit ad custodiam, & de Baronibus Quinque Portuum congregationem habere voluerit, ad ea quæ Custodiam suam de jure pertinent. faciend. solet mandare literas suas de summon. per xl dies ante diem de Shipweya, quod Majores & Ballivi de qualibet villa, vel Ballivus ubi Major non adest, & sex probi homines sint coram eo tali die pro certis causis ad curiam de Shipweya pertinent. Si vero summon. non fuerint per xl dies ante diem de Shipweya, non solet Major vel Ballivus aut aliquis alius pro non veniendo ibidem culpam recipere, neque amerciari. Si vero summon. sua in forma prædicta competens fuerit, tunc vero habent Major & Ballivi, aliique electi ibidem esse. Tamen potest Major vel Ballivus attornatum suum ibidem facere, si causam rationabilem de se absentare de inde habuerit ; & hoc per literas sigillo communitatis suæ consignatas ipsum attornatum testificantes. Et si quis Major, vel Ballivus, ubi Major non adest, absens fuerit, & attornatum non habuerit, solet amerciari ad dimidium marci.

Tamen non solet teneri curia de Shipweya, nisi Custos ibi fuerit sedens in propria persona sua, & cum eo sedebunt omnes Majores & Ballivi qui pro tempore fuerint ibidem, ex utraque parte prope eum. Et si aliquod judicium ibidem dari debet de assensu Majorum, & Ballivorum ubi Majores non fuerint, per

Barons of the *Cinque Ports* they shall appear, they are to hear of the said Warden the Cause of their gathering together there ; which also when the same Warden shall declare to them, and shew to them the Commission of the Office of his Wardenship, as is meet **ᵍ**, one of the Barons aforesaid, chosen by *s As becometh.* consent of all the Barons there present, shall say to him, The Manner and Custom of this Court is, that whosoever shall come to be accepted for Warden shall take his Oath upon the holy Evangelists **ʰ**, touching the Book, **ʰ** *Gospel.* that he shall keep and maintain the Liberties, Usages and Customs of the *Cinque Ports,* according to his Power, inviolate **i** ; and his **i** *Inviolable or* Oath is in this manner : *inviolably.*

I N. by my Oath taken to our Lord the • King of *England,* and by my Knighthood, all the Liberties, Usages and Customs of the *Cinque Ports,* according to my Power, inviolate will keep and maintain.

And it is to be known, that of ancient Time hitherto it is used, that whosoever shall be Warden of the *Cinque Ports* shall be a Knight, and of the King's Council ; which Warden, if he shall refuse to make such Oath, may not be admitted for Warden until he make it. And which Oath being made, the Mayors, Bailiffs, and others, which on the Part of the Commonalty shall be there assigned, were wont jointly to give to the said Warden so received some Gift or solemn Promise, as shall seem fit ; and that Day nothing further may be done there.

And when the Warden of the *Cinque Ports,* after he shall be received to the Wardenship, and shall will to have an Assembly **k** of the **k** *Congregation.* Barons of the *Cinque Ports,* for those Things which to his Wardenship of Right appertain to be done, he is wont to send his Letters of Summons by forty Days before the Day of *Shepway,* that the Mayors and Bailiffs of every Town, or the Bailiff where a Mayor is not, and six good Men, may be before him such a Day for certain Causes to the Court of *Shepway* appertaining. But if the Summons shall not be by forty Days before the Day of *Shepway,* the Mayor or Bailiff, or any other, are not to receive Blame **l** for **l** *Guilt,* not coming there, nor to be amerced. But if their **m** Summons in form aforesaid shall be **m** *this.* competent, then the Mayor and Bailiff, and others elected, are to be there. Notwithstanding the Mayor or Bailiff may make his Attorney to be there, if he shall have Cause reasonable to absent himself therefrom, and this by Letters with the Seal of their Commonalty sealed, testifying the same Attorney. And if any Mayor, or Bailiff, where a Mayor is not, shall be absent, and have not an Attorney, he is wont to be amerced at half a Mark.

Notwithstanding the Court of *Shepway* is not wont to be holden, except the Warden **n** *An.14 Ed.II.* shall be there sitting in his proper Person **o**, and *The King sends* with him shall sit all the Mayors and Bailiffs, *his Writ to the* which for the Time shall be there, on each *Ports to hold a* side **o** near him. And if any Judgment is *Court before the* to be given with the Assent of the Mayors, *Lieutenant of* and of the Bailiffs where Mayors are **p** not, *the Warden.*

o *Pers.* **p** *The Latin Copy in both,* non assuerint, *now obsolete, may be,* are not, *or* shall not be.
U   it

ANNOTATIONS.

per os Custodis folet dari & revelari. Et notandum eft, quod curia illa particularibus fubfequentibus tantummodo deferviëtur.

Inprimis, Inquirendum eft per xii Juratos ibidem de hiis qui pro tempore fuerint ibidem fummon. fi quis prolocutus fuerit feditionem Domino Regi aut Reginæ. Item, fi quis contrafecerit figillum Domini Regis. Item, fi quis falfaverit monetam Domini Regis, aut eundem dicti Domini Regis contrafecerit. Item, fi quis de libertate Quinque Portuum invenerit thefaurum abfconditum fubter terram vel alibi. Item, fi quis Major, aut Ballivus, ubi Major non adeft, vel Jurati aliquod falfum judicium dederit vel dederint alicui inter fe placitanti. Item, fi aliqua villa Quinque Portuum cum fuis Membris fe retraxerint a fervitio Domini Regis, & illud non fecerit prout de jure tenetur, ita tamen, fi de hoc debite præmunita fuerit prout decet. Item, fi quis Ballivus acceperit aliter cuftumam fuam quam debet, aut fi non fecerit debitam executionem, prout de jure ad officium fuum pertinet, aut fi libertate illæferit quovis modo feu injufte contraxerit.

Et nota, Quod Inquifitio illa debet fieri per duos vel tres, prout negiaverint, de qualibet villa ufque ad numerum duodecem, quia omnes Quinque Portus intendunt fe fore & funt folummodo una communicas. Et fecundum quod inquifitio illa de articulis de fe interrogatis dixerit, quod fi quis de libertate Quinque Portuum reus erit in feditione Domini Regis aut Reginæ, aut contrafacto figilli Domini Regis, five falfant. monetam Domini Regis vel contrafacient. cuneam Domini Regis, ftatim per os Cuftodis de affenfu Majorum, & Ballivorum, ubi Major non adeft, adjudicabitur ; quod ille qui reus reperitur, fi præfens fuerit, in circuitu plateæ de Shipweya cum equis detrahetur, & incontinent. in confpectu omnium ibidem exiftentium fufpendatur. Et fi non fuerit præfens, idem Cuftos firmiter injunget ex parte Domini Regis omnes Majores, Ballivos, omnefque alios Quinque Portuum ibidem exiftentium, quod cum talis convictus infra villam aliquam Quinque Portuum inveniatur, quod ftatim captatur & in prifona Domini Regis falvo cuftodiatur, & immediate poft captionem dicto Cuftodi inde certificetur, ut judicium fuum in loco & præfentia ubi prius, quam cito ad hoc dictus Cuftos vacare poterit, recipere valeat. Et hoc non omittent ipfi Majores vel Ballivi, & alii, fub forisfacturam omnium quæ verfus Dominum Regem forisfacere poterunt. Item, fi quis convictus fuerit de thefauro invento, & Dominum Regem aut dictum Cuftodem inde non certificaverit, adjudicabitur ille, quod omnia bona fua ad voluntatem Domini Regis, & nihilominus ipfe in fua gratia, fed pro hujus * non patietur ✝ mortem.

Si vero aliquis Major, vel Ballivus, ubi Major non adeft, aut Jurati fuper falfo dato judicio convictus fuerit, ftatim de fede fua amoveatur

it is to be given and declared ᵖ by the Mouth ᵠ *Revealed.* of the Warden. And it is to be noted, that that Court is kept only for the fubfequent Particulars ʳ.   ʳ *Articles.*

Prefs, It is to be enquired by twelve Jurats there, of thofe which for the Time fhall be there fummoned, if any one have fpoken fedition ᶠ againft the King or Queen. Alfo, if ᵗ *Sedition for* any have ᵘ counterfeited the Seal of our Lord *Treafon againft* the King. Alfo, if any have falfified the *pur Lord the* Money of our Lord the King, or counterfeited *King.* the Coin of our faid Lord the King. Alfo, if ᵛ *Or fhall have,* any of the Liberty of the *Cinque Ports* have *and fo in the* found Treafure hid under the Earth or elfe- *reft.* where. Alfo, if any Mayor, or Bailiff, where a Mayor is not, or the Jurats, have ᵘ given *Or hath giv-* any falfe Judgment to any pleading amongft ʷ *en.* them. Alfo, if any Town of the *Cinque Ports* ʷ *Amongft, by* with their Members have withdrawn them- *the Senfe may* felves from the Service of our Lord the King, *be, before.* and fhall not have done that as of Right it ˣ ˣ *It or fhe, the* is bound, fo notwithftanding if of this it *Town being the* were duly warned as becometh. Alfo, if any *Antecedent,* Bailiff fhall take otherwife his Cuftom than he *which is Femi-* ought, or if he fhall not have ʸ done due Exe- *nine in the La-* cution, as of Right to his Office appertaineth, *tin.* or if he fhall have hurt or unjuftly abridged ˢ ʸ *Or fhall not* the Liberty in any wife.   *do.*

And Note, That that Inquifition ought to be ᵃ *From Contra-* made by Two or Three, as fhall be needful; *ho, to leffen or* of every Town, unto the Number of Twelve, *draw together* becaufe all the *Cinque Ports* intend ᵃ them- *into a narrow-* felves to be, and are only one Commonalty. *or Compafs.* And according to that which that Inqui- ᵇ *Pretend or* tion, being asked of the Articles of them- *think.* felves ᵇ, fhall fay, That if any one of the Li- ᶜ *feverally.* berty of the *Cinque Ports* fhall be guilty in Se- ᶜ *Sedition ufed* dition ᶜ of our Lord the King or Queen, or *for Treafon, as* counterfeiting of the Seal of our Lord the *before.* King, or falfifying the Money of our Lord the King, or counterfeiting the Coin of our Lord the King, prefently ᵈ, by the Mouth of the ᵈ *Or forthwith.* Warden, of the Affent of the Mayor, and Bailiffs, where a Mayor is not, it fhall be adjudged ; that he which is found guilty, if he fhall be prefent, fhall be drawn with Horfes in the Circuit of the Street of *Shepway,* and incontinently, in the Sight of all there being, hanged ᵉ. And if he be not prefent, the ᵉ *Or may be* fame Warden fhall firmly enjoin on the Part *hanged.* of our Lord the King, all the Mayors, Bailiffs, and all others of the *Cinque Ports* there being, that when fuch convicted Perfon within any Town of the *Cinque Ports* may be found, that forthwith ᶠ he be taken and kept fafe in the ᶠ *Or prefently.* Prifon of our Lord the King, and immediately after the taking, the faid Warden fhall be certified thereof, that his Judgment in the Place and Prefence, where at firft, as foon as the faid Warden fhall be at leffure ᵍ, he may ᵍ *Or vacant,* receive. And this the fame Mayors or Bailiffs, *that is empty* and others, fhall not omit, under the Forfei- *of Bufinefs.* ture of all which towards our Lord the King they can forfeit. Alfo, if any fhall be convicted of Treafure found, and fhall not have certified our Lord the King, or the faid Warden thereof, it fhall be adjudged, that he forfeit ʰ all his Goods at the Will of our Lord ʰ *Forfeit is un-* the King, and yet fo that he be in his Mer- *derftood.* cy ᵢ ; but for this he fhall not fuffer Death. ᵢ *Grace or Fa-*

But if any Mayor, or Bailiff, where a *vour.* Mayor is not, or the Jurats, fhall be convicted upon falfe Judgment given, he that hath given this Judgment may prefently be removed

ANNOTATIONS.

tur ille qui hujus judicium dederit, & a concilio Custodis & Majorum ac Ballivorum assidentium. Et super hoc Custos dei assensu, residuorum Majorum & Ballivorum dabit pro judicio, quod libertas illius villæ sequitur in manus Domini Regis, quousque gratiam Domini Regis de novo poterunt invenire.

Cum vero aliquis prosequitur versus aliquam communitatem pro falso judicio dato, & communitas illa se exinde poterit acquietare, ille qui prosequitur debet attachari & salvo sub custodia ipsius custodis in prisona Domini Regis custodiri, quousque dictæ communitati damna sua per taxationem cæterorum Majorum ibidem inter essentium pro injusta querela sua plenarie satisfecerit.

Item, si aliquis communitas convicta fuerit, quod a servicio Domini Regis se retraxerit, & illud non fecerit prout tenetur, solet idem judicium dari quod de falso judicio determinatur.

Among other Things, by this Record (penned, as I take it, about the Tenth Year of King Henry IV.) it may be collected, that the Six returned with the Head Officer need not be all Jurate; but by the other Record before mentioned, which is elder, and was copied out of the Record it self by Mr. John Helylsheuaite, sometime Bailiff of Lydde, it seems anciently not only a greater Number was returned, and the Writs ran in the King's Name and not in the Wardens, but that other Causes than those Pleas of the Crown before mentioned were heard and determined at this Court of Shepway. Upon this Record I have bestowed the Translation, as I did on the former.

De generali summonitione apud Shepweyam.

REX dilectis & fidelibus suis Ballivis de Hastinges, salutem. Præcipimus vobis quod, omni occasione postposita, sitis apud Shepweyam ad talem diem coram dilectis & fidelibus nostris A. B. &c. Et illuc venire faciatis 24^{or}. de legalioribus & discretioribus Baronibus de Hastinges, & aliis, sicut venire debent & solent ad placeam de Shepweya; ad respondendum coram præfatis justiciariis de capitulis subscriptis. De veteribus placitis coronæ quæ alias fuerunt coram justiciar. apud Shepweyam & non fuerunt terminata. De novis placitis coronæ quæ infra libertatem quersunt tempore pacis, postquam justiciar. ultimo itineraverunt apud Shepweyam. De his quæ fuerunt in misericordia, &c. De Ecclesiis. De Assisa pannorum. De Escaet, &c. De illis qui roboraver. in terra vel in aqua post pacem clamat. De Purprestur. & mensuris. De vino vendit. &c. De Thesauro, &c. De Castallis Francherum, &c. De Flouariis. De Burgatoriis, &c. De Mercat, &c. De Cambio, &c. De Fugativis, &c. De Mercede, &c. De novis Consuetudinibus, &c. De default. de Gaolis, &c. De Rapinis, &c. De Navibus capt. in Guerra & tradit. per Willielm. de Wrotcham, cui tradebantur, & quis ill. habeat, vel quid de ill. actum sit, &c. De illis qui vendiderunt naves vel maremium ad naves fabricand. inimicis præsentis Domini Regis. Faciatis venire coram eisdem justiciar. nostris ad præfatum terminum omnia placita & omnia attachiamenta quæ venire &c.

moved [k] from his Seat, and from the Council there sitting. And upon this the Warden, with the Assent of the Residue of the Mayors and Bailiffs, shall give his Judgment, that the Liberty of that Town be seized into the Hands of our Lord the King, until they may find the Favour of our Lord the King anew [n].

But when any prosecuteth against any Commonalty for false Judgment, and that Commonalty can acquit it self thereof, he which prosecuteth ought to be attached and kept in safe Custody of the same Warden, in the Prison of our Lord the King, until he shall fully satisfy to the said Commonalty their Damages by the Taxation of the rest of the Mayors there being it, for his unjust Complaint [o].

Also, if any Commonalty shall be convicted, that it hath withdrawn it self from the Service of our Lord the King, and that it hath have without done as it is bound, the same Judgment is drawn themto be given that is determined of false Judgment.

The general Summons at Shepway.

THE King to his beloved and faithful the Bailiffs of *Hasting*, Greeting. We command you, That every Occasion laid aside, ye be at *Shepway* at such a Day, before our beloved and faithful A. B. &c. And that ye make to come thither Twenty four of the more legal and discreet Barons of *Hasting*, and others, as they ought, and were wont to come to the Place of *Shepway*; to answer before the aforesaid Justices of the Chapters underwritten. Of the old Pleas of the Crown, which otherwise were before the Justices at *Shepway*, and were not determined. Of the new Pleas of the Crown which have happened within the Liberty in the Time of Peace, after the Justices last journeyed at *Shepway*. Of those which were amerced, &c. Of Churches. Of Assise of Cloth [c]. Of Escheats, &c. Of those which have robbed by Land or Water after Peace proclaimed [f]. Of Purprestures and Measures. Of Wines sold, &c. Of Treasure, &c. Of the Castles of French, &c. Of Flowers [g]. Of Burghers [h], &c. Of Merchants, &c. Of Exchange, &c. Of Fugitives, &c. Of Wages, &c. Of new Customs, &c. Of Default of Gaols [k], &c. Of Rapines [l], &c. Of Ships taken in War and delivered by *William de Wrotcham* [m], to whom they were delivered, and who hath them, and what is done with them, &c. Of those which have sold Ships, or Timber to build Ships to the Enemies of our now Lord the King. That ye make to come before the same our Justices, at the Term aforesaid, all Pleas, and all Attachments which ought and

[marginal notes:]
[k] *Amoved or put from.*
[l] *Or with the before.*
[m] *Assent, and so before.*
[n] *Or of new.*

[o] *Or present, as before.*

[p] *Or that they drew them-selves.*

[a] *Lawful.*
[b] *Particulars or Articles.*
[c] *Concerning, and so in the rest.*
[d] *It seems in former Times the Justices itinerant had Cognizance of Pleas at Shepway.*
[e] *It is Cloth according to the Latin, but I think it to be intended for Pannum the Genitive plural for Bread.*
[f] *Clamatum for proclamatum.*
[g] *That is such of the Fishermen as catch Herrings along the Coasts, so I take the Latin rather than for Water.*

Burgatoriis *I take for Houses Men Burglaries, because Robbers on the Land or the Water were mentioned before.* [h] Hire or Bribes. [k] Or Gaolers.
[l] Or Rapes. [m] Warden in the Time of K. John.

were

ANNOTATIONS.

& terminari debent & solent coram justiciar. placita tenentibus apud Shepweyam.

Eodem modo, & per eadem verba scribatur Ballivis de Romenall, Ballivis de Heia, Ballivis de Doure, & Ballivis de Sandwic. ita quod quilibet istorum Portuum habeat per se in forma prædicta.

Et quum lis sæpius est inter homines prædictorum Portuum & homines Gernemeue, & de Donvic. fiet breve Vic. Norf. & Suff.

REX Vic. Norf. & Suff. salutem. Sciatis quod summon. fecimus ad talem diem apud Shepweyam omnia placita de Quinque Portubus, sicut teneri debent & solent coram justiciariis apud Shepweyam. Et ideo tibi præcipimus, quod hæc sciari facias hominibus de Gernemuiæ & Ballivis de Donwie. ita quod si aliquis conqueri voluerit de aliquo qui sit de libertate vel infra libertatem Quinque Portuum, tunc sit apud Shepweyam coram præfatis justiciariis nostris querelam suam proponitur. & justiciam inde recepturi. Teste, &c.

Shipweye. *Curia de Shipweya, quæ est iter Baronum Quinque Portuum, tenta ibidem die lunæ proxima ante festum sancti Gregorii, Anno regni Regis Edwardi tertii post conquestum Angliæ xxiiii°. & Franciæ xi°.*

PRæceptum fuit Major. & Ballivis Quinque Portuum, videlicet, quod unusquisque prædictorum venire faceret hic ad hunc diem de qualibet Portu suo xii. probos & legales homines de Juratis cujuslibet villæ Portuum prædictorum una cum scriptis, cum omnibus articulis & aliis admisiculis curiæ prædictæ tangen. antiquitates confuetas facturi & recepturi juxta consuetudinem Portuum prædictorum. fuerit eis injungen. &c. Et modo venerunt omnes Majores & Ballivi Portuum prædictorum, & mandata sua retornant cum nominibus Juratorum, ut patet per retornum suum prædict.

ff. Adhuc, sicut alias, dat. est dies ad proximam curiam, de Shipweya manucaptoribus manucaptorum Roberti Lad, prout in curie præcedente continetur.

ff. Præceptum fuit Majori & Ballivo de la Rye ad curiam præcedentem, quod caperent Willielm. Hoker de la Rye per corpus suum, ita quod eum haberent adesse hic ad hanc curiam, Johannæ quæ fuit uxor Caroli Colyn, prout in curia præcedente, unde dat. est eis dies ulterius ad proximam.

ff. Communitas villæ de Romenale, alias in curia hic, scilicet die lunæ in crastino apostolorum Petri & Pauli, anno regni Regis Edwardi tertii post conquestum Angliæ xxii°. R. vero sui Franciæ x°. coram Stephano de Burgherth tunc custode allocutis per eundem custodem, prout allocuti fuerunt coram Roberto de Kendale

were wont to come, and be determined before the Justices holding Pleas at Shepway.

In the same Manner, and by the same Words, it may be written to the Bailiff of Romney, the Bailiff of Hithe, the Bailiff of Dover, and the Bailiff of Sandwich, so that every of those Ports may have by themselves in Form aforesaid.

And whereas Strife oftentimes is between the Men of the said Ports and the Men of Yarmouth and of Dunwich, a Writ shall be made to the Sheriff of Norfolk and Suffolk.

THE King to the Sheriff of Norfolk and Suffolk, Greeting. Know ye, that we have made to be summoned at such a Day at Shepway all the Pleas of the Cinque Ports, as ought and are wont to be held before the Justices at Shepway. And therefore to thee we command, that thou make to be known these Things to the Men of Yarmouth, and to the Bailiffs of Dunwich, so that if any will complain of any who may be of the Liberty, or within the Liberty of the Cinque Ports, he may be then at Shepway, before the aforesaid our Justices to propound his Complaint, and to receive Justice thereupon. Witness, &c.

Shepway. *The Court of Shepway, which is the Journey of the Barons of the Cinque Ports, holden there on Monday next, before the Feast of Saint Gregory, in the Year of the Reign of King Edward the Third after the Conquest of England the 24th, and of France the 11th.*

IT was commanded to the Mayors and Bailiffs of the Cinque Ports, that is to say, That every one of them should make to come here at this Day of every their Ports Twelve good and lawful Men of the Jurats of every Town of the Ports aforesaid; together with themselves, with all Articles, and other Things touching the Antiquities of the Court aforesaid, accustomed to be done and received according to the Custom [a] of the Ports aforesaid, to them enjoined, &c. And now came all the Mayors and Bailiffs of the Ports aforesaid, and they return their Mandates with the Names of the Jurats, as appeareth by their Returns aforesaid.

ff. Hitherto [b], as otherwise [c], Day is given to the Pledges [d], of the Pledges of Robert Lad, to be at the next Court of Shepway, as in the precedent Court is contained.

ff. It was commanded to the Mayor and Bailiff of Rye, at the precedent Court, that they should take William Hoker of Rye by his Body, so that they should have him to be here at this Court, Johanne, which was the Wife of Charles Colyn, as in the Court precedent, whereupon further Day is given to them at the next [e].

ff. The Commonalty of the Town of Romney, otherwise in the Court here, that is to say, on Monday, in the Morrow of the Apostles Peter and Paul, in the Year of the Reign of King Edward the Third after the Conquest of England the 22d. but of his Reign of France the 10th, before Stephen de Burgherth, then Warden, were allowed by the same Warden, as they were allowed before Robert de Kendale

[a] Or to do and receive after the Customs; or as after the Customs.

[b] Tot, at this Time, or moreover.

[c] Elsewhere, or at another Time, and so in other Places to be taken.

[d] Bail or Mainpernors; captors.

[e] Or to the next Court, and the like afterward.

ANNOTATIONS.

dale quondam cuftode, de eo quod Majorem non habuerunt ex ipfis, prout habere deberent. Et habent diem ut prius ad proximam.

ff. Combarones Quinque Portuum allocuti per Cuftodèm hic in curia, & quæfiti, fi teneantur hic venire tanquam ad curiam intinerant. qui dicunt quod teneantur hic venire coram Cuftode tanquam jufticiar. itinerant. &c. Et non alibi coram aliquo alio juftici- *vid.Bracton.* ario *.

ff. Hic ad hanc curiam dies dat. eft omnibus Baronibus Quinque Portuum, die lunæ proximo poft feftum fancti Gregorii, apud London ad certificand. Cuftodi de Articulis libertat. & confuetudines fuas tangen. fub figillis eorum divifim, quæ clamant ratione libertatis fuæ.

ff. Johannes Archer hic in curia queritur fe verfus Johannem Monyn de Dovor. de placito tranfgr. & unde queritur quod prædictus Johannes Monyn, die lunæ proximo poft feftum fancti Petri in cathedra, anno Regni Regis Edwardi tercii poft conqueftum Angliæ xxiii°, prædictum Johannem Archer in villa Dovor. cepit & imprifonavit, & in prifona per feptem feptimanas proxim. fequentes eum detinuit minus jufte, ad dampn. xxti marcarum, & inde producit fectam; &c: Et prædictus Johannes Monyn venit & defendit; & dicit quod prædictus Johannes jufte imprifonatus erat, dicit enim quod obligatus erat Willielmo Archer fratri fuo in quadam fumma pecuniæ per unum fcriptum obligatorium, pro qua attachiatus erat ad refpondend. prædicto Willielmo fratri fuo, qui venit in curiam Dovor. refponf. prædicto Willielmo fratri fuo, & dedixit illud fcriptum obligatorium effe factum fuum: Et fuper hoc convictus erat per xii. &c. quod erat factum fuum, & fic erat imprifonatus, & non aliter. Et prædictus Johannes Archer hic in curia dixit, quod non dedixit illud fcriptum obligatorium effe factum fuum, fed cognovit & allegavit in curia Dovor. prædict. quod virtute illius facti de prædicto debito non debuit refpondere, pro eo quod tempore confectionis facti prædicti erat imprifonatus per ipfum Willielmum Archer fratrem fuum, &c. & in prifona illud fcriptum obligatorium factum fuit, &c. & inde petit judicium, &c. Et prædictus Johannes Monyn dicit, quod prædictus Johannes Archer omnino dedixit illud effe factum fuum, &c. Et hoc petiit quod per record. & proceffum curiæ Dovor. prædict. poffit teftificar. Et data eft ei dies habend. record. & proceffum prædict. ad januam Caftri Dovor. die fabati proximo poft feftum fancti Gregorii papæ proxim. fequen. &c. Et eadem dies dat. præfato Johanni Archer, &c. receptur. & acceptur. ibidem quod judicia fuadebit, &c. Ad quem diem prædictus Johannes Archer venit, &c. & prædictus Johannes Monyn non venit cum recordo & proceffu prædictis, prout habuit diem, coram Cuftode, &c. fuper quo prædictus Johannes Archer petit judicium, &c. Et dat. eft ei dies coram dicto Cuftode ad proxim. advent. fuum ad Caftrum Dovor. &c.

dale, fometime Warden, for that, that they have not a Mayor of themfelves, as they ought to have. And they have Day as before at the next.

ff. The Combarons of the *Cinque Ports* were allowed [f] by the Warden here in Court, and [f] *The Ports be-* enquired, if they were bound to come here as *ing allowed* to the Court itinerant, which fay that they *their Liberty* are bound to come here before the Warden as *according to* Juftice itinerant, &c. and not other where *their Demand,* before any other Juftice. *it feemeth by*

ff. Here at this Court, Day is given to all *this the War-* the Barons of the *Cinque Ports,* on *Monday den was their* next after the Feaft of Saint *Gregory,* to cer- *Chief Juftice* tify [r] the Warden at *London* of the Articles *in Eire.* touching their Liberties and Cuftoms, under [r] *By this it is* their Seals feverally, what they claim by rea- *very probable,* fon of their Liberty. *the Warden be-*

ff. *John Archer* here in Court complaineth *fore whom this* himfelf againft *John Monyn* of *Dover,* of a Plea *Court was kept* of Trefpafs ; and whereupon he complaineth, *had not been* that the aforefaid *John Monyn,* on *Monday* next *long in the Of-* after the Feaft of St. *Peter* in the Chair, in the *fice, for this* Year of the Reign of King *Edward* the Third, *Practice is ftill* after the Conqueft of *England* the Twenty *ufual to the* Third, the aforefaid *John Archer,* in the *New Warden,* Town of *Dover,* took and imprifoned, and in *fometimes* the Prifon by feven Weeks next enfuing him *jointly, and* detained unjuftly, to the Damage of Twenty *fometimes fe-* Marks, and thereof he produceth Suit, &c. *verally.* And the aforefaid *John Monyn* cometh and defendeth, and faith, That the aforefaid *John Archer* was juftly imprifoned ; for he faith, that he was bound to *William Archer* his Brother in a certain Sum of Money by one Writing obligatory, for which he was attached to anfwer to the aforefaid *William* his Brother, who came into the Court at *Dover,* anfwered to the aforefaid *William* his Brother, and denied [u] that Writing obligatory to be his Deed : [u] *Or gainfaid.* And upon this he was convicted by Twelve, &c. that it was his Deed, and fo he was imprifoned, and not otherwife. And the aforefaid *John Archer* here in Court faid, that he did not deny [w] that Writing obligatory to be [w] *Or hath not* his Deed, but acknowledged it, and alledged *gainfaid.* in the Court of *Dover* aforefaid, that by virtue of that Deed of the aforefaid Debt he ought not to anfwer, for that, that in the Time of the making of the Deed aforefaid, he was imprifoned by the fame *William Archer* his Brother, &c. and in Prifon that Writing obligatory made [x], &c. and thereof he prayed judgment, [x] *Or was made.* &c. And the aforefaid *John Monyn* faith, that the aforefaid *John Archer* altogether gainfaid [y] that to be his Deed, &c. and this he [y] *Or denied, as* prayed, that by the Record and Procefs of the *before.* Court of *Dover* aforefaid it might [z] be teftifi- [z] *Or may.* ed. And Day is given to him to have the Record and Procefs aforefaid at the Gate of the Caftle [a] of *Dover* on *Saturday* next after [a] *This Adjourn-* the Feaft of St. *Gregory* the Pope next enfuing, *ment of Caufes* &c. and the fame Day is given to the afore- *from hence to* faid *John Archer,* &c. to receive and accept Dover *Caftle,* there that which Juftice fhall perfuade, &c. *brought this* at which Day the aforefaid *John Archer* came, *Court of Shep-* &c. and the aforefaid *John Monyn* came not way *out of re-* with the Record and Procefs aforefaid, as he *queft at laft.* had Day, before the Warden, &c. upon which the aforefaid *John Archer* prayeth judgment, &c. and Day is given to him before the faid Warden at his next coming to the Caftle of *Dover,* &c.

CHARTERS.

quod hujufmodi Major & Jurati,
Ballivus & Jurati, ac etiam Jurati prout fuperius limitantur,
omnia & fingula placita fupradicta (except. præexcept.) habeant & teneant coram eis infra
quem-

TRANSLATION.

that fuch Mayor and Jurats,
Bailiff and Jurats, and alfo Jurats as above are limited, all
and fingular the Pleas abovefaid
(except before * excepted) may
have and hold before them within
every

ANNOTATIONS.

The Twelve Jurats here mentioned are not to be underftood Jurats on the Bench, for then every Town fhould return to the Court of *Shepway* all the Jurats they had, and leave none for a Deputy-Mayor or Bailiff to adminifter Juftice in their refpective Places during the Sitting of this Court; but rather to be taken for Barons, as before, fworn Freemen, who had all taken Oath for the Maintenance of the Liberties and Cuftoms of the Ports, yet might the moft of them be Jurats. And I find, befides the Mayor there were five Jurats and one Commoner returned to the Court of *Shepway*, holden *Auguft* 20, 1629. when *Theophilus*, the Earl of *Suffolk*, was fworn. And when the Lord *Zouche* was fworn, the Mayor and only five Jurats were return-ed, which might be, becaufe in his Lordfhip's Summons he required fix, five, or four Jurats, as by the Copy, and Return thereof following, will appear.

EDward Lord *Zouche*, S^t. *Maure* and *Cantelupe*, Conftable of the Caftle of *Dover*, Lord War-den, Chancellor, and Admiral of the *Cinque Ports, Two Ancient Towns*, and their Members, and one of his Majefty's moft honourable Privy Council, To all and fingular Mayors, Bailiffs and Jurats, of the faid *Cinque Ports, Two Ancient Towns*, and Members of the faid *Cinque Ports* and *Towns*, and every of them, Greeting. For certain good Caufes and Confiderations me thereunto efpecially moving, I have thought it neceffary to notify unto you by thefe Prefents, that I purpofe and am refolved, by God's Grace, to be at *Shepway* in *Kent*, within the Liberty of the faid *Cinque Ports*, upon the fifth Day of *September* next enfuing, by Eight of the Clock in the Forenoon, then and there to make folemn Seremont, and promife to uphold and maintain the Liberties and Privileges of the faid *Cinque Ports* to the beft of my Power according to the ancient Ufage and Cuftom of the faid *Cinque Ports*. Therefore, by Authority of my faid Office, thefe are in his Majefty's Name ftrictly to charge and command you, and every of you, to give good Summons and lawful Warning unto fix, five or four Jurats, and others of the beft and

*Here were not appear before me at *Shepway* aforefaid, on the faid fifth Day of *September* * next coming, at
40 Days from Eight of the Clock in the Forenoon of the fame Day. And that alfo you the faid Mayors and
the Date, as it Bailiffs, and every of you, be likewife then and there perfonally prefent, to do as to you and
fhould have them hath been accuftomed and belongeth. And that you do then and there certify under the
been. feveral Seals of your Office, what you fhall have done in the Accomplifhment of the Premifes, certifying me alfo then and there the Names of all thefe Perfons whom you fhall fo have fum-moned and warned as aforefaid, and therewith returning back unto me then and there this Mandate; whereof fail you not, nor any of you do fail, upon Pain of an Hundred Pounds. Dated at *Philip Lane* in *London*, under the Seal of my Office, the third Day of *Auguft*, in the Years of the Reign of our Sovereign Lord *James*, by the Grace of God, *&c. viz.* of *England*, *France* and *Ireland*, the xiiith, and of *Scotland* the xlixth.

TO all thofe to whom thefe Prefents fhall or may appertain, and efpecially to the Right
Honourable *Edward* Lord *Zouche*, S^t. *Maure* and *Cantelupe*, Conftable of the Caftle of *Dover*, Lord Warden, Chancellor, and Admiral of the *Cinque Ports, Two Ancient Towns*, and the Members of the faid *Cinque Ports* and *Towns*, and every of them, and one of his Majefty's moft Honourable Privy Council, We the Mayor, Jurats and Commonalty of the ancient Town of *Rye* in the County of *Suffex*, of the Liberties of the faid *Cinque-Ports*, with all due Reve-rence fend Greeting. May it pleafe your good Lordfhip to be advertifed, that we have nomi-nated, elected, appointed and chofen our welbeloved Combarons, *Mark Thomas*, now Mayor of the Town of *Rye* aforefaid, *Richard Fowtrell, Thomas Enfing, Matthew Toung, John Palmer*, and *Richard Gibbridge*, of the fame Town, Jurats, to be and appear before your Honour at *Shepway* in the County of *Kent*, within the Liberties of the faid *Cinque Ports*, on the fifth Day of *September* next coming, by Eight of the Clock in the Forenoon of that Day, then and there to do fuch Service as to us appertaineth to be done, by the ancient Ufages and Cuftoms of the faid *Cinque Ports* and their Members, at the Solemnization of the Serement or Promife of the Lord Warden of the faid *Cinque Ports*, at his firft Entry into the faid Office, according to your Lordfhip's Commandment and Pleafure, contained in your Letters of Summons therein of late to

*Some other us, among others, made †, bearing Date the Third Day of *Auguft* laft paft, wherein we do here-
Returns add by ratify, confirm, and allow all and whatfoever the faid *Mark Thomas, Richard Fowtrell*,
here the Word *Thomas Enfing, Matthew Toung, John Palmer*, and *Richard Gibbridge*, or the moft part of them
known. fhall do or confent to be done in the Premifes. In witnefs whereof we hereunto caufed the Common Seal of the Town of *Rye* to thefe Prefents to be affixed. Dated the laft Day of *Auguft*, in the Years, *&c.* 1615.

* *Except before*, that is the Pleas of Treafon laft above fpecified.

P *Court.*

CHARTERS.

qtemlibet hujufmodi Portum five Membrum, in our. ejufdem Portus five Membri, & omnia placita hujufmodi audient & terminent, & judicia inde reddita juxta legem & confuetud. regni noftri Angliæ, vel confuetud. prædictorum Quinque Portuum, ad ipforum electionem exequantur. Et infuper quod nullus prædictorum Baronum, proborum hominum, aut hæredum vel fubcefforum fuorum aut refidentium prædict. per aliqua warranta, præcepta feu mandata Conftabular. Caftri prædict. aut Cuftodis Quinque Portuum prædictorum, feu Admiralli infra Portus & Membra prædicta, ad refpondend. fuper aliquo hujufmodi placito de cætero capiatur, areftetur, feu attachietur, nec ea de caufa coram eodem Conftabulario, Cuftode five Admirallo, vel ejus Locumtenente five Deputato, comparere aliqualiter teneatur nifi in defectu juftitiæ tantum, ut prædictum eft. Et quod nullus Baronum, proborum hominum, aut hæredum fuorum five hujufmodi refidentium, ad feu in fervitium noftrum feu hæredum noftrorum,

TRANSLATION.

évery fuch Port or Member, in the Court [p] of the fame Port or Member, and fhall hear and determine all fuch Pleas, and the Judgments thereupon rendred [q] may execute according to Law, and the Cuftom of our Kingdom of *England*, or the Cuftom of the aforefaid *Cinque Ports*, at their Choice [r]. And moreover, that none of the aforefaid Barons, good Men, or their Heirs or Succeffors, or of the Refidents [f] aforefaid, by any Warrants [s], Precepts [t] or Mandates [u] of the Conftable [v] of the Caftle aforefaid, or of the Warden [w] of the *Cinque Ports* aforefaid, or Admiral within the Ports and Members aforefaid, to anfwer upon any fuch Plea, from henceforth may be taken, arrefted [x], or attached, nor for the fame Caufe [y], before the fame Conftable, Warden or Admiral, or his Lieutenant or Deputy, be bound to appear in any wife, except in default of Juftice only, as is aforefaid. And that none of the Barons, good Men, or their Heirs, or fuch Refidents, to or for the Service of us or of our Heirs,

ANNOTATIONS.

[p] *Court.* Albeit the Word is abbreviated in the printed Copy, as here, in the old Copy it was in the Singular, *Curia.*

[q] *Rendred* or given, *reddita* being ufed for *data.*

[r] *Choice.* Where fome Difference happens between the cuftomary Proceedings in the Courts within the Ports, and the common Law or Cuftom of the Kingdom, the Ports may purfue their Cuftoms, or reduce them to the Manner of other the King's Courts of Record, as they fhall pleafe.

[f] *Refidents* or Refciants, as before, and feveral Places afterward.

[s] *Warrants,* from the French *Garrantir,* to *keep fafe,* or *defend the Officer that executes it.*

[t] *Precepts,* from *præcipio,* to *command.*

[u] *Mandates* or Commandments.

[v] *Conftable,* fo it is in the old Copy, although in the printed Copy, as here, by reafon of the Abbreviation, it be uncertain whether in the fingular or plural.

[w] *Or of the Warden.* Here, as before noted, thefe Offices, though joined in the Diftinctive, yet do not imply feveral Officers.

[x] *Arrefted,* derived from the French, and taken fometimes for a *Seifure of,* or *Execution* ferved upon a Man's Perfon or Goods; fometime for a *Stop* or *Reftraint,* as in a Suit after a Verdict, when Caufes are moved in Arreft of Judgment ; the Judgment in that Caufe is ftayed till the Caufes of Arreft are examined ; and fometime for a Sentence, Decree or Order of a Court. Here, in the firft Senfe, for the Attachment of a Perfon.

[y] *Same Caufe* or for fuch Caufe.

M

[z] *Upon*

CHARTERS.

noftrorum, fuper mare faciend. nifi ad fervitium ipforum Baronum nobis & hæredibus noftris cum navibus fuis, ut prædict. faciend. per aliquem Officiar. feu Miniftrum noftri vel hæredum noftrorum, de cætero capiatur, attachietur feu areftetur quovifmodo. Conceffimus infuper præfatis Baronibus & probis hominibus, quod ipfi, hæredes & fucceffores fui, & alii refidentes quicunque eorum hæredum & fucceffor. infra Portus & Membra prædicta, ad fervitium & navigium prædict. contribuentes, vel qui erunt contribuentes, imperpetuum fint quieti de omnibus auxiliis, fubfidiis, contributionibus, tallagiis, & quotis quibufcunque, quæ ab ipfis feu aliquo ipforum, ratione terrarum, tenementorum, & reddituum, aut bonorum & catallorum

TRANSLATION.

Heirs, to be done upon the Sea [a], except to the Service of the fame Barons to us and our Heirs with their Ships, as aforefaid, to be done, by any Officer or Minifter of us or of our Heirs from henceforth may be taken, attached or arrefted in any wife. We have granted [b] moreover to the aforefaid Barons and good Men, that they, their Heirs and Succeffors, and other Refidents whofoever, their Heirs and Succeffors, within the Ports and Members aforefaid, Contributors [b], or which fhall be Contributors [b], to the Service and Shipping aforefaid, may for ever be quit of all Aids, Subfidies [c], Contributions, Tallages and Scots [d] whatfoever, which from them, or any of them, by reafon of their Lands, Tenements [e] and Rents, or their Goods and Chattels,

ANNOTATIONS.

[a] *Upon the Sea.* The Inhabitants and Refciants of the Ports and Members were not wont (according to this Charter, and the Ufage there long before) to be impreffed to ferve at Sea in the Royal Navy, other than in the Service of their Fifty feven Ships aforefaid. Nor yet were any to be drawn out of the Ports to ferve in the Wars at Land longer than the King himfelf abides perfonally in the Field, nor by the old Cuftoms are any of the Ports to be fent to any foreign Wars, though the King himfelf go in Perfon. The firft Attempt, that I find, ufed to break this Privilege was *Anno* 15 *Henry* VIII. when Sir *Edward Guldeford*, Knight, then but Deputy Warden, commanded certain Men out of every Port to go to the Wars beyond Sea, and about that Time were Seamen impreffed; fince which, this latter hath been ufed when the Ports Ships are not to be fet out; but the other, though endeavoured *Anno* 1639. againft the *Scots* (as at fome other Times) have been, upon the Ports Petition, fuperfeded.

[b] *We have granted.* This Grant, to be free of Aids, Subfidies, &c. by King *Edward* IV. is no more new, than fome other Things before fo mentioned, for it is expreffed in a Writ of King *Edward* VI. under his Privy Seal, bearing Date *March* 18, in the firft Year of his Reign, directed to the Treafurer and Barons of his *Exchequer, That the Barons, Inhabitants and Refciants of the Five Ports, and of all and fingular Members of the fame, and to the fame, or any of them, by any means united, annexed or belonging, or which have been known, reputed or taken as part and parcel or Members of the faid Five Ports, have ever, Time out of mind, claimed, and have enjoyed, to be quit and free, amongft other Things, from and the Payment of all and all manner of Quinzifmes, Difmes and Subfidies, to us, our late Father, or any our Predeceffors, granted by*

* And not only K. R. II. in the 6th and 9th Years of his Reign, by his Writs to the Collectors of his 10th and 15th, certifies the Freedom of the Ports from Payment thereof, but long before,

Act of Parliament, or otherwife, as well for their own Perfons, as for their Goods and Chattels, Lands and Tenements, within the faid Five Ports and Members of the fame, or elfewhere, within any other Place or Places without the fame Ports and Members, &c [e].

[b] Contributors or contributing, as before.

[c] *Subfidies,* an Aid or Affiftance, Tax or Tribute, affeffed by Parliament, and granted by the Commons there, to be levied of every Subject according to the Value of his Lands or Goods, moft commonly after the Rate of Four Shillings in the Pound for Land, and Two Shillings and Eight Pence for Goods, &c †.

[d] *Scots.* So have I feen it rendred, and accordingly tranflated it here, and in other Places; but properly *Quota's* fignifies *Portions* or *Proportions* of any greater Sum to be raifed in the whole.

[e] *Tenements,* from *Teneo,* to hold, under which Lands, Offices, Rents, Commons, &c. may pafs and be included.

Anno 9 K. H. III. Clauf. Rot. Mem. 14. *the Collectors then were commanded to receive none of the Lowye of Pevenfey, which then was of the Liberty of Hafting.* † *One Subfidy amounted to about* 70000 l.

[f] *Exact;*

CHARTERS.

tallorum fuprum, feu alicujus ipforum, quæ jam habeant, & ex
nunc fint habituri, per nos feu
hæredes noftros, aut Ballivos feu
Miniftros noftros feu hæredum
noftrorum, exigi deberent feu poffunt, fi prædicta conceffio eis facta
minime extitiffet. Et quod quandocunque communitates comitatum regni noftri Angliæ, aut
cives & burgenfes civitatum &
burgorum dict. comitatum ipfius
regni decimam, quintamdeci-
mam, feu aliam quotam vel tax-
am quamcunque, de bonis fuis
mobilibus, aut terris, tenementis feu redditibus fuis, nobis, hæred. feu fucceforibus noftris,
qualitercunque conceferunt; feu
nos vel hæred. noftri decima noftra per Angliam fecerimus taliari, Barones prædicti, eorum hæred. & fucceffores, ac Portus &
Membra prædicta, terras, tenementa, ac bona & catalla Baronum

TRANSLATION.

tels, or of any of them, which
now they may have, and from
henceforth may have, by us or
our Heirs, or the Bailiffs or Minifters of us or our Heirs, ought
or might be exacted [f], if the
aforefaid Grant to them had not
been made. And that whenfoever the Commonalties [g] of the
Counties of our Kingdom of
England, or the Citizens [h] and
Burgeffes [i] of the Cities [j] and
Boroughs [k] of the faid Counties
of the fame Kingdom, have
granted a Tenth [l], Fifteenth [m],
or other Scot or Tax [n] whatfoever, of their moveable Goods,
or their Lands, Tenements or
Rents, to us, our Heirs or Succeffors, in any wife; or we or
our Heirs fhall make to be taxed [o] our Tenths throughout
England, the Barons aforefaid,
their Heirs and Succeffors, and
the Ports and Members aforefaid,
the Lands, Tenements, and the
Goods and Chattels of the aforefaid

ANNOTATIONS.

[f] *Exacted*, asked or demanded.

[g] *Commonalties*, here taken ftrictly for the Knights of the Shire elected to fit and ferve in Parliament, reprefenting the Commonalty or Common People of the Counties for which they are
fo elected.

[h] *Citizens*, thefe are they which are elected to ferve in Parliament for Cities.

[i] *Burgeffes*, fuch as are elected to ferve there for Borough Towns; and by this Term are all
the others alfo called Burgeffes; neverthelefs thofe chofen for the Ports are fometimes called Barons: Thefe three Sorts, of Knights, Citizens and Burgeffes, make up the Houfe of Commons,
or Lower Houfe of Parliament, and are all equally and alike privileged in voting and acting
there, though called by thefe diftinct Names.

[j] *Cities*. A City is fuch a Burgh or Borough incorporate as hath or hath had a Bifhop.

[k] *Boroughs*, a Burgh or Burough, alfo wrote Borough and Borow, is a Town that fendeth
Burgeffes to the Parliament: Of old it was taken for one of thofe Companies of Ten that were
Pledge one for another. *Bowboe* in the *Saxon* Tongue fignifying a *Pledge*.

[l] *Tenth*, not taken here for Tithes, nor yet for that yearly Portion of Tribute which all Ecclefiaftical Livings now yield to the King; but for a Tax or Tribute granted by Parliament to be
levied of the Temporalty out of Cities and Boroughs in the Name of a tenth Part of their Goods
and Moveables.

[m] *Fifteenth*, a Tribute or Impofition of Money laid by Parliament upon every City, Borough,
and other Town through the Realm; not by the Poll, but upon the whole City or Town;
called a Fifteenth, becaufe it amounts to one fifteenth Part of that which the City or Town
hath been valued at of old. That now commonly called the Fifteenth is truly, and was anciently called *The Tenth and Fifteenth*; for the Tenth being fuch part of the Tax as was levied out
of Cities and Boroughs, the Fifteenth was the Refidue of the whole Tax, originally and properly due out of the Uplandifh and Country Towns and Villages, as a fifteenth Part of their
Goods and Moveables, abating out of the faid Tenth and Fifteenth Six Thoufand Pounds, according to the general Commiffion of King *Henry* VI. in refpect of the Poverty of fundry decayed Cities and Towns. *Coke* faith it was anciently Twenty nine Thoufand Pounds or thereabouts.

[n] *Tax*, a general Word for any Affeffment or Tribute laid upon the Subject.

[o] *Taxed*. The old Verb *Talio*, from whence *Taliari* in the Infinitive Mood of the Paffive
Voice, is now grown obfolete. I take it properly to fignify the rating or affeffing any Tallage.

Y   [p] Shall

CHARTERS.

num, hæredum & succefforum suorum, ac aliorum refidentium prædictorum, & eorum cujuflibet, five infra libertatem dictorum Portuum & Membrorum fuerint, five extra in com. Kanc. & Suffex, ad opus noftrum vel hæredum noftrorum non taxentur, nec aliquid de decimis, quintifdecimis, & aliis quotis feu tallagiis prædictis quoquomodo, ad opus noftrum vel hæredum noftrorum levetur; nec iidem Barones, hæred. feu succeffores sui, aut alii refidentes prædicti, in terris, tenementis, feu bonis suis prædictis, hiis occafionibus diftringantur, moleftentur, in aliquo feu graventur; fed quod ipfi, eorum hæredes & succeffores de omnimodis decimis, quintifdecimis & aliis quotis & tallagiis hujufmodi imperpetuum fint quieti, licet ipfi fint hujufmodi conceffionibus partes agentes, vel eorum aliquis pars agens five concedens. Et ulterius conceffimus pro nobis & hæred. noftris præfatis Baronibus & probis hominibus, quod nullus eorum aut hæred. feu succeffor. fuorum de cætero ponatur in aliquibus affifis, juratis, recognitionibus, attinctis, feu aliis inquifitionibus quibufcunque extra Portus & Membra prædicta, licet tangunt nos vel hæredes noftros; nec

TRANSLATION.

faid Barons, their Heirs and Succeffors, and other Refidents, and every of them, whether within the Liberty of the faid Ports and Members they fhall be, or without in the Counties of *Kent* and *Suffex*, to the Ufe of us or of our Heirs fhall not [p] be taxed, nor any Thing of the Tenths, Fifteenths, and other Scots or Tallages aforefaid whatfoever, to the Ufe of us or of our Heirs fhall be levied; nor the fame Barons, their Heirs or Succeffors, or other the Refidents aforefaid, in their Lands, Tenements, or Goods aforefaid, by thefe Occafions fhall be diftrained [q], molefted, or in any Thing grieved [r]; but that they, their Heirs and Succeffors, of all manner of Tenths, Fifteenths, and other fuch Scots and Tallages for ever may be quit, although [f] they may be Parties Agents [s], or fome one of them part Agents [s], or granting to fuch Grants. And further we have granted for us and our Heirs to the aforefaid Barons and good Men, that none of them, or their Heirs or Succeffors, from henceforth may be put in any Affizes, Juries, Recognitions, Attaints [t], or other Inquifitions [u] whatfoever without the Ports and Members aforefaid, although they touch us or our Heirs; nor

ANNOTATIONS.

[p] *Shall not* or may not be taxed; for *fhall* may be read *may.*

[q] *Diftrained,* fee afterward.

[r] *Grieved* or burdened, as Men under a Weight or heavy Load.

[f] *Although.* The Ports Burgeffes confenting to fuch Taxes in Parliament fhall not bar them.

[s] *Agent,* doing or doers.

[t] *Attaints.* Attaint is fometimes taken for convict by Judgment; for if a Man have committed Treafon, Felony, &c. and thereof hath been indicted, arraigned, found guilty, and hath Judgment thereupon, he is faid to be Attaint. So fome Award in nature of a Judgment in the higher Courts is called an Attainder, that is, fuch as takes, overtakes, touches or ftains the Party. In inferior Courts it is taken fometimes for a Writ of falfe Judgment, and here for a Writ that lieth where a falfe Verdict is given in a Court of Record upon an Iffue joined by the Parties Subjects, whereby the petty Jury are, as it were, *tinctus,* ftained with Perjury.

[u] *Inquifitions.* A general Word for the Inquiries made by Juries, from whence they are called Inquefts or Enquefts.

CHARTERS.

nec quod fit neque fiat affeffor, taxator feu collector decimarum, quintarum-decimarum, aut alicujus inde parcellæ feu aliorum fubfidiorum, tallagiorum, taxarum feu quotarum quarumcunque, nobis aut hæred. noftris concefs. five concedend. nec collector rationabilis auxilii ad primogenitum filium noftrum & hæredum noftrorum militem faciend. aut ad primogenitam filiam noftram vel hæredum noftrorum maritand. nec eorum aliquis ordinetur feu affignetur Conftabularius, Ballivus, aut alius Officiarius feu Minifter nofter aut hæredum noftrorum, extra Portus & Membra prædicta contra voluntatem fuam: Et in cafu quod aliquis prædictorum Baronum, proborum hominum, aut hæred. vel fucceflorum fuorum, ad aliquid onerum, officiorum five occupationum prædictorum, vel ad aliquid aliud officium fubeund. faciend. vel occupand. de cætero eligatur, ordinetur aut affignetur contra vim, formam & efficaciam præfentis conceffionis noftræ, quanquam ipfe officia five onera illa fubire, facere vel occupare recufaverit, ipfe tamen ea occafione finem, contemptum, forisfactur. deperditum vel dampnatum aliquid in corpore feu bonis fuis nullatenus incurrat; fed

TRANSLATION.

nor that he be nor be made Affeffor [v], Taxor [w] or Collector [x] of the Tenths, Fifteenths, or of any Parcel thereof, or of other Subfidies, Tallages, Taxes or Scots whatfoever, granted or to be granted to us or to our Heirs, nor Collector of the reafonable Aid to make the firft born Son of us and our Heirs Knight, or to marry the firft born Daughter [y] of us or our Heirs; nor any of them fhall be ordained or affigned Conftable [z], Bailiff, or other Officer [a] or Minifter of us or of our Heirs, without the Ports and Members aforefaid againft their Will: And in cafe that any of the aforefaid Barons, good Men, or their Heirs or Succeffors, to any [b] of the Charges [c], Offices or Occupations [d] aforefaid, or to any other Office, may for the Time to come be elected, ordained or affigned to undergo, do or occupy againft the Force, Form and Effect [e] of this our prefent Grant, although he thofe Offices or Charges to undergo, do or occupy, fhall refufe, notwithftanding he by that Occafion may incur by no means any Fine, Contempt, Forfeiture, Lofs or Damage in his Body or Goods; but

ANNOTATIONS.

[v] *Affeffor*, one that fets the Rates or Proportions of a Tax or Scot to be paid upon feveral Perfons, Lands or Goods.

[w] *Taxor*, the fame with Affeffor.

[x] *Collector*, one that gathers up or receives the Tax or Scot fo affeffed.

[y] *Firft born Daughter*. Here I have deviated from the printed Copy, and followed the old Copy both in the *Latin* and *Englifh*, for there it is *primogenitam filiam noftram*, and not *primogenitum filium noftrum*, as in the printed Copy.

[z] *Conftable*. Taken here for the ordinary Officer of the Hundred or Divifion thereof, as the High Conftable or Petty Conftable.

[a] *Other Officer*, as Headborough, Borfholder, Tything-Man, &c.

[b] *Any*, for *aliquid* in the printed Copy is *aliquod* in both Places in the old Copy.

[c] *Charges* or Burdens, the Word *Onus* implying both.

[d] *Occupations*, here taken for Imployment or Exercife of the Offices aforefaid; but properly Occupation, now taken for a Poffeffion of a Freehold, whether lawful or unlawful, of old denoted a putting one out of his Freehold in Time of War and poffeffing it, that is to fay, an unlawful Poffeffion of that kind.

[e] *Effect* for Efficacy; and *p*. 84. *l*. 9. in both which Places it was *Effect* in the old Copies.

[f] *Plaæ*

CHARTERS.

TRANSLATION.

fed quod præfentes literæ noftræ per eum coram quibufcunque Jufticiariis & Miniftris noftris & hæred. noftrorum in quocunque loco de recordo per totum regnum noftrum Angliæ demonftrat. fuper demonftrationem illam in fuis robore permaneant & efficacia, & eis allocentur abfque aliquo brevi feu proceffu inde ulterius profequend. Et quod quandocunque contigerit aliquas inquifitiones coram Conftabulario noftro Caftri noftri Dover. aut Cuftode Quinque Portuum prædictorum vel Admirallo eo-rundem *, inquifitiones hujufmodi habeantur, capiantur & fiant infra illum Portum, five

but that thefe our prefent Letters by him fhewn before whatfoever the Juftices and Minifters of us and our Heirs in whatfoever Place of Record [f] throughout our whole Realm of *England*, upon that fhewing they fhall remain in their Strength and Efficacy [g], and be allowed to them without any Writ [g] or Procefs [h] thereupon further to be profecuted: And that whenfoever there fhall happen any Inquifitions before our Conftable of our Caftle of *Dover*, or Warden of the *Cinque Ports* aforefaid, or Admiral of the fame *, fuch Inquifitions may be had, taken and made within that Port [i], or

Here I find both the printed Copy, and fome of the Exemplifications different from feveral old Copies, and, as I prefume, the Charter it felf of K. Ed. IV. in leaving out the Words following, viz. to follow next after Admirallo eorundem [aut aliujus eorum locuntenente feu deputato, vigore vel virtute literarum, brevis, aut brevium noftrum vel hæredum noftrorum, vel virtute officii ad fectam noftram vel hæredium noftrorum, feu ad fectam partis infra Portus & Membra prædicta capi, fieri vel haberi, tunc volumus, & per præfentes concedimus pro nobis & hæredibus noftris, quod omnes] *in Englifh thus* [or any Lieutenant or Deputy of them, by force or virtue of Letters, Writ, or Writs of us or our Heirs, or by virtue of their Office at the Suit of us or our Heirs, or at the Suit of any Party within the Ports and Members aforefaid to be taken, made or had, then we will, and by thefe Prefents grant for us and our Heirs, that all] *which if they be omitted makes not this Claufe in the Charter to run fo fmooth as others, but more harfh in the conftruing, and chufed in the Senfe of what was hereby intended; and this makes me conclude, that every latter Exemplification or Confirmation of the old Charter being tranfcribed by the foregoing, when once omitted it became omitted in all the reft for want of Retrofpection into the former Confirmations or the Charter it felf.*

ANNOTATIONS.

[f] *Place of Record* or Court of Record.

[g] *Writ.* A Writ contains a brief Declaration of the Caufe of a Suit, and from hence came the Name *breve:* They are original or judicial; original, according to the Nature of the Action, *viz.* real, perfonal or mix'd.

[h] *Procefs*, becaufe proceeding out of fome Court, or from fome Judge or Juftice; a general Term for all Writs, Summons, Warrants, &c.

[i] *Within that Port.* The Ports Men of one Town are not to be drawn out, though to another of the Ports, for the taking of fuch Inquifitions, nor were they before the making of this Charter; but Inquifitions of this kind were taken where the Jury Men lived, though for the King: And I have feen the Record of an Inquifition taken for the King in the Thirteenth Year of King *Henry* VI. before *Galfrido Louthun*, then Lieutenant of *Dover* Caftle, at *Winchelfea*, by Writ from the King directed to the Conftable of the Caftle of *Dover*, &c. to inquire touching the Cuftoms of Ships and Fifhing Boats on the Sea, called Shares, and the Cuftoms called Anchorage and Bulgate: And I have known the like taken in other Ports, and can produce the Prefidents. Neverthelefs, as well fince the making of this Charter, as before, fome of the Officers of the Caftle have fometimes iffued forth their Mandates to call the Ports Men from the Places where they dwell to ferve in Juries, which, perhaps through Ignorance, fome Ports Men have yielded to; yet have the Ports Men always looked on it as a Grievance, and in fit Seafon complained thereof; and fometimes denied Obedience to fuch Mandates, as, among other Inftances, appears in this following, which I tranfcribed out of the Records of *Winchelfea*, and have here tranflated thus:

HUmfridus, dux Buck. Conftabularius Caftri Dovorr. & Cuftos Quinque Portuum, Majori & Ballivo de Wynchelfe, falutem. Virtute officii noftri Cuftode Quinque Portum prædictorum vobis mandamus quod venire faciatis corporaliter coram nobis feu locum noftrum tenente apud ecclefiam fancti Jacobi Dovorr. xxvii^{mo}. die

HUmfry, Duke of *Buckingham*, Conftable of the Caftle of *Dover*, and Warden of the *Cinque Ports*, To the Mayor and Bailiff of *Winchelfea*, Greeting. By virtue of our Office of Wardenfhip of the *Cinque Ports* aforefaid, to you we command, that you make to come corporally before us or our Lieutenant, at the Church of St. *James* in *Dover* the 27th Day

ANNOTATIONS.

die Januarii proximo futuro, xviii. bonos & legales homines, de melioribus & difcretioribus combaronibus villæ veſtræ prædictæ, quorum Ricardus Hawly, Robertus Moris, Robertus Raawod, Willielmus Buckherſt, Stephanus Sevenoke & Laurentius Bryce, ſix eſſe volumus, ad inquirendum & veritatem dicendum de & ſuper certis articulis Officium noſtrum Cuſtod. Quinque Portuum prædictorum tangent. Et habeatis tunc ibidem hoc mandatum, nobis ſeu locum noſtrum tenenti de executione ejuſdem ſub ſigilliis veſtris diſtinctè & aperte certificant. Et hoc ſub pœna ducent. libraium & periculi incumbent. nullatenus omittatis, pro qua quidem pœna Domino noſtro Regi & nobis reſpondere volueritis. Dat. apud Caſtrum prædictum ſub ſigillo Officij noſtri ibidem xiiiº die Januarij, Anno Regni Regis Henrici ſexti xxxviᵗʰ.

SEreniſſimo principi & domino, domino Humfrido duci Bucks, cuſtodi Quinque Portuum & conſervatori libertatum & liberarum conſuetudinum eorundem, ſeu ejus locum tenenti, Nos Major & Balliuus Domini noſtri Regis villæ ſuæ de Wynchelſe ſignificamus, quod cum inter cæteras libertates & liberas conſuetudines, per cartas noſtras per dictum Dominum Regem & ſuos nobiliſſimos progenitores, dudum Angliæ Reges, Baronibus Quinque Portuum conceſſas, & per eoſdem Barones, anteceſſores & prædeceſſores ſuos a tempore immemorato, cujus contrarii memoria non exiſtit, uſitatas, prædicti Barones uſi fuerunt, debuerunt & conſueverunt, quod ipſi ad quaſcunque Inquiſitiones captas ad inquirend. & veritat. dicend. de & ſuper aliquibus articulis Officium Cuſtodiæ tangent. coram Domino Cuſtod. Quinque Portuum pro tempore exiſtente, in Curia de Shipweya, & non alibi, impanellati fuerunt, debuerunt, ac conſueverunt, nec pro aliquibus hujuſmodi articulis Officium Cuſtodiæ eorundem Quinque Portuum tangent. alibi quam in prædicta Curia de Shipweya impanellari ſeu venire debent neque tenentur, prout prædictæ Cartæ & liberæ conſuetudines eorundem Quinque Portuum rationalibit. teſtantur ; qua-propt. ad venire faciend. corporaliter coram vobis ſeu locumtenente veſtro, ad diem & locum infra contentos, xviii. homines, prout per mandatum veſtrum nobis mandat. habere, non debemus nec tenemur contra tenorem cartarum & conſuetudinum prædictar. propter enervationem libertatum & liber. conſuetud. Portuum prædict. Quapropter humiliime ſupplicamus quod placeat celſitudini & graciofæ Dominationi Domini noſtri Ducis prædicti, Cuſtodis Quinque Portuum, & Conſervatoris libertatum & conſuetudinum eorundem, graciofe conſiderare, quod placuit Dominationi veſtræ in prima Curia de Shipweya coram vobis tenta, per ſacramentum veſtrum Domino Regi Angliæ præſtitum, & militiam veſtram, publice declarare & pronunciare, quod omnes libertates, uſus & conſuetudines Quinque Portuum pro poſſe veſtro inviolat. ſervaretis & manuteneretis. Idcirco humiliime ſupplicamus quod prædictas libertates & conſuetudines in omnibus conſervetis & manuteneatis, juxta vim, formam & effectum prædictarum Cartarum & conſuetud. Portuum prædictorum.

Day of *January* next to come, eighteen good and lawful Men, of the better and more diſcreet Combarons of your Town aforeſaid, of whom *Richard Hawly, Robert Moris, Robert Rawwod, William Buckherſt, Steven Sevenoke*, and *Laurence Bryce*, we will to be ſix, to inquire and truth to ſpeak of and upon certain Articles touching our Office of Warden of the *Cinque Ports* aforeſaid. And have ye then there this Mandate, certifying to us or our Lieutenant of the Execution thereof, under your Seals diſtinctly and plainly. And this under the Penalty of two hundred Pounds, and the Peril incumbent, by no means ye omit, for which Penalty ye will anſwer to our Lord the King and us. Dated at the Caſtle aforeſaid, under the Seal of our Office there, the 13ᵗʰ Day of *January*, in the Year of the Reign of King *Henry* the Sixth the 36ᵗʰ.

TO the moſt excellent Prince and Lord, the Lord *Humphry* Duke of *Bucks*, Warden of the *Cinque Ports*, and Conſerver of the Liberties and free Cuſtoms of the ſame, or to his Lieutenant, We the Mayor and Bailiff of our Lord the King of his Town of *Winchelſea* ſignify, that whereas among other Libert es and free Cuſtoms by our Charters by our ſaid Lord the King and his moſt noble Progenitors, late Kings of *England*, granted to the Barons of the *Cinque Ports*, and by the ſame Barons, their Anceſtors and Predeceſſors time out of mind, the contrary whereof Memory is not, uſed, the aforeſaid Barons have uſed, ought and were wont, that they to whatſoever Inquiſitions taken, to inquire, and Truth to ſpeak of, and upon any Articles touching the Office of Wardenſhip, before the Lord Warden of the *Cinque Ports* for the time being, in the Court of *Shepway*, and not elſewhere, have been, ought, and were wont to be impanelled ; nor for any ſuch Articles touching the Office of Wardenſhip of the ſame *Cinque Ports*, other where than in the aforeſaid Court of *Shepway*, ought nor are bound to be impanelled, or to come, as the aforeſaid Charters, and free Cuſtoms of the ſame *Cinque Ports* do reaſonably teſtify ; wherefore to make to come corporally before you or your Lieutenant, at the Day and Place within contained, the 18 Men, as by your Mandate to us is commanded to have, we ought not nor are bound againſt the Tenor of the Charters and Cuſtoms aforeſaid, becauſe of the weakening of the Liberties and free Cuſtoms of the Ports aforeſaid. Wherefore moſt humbly we pray, that it may pleaſe the Highneſs and gracious Lordſhip of our Lord the Duke aforeſaid, Warden of the *Cinque Ports*, and Conſerver of the Liberties and Cuſtoms of the ſame, graciouſly to conſider, that it pleaſed your Lordſhip, in the firſt Court of *Shepway* held before you, by your Oath taken to our Lord the King of *England*, and by your Knighthood, publickly to declare and pronounce, that all the Liberties, Uſages and Cuſtom of the *Cinque Ports*, according to your Power, you would keep and maintain inviolately. Therefore moſt humbly we beſeech, that the aforeſaid Liberties and Cuſtoms in all things you may conſerve and maintain, according to the Force, Form and Effect of the aforeſaid Charters and Cuſtoms of the Ports aforeſaid.

CHARTERS.

five Membrum Portuum & Membrorum prædictorum, ubi illi de Portubus & Membris illis, per quos Inquifitiones illæ captæ erunt, morantur & refident, & non alibi; quodque ipfi Inquifitionibus prædictis pofiti & impannellati ad onus fuum capiend. vel veredictum fuum dicend. Portum five Membrum hujufmodi exire vel aliquem alium locum adire non teneantur, compellantur, neque arctentur quoquomodo; nec ea occafione contemptum, amerciamentum, pœnam, forisfacturam feu deperditum aliquod erga nos vel hæredes noftros incurrant, nec eorum aliquis incurrat quovifmodo. Quare volumus & firmiter præcipimus pro nobis & hæred. noftris, quod prædicti Barones & probi homines Portuum prædictorum, hæredes & fucceffores fui, habeant omnes & fingulas libertates & quietaneias prædictas, ac omnia præmiffa per nos eifdem de novo conceffa, & eis & eorum quolibet futuris temporibus abfque impedimento noftri vel hæredum noftrorum vel miniftrorum noftrorum quorumcunque gaudeant & utantur imperpetuum. His teftibus, venerabili præfule Tho. Archiepifcopo Cantuar'. totius Angliæ Primate, Charif-

TRANSLATION.

or Member of the Ports and Members aforefaid, where thofe of the Ports and their Members, by whom thofe Inquifitions fhall be taken, are abiding [i] and refident, and not elfewhere; and that they which are put and impannelled [k] in the Inquifitions aforefaid, to take their Charge [l], or to give their Verdict [m], may not be bound, compelled nor conftrained [n] in any wife to go out of fuch Port or Member, or to go to any other Place; nor by that Occafion may they incur [o], nor any of them incur in any wife any Contempt [p], Amerciament, Penalty, Forfeiture or Lofs towards us or our Heirs. Wherefore we will and firmly command, for us and our Heirs, that the aforefaid Barons and good Men of the Ports aforefaid, their Heirs and Succeffors, may have all and fingular the Liberties and Freedoms aforefaid, and all the Premiffes by us to them of new granted, and them and every of them in times to come [q], without Impediment of us or our Heirs, or of our Minifters whatfoever, they may enjoy and ufe for ever. Witneffes to thefe Prefents [r], the venerable Prelate [r], Thomas [s] Archbifhop of *Canterbury* [u], Primate of all *England*; our

ANNOTATIONS.

[i] *Are abiding*, or do dwell and refide.

[k] *Impannelled.* So called from *Pannellum* or *Panellum*, ufed for a little Piece of Parchment whereon the Names of the Jurors are wrote, annexed to the Writ and returned with it.

[l] *Charge.* The Articles or Particulars the Jury is charged to enquire of.

[m] *Give their Verdict*, or render their Verdict; which is the Anfwer of a Jury or Inqueft made upon any Caufe committed by the Court to their Confideration or Trial. It is two fold, General or Special, and called Verdict, *q. f. dictum veritatis*, a declaration or faying of the Truth.

[n] *Conftrained* or forced.

[o] *Incur*, or run into; and fo before and afterward.

[p] *Contempt.* Refufal to obey fuch Command fhall be no Contempt of Authority.

[q] *Times to come*, or time to come.

[r] *Witneffes to thefe Prefents*, or thefe being Witneffes; and fo it may be rendered, p. 37.

[r] *Prelate.* Inftead of *Præfule* in the printed Copy, which I here follow, the old Copies have *Patre*; and the Word Father is commonly the Title of Bifhops.

[s] *Thomas.* This was *Thomas Bourchier* then Archbifhop of *Canterbury*.

[u] *Canterbury.* The chief City in *Kent*, to which the Archbifhoprick was gotten from *London* by *Auftin*, contrary to the Epiftle of Pope *Gregory* himfelf.

[w] *Richard.*

CHARTERS.

Chariffimis Fratribus noftris Georgio Clarenciæ & Richardo Glouc. Ducibus, venerabilibus patribus Geo. Exon. Cancellario noftro Angliæ, & T. London. Epifcopis, & Ricardo Warr. & Sarum, & Johanne Northumber. Comitibus, Confanguineis noftris chariffimis, nec non dilectis & fidelibus noftris Magiftro Roberto Stillington, Cuftode privati Sigilli noftri, & Waltero Blunt Milite. Thefaur. noftro Angliæ, & aliis. Dat' per manum noftram apud Weftm. vicefimo tertio die Martii, Anno Regni noftri quinto. Nos autem Cartas & Literas prædictas, ac omnia & fingula in eifdem contenta rata habentes, & grata ea pro nobis & hæred. noftris, quantum in nobis eft, acceptamus & approbamus; ac dilectis nobis nunc Baronibus & probis hominibus dictorum Quinque Portuum & Membrorum fuorum, & corum hæredibus & fucceforibus, tenore præfentium ratificamus & confirmamus, prout cartæ & literæ prædictæ rationabiliter teftantur. In cujus rei teftimonium has literas noftras fieri fecimus patentes. Tefte me ipfo apud Weftm. tertio decimo die Decembris, Anno Regni noftri tertio. Nos autem cartas & literas prædictas, ac omnia & fingula in eifdem contenta rata habentes, & grata

TRANSLATION.

our moft dear Brothers, *George* of *Clarence*, and *Richard* [w] of *Gloucefter*, Dukes; the venerable Fathers, *George* of *Exeter* [x] our Chancellor of *England*, and *T.* of *London* [x], Bifhops; and *Richard* of *Warwick* [y], and *Salisbury*, and *John* of *Northumberland* [z], Earls, our moft dear Coufins; alfo our beloved and faithful Mafter *Robert Stillington*, Keeper of our Privy-Seal, and *Walter Blunt* Knight, our Treafurer of *England*, and others. Dated by our Hand at *Weftminfter*, the twenty third Day of *March*, in the fifth Year [a] of our Reign. And we [b] the Charters and Letters aforefaid, and all and fingular in the fame contained, having ratified, and freely the fame for us and our Heirs, as much as in us is, do accept and approve; and to our beloved the now Barons and good Men of the faid *Cinque Ports* and their Members, and to their Heirs and Succeffors, by the Tenor of thefe Prefents, we do ratify and confirm, as the Charters and Letters aforefaid do reafonably teftify. In witnefs whereof we have made thefe our Letters Patents. Witnefs my felf at *Weftminfter*, the thirteenth Day of *December*, in the third Year of our Reign. And we [c] the Charters and Letters aforefaid, and all and fingular in the fame contained, having ratified, and freely

& Membrorum fuorum, ac corum hæred. & fucceff.

ANNOTATIONS.

[w] *Richard.* He afterwards ufurped the Crown by the Name of King *Richard* III.

[x] *London.* The chief City in *England*, though fpoiled by *Auftin* the Monk of the Archbifhoprick, yet remains an Epifcopal See in Place next the two Archbifhops; and though here the Bifhop of *Exeter* be named before him, it was becaufe he was Lord Chancellor.

[y] *Warwick.* A Shire and City therein of the fame Name.

[z] A County in the North bordering to *Scotland*.

[a] *Fifth Year.* The Date of the Charter of King *Edward* IV. being *March* 23, *Anno* 5 of his Reign, was *Anno Domini* 1464.

[b] *And we.* Here followeth the Confirmation of King *Henry* VII. which bearing Date the 13th of *December*, in the third Year of his Reign, makes the Year of our Lord 1487.

[c] *And we.* Here followeth the Confirmation of King *Henry* VIII. whofe Date being the 4th Day of *March*, in the firft Year of his Reign, was *Anno Domini* 1509.

And

CHARTERS.

grata ea pro nobis & hæred.
noftris, quantum in nobis eft, acceptamus & approbamus ; ac dilectis nobis nunc Baronibus &
probis hominibus dictorum Quinque Portuum & Membrorum
fuorum, ac eorum hæred. & fuccefforibus, tenore præfentium ratificamus & confirmamus, prout
cartæ & literæ prædictæ rationabiliter teftantur. In cujus rei
teftimonium has literas noftras
fieri fecimus patentes. Tefte me
ipfo apud Weftm. quinto die
Martii, Anno Regni noftri primo.
Nos autem cartas & literas prædictas, ac omnia & fingula in
eifdem content. rata habentes, &
grata ea pro nobis & hæred.
noftris, quantum in nobis eft, acceptamus & approbamus; ac dilectis nunc Baronibus & probis
hominibus dictorum. Quinque
Portuum & Membrorum fuorum,
& eorum hæred. & fuccefforibus,
tenore præfentium ratificamus &
confirmamus, prout cartæ & literæ prædictæ rationabiliter teftantur. In cujus rei teftimonium
has literas noftras fieri fecimus
patentes. Tefte me ipfo apud
Weftm. vicefimo die Novembris,
Anno Regni noftri fecundo. Nos
autem cartas & literas prædictas, ac omnia & fingula in eifdem
contenta rata habentes; & grata
ea pro nobis & hæred. noftris,
quantum in nobis eft, acceptamus
& approbamus ; ac dilectis nobis
nunc Baronibus & probis hominibus dictorum Quinque Portuum
& Membrorum fuorum, ac eorum
hæred. & fuccefforibus) tenore
                   præfentium

TRANSLATION.

freely the fame for us and our
Heirs, as much as in us is, do
accept and approve ; and to our
beloved the now Barons and
good Men of the faid *Cinque
Ports* and their Members, and
to their Heirs and Succeffors, by
the Tenor of thefe Prefents, we
do ratify and confirm, as the
Charters and Letters aforefaid
do reafonably teftify. In witnefs
whereof thefe our Letters we
have made Patents. Witnefs my
felf at *Weftminfter*, the fifth Day
of *March*, in the firft Year of
our Reign. And we ᵈ the Charters and Letters aforefaid, and
all and fingular in the fame contained, having ratified, and freely the fame for us and our Heirs,
as much as in us is, do accept
and approve ; and to our beloved
the now Barons and good Men
of the faid *Cinque Ports* and
their Members, and to their
Heirs and Succeffors, by the
Tenor of thefe Prefents, we do
ratify and confirm, as the Charters and Letters aforefaid do
reafonably teftify. In witnefs
whereof thefe our Letters we
have made Patents. Witnefs
my felf at *Weftminfter*, the
twentieth Day of *November*, in
the fecond Year of our Reign.
And we ᵉ the Charters and Letters aforefaid, and all and fingular in the fame contained, having
ratified, and freely the fame for
us and our Heirs, as much as in
us is, do accept and approve ;
and to our beloved the now
Barons and good Men of the faid
Cinque Ports and their Members, and to their Heirs and Succeffors, by the Tenor of thefe
                   Prefents,

ANNOTATIONS.

ᵈ *And we.* Here followeth the Confirmation of King *Edward* VI. The Date whereof is
the 20ᵗʰ Day of *November,* in the fecond Year of his Reign, that is, *Anno Domini* 1548.
ᵉ *And we.* Here followeth the Confirmation of Queen *Mary,* bearing Date the 27ᵗʰ Day of
October, in the firft Year of her Reign, that was, *Anno Domini* 1553.

                                       ᶠ *And*

CHARTERS.

præfentium ratificamus & confirmamus, prout cartæ & literæ prædictæ rationabiliter teftantur. In cujus rei teftimonium has literas noftras fieri fecimus patentes. Tefte me ipfo apud Weftm. vicefimo feptimo die Octobris, anno regni noftri primo. Nos autem cartas & literas prædictas, ac omnia & fingula in eifdem contenta, rata habentes, & grata ea pro nobis & hæred. noftris, quantum in nobis eft, acceptamus & approbamus; ac dilectis nobis nunc Baronibus & probis hominibus dictorum Quinque Portuum & Membrorum fuorum, ac eorum hæred. & fuccefforibus, tenore præfentium ratificamus & confirmamus, prout cartæ & literæ prædictæ rationabiliter teftantur. In cujus rei teftimonium has literas noftras fieri fecimus patentes. Tefte me ipfo apud Weftm. octavo die Martii, anno regni noftri primo. Infpeximus etiam alias literas patentes dictæ dominæ nuper Reginæ Elizabethæ, de conceffionibus Baronibus dictorum Quinque Portuum & villarum de Rye and Winchelfea, & Membrorum eorundem Portuum & villarum, & eorum cujuflibet, & fuccefforibus fuis Baronibus dictorum Quinque Portuum, villarum & membrorum, fact. in hæc verba:

TRANSLATION.

Prefents we do ratify and confirm, as the Charters and Letters aforefaid do reafonably teftify. In witnefs whereof thefe our Letters we have made Patents. Witnefs My felf at *Weftminfter*, the twenty feventh Day of *October*, in the firft Year of our Reign. And we [f] the Charters and Letters aforefaid, and all and fingular in the fame contained, having ratified, and freely the fame for us and our Heirs, as much as in us is, do accept and approve; and to our beloved the now Barons and good Men of the faid *Cinque Ports* and their Members, and to their Heirs and Succeffors, by the Tenor of thefe Prefents we do ratify and confirm, as the Charters and Letters aforefaid do reafonably teftify. In witnefs whereof thefe our Letters we have made Patents. Witnefs My felf at *Weftminfter* the eighth Day of *March*, in the firft Year of our Reign. We have feen [g] alfo other Letters Patents [h] of the late Lady Queen [i] *Elizabeth*, of Grants made to the Barons of the faid *Cinque Ports* and Towns [k] of *Rye* and *Winchelfea*, and Members of the fame Ports and Towns, and every of them, and to their Succeffors, Barons of the faid *Cinque Ports*, Towns and Members, in thefe Words:

Elizabeth,

ANNOTATIONS.

[f] *And we.* Here followeth the Confirmation of Queen *Elizabeth*, which bears Date *March* 8, in the firft Year of her Reign, that was *Anno Domini* 1558.

[g] *We have feen.* This *Infpeximus* is of King *Charles* II.

[h] *Other Letters Patents.* That is, the *Englifh* Charter of Queen *Elizabeth* about the Fifteenth, which beginneth with the next Page.

[i] *Queen.* Commonly taken for the Wife of a King; but here, and in other Places of thefe Charters, for one that was fole and fovereign Governefs and Commandrefs of the Realm, without a King, but of equal Power, Authority and Majefty.

[k] *Towns.* The ancient Towns of *Rye* and *Winchelfea*, of which more hereafter in the Annotations upon that *Englifh* Charter.

CHARTERS.

Elizabeth, by the Grace of God, Queen of *England*, *France*, and *Ireland*, Defender of the Faith, &c. to the Treafurer, Chancellor¹ and Barons² of our *Exchequer*³ for the Time being, and to all other the Officers, Minifters and Subjects of us, our Heirs and Succeffors, for the Time being, or which hereafter fhall be, To whom it fhall or may appertain, and to every of them, Greeting. Whereas it appeareth unto us, by one Record remaining in our *Exchequer*, amongft the Records of the Term of *Eafter*, in the fixth Year of the Reign of our moft dear Grandfather King *Henry* the Seventh, That *John Comvers* of *Winchelfea*, and *William Warwyn* of *Dover*, Combons⁴ of the *Five Ports*, did come before the Barons of the fame *Exchequer*, the feventh Day of *May* in the fame Term of *Eafter*, in their proper Perfons, and did exhibit to the faid Court there a certain Letter of Attorney⁵, fealed with the common Seal⁶ of the Mayors, Bailiffs, Jurats and Barons of the *Five Ports*, and directed to the Treafurer and Barons of the fame *Exchequer*; the Tenor whereof followeth in thefe Words: *To the right Mighty and noble Lord* John Dynham, *Knight, Lord* Dynham, *High Treafurer*⁷ *of England; and To the full Honourable the Barons of our Sovereign Lord the King's* Exchequer *at* Weftminfter *that now is, We the Mayors, Bailiffs, Jurats and Barons of the Towns and Ports of* Hafting⁸, Winchelfea, Rye, Romney, Heth, Dover, *and* Sandwich, *at our Brotheryeeld*⁹ *General, at*
the

ANNOTATIONS.

¹ *Chancellor*, that is the *Chancellor of the Exchequer*, not the *Lord High Chancellor* of England.

² *Barons*, for the Judges of the Court of *Exchequer*, of which the Chief is called *The Lord Chief Baron*.

³ *Exchequer*, fo called, fome fay, from a *Table*, others from a *Pavement*, fometime there of Chequer Work. A Court that takes care that the Revenues and Treafure of the Crown may be duly received.

⁴ *Combons*, wrote as an Abbreviation for *Combarons* or *fellow Freemen*.

⁵ *Attorney*. An Attorney is one fet in the Turn, Place or Stead of another, and the Writing whereby he is fo appointed is called a *Letter of Attorney*.

⁶ *Common Seal* is the Seal belonging to the Corporation of Mayor, Jurats and Commonalty, or Bailiff, Jurats and Commonalty. The Mayor and Jurats, or Bailiff and Jurats, have another fmaller Seal, ferving to feal all Writs and Procefs iffuing out of the Courts holden before them; this is called *The Seal of Office*. But that called here *the Common Seal* is not either of thefe, but the Common Seal belonging to all the whole Affembly of the Corporations of the Ports in the Court of their *Brotherhood*, ferving to feal the Procefs iffuing thence, or from the Court of *Guestling*.

⁷ *High Treafurer*, becaufe there is another Officer in the faid Court of *Exchequer* called *The Under Treafurer*.

⁸ *Hafting*. Of this, and the other Towns and Ports here named, fee afterward.

⁹ *Brotheryeeld*. The *Cinque Ports* and *Two Ancient Towns* being alike and equally privileged, and under the joint Charge of Shipping (as aforefaid) to be provided according to their Charters, it could not be long but of necessity they muft enter into a joint Affociation and brotherly Community one with another (the more eafy to be effected by reafon of their Neighbourhood) becaufe whenever the Ships they were to equip were to be fitted, according to the Number commanded (which fometimes were lefs in Number than thofe mentioned in the Charters, though perhaps bigger in quantity, and fo as coftly) to be made ready, there muft be a brotherly Conference had amongft them for the Provifion thereof, and levying the Charge proportionable for the fame. And this Affembly of them is that which is now called a *Brotherhood*, formerly *Brodall*, *Brodhull* and *Brodhill*; which latter I take to be corrupt, but the former fignifies, *All Brethren, or the Hall, or Body of the Brethren*, and is the fame with that in the Charter, *Brotheryeeld*, as much as *Guilds fraternitatis* (by which *Latin* Name I have feen it called) *The Meeting together or Affembly of the Brotherhood*; *Yeeld* and Guild being one, as *Yeeldhall* and *Guildhall* in *London*, the firft only of moft Antiquity. Befides, the Staple Trade of thefe Towns confifting much in Fifhing, not only of frefh Fifh at home, but of Herring every Year in the Seafon thereof at *Yarmouth* (before mentioned) where bringing them to fhore, in the Sale and Delivery among the Multitude, divers Differences and Stirs arofe for want of a fettled Order in that Town, as was faid before, or as Tradition ftill reports, before there was any Town, or
any

ANNOTATIONS.

any other Shew of a Town than some Huts or Cabins set up near the Water side, like the Booths or Tents in a Fair, and that but during the Time of this Herring Fair there; the Ports were forced to agree and join together yearly to elect and send thither their Bailiffs (before spoken of) to abide there during the Herring Season, allowing them a certain Sum for their Expences. And the Approbation of these Bailiffs, and hearing the Reports of their Proceedings there, and the raising these Allowances, were other necessary Causes of arrearing this their Court of Brotherhood. And moreover, for joint Advice and Assistance one of another in all Emergencies, prudent Policy enforced them to acquaint each other with the State and Condition of their Affairs in relation to their Charters and Customs, and to an unanimous Defence thereof. For if any Particular of them should be impeached or invaded (they being all equally enfranchised) the Mischief might not only have been prejudicial, and so of ill Consequence to the rest in their like loss, but would have been prejudicial to the whole, who must have made good the Total of what was jointly charged on them in general to perform, though some part had been disabled to furnish his *quota* thereof. And these Things also, with others, made it necessary sometimes for these *Ports* and *Two Towns* to have conference with their Members, whereupon arose another ancient Court among them called a *Guestling*, where the Members that are corporate, as Guests invited, appear and sit with those of the *Ports* and *Ancient Towns* to consult about the general State of their Affairs; for the Members cannot raise or appoint this *Guestling* of themselves, but the *Ports* and *Two Towns*, by consent of the major part of them, can and do rear it, and call the Members together when and where they please. By the same Name of a *Guestling* I find also a Court called that consisteth but of part of the *Ports* and *Two Towns*, as suppose *Hastings*, *Winchelsea* and *Rye*, raised upon request of one of them; where by consent, and as by brotherly Invitation, they appear to agree on something necessary to their respective Towns, but not by Compulsion or Penalty; wherein in the Brotherhood, and other Guestling, if the Persons or Members of any Corporation fail to appear, the Corporation is fined to the Use of the whole Ports and Members. Of these *Brotherhoods* and *Guestlings* there are two Sorts, general and special. The general is that Court which is raised to sit at the usual Time of holding it, and appears with the full Number of Persons to be returned thither (Defaulters excepted.) The Special is summoned to sit at some unusual Time about some special Business, and with a smaller Number of Persons than the General, as perhaps but two or three of each Town. The usual Times for the General Brotherhood were formerly Two in every Year, viz. the *Tuesday* after the Close of *Easter* (where was heard the Report of the Bailiffs at *Yarmouth* the fishing Season last before.) And the *Tuesday* next after the Feast of St. *Margaret* (where the Bailiffs then to be at *Yarmouth* the next Herring Season after were approved.) Afterwards both the Reports of the one and Approbation of the other were found to be as conveniently done at the latter Brotherhood, and so this grew to be the only Brotherhood held in the Year. At the end of which Brotherhood is the general *Guestling* to begin, when one is summoned to be held. The Number of Persons to appear at these general Courts were of every Corporation of the *Ports* and *Two Towns* in the Brotherhood, Seven, viz. the Head Officer, whether Mayor or Bailiff, or else his Deputy in his stead, three of the Jurats (among which commonly the last and next Bailiff to *Yarmouth* of the Towns happening to send were part) and three of the Commoners or Freemen (of whom usually the Town Clerk and Chamberlain were two) and the like Number of Persons of every of the corporate Members were to appear, and sit with them in the general *Guestling*. But afterward by Decree of each Court the Number was reduced to five, viz. the Mayor or Bailiff, two Jurats and two Commoners. In both these Courts, the Head Officer or his Deputy of one of the *Cinque Ports*, or *Two Ancient Towns*, sat as Chief, and installed in Speeches addressed to him. Mr. *Speaker*, on each side of him sit next the other Mayors and Bailiffs, then the Bailiffs to *Yarmouth*, and below them the other Jurats, the Clerks in their Places about a Table, and the other Freemen below the Jurats. The *Speakership* goes orderly through the *Cinque Ports* and *Two Ancient Towns*, and continues a Year in each Town. It begins at *Hastings*, goeth to *Winchelsea*, so to *Rye*, then to *Romney*, &c. and after that *Sandwich* hath been *Speaker* a Year, it returns to *Hastings* again. The summoning of these Courts is thus: The Town that is *Speaker*, at the beginning of its *Speakership* (which now is the first Day of *June*, as I take it) sends a Letter to the other Ports and ancient Towns to know their Opinion, whether a *Brotherhood* and *Guestling* be necessary to be arreared that Year (upon this back-side of which every of them indorse their Answer) in such or the like Form as followeth, supposed to come from *Hastings*. ...

L Oving Brethren, Combarons and Friends, our right hearty Affections and Salutations to you presented. Whereas by supernary Revolution the *Speakership* of the Ports is now devolved upon us, we have thought meet to issue forth these our timely Letters to you, whereby we pray and brotherly require your Advice and Subscriptions, whether, as our Affairs now stand, a *Brotherhood* or *Guestling*, or either of them, is necessary to be arreared this Year. We for our Part considering, &c. [*here inserting some one or two Particulars as Causes for their assembling*] are of Opinion, and think fit, that both a *Brotherhood* and *Guestling* be summoned to meet at the Town and Port of *New Romney* in the County of *Kent*, on the *Tuesday* after the Feast of St. *Margaret* next ensuing, at the Hour accustomed: Nevertheless we submit to your grave Wisdoms and Determinations in the Premisses. And so we commit you to God, and rest,

From Hasting, under the Seal of Office of Majoralty there, the first Day of June, 1633.

Your very loving Brethren, Combarons and Friends,

The Mayor and Jurats of the Town and Port of *Hasting*, Speaker.

Upon

ANNOTATIONS.

Upon this, if by four or more of these seven Ports and Towns, one or both is thought fit to be holden, then forty Days before the Day of Meeting the Letters of Summons go forth directed, as the former, to the Mayors and Jurats only of the said *Ports* and *Ancient Towns*, if for the *Brotherhood*; and if for a *Guestling* also, then to the Mayors, Bailiffs and Jurats of them and their Members, with the like Title of *Right worshipful Sirs*, &c. (as above) to this Effect :

THAT forasmuch as by the greater Part of the Brethren of the *Cinque Ports* and *Ancient Towns* it is concluded, that a *Brotherhood* and *Guestling* be arreared this Year, these are therefore to pray and brotherly require them to be at the Time and Place appointed on the Hour accustomed (which is Eight of the Clock in the Morning) with the full Number of Persons duly returned and commissionated, according to their ancient Customs and Usages Time out of mind used and approved, &c.

At the Day of Appearance the Persons returned to fit and act in the said Courts bring with them Commissions from their respective Towns, sealed with the common Seal of their Corporation, as to the *Brotherhood* in the Form following for the Persons returned from *Rye*.

TO all Christian People to whom these Presents shall come, and especially to the right Worshipful, our loving Brethren, Combarons and Friends, the Mayors, Jurats and Combarons of the *Cinque Ports* and ancient Town of *Winchelsea* [a], to be assembled at a general *Brotherhood* to be holden at the Town and Port of *New Romney*, one of the said *Cinque Ports*, upon *Tuesday* the six and Twentieth [b] Day of *July* instant, we the Mayor, Jurats and Commonalty of the ancient Town of *Rye* in the County of *Sussex*, send Greeting. Know ye, that we have received your Letters of Summons [*] for the said *Brotherhood*, sent from the Mayor and Jurats of the Town and Port of *Hasting* [c] ; and at a common Assembly of us the said Mayor, Jurats and Commonalty of *Rye* aforesaid, holden at *Rye* aforesaid, the 19th Day of *June* [d] last past, have elected, chosen, constituted, assigned, and appointed our welbeloved *W. B.* Esq; Mayor of *Rye* aforesaid, *T. G.* Bailiff [*] elect to *Great Yarmouth* for the Year to come, *A. G.* and *T. P.* Jurats, *S.* [and] common Clerk, *T. H.* Chamberlain, and *M. C.* Commoners and Freemen of the said Town, (Persons who have each of them taken a corporal Oath for the Maintenance of the Charters, Liberties and Customs of the said *Ports, Ancient Towns and their Members*) to be and appear for us, and in our Name, Place and Stead, at the said *Brotherhood* at the said Town and Port of *New Romney*, the Day aforesaid, at the Hour accustomed, as well to hear the Relation of the Bailiffs for the *Cinque Ports* from the Town of *Great Yarmouth* for the Year past, as also to agree and consent to the Admittance of the new Bailiffs for the *Cinque Ports* to the same Town of *Great Yarmouth* this Year now coming, and all Things incident to the said Relation and Admittance of the said Bailiffs, And we do by these Presents give and grant unto the said Persons [*], and every of them jointly and severally, our full and whole Power and Authority for us and our Successors, to do, consent and agree unto all and every such Acts, Ordinances, Decrees and Things, which at the said *Brotherhood*, by the said Mayors, Jurats and Commons of the said *Cinque Ports* and *Two Ancient Towns* there assembled, or the greatest part of them, shall be enacted, ordained, established and decreed for the Weal publick of the said *Cinque Ports, Two Ancient Towns, and their Members*. And we do, for us and our Successors, ratify and allow, and hold firm and stable All and whatsoever the said Persons before named, or the greatest part of them at the said Assembly, shall, or in the said *Brotherhood*, ordain, make, content unto, or establish as aforesaid. In witness whereof our common Seal is hereunto affixed. Dated [here, and again] at *Rye* aforesaid the 40th Day of *July*, in the Year of our Lord 1653.

The Form of the Commission for the *Guestling* is little different from this for the *Brotherhood*, only in the Clause touching the Relation and Admittance of the *Yarmouth* Bailiffs ; which is wholly omitted, and usually the Form is according to that prescribed by Order of the *Guestling* holden at *Romney*, *July* 22, 1601. An°. Eliz. 43.

The Persons thus returned, after they are set in their Places, the Clerk of the House reads first the Speaker's Letters abovementioned, and the several Commissions ; then are they all called over, and answer to their Names, and if any be Defaulters of the Persons returned, they are noted in order to be fined ; and if any Corporation fail in returning, or their Return be insufficient, that Corporation is fined. But if the Representatives of the greater part of all the Corporations appear, that is four of the seven, and eight of the fourteen, they may proceed in either of the Courts. After the calling over of the House, the Speaker makes a short Speech to declare the Occasion of their Meeting, and then the other Business proceeds, which at the *Brotherhood* was wont to be; First, The Report of the last Bailiffs to *Yarmouth*, who going to the Bar, and standing uncovered, made Relation of their Proceedings, and upon well behaving themselves in their Office, received the Thanks of the House, and were dismissed; if otherwise adjudged by the House, upon Complaint and Proof, fined. Then the Bailiffs elect were called to the Bar, and if nothing found to excuse them, were approved and took their Places in the House. Other Things, both here and at the *Guestling*, are brought into the House by Petition, or by Motion of some Member thereof ; to which Matter in question every Person, Member of the House, hath liberty to speak his Mind freely, as in the Parliament, and directs his Speech always to the Speaker, who after the Matter is debated, puts it to the Vote, and according to the Majority of Votes is the Matter concluded, and the Clerk of the House enters the Order and Decree of the House accordingly. Both these Courts are ancient, but especially that of the *Brotherhood*, under which Name I find the *Guestling* of old included ; so that, as well when the Members sat with the Ports, as not, it was called a *Brodhull*, as aforesaid. But afterward much of the ordinary Business being about the Bailiffs to *Yarmouth*, with whom the Members were not concerned (they always being chosen out of the Ports and ancient Towns) it was thought

fit

Margin notes

[a] Or, and Two Ancient Towns, leaving out Winchelsea.

[b] According to the Day appointed for the Meeting.

[*] Summonance in some old Copies.

[c] According to the Town that New Romney is Speaker.

[d] Answerable to the Day of Election.

[*] When it is the Bailiff last there, it is said and the late Bailiff, &c.

[*] Sometimes instead of Persons the Names are repeated, and again afterward in the Commission.

ANNOTATIONS.

fit to spare the Members their usual Attendance till they were called or summoned; whereupon as Guests invited, as aforesaid, they come to this Court of *Guestling*. But that the Ports, ancient Towns and corporate Members did before fit together under the Name of a *Brodhull*, seems clear by an Order I have seen in *French* (wherein, and in *Latin* formerly, as the old Acts of Parliament, were recorded the Orders and Decrees of this Court.) The Copy whereof, with the Translation, here followeth.

Soumz chose a toutz gentz: Que come le manessie on la fest de seint Barnabe l'appostell, l'an du Reign de Roy Richard secunde Dengleterre quinszisme, en pleyn Brodhull a Romeney tenustz par les Maires, Bailliffes, Jurees & Comunes tlousques a ceo, par lour comunes assent assemblas, assoit lez une Endenture en cestes paroles:

Sounts chose a toutz cest escript endente veisuntz ou oisauntz: Que come grauntz debatz estoient moeves par entre les Barons des Sink Portes & lour Members, par reason, des taillages, assises & payments, & alterez diverses charges & costages sovent eschoisuntz entre eux; des queux debatz null certayns allouuantz ne amendementz neyent est ordeigne ne faite de sa en arere, a graunt damage de eux toutz aleatreen; le mardie procheyn apres le fest de saint Dunstan, l'an de Reign de Roy Edwarde, fitz le Roy Henry trentisme quinte, en pleyn court de Shepwey, devaunt Sr. Henry de Cobham adonques Gardem. de Sink Portes, a contenutz est & assentuz entre aux de bone valunte, que toutz les dites, deuuz auaunt cell marsdie auaunt dite, ficome pluis pleinement est contenutz en une chartre d'accompt par entre le dit nostre Seigneur le Roy & les Barons des Sink Portes, soient levez par porgion. cestassavoir, la Port de Hastynges la tairce partie, la Port de Romenall & Dovorr. la tierce partie; la Port de Sandwych & de Hethe la tierce partie; issint nepour quaunt que tres toutz les paimentz, assifes & taillages, & altres diverses charges & costages que sount a grraunt, ou a lever. entre eux ou par eux, en quel manere ou en quel fourme que ceo soit, ou pour quel chose, que de cele maessly on enauant soient leves, par chateux & par moebies de les cestes que les dement dedeins la fraunchise de Sink Portes, issint que chescun home port sa charge ouelment de ceo qu'il avera faive partie dite fraunchise de Sink Portes; salve nepourquaunt les costages a mettre on le service nostre saign. le Roy due a luy en sa guerre, de quel service chescune Port est de droit tenutz a som. certeyn. Et si null. promesse ceo face de ceo jour en auant faunz assent de t'stoutz les Sink Portz, que cell promesse soit al perill com'aus. costages de celuy ou de ceux que fera ou ferrount la promesse. Et si null assise ou paiment ou autres charges ou costages de cest jour en auant aviegment par lour assent encountre la fourm. de cest escript auaunt dit, que cell taillage, assise ou payment ne face prejudice a cest escript auant nome, mes que cest escripe. de surdit se tiegn. en sa force a toutz jours. En testmoignance de quel chose nous auantditz Barons dez Sink Portes, cestassavoir Haslynges, Wynchelsee, Rie, Pevense, Romeney, Heth, Dovorr. Sandwiche, Fordwich & Feversham pur nous & pour toutz nous membres auons a cest escript endente pendits nous communes seales.

Sur

These Things * to all Men: That *whereas the* * These Things Tuesday in the Feast of Saint *Barnabas the* are to all Men, Apostle, in the Fifteenth Year of the Reign or all Men may of Richard the Second King of England, is know, and the full Brodhull holden at Romney by the like below. Mayors, Bailiffs, Jurats and Commons there, by their common Assent assembled, was read one Indenture in these Words:

These Things to all that may see or hear this Writing indented: That whereas great Debates being † moved between the Ba- † Or have been. rons of the *Cinque Ports* and their Members, by reason of the Tallages, Assessments and Payments, and divers other Charges and Costs that have been amongst them; of which Debates no certain Allowances ‡ or Amend- ‡ Or approved ments have been ordained nor made for the Remedy. since in Arrear, to the great Damage of them all concerned; the Tuesday next after the Feast of Saint Dunstan, in the Thirty fifth Year of the Reign of King Edward, the Son of King Henry, in full Court of Shepway, before the Lord Henry of Cobham then Warden of the *Cinque Ports*, it is now concaunted and assented between them of good will, that all the said Dues before this Tuesday aforesaid, as more fully is contained in one Charter of Accompt between our said Lord the King and the Barons of the *Cinque Ports*, may be levied by Portions; that is to say, The Port of Hasting the third Part; the Ports of Romney and Dover the third Part; the Ports of Sandwich and Hithe the third Part; so nevertheless that all Three the Payments, Assessments and Tallages, and divers other Charges and Costs, which are to be granted or levied between them or by them, in what Manner or in what Form soever they be, or for what Thing, that from this Tuesday forward may be levied, be levied by the Chattels and Moveables of those within the Franchise of the *Cinque Ports*, so that every Man bear his Charge equally of that, which he shall have safe-by-the-said Franchise of the *Cinque Ports*; saved nevertheless the Costs to send into the Service of our Lord the King, that is due to him in his War, of which Service every Port is of right bound to a Sum certain. And if any Promise be made from this Day forward without assent of all those * of the *Cinque Ports*, * Or of all the that that Promise be at the Peril, as also the Cinque Ports. Costs of him or them which shall make that Promise. And if any Assessment or Payment, or other Charges or Costs from this Day forward, come by their Assent against the Form of this Writing aforesaid, that that Tallage, Assessment or Payment be not to the Prejudice of this Writing aforenamed, but that this Writing from henceforth be holden always in its force. In witness whereof we the aforesaid Barons of the said *Cinque Ports*, that is to say, of *Hasting, Winchelsea, Rye, Pevensea, Romney, Heth, Dover, Sandwich, Fordwich* and *Feversham*, for us, and for all our Members, have to this Writing indented hung our common Seals.

Upon

ANNOTATIONS.

Sur quoy, par bon avis & deliberacion des Maires, Bailiffs, Jures & Cominaltes avantnomes, accorde se prist a dures de cest jour en avant; cestassavoir, que quant auscun des Maires, Bailliffs, Jurres, Cominaltes, ou singuler person, dascune des villes ou membres des Sink Portes, soit ou soient enpeches ou enpledes, enpledent ou enpechent ascune autre denizen. ou foreyn. & en les ditz enpechement ou plee movee d'une partie ou dautre, debate ou travers soit dascune point ou clause contenutz en lour comune chartre, ou dascune point tochaunt lour comunes usages ou fraunchises, soit mountenaunt Brodhull assignee, al request del ville ou Membre, Cominalte ou singuler person, que soy font greve; a quel Brodhull chescun ville ou Membre que de custume doit vener per somons ou garnisment al dite Brodhull, & ne viegne mye due contribucion a ceo que la greindre partite de la dite Brodull voet assenter. encourge le peyn de vinte livers, outre ses autres des diutes, a levez en mesme la manere come dette adjugge, a la suyte dascune partie des dites villes ou Membres envers ascune autre partie demurrant en autre ville est a lever. En testmoign. de quel chose nous avanditz Barons dez Sink Ports, cestassavoir, Hastyngs, Wyndechelsee, Rie, Pevense, Romeney, Heth, Dovorr, Sandwiche, Fordwich, & Feversham, pour nous & pour toutz nous Membres avoms a cest escript endente penditz nous comons sealx.

Upon which, by good Advice and Deliberation of the Mayors, Bailiffs, Jurats and Commonalties aforenamed, it is readily accorded to endure from this day forward, that is to say, that when any of the Mayors, Bailiffs, Jurats, Commonalties, or single Person, of any of the Towns or Members of the *Cinque Ports*, be impeached or impleaded, impeach or implead, any other Denizen or Foreigner; and in the said Impeachment or Plea moved of the one Part or of the other, the Debate or Traverse be of any Point or Clause contained in their common Charter, or of any Point touching their common Usages or Franchises, there be forthwith a Brodhull assigned, at the Request of the Town or Member, Commonalty or single Person, which may be grieved; at which Brodhull, every Town or Member, which of Custom ought to come by Summons or Warning to the said Brodhull, and cometh not, nor pay the due Contribution to that which the greater Party of the said Brodhull shall assent to, shall incur the Penalty of twenty Pounds, besides the other Duties, to be levied in the same manner as Debt adjudged, at the Suit of any Party of the said Towns or Members against any other Party dwelling in another Town, is to be levied. In witness whereof we the aforesaid Barons of the *Cinque Ports*; that is to say, *Hasting, Winchelsea, Rye, Pevensea, Romney, Heth, Dover, Sandwich, Fordwich* and *Feversham*, for us and for all our Members, have to this Writing indented hung our common Seals.

By this Order, and the other Records of these Courts, appeareth the Authority and Practice thereof about raising of Money to defray the publick Charges; which in the Brotherhood is but one only way, called Purses, settled by virtue of a Decree made at a General Brodhull holden at *Romney* the *Tuesday* next after the Close of *Easter* in the 10th Year of King *Henry* VII. The Copy whereof followeth.

HYT is ordeyned, for divers Considerations movyng the Bretheryn at thys present Brodehill assembled, that every Meyre and Bailliff of every Towne of the v Ports for the tyme beyng, pay at every general Brodhull yerely here to be holden the *Teuesday* next after the Close of *Ester*, for hym and hys Membres, a certayne Somme of Money unther wrytten, for the common Relief and Aid of all the Portes and there Membres; that is to say,

Hastyng and hys Membres	xiii s. viii d.
Wynchelse	vi s. viii d.
Rie, for hym and hys Membr.	x s.
Romeney, for hym and hys membr.	xi s. viii d.
Hythe	vi s. viii d.
Dovorr, for hym and hys Membr.	xviii s. iiii d.
Sandwych, for hym and hys Membr.	xx s.

Sm. iiii l. vii s.

And that under payne of forfaiture of every Towne so faillyng to the wele of all the v Ports v Marks; and for the more Knowlich, every Town and Membr of the fyve Portes, wyth there Membres, is assessed for his Part as it followeth.

Hastyng	vi s. viii d.	*Hythe*		vi s. viii d.
Pevensa	iii s. iiii d.	*Dovorr*		vi s. viii d.
Bulverbythe	xx d.	*Feversham*		v s.
Parva Heigham	xii d.	*Folkeston*		v s.
Bekysborne	xii d.	*Margat*		xx d.
Wynchelse, having no Membre,	vi s. viii d.	*Sandwich*		vi s. viii d.
Rye	vi s. viii d.	*Ramsgate*		iii s. iiii d.
Tenterden	iii s. iiii d.	*Fordwich*		iii s. iiii d.
Romeney	vi s. viii d.	*Serre*		iii s. iiii d.
Old Romeney	xx d.	*Dele* and *Walmer*		iii s. iiii d.
Lyde	iii s. iiii d.			

And so, according to the Sum to be raised, are more or less Purses granted, and sometimes half a Purse; whence came the Proverb of cutting of Purses at the Brotherhood, from the Sum of

ANNOTATIONS.

of a Purſe cut or parted in two. But at the Gueſtljng there are divers Ways of raiſing Money. One by virtue of the former Indenture made at the Court of *Shepway*, in the Reign of King *Edward* I. and the Order of Brotherhood thereupon in the Reign of King *Richard* II. as aforeſaid, which is called Compoſition, whereto the Members pay nothing, as they do not to the Purſes at the Brotherhood. Another is that called Shipping, when every Port Town and Member pays according to the Number of Ships they are to find ; and accordingly the Benefit of the five hundred Pounds mentioned afterwards in this Charter of Queen *Elizabeth*, when received, is divided among them as the Charge of Shipping was and ought to be incumbent upon them. The other Way of levying Money is by Proportion, commonly now uſed for Charges, not concerning Shipping, but for defence of their Charters and Cuſtoms ; and is this, where every one of the Ports, and two ancient Towns, pay twenty Shillings, *Seaford* ſhall pay ten Shillings, and every one of the other corporate Members thirteen Shillings and four Pence ; that is, *Seaford* but half as much as a Port ; and the reſt of the Members two Thirds as much . *Seaford*, by reaſon of Poverty, having been abated of its old Proportion ; for formerly the Proportions appear ſomewhat different. The Members not corporate pay nothing here in the Gueſtling, nor their Head-Ports for them, as they do to the Purſes of the Brotherhood. When Money is raiſed by Compoſition, *Dover* and *Romney* pay the third Part by equal Portions ; and *Sandwich* and *Hithe* another third Part by equal Portions ; but to *Haſtings* third Part *Winchelſea* and *Rye* aſſiſt, as by an Indenture made between them in the 17ᵗʰ Year of the Reign of King *Richard* II. appeareth ; the Copy whereof followeth, with the Tranſlation out of *French* thus :

CEST Endenture tripartie, ſacte par ent. les Bayliſſ, Jurres & la Comaynalte de la ville de Haſtyng, d'une partie ; les Maire, Bayliſſe, Jurres & la Comynalte de la ville de Wyncheſſee, d'altre partie ; & les Maire, Bayliſſ, Jurres & la Comynalte de la ville de Rie, de tierce partie, teſmoyne, que come grauntz debates eſtoyent moevez par entre les Maires, Bailliſſs, Jurres & Comynaltes des villes avauntditz ſur le port les certains & diverſis charges ſovent eſcheauntz entre eux, des queux debates & diſcordes nulle certeyn. allegeaunce ne remedie eſtoit pleynement ordeigne ne purven. tanq'en cea ; ſurquoi par mediacion des amys d'une part. & d'altre, & auxi par lour comun. accord. & aſſent, les parties avauntz, pour final pees, tranquylite & quiete par entre eux a durer pour tout temps avenir, accorderent en maner purſuyt, ceſtaſavoir, que touchant la charge, coſtages & diſpenſes, & la general ſervice a ſaire a noſtre Seignour le Roy de la navey en ſa voyage, que la dite ville de Haſtyng, oue ſes membres, trovera en la dite voiage ſynk nyeſſi, avec toute le mayne & l'appareill. a ceux apportennes, accordaunt a lour auncyene uſage & cuſtomes. La ville de Wyncheſſe diez nyeſſi, & la ville de Rye ſynk nyeſſi, avec le maynire & l'appareill. a ceux ſeverallment appurteuntz, accordaunt a lour uſage & cuſtome de tout temps entre eux approve. Et que touchant la Baylie de Jernemuth d'an en an. que la dite ville de Haſtyng, oue ſes membres apart, trovera a lour coſtages un prod. home de continuer & occupier la Bayliye avant dite. Lez ditez villes de Wyncheſſe & la Rye un--aut. prod. home come Bailliſſe, a lour Comune coſtages, cheſcune an. en manire come enſuyt, ceſtaſſavoir que la dite ville de Wyncheſſee maundera la dyte perſon come Bailiſſ a ſervir & continuer la Bailiſſ en un. an. & la dite ville de la Rie maundera une autre perſon. come Bailiſſ pur occupier la dite Baylye en la procheyn an. viſuaunt iſſint que l'une de les villes de Wyncheſſe & de la Rye avantz, dount null. perſſne. come Bailiſſ eſt maunde ſerra gree & contribucon. a la dite ville que maund. la perſon. pour ceſt an. des coſtages & deſpences ſactes ou a ſaires duraunt le temps de la demme illeſques de la Bailliſſ avantdite.

Iſſint

THIS Indenture tripartite, made between the Bailliff, Jurats and Commonalty of the Town of *Haſting*, of the one Part ; the Mayor, Bailiff ᵃ, Jurats and Commonalty of ᵃ *The Bailiff mentioned in* the Town of *Winchelſea*, of the other Part ; and the Mayor, Bailiff ᵃ, Jurats and com- Winchelſea monalty of the Town of *Rye*, of the third Part, *and Rye is the* witneſſeth, that whereas great Debates have *King's Bailiff, commonly called* been moved between the Mayors, Bailiffs, *the Water Bai-* Jurats and Commonalties of the Towns afore- *liff.* ſaid, upon the bearing of certain and divers ᵇ Charges that have grown amongſt ᵇ them ; of ᵇ *Between.* which Debates and Diſcords no certain Al- ᶜ *Redreſs that* lowance ᶜ nor Remedy hath been fully ordain- ᶜ *ed nor provided hitherto* ᵈ ; whereupon, by ᵈ *hath been al-* the Mediation of Friends of the one Part and *loved of by all* of the other ; and alſo by their common Ac- *as a Law.* cord and Aſſent, the Parties aforeſaid, for ᵉ *Concerning* final Peace, Tranquillity and Quietneſs be- *the ſame.* tween them to endure by all times to come, do accord in manner following ; that is to ſay, that touching the Charge, Coſts and Ex- pences, and ᵉ the general Service to be done to ᵉ *This, and,* our Lord the King of the Navy ᶠ in his *one Copy hath,* Voyage, that the ſaid Town of *Haſting*, with of. its Members, ſhall find in the ſaid Voyage ᶠ *For his Navy* five Ships with all the Mariners ᶠ and ᶠ Ap- *in his own* parel to them appertaining, according to their *Voyage.* ancient Uſage and Cuſtoms. The Town of ᵍ *Men, ſo one Winchelſea* ten Ships, and the Town of *Rye* five ᵍ *Tranſlation* Ships, with the Mariners and the Apparel to ᵍ *hath it, the* them ſeverally appertaining, according to their *like afterward.* Uſage and Cuſtom by all times amongſt them approved. And that touching the Bailiage of *Tarmouth* from Year to Year, that the ſaid Town of *Haſting*, with its Members apart, ſhall find at their Coſts one prudent Man to continue and occupy the Bailiage aforeſaid. The ſaid Towns of *Winchelſea* and *Rye* an- other Man as Bailiff, at their common Coſts, every Year, in the Manner as enſueth ; that is to ſay, that the ſaid Town of *Winchelſea* ſhall ſend the ſaid Perſon as Bailiff to ſerve and continue the Bailiff in one Year ; and the ſaid Town of *Rye* ſhall ſend another Perſon as Bailiff, for to occupy the ſaid Bai- liage in the next Year. So that one of the Towns of *Winchelſea* and *Rye* aforeſaid, out ˢ Gree, *is the* of which no Perſon as Bailiff is ſent, ſhall *French, is pro-* grant ˢ and contribute to theſaid Town which *perly* to agree ; ſendeth the Perſon for that Year, to the Coſts *but here and* and Expences made or to be made during the *elſewhere uſed* time of the Abode there of the Bailiff aforeſaid. *for* pay.

So

ANNOTATIONS.

Iſſent que cheſcun an. la dite ville de Haſtyng, ou ſes membres, trovera & maunders une perſonne convenable a ſez coſtages ſeverals, & lez ditz villes de Wynchelſee & de la Rie une autre perſonne convenable, a lour comune coſtages, en manire come dite eſt devant. Auxint que touchaunt aſcune generall promeſſe fait ou faire en temps avenir par les Maires, Baillifs, Jures au Cominaltes de tous lez villes dez Cinque Ports, de quele promeſſe generall les ditz villes de Haſtyng, Wynchelſee & la Rie per auncient cuſtume & uſage porterount le charge de la tierce perte par my & par tout en man. enſuaunt; ceſtaſſavoir, que la dite ville de Haſtying paiera & ferra gree le quart parte, la dite ville de Wynchelſee la moite, & la dite ville de la Rie la quart. parte de tout la tierce parte du generall promeſſe avant dite. Purdeen toutſfaitz que ſi aſcune promeſſe ſoy face en temps avenir, par aſcune de villes membres des Sinq. Ports, ou ſingler perſonne reſeaunt dedeins icels, ſaunz aſſent ou volunte de treſtoutz; que celle ville membr ou ſingler perſonne que faite, ou ferra la promeſſe, potera la charge ſeveralment del promeſſe avandite, come en certeins Endentures par entre toutz les villes de Sinq. Ports nadgariz faitz pluis ploy_nement eſt conteaue. Et que touchaunt le generall charge & coſtages de aſcunz perſonnes ou perſonne demiraunte ou demiraunt al parlament en le nom. de toutz, ou pour toutz les villes membres & cominaltees de SinkPortes, ou pour purſuyt a faire un diſchauge de la diſme & quinziſime graunt a noſtre Sr. le Roy quaunt il eſtehte des queux charges, coſtages, diſpences & paymentz, lez ditz villes de Haſtyng, Wynchelſee & de la Rie d'antiquite ount porte la tierce parte; & de toutz autres charges, taillages, ſubſidies ou autres manners coſtages, que conq. ſur toutz lez villes & pour toutz les villes de Sink Portes graunteo, ou en temps aven. a grauntiers, faites ou a faire en generall come deſuis eſt dit; de quel tiert partie les ditz villes de Haſtyng, Wynchelſee & la Rie porterint lour charge cheſcune de eux ſeveralment, en le forme qu'enſuyt; ceſtaſſavoir, que quaunt la charge ſur lez ditz villes de Haſtyng, Wynchelſee & la Rie ſeſtent a la ſomme de ſept livres, que la dite ville de Wynchelſee paiera & ferra gree a cell ſomme trois livres, & lez ditz villas de Haſtyng & de la Rie quartre livres, par queles porcions; & iſſiut pour tout temps avenir ſolunq. la quantite de la ſomme greindre. Purven. toutefoitz pour tout le temps que aſcuns perſonnes ou perſone maundes ou maunde par cheſcun de villes des Sink Portes al Parlament par brief noſtre Sr. le Roy; ceſtaſſavoir, de cheſcun ville deux perſonnes come ils ſolient vendr. ou que aſcuns des villes ou ſingler perſonne ſoit en peche apart ſeveralment de choſe que ne le touche la generall fraunchiſe ou comane uſage de Sink Ports avantditz, que cheſcun de villes avantditz, ou ſingler perſonne, porterount & cuſtodiendrount lour charge ſeveralment. Et que pour tout le temps que les villes de Sink Portes ſount en lour congregation pur eux nutz & en nom. de toutz come a Brodhell, Shyypweye, ou ayllours, en congregation de eux appartient d'eſtre fait, que cheſaun de villes des Sink Portes ſeveralment ſerra a ces coſtages, cheſcun ville apart en manire & *ſourme*

So that every Year the ſaid Town of *Haſting,* with its Members, ſhall find and ſend one fit [h] Perſon at their ſeveral Charges, and [k] *In both the* the ſaid Towns of *Wincheljea* and *Rye* an- *places it may* other fit [h] Perſon, at their common Coſts, in *be ſufficient; or* manner as before is ſaid. Alſo that touching *convenient.* any general Promiſe made, or to be made in time to come, by the Mayors, Bailiffs, Jurats or Commonalties of all the Towns of the *Cinque Ports,* of which general Promiſe the ſaid Towns of *Haſtings, Winckelſea* and *Rye,* by ancient Cuſtom and Uſage, ſhall bear the Charge of the third Part wholly, and of every Part thereof in manner enſuing; that is to ſay, that the ſaid Town of *Haſting* ſhall pay and grant * the quarter Part; the ſaid Town * *Or make a-* of *Winchelſea* the Moiety; and the ſaid Town *greement for.* of *Rye* the quarter Part of all the third Part of the general Promiſe aforeſaid. Provided always, that if any Promiſe be made in time to come by any of the Towns, Members of the *Cinque Ports,* or ſingle Perſon reſiant within the ſame, without the Aſſent or Will of the Whole; that the ſaid Town, Member, or ſingle Perſon, which made or ſhall make the Promiſe, ſhall ſeverally bear the Charge of the Promiſe aforeſaid, as in certain Indentures between all the Towns of the *Cinque Ports,* late made, more fully is contained. And that touching the general Charge and Coſts of any Perſon or Perſons abiding at the Parliament in the Name of all, or for all the Towns Members and Commonalties of the *Cinque Ports*; or in purſuit to get a Diſcharge of the Tenth and Fifteenth granted to our Lord the King whom it happeneth, of the which Charges, Coſts, Expences and Payments, the ſaid Towns of *Haſting, Winchelſea* and *Rye,* anciently have born the third Part; and of all other Charges, Tallages, Subſidies, or other manner of Coſts, which ſhall be changed [i] upon [i] *Or concern all.* all the Towns, and by all the Towns of the *Cinque Ports* granted, or in time to come to be granted, made or to be made, in general as aforeſaid; of the which third Part, the ſaid Towns of *Haſting, Winchelſea* and *Rye* ſhall bear their Charge, every one of them ſeverally in the Form that followeth; that is to ſay, that when the Charge upon the ſaid Towns of *Haſting, Winchelſea* and *Rye* amounteth to the Sum of ſeven Pounds, then the ſaid Town of *Winchelſea* ſhall pay and anſwer * of that * *Or make a-* Sum three Pounds; and the ſaid Towns of *greement for* *Haſting* and *Rye* four Pounds, by equal Por- *the Sum,* &c. tions; and ſo by all times to come, according to the Quantity of the Sum, greater. Provided always, that for all the time that any Perſon or Perſons be ſent by any of the Towns of the *Cinque Ports* to the Parliament by Writ of our Lord the King; that, is to ſay, of every Town two Perſons, as they were wont to come [k]; or that any of the Towns, or [k] *Or accuſtom:* ſingle Perſon, be impeached apart ſeverally of *ed to do.* a thing [m] which toucheth not the general * *For matter* Franchiſe or common Uſage of the *Cinque* *which toucheth* *Ports* aforeſaid, that every of the Towns afore- *not,* &c. ſaid, or ſingle Perſon, ſhall bear and keep their Charge ſeverally. And that for all the time that the Towns of the *Cinque Ports* be in their Aſſembly for them all, and in the Name of all, as at a Brotherhood, Shepway, or elſewhere, in the Aſſemblies appertaining to be made by them, that every of the Towns of the *Cinque Ports* ſhall be ſeverally at their own Coſts, every Town apart in manner and *form*

ANNOTAIONS.

fourme d aunce temps ufee. Enfeinment purven. toutefoitz, que fi afcunes ou afcun des
villes ou ville de Haftyng, Wynchelfee ou la
Rie fufditz, en feverall, foient ou foit en contrarie de faire contribucion, gree ou fatisfac-
cion de la tierce partie de les generall charges,
ou generall charge, en le man. avantdite, ceftaffavoir, chefcune des villez avantditz eu man.
& en fourme prefditz, foluntz rate & porcion.
feversalment, come præfcript. eft, encourgent ou
encourge, chefcun des villes avantditz, le
payne des diez liures d'eftre leve de ceft ville
ou villes, que foit ou fount en defaute, en la
manire enfuaunt, ceftaffavoir, que la ville ou
villes que foit ou fount gravez ou grevez a
contrarie de covenauntz & accordes avantditz, & maunde ou maundent al Mair,
Bayliffes, Jurres &Cominaltees de les ditz villes
ou ville, que eft ou foient en defaut, lours
lettres ou lettre tefmoinialz ou tefimoniall,
& ficut alias, defouche le feall. d'office, & ficut plures, defoutz lours comunes fealles ou
feall. & fur feo prendre withername, & tenir
tanq. gree foit fait, enfemblement avec coftages,
damages & expences en nature de dett ajugge
entre partie & partie, en fembleable cas come
avant fes heeurs ad effee ufee. En tefmoign-
aunc. de quel chofe a ceftes endentures tri-
parties chefcun deux des trois villes avantditz
ount mys lours comunes fealx a la tierce ville.
Don. le victifme jour del mois de fevrier, l'an
du Reign. le Roy Richard feconde dife &
feptifme.

form of ancient time ufed. Likewife provided
always, that if any of the faid Towns, or Town
of *Hafting*, *Winchelfea* or *Rye* aforefaid, in feveral, be contrary [1] to make Contribution, [1] *Refufe or a-*
Payment [a] or Satisfaction of the third Part of *verfe.*
the general Charges, or general Charge, in [a] *Agreement as*
manner aforefaid ; that is to fay, every of the *before.*
Towns aforefaid in manner and form before
fpecified, according to the Rate and Portion [m m] *Or Propor-*
feverally, as is before preferibed ; then they *tion.*
fhall incur, every of the Towns aforefaid, the
Penalty of ten Pounds, to be levied of the faid
Town or Towns, which fhall be in default, in
the manner enfuing ; that is to fay, that the
Town or Towns which be burdened or grieved
to the contrary of the Covenants and accords aforefaid, do fend to the Mayors, Bai-
liffs [n], Jurats and Commonalties of the faid [n] *Or Mayor,*
Towns or Town, which is or are in default, *Bailiff.*
their Letters or Letter. teftimonials or tefti-
monial, & *ficut* [o] *alias*, under the Seal of [o] *Or as other-*
Office, & *ficut plures* [v], under their Common *wife or again,*
Seals or Seal ; and upon this fhall take with- *that is, the fe-*
ernam, and hold the fame till Payment be made, *cond Letter,*
together with the Cofts, Damages and Ex- *which is called*
pences in the nature of Debt adjudged be- *an alias, and*
tween Party and Party, in fuch Cafe as before *hath thefe*
this time [h] hath been ufed. In witnefs *Words*, ficut
whereof, to thefe Indentures tripartite every alias *therein.*
two of the three Towns aforefaid have put [p] *Or as often,*
their Common Seals to the third Town. *or many times;*
Given the twentieth Day of the Month of *thefe Words*, fi-
February, in the feventeenth Year of the Reign cut plures, *are*
of King *Richard* II. *in the third*
Letter, which
is alfo called a

Moreover, befides the Authority of thefe Courts in the Matters aforefaid, they have alfo Jurifdiction to correct and amend Defects of Juftice and Irregularities in the Officers of Juftice *Plures.*
and *Proceedings therein* in any of the Ports, Towns and Members ; and the Decrees and [a] *According to*
Orders here made fhall be directory and binding to the Whole : And *Caufes* fometimes ad- *the French,*
journed hither have been heard and determined ; as if needful I could give Inftances enough *thefe Hours.*
Yet neverthelefs though they act within and amongft themfelves here jointly, like a County
Palatine, as to the Government and for the Maintenance and Defence of the Liberties of the
Whole : Every particular Corporation in each Town acts feverally and diftinctly within the
Limits thereof, as to Matters of Law and Juftice (notwithftanding liable for Miftakes and
Failures therein, as aforefaid, to be corrected by the Judgment of thefe Courts) and have born
many of their particular Burdens and Loffes without affiftance of their Brethren.
To the bearing of which Particulars when happening, but efpecially the publick and ge-
neral Charges, the Members feem to be added at firft to the Ports ; left any of them failing, the
Burden fhould be infupportable to the reft, and make them fail too, to the utter Decay of the
Service. For the *Cinque Ports* and two ancient Towns being, as aforefaid, equally privileged,
and thus affociate into one Society or Fellowfhip, quickly gave occafion to their being taken and
confidered as one Body, and jointly together have their Liberties and free Cuftoms confirmed to
them by *Magna Charta*, cap. 9.by the Name of *the Barons of the Five Ports* ; under which Name,
or the like, they and their Members are included in divers other Charters, Statutes, Writs,
and Book-cafes. And in the Days of King *Edward* I. as before is feen (if not before that)
obtained one general Charter concerning them, which by *Infpeximus* hath received Confirmation, and fometimes with Additions, from moft of the Kings and Queens of *England* that have
fince fucceeded him in the Throne. Other particular Charters to any of the Towns, and addition of Members united at any time after their general Charter and Affociation, have been (as
the Exigence of their Affairs and Condition required) obtained as Acts of Favour of their
Princes then regnant, the better to enable them to perform their Services, and to alleviate the
Charge thereof ; with which Member, fuch Town to whom it was annexed, after fome fpace
of time, agreed or compounded what certain Sum to receive of them toward the fame ; as appeareth by the Compofition between *Rye* and *Tenterden*, the Copy whereof followeth :

The Englifh thus:

HÆC Indentura, facta vicefimo primo die,
menfis Septembris, Anno regni Regis
Henrici feptimi poft conqueftum Angliæ
octavo, inter Henricum Swan, Majorem Portus
& ville de Rye, ac communitatem ejufdem
villæ, ex parte una ; & Hugonem Parker,
Ballivum villæ & hundred. de Tenterden,
& communitatem eorundem villa & hundred,

THIS Indenture, made the twenty firft
Day of the Month of *September*, in the
eighth Year of the Reign of King *Henry* VII.
after the Conqueft of *England*, between *Henry
Swan*, Mayor of the Port and Town of *Rye*,
and the Commonalty of the fame Town, of
the one Part ; and *Hugh Parker*, Bailiff of the
Town and Hundred of *Tenterden*, and the
Commonalty of the fame Town and Hundred,

C c

ANNOTATIONS.

ex parte altéra, testatur, quod cum prædicti Major & communitas predict. Portus & villæ de Rye, & cæteri Barones Quinque Portuum, quam pluribus libertatibus & franchesiis, privilegiis, immunitatibus, eis per cartas & literas patentes diversorum Regum Angliæ concessis, ac per cartas Domini Regis nunc confirmat. ratificatis & approbatis, usi fuerint & gavisi, a tempore de quo memoria hominum non existit, pro navigio quod ipsi Barones Domino Regi, & hæred. suis Regibus Angliæ ad summonicionem ipsius Domini Regis & hæred. suorum Angliæ Regum, per quadraginta dies, præparare & invenire debent, quando ipse Dominus Rex, vel aliquis hæred. suorum Angliæ Regis, ad aliquas partes exteras transfretaverit ; videlicet, quinquaginta & septem naves, & in qualibet nave viginti & unum homines, ad custag. dictorum Baronum Quinque Portuum, hæred. & successor. suorum per quindecim dies, prout in dictis literis patentibus plenius continetur. Unde vero dicti Major & Communitas Portus & villæ de Rye, pro porcione sua eis contingent. quinque naves & homines in qualibet nave de numero supradicto, invenire & præparare, debent, & præparare solebant a tempore supradicto. Et quia Major & communitas dict. Portus & villæ de Rye, propter magnam destruccionem, devastacionem, exilium & depauperacionem ejusdem villæ, ut per fluxum & refluxum maris, ac per combustionem inimicorum Domini Regis sæpe fact. onus inter se propriis facultatibus suis absque eorum expensis importabilibus facere & invenire non sufficiebant, Dominus Henricus nuper Rex Angliæ sextus, de gra. sua speciali, & ex mero motu & certa scientia suis in præmissis, primo die Augusti, Anno regni sui vicesimo septimo, per literas suas patentes concessit, quod prædict. villa & hundred. de Tenterden sint membrum dictæ villæ de Rye, annexum & unitum, ac dict. villam & Hundred. de Tenterden ad dict. Portum & villam de Rye annexuit & univit, ac a Com. Kanciæ separavit. Volensque quod dict. villa & Hundred. de Tenterden, sic annexa, unita, & separata, membrum Quinque Portuum prædictorum, prædict. Portui & villæ de Rye sic annexum, unitum & pertinens, reputetur & habeatur. Et quod ipsi Ballivus & communitas villæ & Hundred. de Tenterden prædict. hæred. & successores sui quam plurimis libertatibus, franchesiis, privilegiis & quietanciis in dictis literis dicti Domini Regis Henrici sexti patentibus contentis, necnon omnibus & omnimodis libertatibus, privilegiis, quietanciis & liberis consuetudinibus, quibus Barones Quinque Portuum prædictorum, ante hæc tempora, melius, uberius, & honorificentius usi & gavisi fuerunt, dicti Ballivus & communitas villæ & Hundred. prædict. hæc. & successores sui plene se plenarie in omnibus & singulis gaudeant & imperpetuum utantur. Ita quod ipsi Ballivus dictorum villæ & Hundred. de Tenterden. hæredes & successores sui contribuant cum prædictis Baronibus dict. Portus & villæ de Rye, videlicet, quilibet eorum juxta facultates suas ad faciend. serviciam ipsius Domini Regis, & hæred.
suorum

of the other Part, witnesseth, that whereas the aforesaid Mayor and Commonalty of the aforesaid Port and Town of *Rye*, and other the Barons of the *Cinque Ports*, very many Liberties and Franchises, Privileges and Immunities to them, by the Charters and Letters Patents of divers Kings of *England*, granted, and by the Charters of our Lord the King now confirmed, ratified and approved, have used and enjoyed, from the time * of which the * *Or time out* Memory of Men is not , for the Shipping that *mind.* they, the said Barons, to our Lord the King, and his Heirs Kings of *England*, at the Summons of our said Lord the King, and his Heirs Kings of *England*, by forty Days, ought to prepare and find, when he, our said Lord the King, or any of his Heirs the Kings of *England*, shall pass † to any foreign Parts ; that is † *Or cross the* to say, fifty and seven Ships, and in every *Seas.* Ship twenty and one Men, at the Costs of the said Barons of the *Cinque Ports*, their Heirs and Successors, by fifteen Days, as in the said Letters Patents more fully is contained. And whereof ‡ the said Mayor and Commonalty of ‡ *Or but* the Port and Town of *Rye*, for their Portion ‖, *whereof.* belonging to them, five Ships, and Men in ‖ *Or Proportion.* every Ship of the Number aforesaid, ought to find and prepare, and were wont to prepare from the time aforesaid. And because the Mayor and Commonalty of the said Port and Town of *Rye*, by great Destruction, Devastation, Exile * and Impoverishment of the * *Departure of* same Town, as by the flowing and reflowing *the Inhabi-* of the Sea, and by the Fire of the Enemies of *tants ; or if* our Lord the King oft made, were not suffi- *the Latin were* cient to bear † and find the Charge of them- *intended for* selves of their own Estates ‡, without their in- *exitium, then* supportable Expences , the Lord *Henry* late *it is to be ren-* King of *England* the Sixth, of his special *dered* Ruin. Grace, and of his mere Motion, and certain † *Do or make.* Knowledge in the Premisses, the first Day of ‡ *Substance or* *August*, in the twenty seventh Year of his *Faculties.* Reign, by his Letters Patents, granted, that the aforesaid Town and Hundred of *Tenterden*, may be a Member annexed and united to the said Town of *Rye* ; and the said Town and Hundred of *Tenterden* to the said Port and Town of *Rye* did annex and unite, and from the County of *Kent* separated. Willing * also * *Or and wil-* that the said Town and Hundred of *Tenterden, ling.* so annexed, united and separated, be reputed and accounted † a Member of the *Cinque Ports* † *Had or* aforesaid, to the aforesaid Port and Town of *esteemed.* *Rye* so annexed, united and appertaining : And that, the said Bailiff and Commonalty of the Town and Hundred of *Tenterden* aforesaid, their Heirs and Successors, the many Liberties, Franchises, Priviledges and Freedoms in the said Letters Patents of the said Lord King *Henry* the Sixth contained ; also all and all manner of Liberties, Priviledges, Freedoms and free Customs which the Barons of the *Cinque Ports* aforesaid, before these times, better, more plentifully, and more honourably have used and enjoyed, the said Bailiff and Commonalty of the Town and Hundred aforesaid , their Heirs and Successors fully and largely in all things and every thing might enjoy and use for ever. So that the said Bailiff of the said Town and Hundred of *Tenterden*, their Heirs and Successors, should contribute with the aforesaid Barons of the said Port and Town of *Rye* ; that is to say, every of them, according to their Estates ‡, to do the Service † *Substance or* of our said Lord the King, and of his Heirs *Faculties.*
Kings

fuorum 'Angliæ Regum, cùm ab ipfo Domino
Rege, vel hæredibus fuis Angliæ Regibus,
hoc haberent in mandatis, prout alii Barones
Quinque Portuum prædictorum per antea, ut
prædicitur, habuerint. Quapropter prædicti
Major & communitas dict. Portus & villæ
de Rye, & prædicti Ballivus villæ & Hundred.
de Tenterden, & communitas eorundem, ad onus
& fervicium Domini Regis fuprædict. inter eos
faciend. agend. & fupportand. de cætero in futur. per eorum mutu. affenfu. & confenfu. talem
inter fe inierunt & ceperunt convenationem &
concordiam, prout inferius plenè liquet, tàm ex
una parte quàm ex altera parte, pro imperpetuo
obfervand. videlicet : Si & quandocunque Dominus Rex, hæredes vel fucceffores fui, pro in-
tegro navigio prædicto habend. quàm ipfe Dominus Rex, vel aliquis hæred. fuorum Angliæ
Regum, transfretare propofuerit, & breve fuum
de fummonicione Cuftodi Quinque Portuum
prædictorum, vel ejus in hac parte locumtenenti,
mandaverint ; & idem cuftos five locumtenens
fuper hoc mandatum ftatim præfat. Majori &
Baronibus dict. Portus & villæ de Rye di-
rexerit ; quòd tunc dicti Major & communitas
dict. Portus & villæ de Rye, hæredes & fucceffores fui, illud mandatum dicti Cuftodis five
locumtenentis de fummonicione prædicta, fic
eis directa, dictis Ballivo & communitati villæ
& Hundred. de Tenterden, hæred. & fuccefforibus fuis, infra tres dies proxim. poft recepcio-
nem ejufdem mandati dirigent, transmittent &
deliberari facient. Et tunc dicti Ballivus &
communitas dictorum villæ & Hundred. de Tenterden, hæredes & fucceffores fui, unam navem,
& homines in eadem nave juxta numerum
prædictum, ad diem & locum in dicto mandato
fpecificat. præparare & invenire debent, per
dies præfpecificat. fumptibus fuis propriis & expenfis. Vel fi & quandocunque Dominus Rex
nunc, hæred. & fucceffores fui Angliæ Reges,
breve fuum de fummonicione pro medietate
vel parte navigii fui quinquaginta & feptem
navium habend. feu præparand. mandaverint,
extunc dict. Ballivus & communitas dict. villæ
& Hundred. de Tenterden, hæred. & fucceffores fui, invenient quintam partem omnium
folucionum & expenfarum circa præparacionem
& invenicionem navium & hominum, de & in
proport. dicti navigii faciend. Provifo femper
quòd dict. Ballivus & communitas dictorum
villæ & Hundred. de Tenterden, hæred. & fucceffores fui, fine fecreti & convocati tàm ad
præparacionem navium & hominum prædict.
quàm ad folucionem expenfarum & cuftagio-
rum, ut prædicitur, faciend. Et ulterius, prædicti Ballivus & communitas villæ & Hundred. de Tenterden, hæred. & fucceffores fui,
pro & in nomine plena ac pithariæ porcionis
& contribucionis, juxta facultates fuas, ad
facturam reperacionem, fuftentacionem ac inventionem aliarum navium, omnium & fingulorum porcion. Majoris & communitatis dict.
Portus & villæ de Rye, Domino Regi Angliæ,
hæred. & fucceffiribus fuis Angliæ regibus,
in & de navigio fuo prædicto invenire incumbent. five pertin. contribuet, folvant &
folvere teneantur, ac per præfent. concedunt
prædictis

Kings of *England*, when of our faid Lord the
King, or his Heirs Kings of *England*, they
fhould have it in commandment, as other
Barons of the *Cinque Ports* aforefaid before
time, as aforefaid, have had. Wherefore the
aforefaid Mayor and Commonalty of the faid
Port and Town of *Rye*, and the aforefaid
Balliff of the Town and Hundred of *Tenterden*, and Commonalty of the fame, to make,
do and fupport the Charge and Service of our
Lord the King aforefaid between them, from
henceforth for the future, by their mutual
Affent and Confent, have entered into and
taken fuch Covenant and Concord amongft
themfelves, as beneath fully may appear, as
well of the one Part as of the other Part, for
ever to be obferved, that is to fay: If and
whenfoever our Lord the King, his Heirs or
Succeffors, for the whole Shipping aforefaid to
be had, when the faid Lord the King, or any
of his Heirs, Kings of *England*, fhall propofe
to crofs the Seas, and fhall fend his Writ of
Summons to the Warden of the *Cinque Ports*
aforefaid, or his Lieutenant in this behalf;
and the fame Warden or Lieutenant upon this
fhall direct his Mandate to the aforefaid
Mayor and Barons of the faid Port and Town
of *Rye*; that then the faid Mayor and Commonalty of the faid Port and Town of *Rye*,
their Heirs and Succeffors, that Mandate of the
faid Warden or Lieutenant of Summons aforefaid, fo to them directed, to the faid Balliff and
Commonalty of the Town and Hundred of
Tenterden, their Heirs and Succeffors, within
three Days next after the Receipt of the fame
Mandate, fhall direct, tranfmit and caufe to be
delivered. And then the faid Balliff and Commonalty of the faid Town and Hundred of
Tenterden, their Heirs and Succeffors, one
Ship, and Men in the fame Ship according to
the Number aforefaid, at the Day and Place in
the faid Mandate fpecified, ought to prepare
and find, by the Days before fpecified, at
their proper Cofts and Expences. Or if and
whenfoever our now Lord the King, his
Heirs and Succeffors, Kings of *England*, fhall
fend his Writ of Summons for the Moiety or
Part of his Shipping, of fifty and feven Ships,
to be had or prepared; then the faid Balliff
and Commonalty of the faid Town and
Hundred of *Tenterden*, their Heirs and Succeffors, fhall find a fifth Part of all Payments
and Expences about the Preparation and finding of the Ships and Men of and in proportion
of the faid Shipping to be made. Provided
always that the faid Balliff and Commonalty
of the faid Town and Hundred of *Tenterden*,
their Heirs and Succeffors, may be privy [*] and * *Or fecret.*
called always, as well to the Preparation of
the Ships and Men aforefaid, as to the Payment of the Expences and Cofts as aforefaid
to be made. And further, the aforefaid Balliff
and Commonalty of the Town and Hundred
of *Tenterden*, their Heirs and Succeffors, for
and in the Name of a full and ample Portion
and Contribution, according to their Eftates [*], * *Subftance or*
to the making reparation, fuftentation and   *faculties.*
finding the other Ships, of all and fingular the
Portion of the Mayor and Commonalty of the
faid Port and Town of *Rye* to our Lord the
King of *England*, his Heirs and Succeffors, Kings
of *England*, incumbent, or appertaining to
find for and concerning his Shipping aforefaid, fhall contribute, pay, and are bound to
pay, and by thefe Prefents do grant to the

aforefaid

ANNOTATIONS.

prædictis Majori & communitati Portus & villæ de Rye, hæred. & succeſſoribus ſuis, annuatim imperpetuum ſex marcas legalis monetæ Angliæ, videlicet, ad feſta annunciationis beatæ Mariæ virginis & ſancti Michaelis archangeli, æquis portionibus ſolvend. Pro qua quidem contributione ſex marcarum annuatim, ut præfertur, dictis Majori & communitati Portus & villæ de Rye, hæred. & ſucceſſoribus ſuis, imperpetuum ſolvend ac dict. navis & homin. in eadem nave, ut præfertur, modo & forma prædictis præparand. & inveniend. dicti Major & communitas dict. Portus & villæ de Rye, hæred. & ſucceſſores ſui, ſingulariter per ſe ſumptibus ſuis propriis & expenſis, tam pro eis & communitate ſua, quam pro prædictis Ballivo & communitate dictorum villæ & hundred. de Tenterden, hæred. & ſucceſſoribus ſuis, de reſiduo navium in viagio dicti Domini Regis Angliæ & hæred. ſuorum Angliæ Regum, ut præmittitur, inveniend. omnimod. cuſtagia & expenſas facient, ſupportabunt, & ſolvent; ac etiam de cuſtagiis Baronum ad parliamentum, Ballivorum apud Jernemuthum, ad coronationem Regis ſive Reginæ inveniend. muneris ſive doni alicui Cuſtodi Quinque Portuum in ſua primaria dand. ſive conferend. Necnon de omnibus & ſingulis aliis quibuſcunque ſerviciis, ſolutionibus oneribus, auxiliis, donis, & cuſtagiis Baronum Quinque Portuum prædictorum qualitercunque ſpectant. incumbent. ſive de jure pertinent. de Majore & communitate Portus & villæ de Rye, ſuprædict. hæred. ſive ſucceſſoribus ſuis exeunt. exigent. petit, conceſſis, ſeu in futur. exigend. ſive concedend. ipſos Ballivum & communitatem dictorum villæ & hundred de Tenterden, hæredes & ſucceſſores ſuos, exonerabunt, defendent, acquietabunt, & imperpetuum indempnes conſervabunt. Et prædicti Major & communitas prædict. Portus & villæ de Rye, & ſucceſſores ſui, allocabunt & exonerabunt prædict. Ballivum & communitatem villæ & hundred. de Tenterden ac ſucceſſores ſuos, ac dict. villam & hundr. de Tenterden de xv l. xiii s. iiii d. ad quamlibet integram x[am]. & xv[am]. impoſterum Regibus Angliæ de villa & hundr. de Tenterden concedend. Et ſi xv l. xiii s. iiii d. plene exonerare dict. villam & hundred. de Tenterden pro integra decima & xv[ma]. non poterit, tunc reſidm. xv°. & xme de villa & hundred. prædict. ſic conceſſ. ultra prædict. xv l. xiii s. iiii d. propriis cuſtagiis & expenſis villæ & hundred. de Tenterden prædict. ſupportentur & exonerentur. Et ſi contingat dictos Ballivum & communitatem dict. villæ & hundred. de Tenterden, hæred. & ſucceſſores ſuos, ſeu eorum aliquem, pro aliquibus rebus vel cauſis quibuſcunque forinceſis (hoc de decimis & quintiſdecimis ante dictis dictam ſummam xv l. xiii s. iiii d. excedente omnino excepto) contra tenorem libertatum & francheſ. contentarum in dictis literis patentibus dicti nuper Regis Henrici ſexti eis conceſſarum, aut contra aliquas alias libertates ſive francheſ. Baronum Quinque Portuum, perturbari & inquietari, extunc dicti Ballivus & communitas dict. villæ & hundred. de Ten-

aforeſaid Mayor and Commonalty of the Port and Town of *Rye*, their Heirs and Succeſſors, yearly for ever, ſix Marks of lawful Money of *England*, that is to ſay, at the Feaſt of the Annunciation of the Bleſſed Virgin *Mary*, and of St. *Michael* the Archangel, by equal Portions to be paid; for which ſaid Contribution of ſix Marks yearly, as aforeſaid, to the ſaid Mayor and Commonalty of the Port and Town of *Rye*, their Heirs and Succeſſors, for ever to be paid, and the ſaid Ship and Men in the ſame Ship, as aforeſaid, in manner and form aforeſaid to be prepared and found, the ſaid Mayor and Commonalty of the ſaid Port and Town of *Rye*, their Heirs and Succeſſors, ſeverally by themſelves, at their proper Coſts and Expences, as well for them and their Commonalty, as for the aforeſaid Bailiff and Commonalty of the ſaid Town and Hundred of *Tenterden*, their Heirs and Succeſſors, of the Reſidue of the Ships in the Voyage of our ſaid Lord the King of *England*, and of his Heirs Kings of *England*, as aforeſaid, to be found, ſhall make, ſupport and pay all manner of Coſts and Expences; and alſo of the Coſts of Barons to the Parliament, Bailiffs at *Yarmouth*, at the Coronation of the King or Queen to be found ; of the Gift or Preſent to any Warden of the *Cinque Port*, in his Entrance to be given or conferred , alſo of all and ſingular other whatſoever Services, Payments, Charges, Aids, Gifts and Coſts of the Barons of the *Cinque Ports* aforeſaid, in any wiſe belonging, incumbent, or of Right appertaining, of the Mayor and Commonalty of the Port and Town of *Rye* aboveſaid, their Heirs or Succeſſors, iſſuing, exacted *, asked, *As I take it granted, or in Time to come to be exacted or *in the Inden-* granted, the ſame Bailiff and Commonalty of *ture it is exi-* the ſaid Town and Hundred of *Tenterden*, gend. their Heirs and Succeſſors, ſhall diſcharge, defend, acquit, and for ever ſhall keep indemnified. And the aforeſaid Mayor and Commonalty of the aforeſaid Port and Town of *Rye*, and their Succeſſors, ſhall allow and diſcharge the aforeſaid Bailiff and Commonalty of the Town and Hundred of *Tenterden*, and their Succeſſors, and the ſaid Town and Hundred of *Tenterden* of 15 l. 13 s. 4 d. at every whole Tenth and Fifteenth hereafter to be granted to the Kings of *England* from the Town and Hundred of *Tenterden*. And if 15 l. 13 s. 4 d. cannot fully diſcharge the ſaid Town and Hundred of *Tenterden* for the whole Tenth and Fifteenth, then the Reſidue of the Tenth and Fifteenth ſo granted from the Town and Hundred aforeſaid, beyond the aforeſaid 15 l. 13 s. 4 d. at the proper Coſts and Expences of the Town and Hundred of *Tenterden* aforeſaid ſhall be born and diſcharged. And if it happen the ſaid Bailiff and Commonalty of the ſaid Town and Hundred of *Tenterden*, their Heirs and Succeſſors, or any of them, for any Things† or Cauſes† *Or Matters* foreign whatſoever (this of Tenths and *or foreign Cau-* Fifteenths aforeſaid exceeding the ſaid Sum of *ſes.* 15 l. 13 s. 4 d. altogether excepted) againſt the Tenor of the Liberties and Franchiſes contained in the ſaid Letters Patents of the ſaid late King *Henry* VI. to them granted, or againſt any other Liberties or Franchiſes of the Barons of the *Cinque Ports*, to be diſturbed and vexed ǁ ; then the ſaid Bailiff and Com- ǁ *Troubled and* monalty of the ſaid Town and Hundred of *unquiet.* Ten-

ANNOTATIONS.

Tenterden Majori & communicati Portus &
villæ de Rye inde ſcire fac. & ſuper hoc dicti
Major & communitas de Rye remedium congruum ſuis expenſis providebunt ; proviſo
quod aliqui de dict. villa & hundred. de Tenterden parati erunt ad curiam de Brodhill ad
ibidem oſtendend. & ſcire facer. Baronibus
Quinque Portuum materias & cauſas in quibus
ſic perturbantur & inquietantur, cum ad hoc
erunt requiſiti. Et ſi aliqua ſupplicatio ſive
biila concepta fuerint, aliquo tempore futuro, &
Domino Regi nunc, hæred. ſive ſucceſſoribus
ſuis Angliæ Regibus præſentat. ad reſumend.
libertates & privilegia per dictum Dominum
Henricum nuper Regem per literas ſuas patentes prædictas dictis Ballivo & communitati dictorum villæ & hundred. de Tenterden, hæredibus & ſucceſſoribus ſuis, conceſſas ; ex tunc
partes prædictæ volunt & per præſentes concedunt pro ſe, hæred. & ſucceſſoribus ſuis, quod
ipſi conjunctim ex æarum partium expenſis
æqualibus, melioribus modis & viis quibus
ſcire poterint, tam in conſervationem libertatum prædict. quam obſervacionem dict. contributionis indifferent. ad ultimum laborabunt.
Et ſi dictæ libertates per dictum Dominum
Henricum nuper Regem, ut prædict. dictis Ballivo & communitati de Tenterden, hæred. &
ſucceſſoribus ſuis, conceſſæ, in manus Domini
Regis nunc, ſeu hæred. ſuorum Angliæ Regum,
reſumptæ fuerint, aut dictæ literæ Domini
Regis Henrici vi[ti]. patent. auctoritate alicujus
parliamenti ſeu aliter revocari, adnullari ſeu
cancellari contigerint, quod abſit ; extunc dicti Ballivus & communitas dictorum villæ &
hundred. de Tenterden, hæred. & ſucceſſores
ſui, pro præparatione & inventione navium &
hominum prædict. ac ſolutione contributionis
ſex marcarum, penitus ſint inde quieti & imperpetuum exonerati. Et ſi dicti Major & communitas dict. Portus & villæ de Rye, hæred. &
ſucceſſores ſui, pro præparatione & inventione
navium & hominum prædictorum, ac ſolutione
contributionis dictarum ſex marcarum annuatim,
ut prædicitur, ſolvend. dictos Ballivum & communitatem dict. r.villæ & hundred.deTenterden,
hæred. & ſucceſſores ſuos ac eorum quemlibet,
tam erga Dominum Regem de reſiduo dictarum navium & hominum in viagio Domini
Regis Angliæ & hæred. ſuorum, portioni Majoris & communitatis dict. Portus & villæ de
Rye inveniend. pertinent. ſive incumbent.
quam erga omnes alios & ſingulos quoſcunque,
ut prædict. eſt, non exoneraverint, acquietave-
rint, nec defend. ſeu negligent. fuerint & re-
miſi in præmiſſis ſeu in aliquo præmiſſorum ;
quod tunc Major & communitas dict. Portus
& villæ de Rye volunt, & pro ſe, hæred. &
ſucceſſoribus ſuis concedunt, quod dicti Ballivus & communitas dict. villæ & hundred. de
Tenterden, hæred. & ſucceſſores ſui, de ſolutione dictæ contributionis dictarum ſex marcarum ceſſent, quouſque dampna, miſræ, & expen-
ſæ, occaſione ſive occaſionibus prædictis, ſeu aliis
cauſis rationabilibus emergentibus, Ballivo &
communitati dictorum villæ & hundred. deTen-
terden plenarie ſint ſatisfact. & perſolut. ita
quod dict. Major & communitas dict. Portus &
villæ de Rye, & ſucceſſores ſui, ſecreti fiant,
&

Tenterden ſhall make ‡ it known to the Mayor ‡ *Thereof ſi ait*
and Commonalty of the Port and Town of *make to know*,
Rye, and upon this the ſaid Mayor and Commonalty of Rye ſhall provide meet Remedy at
their Expences ; provided that ſome of the
ſaid Town and Hundred of *Tenterden* ſhall be
ready at the Court of *Brotherhood* to ſhew
there, and to make * known to the Barons of * *Or make to*
the *Cinque Ports* the Matters and Cauſes in *know*.
which they are ſo diſturbed and vexed †, † *Or unquiet*,
when to this they ſhall be requeſted. And if as above.
any Supplication || or Bill ſhall be conceived, || *Or Petition*;
at any Time to come, and preſented to our
now Lord the King, his Heirs or Succeſſors,
Kings of *England* to reſume ‡ the Liberties and ‡ *Or retake*,
Privileges by the ſaid Lord *Henry*, late King,
by his Letters Patents aforeſaid, granted to
the ſaid Bailiff and Commonalty of the ſaid
Town and Hundred of *Tenterden*, their Heirs
and Succeſſors ; then the Parties aforeſaid will,
and by theſe Preſents grant for themſelves, their
Heirs and Succeſſors, that they jointly, at the
equal Expences of both Parties, by the beſt * * *Better after*
Ways and Means they can know, as well for the *Latin*.
Preſervation † of the Liberties aforeſaid, as † *Or Conſerva-*
for Obſervation of the ſaid Contribution in- *tion*.
differently, ſhall labour to the utmoſt. And
if the ſaid Liberties by the ſaid Lord *Henry*,
late King as aforeſaid, granted to the ſaid
Bailiff and Commonalty of *Tenterden*, their
Heirs and Succeſſors, ſhall be reſumed || into || *Retaken or*
the Hands of our now Lord the King, or his *reſeized*,
Heirs, Kings of *England*, or the ſaid Letters
Patents of the Lord King *Henry* the Sixth by
Authority of any Parliament, or otherwiſe,
ſhall happen to be revoked, adnulled or can-
celled, which God forbid ; then the ſaid
Bailiff and Commonalty of the ſaid Town
and Hundred of *Tenterden*, their Heirs and
Succeſſors, for the Preparation and finding of
the Ships and Men aforeſaid, and Payment of
the Contribution of ſix Marks, altogether
may ‡ be thereof quit and for ever diſcharged. ‡ *Or ſhall bri*
And if the ſaid Mayor and Commonalty of the
ſaid Port and Town of Rye, their Heirs and
Succeſſors, for the Preparation and finding of
the Ships and Men aforeſaid, and the Payment
of the Contribution of the ſaid ſix Marks
yearly, as aforeſaid, to be paid, the ſaid Bailiff
and Commonalty of the ſaid Town and Hundred of *Tenterden*, their Heirs and Succeſſors,
and every of them, as well towards our Lord
the King, concerning the Reſidue of the ſaid
Ships and Men in the Voyage of our Lord the
King of *England*, and his Heirs, the portion
incumbent to be found or appertaining to the
Mayor and Commonalty of the ſaid Port and
Town of Rye, as towards all and ſingular
others whomſoever, as is aforeſaid, ſhall not
diſcharge, acquit nor defend, or ſhall be negligent and remiſs in the Premiſſes, or in any
of the Premiſſes ; that then the Mayor and
Commonalty of the ſaid Port and Town of
Rye will, and for themſelves, their Heirs and
Succeſſors, grant, that the ſaid Bailiff and
Commonalty of the ſaid Town and Hundred
of *Tenterden*, their Heirs and Succeſſors, of
the Payment of the ſaid Contribution of the
ſaid ſix Marks may ceaſe, until the Damages,
Coſts and Expences, by the Occaſion or Occaſions aforeſaid, or other reaſ nable Cauſes
happening *, be fully ſatisfied and paid to * *Ariſing or*
the Bailiff and Commonalty of the ſaid Town *emergent*.
and Hundred of *Tenterden*, ſo that the ſaid
Mayor and Commonalty of the ſaid Port and
Town of Rye, and their Succeſſors, be made
Privy,

D d

ANNOTATIONS.

& perfectam noticiam habeant de dampnis, missis & expensis prædictis. Et si Ballivus & communitas dict. villæ & hundred. de Tenterden, hæred. sive successores sui, de præparatione & inventione navis & hominum in viagio Domini Regis, seu de solutione quintæ partis omnium expensarum & solutionum circa navigium prædict. aliquo tempore futur. quando ipsi, ut prædicit. debite summoniti fuerint, negligentes fuerint & remissi, talit. quod dict. navis & homines, ut prædicitur, parati non fuerint ad velificand. cum cæteris navibus per Majorem & communitatem villæ de Rye in viagio aliquo Domini Regis præparand. & servicium prædict. modo & forma prædict. faciend. vel si dicta quinta pars omnium solutionum & expensarum, post summonitionem ut prædicitur, in viagio Domini Regis aliquo tempore futur. a retro sit non soluta, cum prædicti Major. & communitas dict. Portus & villæ de Rye in viagio aliquo dicti Domini Regis super mare faciend. præparent, & dict. modo & forma facient; quod tunc prædicti Ballivus & communitas villæ & hundred. de Tenterden volunt & concedunt pro se & successoribus suis, quod ipsi incurrant in duplicem pœnam omnium custiag. dampn. pœnarum & expensarum, tam circa præparationem & inventionem navis & hominum prædict. quam solutionis quintæ partis omnium solutionum & expensarum prædictarum : seu si dict. annualis contributio dictarum sex marcarum a retro fore contigerit post aliquod festum festorum prædictorum, quo solvi debeat, per quindecim dies post petitionem dicte solutionis per prædictos Majorem & communitatem villæ de Rye vel eorum deputatum ; tunc Ballivus & communitas villæ & hundred. de Tenterden volunt & concedunt pro se, hæred. & successoribus suis, quod ipsi incurrant in pœnam viginti solid. levand. de bonis & catallis suis pro defectu solutionis quarumlibet trium marcarum. Et super hoc necnon, pro prædictis custiagiis, dampnis, pœnis, & expensis pro defectu navis & solutionis prædictarum, dicti Major & communitas dict. Portus & villæ de Rye, hæred. & successores sui, mandent & transmittent dict. Ballivo & communitati dict. villæ & hundred. de Tenterden literas processi. original. & alias sub sigillo officii dicti majorat. de Rye, & sicut plures sub sigillo communi ejusdem villæ ; & super hoc capient Wythernamium, secundum antiquum usum Quinque Portuum, tenend. & retinend. quousque eis satisfact. fuerint, una cum custiagiis, dampnis & expensis, in natura placiti debiti adjudicat. & ab antiquo usitat. inter partem & partem. In cujus rei testimonium uni parti hujus Indenturæ, penes præfat. Majorem & communitatem Portus & villæ de Rye remanenti, prædicti Ballivus & communitas villæ & hundred. de Tenterden prædict. sigillum suum commune apposuerunt ; alteri vero parti hujus Indenturæ, penes præfatos Ballivum & communitatem villæ & hundred. de Tenterden remanenti, prædicti Major & communitas Portus & villæ de Rye prædict. sigillum suum commune apposuerunt. Dat. apud Rye, die & anno supradict.

Privy to, and have perfect Knowledge † of the † *Or Notice.* Damages, Costs and Expences aforesaid. And if the Bailiff and Commonalty of the said Town and Hundred of *Tenterden*, their Heirs and Successors, of the Preparation and finding of the Ship and Men in the Voyage of our Lord the King, or the Payment of the fifth Part of all the Expences and Payments about the Shipping aforesaid, at ‖ any Time to come, ‖ *Or in any.* when they, as aforesaid, shall have been duly summoned, shall be negligent and remiss, so as that the said Ship and Men, as aforesaid, shall not be ready to sail with the other Ships to be prepared by the Mayor and Commonalty of the Town of *Rye* in any Voyage of our Lord the King, and to do the Service aforesaid, in Manner and Form aforesaid ; or if the said fifth Part of all the Payments and Expences, after Summons as aforesaid, in the Voyage of our Lord the King, at ‡ any Time ‡ *Or in any.* to come, be behind * and unpaid, when the * *Or in arrear* aforesaid Mayor and Commonalty of the said *and not paid.* Port and Town of *Rye*, in any Voyage of our said Lord the King to be made upon the Sea, should prepare, and in the said Manner and Form should do ; that then the aforesaid Bailiff and Commonalty of the Town and Hundred of *Tenterden* will, and grant for themselves and their Successors, that they ‖ will ‖ *Or may incur* incur the double Penalty of all Costs, Dama- *or run into the* ges, Penalties and Expences, as well about the *double, &c.* Preparation and finding of the Ship and Men aforesaid, as of the Payment of the fifth Part of all the Payment and Expences aforesaid : Or if the said yearly Contribution of the said six Marks shall happen to be behind ‡, after ‡ *Or in arrear.* any Feast of the Feasts aforesaid, in which it ought to be paid, by fifteen Days after request * of the said Payment by the aforesaid * *Or Petition;* Mayor and Commonalty of the Town of *Rye*, or their Deputy ; then the Bailiff and Commonalty of the Town and Hundred of *Tenterden* will, and grant for themselves, their Heirs and Successors, that they † will incur † *Or may incur* the Penalty of Twenty Shillings, to be levied *or run into the* of their Goods and Chattels for default ‖ of *Penalty, &c.* Payment of every three Marks. And upon ‖ *Or defect, and* this also, for the aforesaid Costs, Damages, *so afterward.* Penalties and Expences for default of the Ship and Payment aforesaid, the said Mayor and Commonalty of the said Port and Town of *Rye*, their Heirs and Successors, shall ‡ send ‡ *Or may;* and transmit to the said Bailiff and Commonalty of the said Town and Hundred of *Tenterden* Letters of Process, *Original* and *Alias*, under the Seal of Office of the said Mayoralty of *Rye*, & *sicut plures*, under the Common Seal of the same Town ; and upon this they shall take *Withernam*, according to the ancient Use † of the *Cinque Ports*, to be held and re- † *Or usage.* tained until they shall be satisfied, together with Costs, Damages, and Expences, in nature of a Plea of Debt adjudged, and of ancient Time used between Party and Party. In witness whereof to one part of this Indenture, remaining with the aforesaid Mayor and Commonalty of the Port and Town of *Rye*, the aforesaid Bailiff and Commonalty of the Town and Hundred of *Tenterden* aforesaid have put their Common Seal ; and * to * *Or but.* the other Part of this Indenture, remaining with the aforesaid Bailiff and Commonalty of the Town and Hundred of *Tenterden*, the aforesaid Mayor and Commonalty of the Port and Town of *Rye* aforesaid have put their Common Seal. Dated at *Rye* the Day and Year abovesaid. 　*　*Wil-

CHARTERS.

the said Town and Port of Romney, *the Day of the Date here-of holden, assembled, that is to say,* William Nepsham ᵘ *Bai-liff* ᵛ *of* Hasting ᵂ, Richard Martham *Mayor of* Winchelsea ˣ, John

ANNOTATIONS.

ᵘ *William Nepsham, &c.* These here named were only the Chief Magistrates of the Town mentioned, who in the Name of the whole *Brotherhood,* and consequently for all the Ports Towns and Members, make this Letter of Attorney. The Places of which these Persons are named, are the *Cinque Ports* and *Two Ancient Towns,* as by their following Charters appear. And here may be noted further, that this is the first of all the general Charters that mention the Names of the said Ports and Towns.

ᵛ *Bailiff,* for so had the Head Officer of *Hasting* been called before ; and after the Time of King *Henry* VII. till turned into a Mayor by particular Charter of Queen *Elizabeth.*

ᵂ *Hasting.* Sometime wrote *Hastinge* and *Hastings,* in *Latin Hastingia* and *Hastinga.* *Camb-den* in his *Britannia* says, it seems to take its Name from the Arch-pirate *Hasting,* for being called in the *Saxon* Tongue *Hastinga-Ceaster,* is as much as *Hasting's Town* ; and that in the Time of King *Athelstane* it had *Officinam monetariam,* which his Translator calls *A Mint-House :* But whether the old or present *Hasting,* tells not. This latter seems to be of Note at the Conquest of King *William,* who landed at or near it with his Army, and by him was made one of the *Five Ports* (as the Lord *Coke* in the fourth Part of his *Institutes* affirms*) and as Tradition tells us, * Cap. 42. fortified it with a Castle built on the Top of an Hill near thereto, part of whose Ruins are yet ₚₐg. 222. to be seen. It gives the Name to the Easternmost of the six Divisions of the County of *Sussex* called *Rapes.* The Barony whereof, and of the Castle, was given by *W. liam* the Conqueror to *John de Britannia,* as *Speed's* Chronicles testify ; and since *Edward* the Fourth conferred, with other Royalties, the Title of Lord of *Hastings* on *William Hastings,* one of his Bed-chamber, in the first Year of his Reign : This hath added to the honourable Titles of the Earls of *Hunting-don,* who enjoyed the Honour and Profits thereof till Queen *Elizabeth's* Time, and then *Henry* Earl of *Huntingdon,* in the Thirty third Year of her Reign, sold the Profits of the *Rape, &c.* to *Thomas Pelham,* Esquire. The present Town of *Hasting* is built between two Hills, in two long Streets, containing two Parishes, between which runs a fresh Water called *The Bourne,* serving for use to both. It is beautified with two Churches, one called by the Name of S^t. *Clement,* and the other *All Saints* ; but by their Custom it seems they had formerly another called S^t. *Michael,* as also S^t. *Mary* of the Castle, *&c.* besides an Hospital of S^t. *Mary Magdalene,* and the Priory near the Town : Populous, besides others, with Fishermen, who bring in great Quantities of fresh Fish. By the Charter of King *James* may be collected, that it was first enfranchised by the Name of *the Barons of the Town and Port of* Hasting, and afterward incorporated by the Bailiff, Jurats and Commonalty of the Town and Port of *Hasting,* by which Bailiff and twelve Jurats it was governed till about the Thirtieth Year of Queen *Elizabeth,* when the Bailiff was changed for a Mayor by particular Charter and Grant from the Queen.

ˣ *Winchelsea,* wrote sometimes *Winchelsee, Winchelsey,* and *Winchelsey,* signifies *Wind-cold-sea,* (*chil,* an old Word, yet in use for *cold*) according to the *Latin Frigmareventus,* for which now the Word *Winchelsea* is used ; and well might the old Town deserve that Name, standing in a low Plain, open both to the Winds and Sea. By *Johnson,* in his *Atlas,* it is reported to have been a City in the Time the *Romans* were here, included with *Rye* under the Land of *Staninges.* It was, as appeareth by a Charter of King *Henry* III. given by *Edward* the Confessor (there called S^t. *Edward*) to the Abbot and Monks of *Fischampe* (vulgarly *Fecham*) in *France,* and afterwards granted and confirmed by King *William* and King *Henry* with their Liberties, free Customs, Pleas, Plaints and Causes ; but after that (for the better Defence of this Realm, and it might be, to conceal from Foreigners the Intelligence of Affairs at home, and stop them of such convenient Ports of Passage) by King *Henry* III. in the Thirty first Year of his Reign, exchanged with the said Abbot and Monks for the Manor of *Chilceham,* sometimes wrote *Chiltenham* and *Chiltham* in *Gloucestershire, &c.* and taken into his own Hands, as appeareth further in the Notes of *Rye;* before which both were adjoined to the Ports, because in that Charter they are then called *Nobiliora Membra* Quinque Portuum, *The more Noble Members of the* Cinque Ports. This Union to the Ports, according to the Lord *Coke,* was after the Con- * For in a Re-queror, and before King *John,* Father of King *Henry* III *.* and by the Charter of King *James,* cord in the first *Winchelsea,* that is the old, seems enfranchised, and incorporated at first by the Name of *the Barons* Year of K. John *of the ancient Town of* Winchelsea, and then by *The Mayor, Jurats and Commonalty of the anci-* they are menti-*ent Town* of Winchelsea. In which State it stood, washed by the *British* Ocean on the South oned to be in and East, and by the Mouth of the River of *Rother* (then running out there) on the North, till *Aid of* Hasting about the beginning of the Reign of King *Edward* I. for in the eighth Year of his Reign, in a to do the Ser-Writ directed to *Ralph* of *Sandwich* his Steward (for to exchange or buy of *John de Langherst* vice of their and *John Bon,* if they would sell, Lands that lay near *Iham,* and fit to the Building of the new Navy. In Dorf. Town of *Winchelsea*) it is mentioned that the greatest part of *Winchelsea* was drowned, and the Sea Cart An°.1 R. prevailing more and more against it, that the rest was hopeless long to stand. In the tenth Jo.par.1.M.12. Year of his Reign he issued forth a Commission to *Stephen de Pencester* and others, to assign Places And in the at *Iham* (being an Hill near) for the Inhabitants of old *Winchelsea* to plant themselves at, the *Charter of K.* Copy whereof follows. John *to* Rye

and Winchelsea, *dated* 6 June, An° 7. *of his Reign, he mentions and confirms to them the Charter of his Father,* *which was* K. Henry II. *and of his Brother* K. Richard I.

                                                                                          Edwardus

ANNOTATIONS.

Edwardus Dei gratia, Rex Angliæ, Dominus Hiberniæ, & Dux Acquitaniæ, dilectis & fidelibus suis Stephano de Pencelir. Iter. Engolisina, & Henrico le Waleys, salutem. Sciatis quod assignavimus vos ad assidend. placias apud Ihame, & eas per certam arrentationem, juxta legalem extentam per vos inde faciend. Baronibus & probis hominibus nostris de Wynch. ædificand. & inhabitand. juxta discretiones vestras committend. Et ideo vobis mandamus, quod vos omnes, vel duo vestrum, quos ad hoc vacare contigerit, in propriis personis vestris apud Ihame accedatis, & placias ibidem assideatis, & eas præfatis Baronibus ædificand. & inhabitand. committatis in forma prædicta ; salva tum Dominis immediatis placiarum prædictarum rationabili extenta cujuslibet acræ per vos assessæ, & ad inhabitan. commissæ, juxta discretiones vestras prædictas, sicut prædictum est. In cujus rei testimonium has literas nostras fieri fecimus patentes. Teste me ipso apud Westm. xxvii°. die Novembris, anno Regni nostri decimo.

And in the eleventh Year of his Reign, his Charter then (for the Barons of *Winchelsea* to enjoy their Liberties in the new Town as in the old) mentions it part drowned, and that it was feared daily to be wholly lost ; and also that the Inhabitants had begun to build at *Iham*, as fully appears by the Charters, &c. following, exemplified afterward by King *Henry*, in one Exemplification whereof that Commission above of the tenth Year is also inserted, the Translation whereof, to avoid prolixity, is omitted.

Henricus Dei gratia, Rex Angliæ, & Franciæ, & Dominus Hiberniæ, omnibus, ad quos præsentes literæ pervenerint, salutem. Inspeximus irrotulamentum quarundam literarum patencium Domini Edwardi, quondam Regis Angliæ primi post conquestum, in rotulis cancellariæ suæ irrotulatarum in hæc verba : Edwardus Dei gratia, Rex Angliæ, & Dominus Hiberniæ, & Dux Acquitaniæ, omnibus, ad quos præsentes literæ pervenerint, salutem. Quia pro villa nostra de Winchelsee, quæ pro majori parte per maris inundationes jam submersa est, & de cujus submercione totali condie veretur, quandam villam novam apud Yhame fieri providimus, & terras & tenementa ibidem Baronibus villæ & portus de Wynche.see committere, & ipsos inde feoffare, ædificand. & inhabitand. volumus & concedimus, pro nobis & hæredibus nostris, quod cum iidem Barones placias suas apud Yhame ceperunt, & eas ædificare inceperunt, ipsi, cum rebus & bonis suis omnibus adeo liberi sint in eadem nova villa & alibi ubique, sicut antea fuerint in prædicta villa de Wynchelsee, & aliis locis quibuscunque ; & easdem libertates & consuetudines habeant, quas habent per cartas prædecessorum nostrorum Regum Angliæ, & eisdem libertatibus & consuetudinibus gaudeant & utantur, quibus rationabiliter usi sunt temporibus retroactis; & cartas nostras eis inde de novo fieri faciemus. In cujus rei testimonium has literas nostras fieri fecimus patentes. T. me ipso apud Acton Burnell, xiii die Octobris, anno Regni nostri undecimo. Inspeximus etiam irrotulamentum cujusdam commissionis prædicti quondam Regis in rotulis Cancellariæ prædictæ irrotulatæ, in hæc verba :

Edwardus Dei gratia, Rex Angliæ, Dominus Hiberniæ, & Dux Aquitaniæ, dilecto & fideli suo Johanni de Cobeham, salutem. Sciatis quod assignavimus vos una cum dilectis & fidelibus nostris Stephano de Penecear. Iter. de Engolisme, & Henrico le Walys, ad assidend. placeas apud Ihamme, & eas per certam arrentationem, juxta legalem extentam per vos & ipsos inde faciend. Baronibus & probis hominibus nostris de Wynchelsee ædificand. & inhabitand. juxta discretiones vestras committend. Et ideo vobis mandamus, quod vos una cum prædictis Stephano, Iter. & Henrico, duobus vel uno eorum, quos vel quem ad hoc vacare contigerit, in propria persona vestra apud Ihamme accedatis, & placeas ibidem unacum ipsis assideatis, & eas prælatis Baronibus ædificand. & inhabitand. committatis in forma prædicta. Salva tum Dominis immediatis placiarum prædictarum rationab. extenta cujuslibet acræ per vos & ipsos assessæ, & ad inhabitand. commissæ, juxta discretiones vestras prædictas, sicut prædictum est. Mandavimus enim præfatis Stephano, Iter. & Henrico, quod vos ad hoc admittant in forma prædicta. In cujus rei testimonium has literas nostras fieri fecimus patentes. T. me ipso apud Roch. quinto die Marcii anno Regni nostri xi°. Inspeximus insuper irrotulamenta quorundam brevium ejusdem quondam Regis in rotulis Cancellariæ suæ prædictæ similiter irrotulatorum, in hæc verba : Quia propter dampnum quod di. & fi. R. Barones Portus R. de Wynchelsee, de villa sua per maris intemperiem, jam diu est, sustiouérunt, ac periculum quod eis indies imminet ibidem, Rex dedit & concessit eisdem Baronibus suis situm & placeam de Ihamme, cum marisco, exceptis decem acris terræ, quas in placea prædicta Rex retinet ad opus suum, quos Rex habuit ex concessione di. & fi. suorum Willielmi Wynd. de Grandisono & Isabellæ uxoris ejus, ad inhabitand. & ad villam suam de Wynchelsee ibidem faciend. & tenend. de Rege & hæred. suis, sibi & hæred. suis. Ita quod ipsi Barones sint ibidem adeo liberi, sicut prius apud Wynchelsee fuerunt, & eisdem libertatibus, quibus apud Wynchelsee, per cartas antecessorum Regis Regum Angliæ, & confirmationem Regis uti consueverunt, de cætero in omnibus gaudeant & utantur ibidem. Et ita quod de firma villæ ejusdem R. respondeatur per annum ad scaccarium Regis per manus Ballivi Regis ibidem, sicut prius de prædicta villa de Wynchelsee responderi consueverint. Mandatum est Vic. Sussex, quod eisdem Baronibus de prædictis situ & placea, cum marisco, plenam seisinam habere fac. salvo jure cujuslibet, & ita quod alteri non præjudicetur, Rex eum in adventu suo in Angliam per se & eosdem Barones singl. jus petentibus in prædicta & clamantibus satisfaciet, nisi per dilectos & fideles Regis prius inde fuerit satisfactum. T. Edm. comite Cornubiæ consf. R. apud Westm. xxiii. die Junii, anno Regni sui sexto decimo. Consimile breve dirigitur eidem vic. quod eisdem Baron. de prædictis situ & placea per metas & bundas inde factas plenam seisinam similiter habere fac. absque conditionibus prædictis. T. ut supra. Sub hujusmodi forma mandatum est Salomoni de Rofs. & sociis suis Justic. itinerantibus in com. Sussex, per duo brevia R. videlicet, perunum cum condicionibus prædictis & aliud absque condicionibus quod prædictos Barones libertatibus prædictis ibidem uti permittant, nec ipsos super hiis in aliquo inquietent coram eis, seu ab aliis inquietari permittant. T. ut supra. Inspeximus similiter tenorem irrotulamenti cujusdam cartæ

†   ‡   Willielmi

CHARTERS.

John Cheefman, *Mayor of* Rye, John Cheyncw,
Jurat

ANNOTATIONS

Willielmi de Grandifono & Sibilla uxori ejus, in ſuperioribus ſæcaſii ... quondam Regis irrotulatæ, quem coram nobis in Cancellar. noftram venire feciñús, ... in hac verba, &c. ... præfentes & futuri, quod nos Willielmus de Grandiſono & Sibilla uxor mea ... concefmus & hac præfenti carta noftra confirmavimus, pro nobis & hæred. noftris, magnifico principi & Domino noftro ligeo Domino Edwardo, Dei gratia Regi Angliæ Illuſtri, in eadem noftra de Jhamne cum advocationibus eccleſiarum, parcis & cum ſedds meſſuag, & cum omnibus alii per ſuis, excepta illa terra quæ fuit Henrici Berrin in Jhamne, habend. & tenend. eidem Domino noſtro Regi & hæred. fuis libere, quiete, abſolute, & integre, imperpetuum, in eſcambium man ... & Dymnok, & quadraginta & ſex libratus, ſex ſolidorum, & trium denar. & unius quale, redd ... tus ann. in Dertford. Et nos & hæred. noftri warrantizabimus prædicta Domino noftro Regi & hæred. fuis eadem materia de Jhamne & Idonæ imperpetuum in eſcambium prædictum, in cujus rei teftimonium præfenti carta ſigilla noftra appoſuimus. His teftibus, venerabili patre J. Bienſi epiſcopo Dom. Rx. Theſaur. Petro de Ceſtr, præpoſito Bryerlaa, J. Romayn de Cichaŋ, Willielmo de Myddeton, Willielmo de Carleton, Baron. de ſaccario, R. de Wytha, Cancellar. ejuſdem ſaccarii, Thoma de Weyland, Johanne de Lincton, Willielmo de Braunton, Ju ... ſtic. de Banco, Rad. de Sandewico, Nich. de Caſtello, Richardo de Standieford, & aliis, ... apud Weftm. viceſimo octavo die Aprilis, an⁰ Regni Rx. Edwardi prædicti quinto decimo. Nos autem tenores irrotulamentorum prædictorum ad requiſitionem nunc homin. dictæ villæ de Wynchelſee duximus exemplificand. per præfentes. In cujus rei teſtimonium has literas noſtras fieri fecimus patentes. T. me ipſo apud. Weftm. quinto decimo die Junii, anno Regni noſtri quinto.

But that old *Winchelſea* was abandoned, and the new built ſo ſoon as 1277, as *Lambard's* marginal Note affirms, I cannot believe; nor do I believe it to be wholly loft till the fixteenth Year of that King *Edward*, for I find by a Memorandum, in a Book remaining with the Records of the Town of *Rye*, theſe Words, *viz.*

M D. quod anno Domino Milleſimo CClxxxvij⁰, in vigilia ſanct. Agathæ virginis, ſubmerſa fuit villa de Wynchelſee, & omnes terræ inter Climeſden uſq. li Vochere de Hiſle. Eodem anno erat tanta copia bladi per univerſ. Angliã, Scotiã, Walliã, regiones, quod vendebatur quarterium frumenti pro duobus ſolidis.

Or Engliſhed thus.

BE it remembered, that in the Year of our Lord 1287. in the Even of St. *Agath* the Virgin, was the Town of *Winchelſea* drowned, and all the Lands between *Climeſden*, and the Voches of *Hiſle*. The ſame Year was ſuch Plenty of Corn throughout all the Countries of *England, Scotland,* and *Wales,* that a Quarter of Wheat was ſold for two Shillings.

Old *Winchelſea* being drowned, the Inhabitants, by favour of the King, and Authority of his Charters and Grants aforeſaid, brought the Name of *Winchelſea* to their new Plantation at *Iham* (which ſeems to be that which was before a Member to *Haſting*, called *Petit Iham*, and the rather, becauſe *Haſting* yet claims that part called St. *Leonard's*) and there built a Town of about forty* Squares, called Quarters, after the Pattern (as is believed) of the old Town, with ſpacious Streets; adorned, beſides the Religious Houſes, with three Churches, called ٭ *Or Thirty* St. *Giles,* St. *Leonard's,* and St. *Thomas* the Apoſtle, of which two former only ſome of the *nine.* Ruins remain to be ſeen, and of the latter but part of the ancient Building, and that no more than ſome ſay was intended only for the Chancel; yet all three were ſtanding, as *Lambard* affirms, within Memory when he wrote, which was 1573. Fortified, beſides the natural Situation on an Hill, with Walls, part of which, and of three of the Gates, are yet ſtanding; that called *Pipewell* leading to *Rye,* another called *Newgate* leading to *Haſting,* and the other called *Strandgate* leading to the Rivulet running near the Foot of the Hill, and ſo into the Sea at *Rye,* formerly called the River of *Ror,* which the Edifying of this new Town is ſuppoſed to have run up navigable beyond *Winchelſea* into the Country, and at the Weſt Side of the Town, in the Place called *Pewes Pond,* conceived to have made the Harbor where Ships lay at Anchor, which the Sea afterwards deſerting, was one Cauſe of the Decay of the Place. But others attribute their Decay to the Fire of the *French* in the Reigns of King *Richard* II. and King *Henry* VI. yet was it not ſo much decayed in 1573. when Queen *Elizabeth* in her Progreſs gave it a Viſit, but that beholding the goodly Situation, ancient Buildings, grave Bench of a Mayor and 12 Jurats in their ſcarlet Gowns, and City like Deportment of the People (there being then ſeveral Gentry) as well as Projection of the Place, ſhe gave it, as ſhe thought deſervedly, the Name of *Little London,* and it is yet a Title of Honour to the noble Family of the *Finches* in *Kent,* who are Earls of *Winchelſea.*

٭ *Rye* or *Riæ,* ſometimes wrote *Riæ,* in *Little Riæ* and *Riæ.* I cannot conclude to derive its Name from *Rie,* the Corn ſo called (as *Rieton* in *Warwickſhire,* in the Opinion of *Lingdale*) becauſe as the Soil thereabout is not very proper to bear it, ſo the People there are generally averſe to it. Nor will I affirm the Name came from the Rivulet *Ror,* before remembred

E e   *in*

ANNOTATIONS.

in *Winchelsea*, nor from *Rhe* or *Rey* sometime used for a River ; though the River of *Rother* on the East, and the Creek of the Sea like a River running up on the West into the Country between *Peasmarsh* and *Udimer*, called yet *Tillingham* Water, from a Farm on *Peasmarsh* side which it washeth, meeting together with the said *Ree*, and running out into the Sea at the South East (and formerly more South) side of the Town, might be supposed so to have first occasioned the Name. But it seems to me rather to take the Name from the *British* Word *Rhy*, signifying a *Ford*, or as some say, a *Bay*; in reference to the former, importing the Place where the Rivers of *Rother* and *Ree* were yet fordable ; and to the latter, the Situation of the Town in the bottom or middle of the Bay made by the Sea, between the Cliff at *Beachy* and those at *Folkstone*, from whence the Sea over against *Rye*, and near the Shore, is still called *Rye Bay*. This ancient Town is compact as a little City, stored with Buildings, and consisting of several Streets, as the lower or longer Street (in which standeth the Grammar School built by *Thomas Peacock*, Gent. one of the Jurats of the Town, *Anno* 1636. and by his Will, *Sept.* 10. 1638. devised to that Use ; and by Order thereof, and Settlement of his Executors, enjoying the yearly Revenue of Thirty five Pounds) besides which are the middle Street, the Butchery (where is the Market Place with the Town Hall) and the Watch-bell Street, with some cross Streets running from one to the other : It is built on a little Hill, now washed, on the South West, South, South-East, East, and North East sides of the Town, by the Flux and Reflux of the Sea, but especially on the two latter, where hath been washed away some Streets, the *Baddings* Gate, and Wall leading therefrom to the Land Gate ; yet the Compass of the Town may be about two Hundred and seventy one Rods : Beautified with a large Church called S'. *Mary*, the goodliest Edifice of that kind in the Counties of *Kent* and *Sussex*, the Cathedrals excepted : Inclosed with Walls, as *Cambden* says, in the Time of King *Edward* III. There are yet standing the Land Gate, called sometimes the North Gate, leading into the Country towards *Kent* ; the Postern Gate leading to the *New Conduit* ; the Strand Gate or South Gate opening towards *Winchelsea*, where the old Harbour was, though now more frequented on the East side of the Town ; the Gun Garden Gate adjoining to *Ipres* Tower, built by *William de Ipre*, Earl of *Kent*, and from him so called, afterwards purchased by the Corporation of one Mr. *Newbery*, about the tenth Year of King *Henry* VII. and used to keep Court in till the Building of the Town Hall aforesaid, whence it got the Name of the Court House, and then was converted into a Prison. And besides the Chapel of S'. *Clare* (now used for a Powder House) the Chauntry of S'. *Nicholas*, the Chancel whereof is still kept for an Ammunition House, where to it was converted *Anno* 17 *Elizabeth*, had a Monastery of the Friers Heremites of S'. *Augustines*, the Chapel whereof is yet standing, erected *Anno* 16 *Henry* VIII. and dissolved by him shortly after with the first Dissolution, in the Twenty seventh Year of his Reign, because the Revenues were not two Hundred Pounds *per Annum*, so as it had but a short standing ; for that it was not elder than the sixteenth Year of that King, I gather from a Passage I found in the Records of this Town, in that Year, which was thus : *Eodem anno, scilicet, quarto die Septembris, erect. fuit tegument. fabrica fratrum heremitarum sancti Augustini infra villam prædictam, ex impensis cujusdam Willielmi Marshe, agricolæ,* i. e. *In the same Year, that is to say, the fourth Day of September, was erected the Roof of the Fabrick of the Friers Heremits of Saint Augustin, within the Town aforesaid, at the Costs of one* William Marshe, *Husbandman.* The Town is of beautiful Prospect to look upon any way, a convenient Passage into *Normandy*, famous for Fishing, as good Fish having been brought to Market (before the *French* spoiled the Fishing Grounds) as any where in *England*, and yet the Fish keep the Name of the Town, as *Rye Herring*, to sell the better in *London*. An ancient Town it is called, and so is, and with its Sister Town, or Twin rather, *Winchelsea*, (though this had the Precedence in its Prosperity, and now the Priority in its Decay and Ruins) hath very near shared equally in Vicissitudes and Misfortunes ; for in the Time of *Edward* the Confessor they were both given to the Abbot and Monks of *Fischampe* (as before noted in *Winchelsea*) and afterwards reassumed in Exchange by King *Henry* III. as by the Exemplification of another King *Henry* following doth plainly appear.

HEnricus Dei gratia, Rex Angliæ, & Franciæ, & Dominus Hiberniæ, omnibus, ad quos præsentes literæ pervenerint, salutem. Inspeximus quoddam breve nostrum de memorando Thes. & Camerar. nostris direct. & nobis in Cancellar. nostram retorn. & in filacus ejusdem Cancellar. residen. in hæc verba: Henricus Dei gratia, Rex Angliæ, & Franciæ, & Dominus Hiberniæ, Thes. & Camerar. suis, salutem. Volentes certis de causis certiorari super transcripto Recordi quarundam literarum patencium per Dominum Henricum nuper Regem Angliæ, tercium, progenitorem nostrum, abbati & monachis de Fischampa fact. vobis mandamus quod scrutatis rotulis & aliis memorandis quæ in Thesaur. nostra sub custodia vestra existunt transcriptum recordi prædictarum literarum patencium, cum omnibus ea tangentibus, nobis in Cancellar. nostram, sub sigillo scaccarii nostri distincte & aperte sine dilacione mittatis & hoc breve. T. me ipso apud Westm. xix°. die Junii, anno Regni nostri vicesimo secundo. Baynbrig. Inspeximusque indorsamentum de & super eodem brevi factum in hæc verba: Responsio Thes. & Camerar. transcript. recordi de quo infra fit mencio, vobis mittimus in scedula huic brevi consut. Inspeximus etiam transcript. recordi quarundam literarum patencium per Dominum Henricum, nuper Regem Angliæ, tercium, progenitorem nostrum, abbati & monachis de Fischampa fact. & nobis in Cancellar. nostram virtute ejusdem brevis nostri retorn. & in filacus ejusdem Cancellar. nostræ residen. in hæc verba: Henricus Dei gratia, Rex Angliæ, & Dominus Hiberniæ, & Dux Acquitaniæ, Archiepiscopis, Episcopis, Abbatibus, Prioribus, Comitibus, Baronibus, Justic. Vicecomitibus, Præpositis, Ministris, & omnibus Ballivis, & fidelibus suis, salutem. Inspeximus cartam nostram quam dudum fieri fecimus abbati & monachis de Fischampa veteri, sigillo nostro signatam, in hæc verba : Henricus Dei gratia, Rex Angliæ, Dominus Hiberniæ, Dux Normanniæ & Acquitaniæ, & Comes Andegaviæ, Archiepiscopis, Episcopis, Abbatibus, Prioribus, Comitibus, Baronibus, Justic. Forestar. Vicecomitibus, Præpositis, Ministris, & omnibus Ballivis, & fidelibus suis, salutem. Cum non solum

ANNOTATIONS.

folum ad fidele regimen Regni noftri, verum eciam imminentibus hujus periculis faluti follicitudine profpicere teneamur, confiderantes undique ipfius Regni noftri ftatum, & maxime in maritima, comperimus per quod per villas de Wynchelfe & de la Rye, quæ nobiliora* Membra Quinque Portuum noftrorum dicuntur, quas abbas & monachi Fifchampæ hactenus poffiderunt, quibus non licet contra inimicos Regni armis materialibus dimicare, poffet nobis & hæred. noftris tempore hoftili irrecuperabile dampn. quod abfit, conting. fi taliter indefenfe in eorum abbatis & mona- chorum manibus remanerent. Quapropter de majorum Regni noftri confilio, & de bona voluntate dictorum abbatis & monachorum Fifchampæ, prædictas villas de Wynchelfe & de la Rye, cum tubus & advocat. ecclefiarum, & cum quarta parte marifci de Northmareys, & annuo redditu trium folidorum & novem denariorum inde folvendorum, & cum aliis pertin. fuis ad noftrum & hæred. noftrorum Dominicum revocavimus per divifas de Wynchelfe fubfcriptas, fcilicet, ficut mare & la Rye, cum pertin. maneria noftra de Chilcenham in com. Glouc. cum hundred. & aliis pertin. fuis; & de Scloutr. in eodem com. cum hundredo de Salemabery & aliis pertin. fuis; & de Navencby in com. Lincoln. cum pertin. fuis, fine aliquo retenemento habend. & tenend. de nobis & hæredibus noftris prædictis abbati & monachis Fifchampæ imperpetuum, adeo libera & quieta ficut antea tenuer. Wyn- chefe & la Rye, ratione donaconis eis factæ a fœlicis memoriæ fancto Edwardo, & conceffionum ac confirmacionum poft modum habitarum a Willielmo & Henrico Regibus Angliæ, de terra Staninges; cum omnibus appendenciis fuis, inter quæ reputabantur Wynchelfe & la Rye, in cujus Regia Willielmi carta continebantur hujufmodi libertates, vid. licet, quod prædicti abbas & monachi Fif- champæ habeant terram de Stanynges, cum omnibus omnino appendenciis fuis, & cum omnibus legibus, libertatibus, liberis confuetudinibus, quietanciis, placitis, querelis & caufis, quæ funt vel fore poffunt, abfque ulla inquietudine, diminucione cujuflibet fecular. vel judiciar. poteftatis, ficut res ad Fifchamp. dominicum pertinentes. Et quod prædicta terra cum omnibus appenden- tiis, poffeffionibus & poffefforibus fuis libera fit & quieta ab om. confuetudine terræve fervitutis & ab dominatione & fubjectione Baronum & Princip. & omn. aliorum. Et prædicti abbas & monachi Fifcam. & eorum miniftri habeant omnem regiam, libertatem & confuetudinem & omnem jufliciam fuam de omnibus rebus & negotiis quæ in terra fua evenient vel poterunt eve- nire; nec aliquis nifi per eos fe inde intromittat, quia hoc totum regale beneficium eft, & ab omn. fervitute quietum, & quod fi aliquis quicquam contra hujufmodi conceffionem præfumat, ad Fifcam. dominicum coactus auri libras centum perfolvat. Quare volumus & firmiter præcipimus pro nobis & hæredibus noftris, quod prædicti abbas & monachi Fifcam. habeant & teneant imper- petuum prædicta maneria de Chilcham cum hundredo & pertin. fuis, de Scloutr. cum hundredo de Salmanbury & pertin. fuis, & de Navencby cum omnibus pertin. fuis, & de Navencby cum omnibus pertin. fuis, & prædicta maneria de Chilcham cum hundredo & pertin. fuis, & libertatibus, liberis confuetudinibus, quietanciis, placitis, querelis & caufis, quæ funt & fore poffunt, abfque ulla inquietudine & diminucione cujuflibet fecular. vel judiciar. poteftatis ficut res ad Fifcam. dominicum pertinentes; & quod eadem maneria & hundred. cum omnibus poffeffi- onibus poffefforibus & pertin. fuis libera fint & quieta ab omni confuetudine terræve fervitutis & ab omni dominacione & fubjectione Baronum & Principium, & omni aliorum. Et quod iidem abbas & monachi Fifcam. & eorum miniftri habeant omnem regiam, libertatem & confuetudi- nem & omnem jufliciam fuam de omnibus rebus & negotiis quæ in eifdem maneriis & hundre- dis & pertin. fuis evenient vel poterunt evenire; nec aliquis nifi per eos fe inde intromittat, quia hoc totum regale beneficium eft, & ab omni fervitute quietum, ficut in cartis prædictorum fancti Edwardi, Willielmi, Henrici Regum, plenius continetur. Si vero aliquis contra prædictam do- nacionem & confirmacionem noftram quicquam præfumpferit, coactus ad Fifcam. dominicum auri libras centum per folvat. Hiis teftibus, venerabilibus patribus, W. Ebor. Archiepifcopo, W. Wynton, & P. Herford, Epifcopis, W. electo Sarum, R. Abbate Weftm. D. Comite Cornubiæ, fratre noftro, R. Comite Glouc. & Herford, S. Comite Leyc. per de Sabaudia, J. Mauntel, Præ- pofito Beverlacenc. R. Paffelewe, Arch. Lewend. J. de Caxton, W. de Cantlup. R. fil. Nicholi B. de Cyroyll, J. de Lexadon, P. Peytre & de Muffegros, & aliis. Dat. per manum noftram apud Windlefores, quinto decimo die Maii, anno Regni noftri tricefimo primo. Et quia prædi- ctum figillum noftrum mutatum eft, cartam prædictam, de verbo ad verbum, innovari, & eam im- preffione figilli noftri, quo nunc utimur, ad inftar prædictorum abbatis & monachorum, fecimus communiri. Hiis teftibus, Rogero de Semeri, Roberto Walerund, Willielmo de fancto Adoma- re, Roberto Agulun, Roberto de Brywer, Johanne de la Lynde, Willielmo de Aette, Williel- mo Belett, Johanne de Turbelvyle, Radolpho de Balkepus, & aliis. Dat. per manum noftram apud Salop. vicefimo quinto die Septembria, anno Regni noftri quinquagefimo primo. Not au- tem tenores prædictas ad requificionem Majoris & Communitatis villæ de Rye duximus exemplifi- cand. per præfentes. In cujus rei teftimonium has literas noftras fieri fecimus patentes. T. me ipfo apud Weftm. quinto die Julii, anno Regni noftri vicefimo fecundo.

Bayobrig.

These Words, The more noble Members, &c. make it plain that not only thefe, but others were Members to the Ports at the granting this Charter

Before which Reaffumption of King *Henry* III. both Towns were added to the Ports, accor- ding as is before afferted; both confiderable fifhing Towns for fo long ago as King *Henry* IV. *Anno* 1400. The *Rippiers* of *Rye* and *Winchelfea*, that furnifhed *London* with fresh Fifh, were,

C H A R T E R S.

Jurat [1] *of* Romney [2], Thomas Walton *Jurat* [3] *of* Heth [4],
Edward

A N N O T A T I O N S.

as *Grafton* says, privileged to fell their Fish there to whom they would ; and the Fishmongers of *London* prohibited to buy it to fell again by retale. Both were burnt by the *French* in the Time of King *Richard* II. as I take it, and King *Henry* VI. about the twenty fixth or twenty feventh Year of his Reign ; in which I suppose the old Records and Charters of the Town of *Rye* perished ; because none elder than his twenty feventh Year, fave only fome Fragments, are to feen ; in which Confumption, as conceived, the old Church was burnt, and this now ftanding built fince, the former ftanding near to *Ipres Tower*, in the Place yet called *the old Church-yard*. It never recovered its ancient Shipping fince the Lofs of the *Bourdeaux* Fleet, as reported in the Time of King *Henry* VII. who, in the third Year of his Reign, thought it worth his Vifit ; as did his Grandchild and Succeffor, Queen *Elizabeth*, in 1573, who, from the noble Entertainment fhe had, accompanied with the Teftimonies of Love and Loyalty, Duty and Reverence fhe received from the People, was pleafed to call it *Rye Royal*. Populous, to its Capacity, it was in her Reign, though much wafted by a Peft in 1563, fo that in the Months of *August*, *September* and *October* were buried 562 Perfons. Afterwards it was replenifhed by the *French*, who fheltered themfelves here from the Maffacre in *France* 1572, and other Troubles of the Proteftants there ; fo that Anno 1582, upon an Accompt taken, were found inhabiting here 1534 Perfons of that Nation. By another Plague it fmarted again, Anno 1596. Succoured the *French* Proteftants afterward, toward the latter End of King *James*, till things looking better in that Country encouraged them to return. It fuffered after this by the Plague Anno 1625, by the Small Pox in the Years 1634 and 1635, and 1654, and 1655. Loft many Veffels in the time of the Wars between the King and Parliament ; all which, with other Things, have added to the Decay and Depopulation thereof. One hundred Years after the Vifit of Queen *Elizabeth*, the prefent Prince, King *Charles* II. was pleafed to fee it, viz. May 1673, when his royal Navy, with the *French* Fleet, lay in the Bay, in fight of the Town.

[1] *Jurat.* Romney, in the Time of King *Henry* VII. had neither Mayor nor Bailiff ; but Queen *Elizabeth* granted them a Charter for the Election of a Mayor ; and fome few Years before her Reign they had a Bailiff.

[2] *Romney*, fome have thought to fignify the Nigh-way or Port to *Rome*, reckoning from *Canterbury*, the head City of the Kingdom of *Kent*, in which Time, as afterward, there was great pofting thither ; but becaufe *Dover* and other Places were as near to take Shipping at as *Romney*, this Etymon is rejected. And though fome times of old it hath been written *Romenal*, as if it were all *Romans*, by occafion of which, and that the Plant called Roman Nettle is found to grow there and about *Lydd* near thereto, in ufe with and fowed by the *Romans* when they came hither, as *Parkinson*, in his Herbal, thinks, he and fome others conceived it took its Name from the *Romans* who either firft landed, or afterwards planted moftly, thereabouts ; and that it was by them called *Romania*, and after corruptly Romney and Romny. Yet being alfo wrote *Rumenal*, *Lambard* and others, with greater Probability, derive the Name from *Rumen ea*, which in the *Saxon* Language imports a large waterifh Place or Marfh ; for ftanding in a low Plain or Marfh, containing 24000 Acres, befides *Walland* and *Eaft Guildford*, or *Guldeford* Marfhes, &c. thereto adjoining, the Name of *Romney* was given not only to the old and new Towns, but alfo to that great Quantity of Land which to this Day is known by the Name of *Romney Marfh*, governed by certain Laws of Sewers made by one *Henry Bath*, a Juftice and Commiffioner for that purpofe in the Time of King *Henry* III. whofe Statutes, faith *Lambard*, Experience in time hath begotten fuch Allowance and liking, that not only all the low Grounds between *Thames* in *Kent* and *Pevensea* in *Suffex* were afterwards ordered to be guided by them ; but they are alfo now become a Pattern to all like Places in the whole Realm, viz. to be governed according to the Cuftoms of *Romney* Marfh. The Town of old *Romney*, according to this Author, was a Place of note before the Conqueft, and had a good and commodious Haven, and abounded with Shipping : And as *Henry* (the Archdeacon of *Huntingdon*) reporteth, in the Reign of *Edward* the Confeffor, Anno 1053, when Earl *Goodwin* and his Sons were exiled the Realm, they armed Veffels to Sea, and fought, by difturbing the Peace of the People, to compel the King to their Revocation, and among fundry other Harms on the Coaft, entered the Haven of this *Romney*, and led away all fuch Ships as they found in Harbour there, in the Conqueror's Time, as appeareth by the Book called *Domefday* or *Doomefday*, in Latin *Liber Judiciarius* (which the Red Book in the Exchequer teftifies to be begun in the fourteenth, and finifhed in the twentieth Year of his Reign) *Romney* was of the Poffeffion of one *Robert Rumney*, and holden of *Odo* (then Bifhop of *Bajeux*, Earl of *Kent*, and Baftard Brother to *William* the Conqueror) in which Town the fame *Robert* had thirteen Burgeffes, who for their Service at Sea were acquitted of all Actions and Cuftoms of Charge, except Felony, breach of the Peace, and Foreftalling. And fo feems to be that Town of the two *Romneys* that had the old Privileges of the Ports before the Conqueft. In the Time of King *Henry* II. Anno 1164. This was the Port, fay fome, where *Thomas Becket* (then Archbifhop of *Canterbury*) having provoked the King to Indignation againft him, to avoid the Trial of Juftice at Home, intending to appeal to *Rome*, took Boat to have efcaped ; but by contrary Winds was driven back again to Land. In this old *Romney* and the Marfh, was great Damage done in the eighth Year of King *Edward* III. by an hideous Tempeft that threw down many Steeples and Tents, and above 300 Mills and Houfings there ; which, or rather the choaking up of the old Harbour, and its falling off to the Eaftward, where the *New Romney* ftands, feems to me not only the Caufe

..   I   of

ANNOTATIONS.

of the Decay of the Old Town, but of the flourishing of the New, which at last got the Preheminence and Superiority of the Old; though the time when I cannot say, but leave to further Discovery; and having got it (not without Displeasure of the Inhabitants of the Old, who, as I have been informed, in discontent burnt the old Charters) hath kept it ever since, and stood in its Glory till the Sea deserted it; and now is neither plentiful in Buildings nor populous in People (though generally those that are, love to be as stately as most in *Kent*) but surely was sometimes more populous, or else would never have had seven Churches, as some say; three of which, St. *Nicholas*, St. *Lawrence* and another were standing in the Time of King *Henry* VIII. for I find, amongst the Expences of *Rye*, at a Brotherhood in the eighteenth Year of his Reign, and several times before, something was given to the three Lights in the three Churches there (as was usual in the Blindness of Popery) the first of which I take to be the only one of the three now standing; and which, as an ancient Gentleman of that Town of my Acquaintance, since deceased, told me, was not the biggest, but the eldest of the three; and, as he was pleased to term it, the Mother Church, and so escaped the fatal Ruin the other suffered. This Town was never walled that I find; contains, besides others, one large and spacious Street running East and West, crossed by the Market-Place with another North and South, in the southern Part whereof, leading to the Church, standeth the Hall or Brotherhood House, where the Mayors, Jurats and Commons of the *Cinque Ports* and two ancient Towns usually keep their Court called a Brotherhood, an ancient Building, but not large enough to hold all the Mayors, Bailiffs, Jurats and Commons of the Members to sit with them in their Court called a Guestling, which therefore is kept in the Church. These Courts are sometimes held in other of the Ports, but most commonly at *Romney*; because *Romney* is well nigh the middle Town to eastern and western Ports and Members, and so frequented for Conveniency, that none might have too far a Journey. It seems, by the Charter of King *James*, and other Records, to enjoy its Privileges and Freedoms first by the Name of the Barons of the Town and Port of *Romney*, as the Old Town did; and afterwards to be incorporated by the Name of the Jurats and Commonalty of the Town and Port of *New Romney*. Not long before Queen *Elizabeth* a Bailiff is mentioned by them in some Letters of Process, and she, by her Charter particular to that Town, granted them a Mayor, in or about the fifth Year of her Reign; so as now they are incorporate by the Name of the Mayor, Jurats and Commonalty of the Town and Port of *New Romney*.

But this with Office whereof they had in

b *Jurat.* Hithe, like *Romney*, it seems, at the time when this Letter of Attorney was made, had neither Mayor nor Bailiff, but acted by Jurats; but, before *Romney*, obtained a Bailiff for at the Decree made on or about the first of *May*, in the seventeenth Year of King *Henry* VIII. *Hithe* had a Bailiff, which was changed into a Mayor afterward by the Charter of Queen *Elizabeth.*

Lease from Tho. Cranmer, Lord Archbishop of Canterbury, as I have

c *Heth*, diversly wrote, as *Heath, Heeth, Hith, Hithe* and *Hyde*, in the *Saxon* Tongue *Hythe*, signifying an Haven, called of *Leland* in Latin, *Portus Hithinus*; and though now but one Parish, and the same a Chapel to *Saltwood*, as *Leland* saith, did once extend itself two Miles in length by the Shore; and had the Parishes of our Lady, St. *Nicholas*, St. *Michael*, and of our Lady at *West Hithe*, which be now destroyed. This Town, by several, is supposed to encrease after the Decay of *West Hithe* and *Lyme* by the Departure of the Sea from them, enjoying the Benefit of an Haven longer than they. Earl *Godwine* and his Sons in their Exile fetched away divers Vessels lying at Anchor here, as they did at *Romney, Anno* 1053. Before this Town, in the Reign of King *Edward* I. a great Fleet of *Frenchmen* shewed themselves at Sea, of which one (furnished with 200 Soldiers) set their Men on Land in the Haven; but the Townsmen came upon them and slew them to the last Man, as *Lambard* saith, *Anno* 1293; whereat the Residue being afraid, hoisted up sail and made no further Attempt. Besides the Fury of the Pestilence which raged here in the Beginning of the Reign of King *Henry* IV. the Town was grievously afflicted by Fire, in which 200 Houses were consumed by the Violence thereof, and five of their Ships lost, and 100 of their Men drowned at Sea; whereby the Inhabitants were so wounded, that they began to devise how they might abandon the Place and build a Town elsewhere. But the King, by his Charter, releasing them for five Turns following (unless a greater Necessity should compel him to require it) their Service of five Ships, one hundred Men and five Boys, which they ought to find at their Charge for fifteen Days, caused them to alter their Intentions. They had here an Hospital of St. *Bartholomew*, erected by *Hamon* of *Hythe* (sometime Bishop of *Rochester*, and named of *Hythe*, because it was his native Town) for continual Relief of ten poor Persons, and endowed with twenty Marks of yearly Profit, or thereabouts. The Town still contains one long Street, but not broad; besides other Buildings ascending the Hill near and towards the Church; against which, near the long Street, is lately built a Market-Place, by the Benevolence of *Philip* Lord Viscount *Strangford*, as I have heard. On the North Side of the Church is a Charnel-House, or *Golgotha*, full of dead Mens Bones, piled up together orderly, so great a Quantity as I never saw elsewhere in one Place; supposed by some to be gathered at the Shore, after a great Sea Fight and Slaughter of the *French* and *English* on that Coast, whose Carcases, or their Bones after Consumption of the Flesh, might be cast up there, and so gathered and reserved for a Memorandum. This *Hithe*, according to the Lord *Coke*, was made one of the Five Ports, together with *Hasting*, by *William the Conqueror*, and seems to have enjoyed the Privileges thereof, first by the Name the Barons of the Town and Port of *Hithe*; and incorporated first by the Name of the Jurats and Commonalty of the Town and Port of *Hithe*; and so continued till after this Letter and their Attorney. Some time after which they had a Bailiff for their chief Magistrate, as I take it; and, as *Romney*, were graced with a Mayor by particular Charter of Queen *Elizabeth*, incorporating them by the Name of Mayor, Jurats and Commonalty of the Town and Port of *Hithe.*

Tet by the Charter of King John, Anno ? of his Reign, certain Freedoms, as of them certain Ancestors had in the Times of King Edward the Confessor, &c.

F f

Dover,

CHARTERS.

Edward Hextall *Mayor of* Dover [a], *and* Thomas Aldy *Mayor of* Sandwich [b], *which send due Recommendations in all humble wise as apper-*

ANNOTATIONS.

[a] *Dover.* Dovor or Dover; in *Latin, Davis, Doveria, Dovéria, Dovorría, Duros* and *Dubr's*; in *Saxon, Dofra* ; all which seem to be drawn from the *British* Words *Dufir,* Water, or *Dugh'a,* high or steep, the Situation of the Castle being on an high Rock, and the Town below near the Water, and part under another steep Cliff. Some fetch the Name from *Doo* afore (faith *Lambard*) meaning stoped at the Mouth before, which they say *Avaringus* did. One calleth it *Dorobrina,* differencing it from *Canterbury,* which he termeth *Dóroborma,* as if the one were *Bowne* and the other *Bryne* ; because the one standeth upon the fresh Water and the other on the Salt. The Town is agreed on by all to be privileged before the Conquest ; and by the Book, called *Domesday* last mentioned, appears of Ability, in the Time of King *Edward* the Conquest,

to arm yearly twenty Vessels to the Sea [a] ly the Space of fifteen Days together, each Vessel having therein twenty one able Persons : For in consideration thereof the same King (as *Lambard* faith) granted to the Inhabitants of *Dover,* not only Freedom from Payment of Tholl, and other Privileges throughout the Realm, but also pardoned them all manner of Suit and Service to any his Courts whatsoever. Yet in those Days the Town seems under the Protection and Governance of *Godwine* Earl of *Kent* ; for *Anno* 1051, when *Euslace* Earl of *Bo-loigne* (who had married *Goda,* King *Edward's* Sister) came over Sea to visit the King his Brother, his Harbinger demeaned himself so unwisely in taking up Lodgings at *Dover,* that a Variance happened between him and the Townsmen, and he killing one of them, the other *Dover* Inhabitants took Arms and killed eighteen of the Earl's Servants, and drove the rest thence. Of which when *Euslace* complained to the King, the Townsmen complain to *Godwine,* whereupon the King and Earl *Godwine* raised Forces one against the other ; for which Earl *Godwine* and his Sons were afterwards banished the Realm. Soon after the coming in of the Conqueror (faith the same Author) the Town was so wasted by Fire, that all, except twenty nine Houses, were reduced to Ashes. And *Anno* 1295, in the Time of King *Edward* I. the *French* landed in the Night, and burnt a great Part of the Town, and some of the Religious Houses, with which it was then stored; for besides the Priory of *St. Martins,* which from the College first erected within the Walls of the Castle by *Eadbald* or *Edbald,* Son of *Ethelbert* (first christened King of the *Saxons*) about the Year 715, was by *Wightred,* a Successor of his, removed into the Town, and stored with twenty two Canons, dedicated to St. *Martin* ; and being suppressed, and a new one built by King *Henry* II. (or rather by *William Corbell* the Archbishop, in the Time of King *Stephen*) stuffed by *Theobald,* his Successor, with *Benedictine* Monks, and called the Priory of St. *Martins,* though commonly afterward it obtained the Name of *the New Work at Dover* ; here was also an Hospital of St. *Mary's,* founded by *Hubert de Burgh* Earl of *Kent* ; and an House of the *Templers,* called *Maison Dieu,* or God's House, founded by King *Henry* III. for the *Knights Templers* ; which Order was suppressed in the Reign of King *Edward* II. This Town towards the Sea was formerly defended with a Wall, in which were three Gates, *Congate, Crossgate,* and the *Boucheriegate,* beautified with Towers, since fallen down. The ancient Harbour decaying was endeavoured to be restored by King *Henry* VIII. with a Piece built at the Cost of 63000 *l.* and again by Queen *Elizabeth,* who, besides her own Gift in the twenty third Year of her Reign, took order by Parliament (as hath been since done) for a general Help upon the Tonnage of Vessels ; and a Pent and Sluce were made to open the Mouth and secure the Bottom of the Haven of the Beach often cast in there by the Rage of the Sea in the *South* and *West* Winds ; yet doth only serve for an Harbour Ships may make for in fair Weather. The Town is indifferently stored with Buildings and Streets ; hath two Churches, called St. *James's* and St. *Mary's,* of which the former gives name (because standing therein) to the fairest Street in Town, leading to the Castle-Hill. The Market-Place is large and handsome, with the Town-Hall built over the same. This Town and Port, by the Charter of King *James,* appears to be first privileged by the Name of the Barons of the Town and Port of *Dover* ; and afterwards incorporated by the Name of the Mayor, Jurats and Commonalty of the Town and Port of *Dover,* and that first, as I conceive, of all the Ports.

[b] *Sandwich*; in the *Saxon, Sandwic*; in old *Latin, Sabulovicum,* takes its Name from *Sand* and *Wic,* that is to say, *the sandy Town or Bank,* because the Coast thereabout aboundeth with Sand, a Word still used, as *Wick* was of old for a Place upon the Edge of the Sea, or a River which is always sandy. King *Canutus,* among other Gifts, gave the Haven of *Sandwich,* with the Royalty of the Water on each Side, so far forth as (a Ship being on float at full Sea) a Man might cast a short Hatchet out of the Vessel unto the Bank, to *Christ's Church* in *Canterbury.* About the Year 787, three Vessels of the North-east Country Men, generally in our Histories called *Danes* (whose Ancestors had before, within the Compass of 140 Years, sacked *Rome* in *Italy* four several times ; and their Offspring afterwards won *Normandy* from the *French* King) shewed themselves on the western Shore of *England,* perhaps to espy the Commodity of the Haven, and Advantage of landing; and setting some of their Men on land, when the Reeve or Officer of *Beorbvricks* or *Brisricke,* King of the *West Saxons,* came to them, and demanded the Cause of their Arrival, and would have carried them to the King's Presence, they slew him ; whereupon the Country adjoyning assembled, and forced them back to their Ships. But after this first Attempt, and another *Anno* 795, in *Scotland* and *Tinmouth,* in the north Part of *England*; by these Experiments emboldened, in the Time of King *Egbert, Anno* 833, with thirty five Sail, they entered the River of *Thames,* and did great Spoil ; and getting the better of the King's

CHARTERS.

*appertaineth: And whereas it hath pleased our Sovereign Lord,
and by the Advice of his Council is agreed, for the Suftentation, Subfidy and Maintenance of our Navy, to do our old Service to our
Sovereign Lord the King, and to his Heirs Kings of England, that
at every whole Fifteenth and Tenth hereafter, by the Commons of
this his Realm, to Him and to his Heirs to be granted, the Collectors of the fame, and every of them, within the Counties of Kent
and Suffex, from thenceforth fhall have Deduction in their Accompts betwixt them by the Certificates of the faid Barons, fo that
they exceed not the Sum of five hundred Pounds Sterling, for the
Allowance of all Refciants and Advocants, of their Allowance*

ANNOTATIONS.

King's Army, they were fo encouraged, that for feveral Years they infefted this Kingdom both at
Sea and Land. In the Year 851, *Athelftane*, King of *Kent* (Son of *Ethelwolfi*) fought at
Sea before *Sandwich*, againft a great Navy of the *Danes*, of which he took nine Veffels, and
difcomfited the Refidue. And afterwards, *Anno* 1006, another Fleet of *Danes* landed at *Sandwich*, and did great Mifchief ; and being worfted afterward in a Fight in *Lincolnfhire*, with-
drew to their Ships at *Sandwich*, and returned to *Denmark* for Recruits. Thus never laft they
their Invafions from time to time, till at laft they fo far prevailed, that King *Ethelred*, in his
Reign, about the Year 980, bought his Peace with great Sums of Money ; but not being able
to hold it, he, by the Advice of *Huna* (General of his Army) wrote Letters to each Part of his
Realm, commanding to fet at once on the *Danes* and kill them ; which Defign, carried on with
great Secrecy, was accordingly executed on St. *Brice's* Day (that is, fay fome) the Morrow
after St. *Martin's* Night, *Anno* 1012. For Revenge of which great Slaughter of the *Danes*,
Sueno, or *Sweyn*, their King, preparing a huge Army, took Shipping *Anno* 1013, and arrived
firft at *Sandwich*, and after in the North Country ; the Terror of whofe coming caufed the
People to fubmit to him, in fuch wife that King *Ethelred*, feeing the Caufe defperate, fled into
Normandy, *Anno* 1014, though after returning put *Canutus* to flight. In the Days of King
Edward the Confeffor, *Anno* 1060, the Danifh Princes (or Pirates) *Lachen* and *Irlinge* landed at
Sandwich, laded their Ships with rich Spoil, wherewith they croffed the Seas to *Flanders* and
made Money thereof. By *Domefday Book* it appeareth, that before the Conqueft of King
William, *Anno* 1064, *Sandwich* lay in *tot* Hundred by it felf ; and that the Town and Romney
did to the King like Service by tenure as *Dover* did. Then it was of the Poffeffions of *Chrift
Church*, as before noted, and was appointed for the Apparyl of the Monks there, to whom it
yielded 40000 Herrings, befides certain Money, and had in it 307 Houfes inhabited. After
the Conqueft *Lewis* of *France* burnt the Town, *Anno* 1217, in the Beginning of the Reign of
King *Henry* III. but it recovered again in the End of his Reign. *Anno* 1272, was there built an
Hofpital of *White Friers Carmelites*, founded by one *Henry Cowfold*, an *Almaine* ; helped alfo it
was by the Staple removed thither for a time by King *Edward* I. In the thirty feventh
Year of King *Edward* III. he gave to *Chrift's Church* the Manor of *Borley* in *Effex*, in exchange for
it, and reunited it to the Crown. *Peter Brice*, Steward of *Normandy*, in the Days of *Henry* VI.
about the Year 1456, landed at *Sandwich*, and with Fire and Sword wafted the Town, and
deftroyed the Inhabitants almoft utterly ; which, with other Loffes, and the Sand choaking
their Harbour, hath taken from the growing Grandeur this Town might have had, whofe Situation is pleafant, a well compact Town of its Bignefs, with three Churches, the Spire Steeples
whereof (many fuch good Sea-marks) are lately all fallen. A Refuge to feveral of the Low
Countries, who abandoning their own Country for the Freedom of their Confciences, in the
Time of Queen *Elizabeth* fettled here. It hath an Hofpital called St. *Bartholomew* (as I take it)
for aged Perfons ; and a Free-School, founded *Anno* 1563, by Sir *Roger Manwood* (Native of
the Place) endowed with Forty Pounds a Year, or thereabouts. A well governed Town ;
though, it feems, for fome former Defect in the chief Magiftrate, the Mayors there ever fince,
as a Badge thereof, carry in their Hand a black Rod, and the Mayor of *Fordwich*, a Member
thereto, likewife : Whereas all the other Head Officers of the Ports Towns and Members carry
white Rods. Like as *Dover*, it feems by the Charter of King *James* to be privileged firft
by the Name of the Barons of the Town and Port of *Sandwich* ; and afterwards incorporated
by the Name of the Mayor, Jurats and Commonalty of the Town and Port of *Sandwich*, and
that long ago.

f *Commons*. The Commons in Parliament.

g *Certificates*. See afterwards the Notes on the fame Word below, and on the Word *Billet*.

h *Five Hundred*. The Sum came now, by King *Henry* VII. to be ftinted, which before was
more or lefs, as the Favour of the Prince was pleafed to allow.

i *Sterling*, (fo called from *Efterlings, i. e. Pruffians, &c.* who formerly were Artifts in fining
Gold and Silver, and taught it to the *Britons*) a general Name or Diftinction for the current
lawful Money of *England*.

k *Refciants*, from the *French*, all one with Refidents in the former Charters ; the Name
whereby Inhabitants in the Ports, though not Freemen, are commonly called,

Combens,

CHARTERS.

of all such Fifteenths as from thenceforth shall be granted to our said Sovereign Lord the King, and to his Heirs Kings of England, and from thenceforth to be gathered ; and that his Highness willeth in that behalf, that we nor our Heirs shall not in any wise exceed the said Sum of five hundred Pounds, and that we should thereupon be bound by Recognizance before his said Barons, in his said Exchequer at Westminster, to the Accomplishment of the same. We the said Mayors, Bailiffs, Jurats and Barons, certify by these Presents, that we, the Day of the making hereof, have given full Power and Authority to our right trusty and right well-beloved Brethren and Combons [1], Mr.* John Convers, *of the said Town of Winchelsea, and* William Warwyn, *of the said Town of Dover, our true and lawful Attornies, jointly and severally in that behalf, by the Advice of learned Counsel, to bind us* [m] *to our said Sovereign Lord the King and to his Heirs, Kings of England, by Recognizance in the said King's Exchequer before the said Barons, in all due and convenient Form, and Sum reasonable after the said Wisdoms and Discretions of the said High Treasurer, and the said Barons, for the Accomplishment of the Premisses ; that is to say, that we nor our Heirs shall not from henceforth exceed the said Sum of five hundred Pounds. In Witness whereof, we the said Mayors, Bailiffs, Jurats and Barons, the Seal* [n] *of our said Brotheryeeld used and accustomed to these Presents, have put at the said Town and Port of Romney, the* 12th *Day of April, in the* 6th *Year* [o] *of the Reign of our said Sovereign Lord King* Henry *the Seventh.* Whereupon the said *John Convers* and *William Warwyn* being then present in the said Court [p] in their proper Persons, and admitted there by the Barons to be the Attornies of the said Mayors, Bailiffs, Jurats and Barons of the aforesaid Ports, to execute and do in all things according to the Tenor of the said Letter; and the said *John* and *William* taking upon them the same, did acknowledge the same Mayors, Bailiffs, Jurats and Barons, to owe to our said Grandfather one Thousand Pounds [q] Sterling, to be paid to our said Grandfather in the Feast of the Nativity of St. *John* [r] *the Baptist* then next coming. And except they did perform it, the said *John* and *William*, in the Stead and Name of the same Mayors, Bailiffs, Jurats and Barons, did grant that our said Grandfather should cause to be levied the said Money of the Lands and Tenements of the said Mayors, Bailiffs, Jurats and Barons, whereof they, or any others, or any other than were seized, and of their Goods and Chattels to whose Hand soever they should come. And made that this Recognizance

ANNOTATIONS.

[1] *Combons,* Combarons or Fellow Freemen.

[m] *Bind us* ; that is, not the Persons only that make this Letter of Attorney, but the whole Ports, Towns and Members in their politick Capacity, and their Successors.

[n] *Seal.* This Seal was set to Precepts or Warrants for the apprehending of Persons and bringing them before the Brotherhood House ; and for the levying of Fines imposed by order of the House; as well as to such like Writings that run in the Name of the whole Ports, Towns and Members. It is the same which before, *p.* 93. is called *the Common Seal.*

[o] *Sixth Year.* The Date of this Letter of Attorney was *Anno Dom.* 1491.

[p] *Court.* Meaning the Court of Exchequer.

[q] *Pounds.* Thus it is in the printed Copy, which I follow ; but seems mistaken for Marks ; because several times afterwards in this Charter, it is mentioned to be one thousand Marks.

[r] *St. John,* that is *June* 24, 1491.

[s] *Certi-*

CHARTER S.

cognizance was under fuch Condition, that if the Collectors of the
Fifteenths and Tenths to our faid Grandfather, then, or to his Heirs
Kings of *England*, in the Counties of *Kent* and *Suffex*, and elfe-
where within this Realm of *England* from henceforth to be granted,
fhould not have Deductions in their Accompts to our faid Grand-
father of fuch whole Fifteenth and Tenth to be yielded by the
Certificates [r] of the Mayors, Bailiffs, Jurats and Barons, or their
Succeffors, from thenceforth to be above the Sum of 500 *l.* And
if the faid Mayors, Bailiffs, Jurats and Barons, their Heirs and
Succeffors, by their Certificates to fuch Collectors in the faid
Counties of *Kent* and *Suffex*, and elfewhere within this Realm of
England, of and for fuch whole Fifteenth and Tenth for the fame
Mayors, Bailiffs, Jurats and Barons, and the Refciants and Advocants of the faid Ports to be made and directed, fhould not exceed
the Sum of 500 *l.* at every fuch Fifteenth and Tenth thenceforth to
be granted, that then the faid Recognizance fhould be void, otherwife it fhould remain in its Strength and Effect, as by the faid Record remaining in the Cuftody of our Remembrancer [s] in our *Exchequer* more at large appeareth. And whereas further it appeareth
unto us by Letters under the Privy Seal of our faid moft dear Grandfather King *Henry* the Seventh, directed to Mr. Treafurer and the
Barons of his *Exchequer*, bearing Date at *Weftminfter* the three and
twentieth Day of *June*, in the ninth Year of his Reign, That
whereas our faid Grandfather was then informed, that of old time [u]
accuftomed, at every Fifteenth granted to the Barons of the *Five
Ports* and their Advocants and Members of them, and every of
them, they were wont to be allowed in the *Exchequer* of our faid
Grandfather of as much and as large Sums of Money as they
would ask by fufficient Billet [w] thereof, at every Fifteenth granted,
till

A N N O T A T I O N S.

[r] *Certificates*, from the *Latin*, fignifying fuch Writings as make certainly known what was
fo received and to be deducted out of the Collectors Accompts ; and here, before and after, are
equivalently ufed with the Word Billet.

[s] *Remembrancer.* An Officer in the *Exchequer* fo called. There are more than one ; but one
is called by the Name of the King's Remembrancer.

[u] *Old Time.* Before the Limitation of 500 *l.* by King *Henry* VII. it appears not only that
the Ports had Allowance out of the *Exchequer* towards their Shipping Charge ; but larger Sums
than 500 *l.* And I have feen a Record which teftifies, out of the Tenth and Fifteenth levied
in the fifteenth Year of King *Edward* IV. upon his Voyage into *France* for regaining the Dutchy
of *Normandy, Gafcoigne, Guyan, Anjou* and *Mayne*, the Allowances to the Ports and their Members were, from *Kent* 455 *l.* 0 *s.* 3 *d* ¼, and from *Suffex* 79 *l.* 5 *s.* 5 *d.* ¼, which are together
534 *l.* 5 *s.* 8 *d.* ½.

[w] *Billet.* The little Bill or Writing fealed with the Seal of Office of the Town or Port
receiving any Part of the faid Allowance, teftifying, that fuch Perfons as are named in the
Bill are Barons of that Port or Town, and pay to the Service of Shipping, were taxed in fuch
a Place, at fuch a Sum, made in fuch Form as followeth, *mutatis mutandis.*

In Englifh thus :

PRæfens billa indentata teftatur, quod hæc
funt nomina quorundam Baronum & inhabitantium villæ & Portus de Rye in com.
Suffex. unius antiquarum villarum Quinque
Portuum Domini Regis, ad navigium fuum
quum acciderit cum Portubus prædictis contri-
buent. & folvent. quorum bona & catalla taxantur in villat. de Hope, infra hundred. de
Golfpore, in Com. prædicto, ad folucionem fe-
cundæ xv^m. & x^m. duarum integrarum xv^marum
&

THIS prefent Bill indented witneffeth,
that thefe are the Names of certain
Barons and Inhabitants of the Town and Port
of *Rye* in the County of *Suffex*, one of the
ancient Towns of the *Cinque Ports* of our Lord
the King, contributing and paying with the
Ports aforefaid, to their Shipping when it fhall
happen ; whofe Goods and Chattels are taxed in
the village [*] of *Hope*, within the Hundred of *Golfpore*, in the County aforefaid, to the Payment of
the fecond 15th and 10th of the two whole 15th's
and

[* *Or Borough.*]

G g

CHARTERS.

till then of late, by Agreement thereof taken, and as between our
faid Grandfather and them, they were ceffed at a certain Sum of
500 *l.* and thereupon they were bound in a Recognizance before
the Treafurer and Barons of our faid Grandfather, in his *Exchequer*,
unto our faid Grandfather in one thoufand Marks *ˣ*, that they
fhould not exceed the faid Sum of 500 *l.* in asking Allowance by
Billet, upon Forfeiture to our faid Grandfather of the faid thoufand
Marks. And whereas our faid Grandfather being informed, that
the Treafurer and Barons of his *Exchequer* did then deny to receive and allow the Bills and Billets *ʸ* under the Seals either of the
Towns of *Winchelfea* or *Rye*, and of the Members of the faid *Five
Ports*, and of every of them, for difcharging of diverfe of the Collectors of our faid Grandfather for diverfe Fifteenths that then
were paft; our faid Grandfather, willing the faid *Five Ports*, the
faid Towns of *Winchelfea* and *Rye*, and the Members of them, and
every of them, to be Partners of the faid Difcharge of 500 *l.* as
they be charged to our faid Grandfather in Service ; and for diverfe
and many other great Confiderations our faid Grandfather fpecially
moving, did, by the faid Letters under the faid Privy Seal, will
and charge *ᶻ* the faid Treafurer and Barons of his *Exchequer*, and
every of them, that they, immediately after the Sight of the fame
Letters, fhould receive and take of the Collector and Collectors of
our faid Grandfather of any fuch Fifteenth all fuch Bills and
Billets for difcharging of the faid Fifteenths before that time granted,
and

ANNOTATIONS.

& xᵐᵃʳᵘᵐ Domino noftro Henrico Regi Angliæ
octavo, Anno Regni fui xxxviiᵐᵒ à laicis in
Parliamento fuo apud Weftm. tento, conceff.
& folvend. citra ultimum diem Junii, An. Dom.
1547, *viz.* Alexander Wellis ad xxᵈ Richard
Whyte ad viiiᵈ ob. & Robertus Edenden ad
viiᵈ ob. Summa iii *s.* In cujus rei teftimonium
figillum officii majoratus villæ de Rye prædicta
præfentibus eft appenfum. Dat. xᵐᵒ die Junii,
Anno Regni Domini noftri Edwardi fexti, Dei
gratia Angliæ, Franciæ & Hiberniæ, Regis,
fidei defenforis, & in terra Ecclefiæ Anglicanæ
& Hibernicæ fupremi capitis, primo, 1547.

and 10ᵗʰˢ granted to our Lord *Henry* the
Eighth, King of *England*, in the 37ᵗʰ Year of
his Reign, from the Laity in his Parliament
holden at *Weftminfter*, and to be paid before
the laft Day of *June*, in the Year of our Lord
1547, *viz. Alexander Wellis* at 20 *d. Richard
Whyte* at 8 *d.* ½, and *Robert Edenden* at 7 *d.* ½.
The Sum 3 *s.* In witnefs whereof the Seal
of Office of Mayoralty of the Town of *Rye*
aforefaid is put to thefe Prefents. Dated the
10th Day of *June*, in the firft Year of the
Reign of our Lord *Edward* the Sixth, by the
Grace of God, King of *England, France* and
Ireland, Defender of the Faith, and in Earth
of the Church of *England* and *Ireland* fupream
Head, 1547.

Thefe Bills, Billets or Certificates, as before they are called (being all one) the Collectors of
the Tax receiving and producing had Deduction of upon their Accompt in the *Exchequer*.
And the Money fpecified in them (if not really charged upon the Goods of Refciants or Advocants of the Ports, Towns or Members aforefaid) the Collectors received and paid to that
Town that fealed thefe Bills, or the Parties taxed upon receipt of thefe Bills paid the Town
and delivered the Bills to the Collector ; who wrote under, *Received by me A. B. the Sum
aforefaid, by way of billeting*, or to the like effect.

ˣ *Thoufand Marks.* And fo all along in the Charter afterward 1000 Marks, and not
1000 Pounds ; which occafions me ftill to conceive, as before was noted in *p.* 111. Pounds
was there miftaken for Marks. A Mark, which is two thirds of a Pound, or 13 *s.* 4 *d.* was a
Denomination ufed much in old time.

ʸ *Bills and Billets*, for Bills or Billets, feeing they were all one ; and fo afterwards in other
Places of the Charters.

ᶻ *Will and Charge*, equivalent to Will and Command ; and in the fame Senfe ufed here and
in other Places.

ᵃ *Parcel.*

CHARTERS.

and thereafter to be granted, as well them that were under the Seals of the said Towns of *Winchelfea* and *Rye*, parcel[a] of the Head Ports, or any of them, as them that were under the Seals of any of the Members, to what manner of Sum that the said Bills or Billets should amount unto. And if the said Bills or Billets should amount to the Sum of 500 *l.* or beneath, at a Fifteen, then our said Grandfather willed and charged them, and every of them, to allow all the Sum of 500 *l.* or any Sum beneath that Sum. And if the said Bills or Billets should amount above the Sum of the said 500 *l.* then our said Grandfather willed the said Treasurer and Barons, that they allow to the said Collectors the said Sum of 500 *l.* and no more. And then our said Grandfather willed, that the said Treasurer and Barons should make as hasty Process as they lawfully might against the said *Five Ports* for the said thousand Marks by them unto our said Grandfather to be forfeited for their exceeding the said Sum contrary to their said Recognizance, as by the said Letters under the Privy Seal[b] of our said Grandfather more at large appeareth. And whereas divers of the most ancient Charters[c] and Letters Patents made to the Barons of the said *Cinque Ports* in that behalf, as also the Inrolment of the same, by length and tract of long Time and many Ages, or otherwise, are perished and utterly worn out, lost or decayed; We considering the good Services which the said Barons of the said *Cinque Ports*, and of the said Towns of *Rye* and *Winchelfea*, and their Members, have done unto us, and the great Charges which they have been at in our late Services upon the Seas, and elsewhere[d] against the *Spaniards*[e], in the Year of our Lord God 1588, and 1596, and willing that the said Barons of the said *Cinque Ports*, and of the said Towns of *Rye* and *Winchelfea*[f], and the Members of them, and every of them, and the Resciants of the said Ports, Towns[g] and Members, and the Advocants of the said Ports and Towns, and every of them, should be discharged of the Sum of 500 *l.* at every Fifteen, and

ANNOTATIONS.

[a] *Parcel.* Such Towns as were equal with the Head Ports, that is the *Cinque Ports*, still not Members thereto.

[b] *Privy Seal.* These Letters under the Privy Seal of King Henry VII. (the Recitation whereof endeth here) bearing Date as aforesaid, *June* 13, in the ninth Year of his Reign, were made Anno Domini, 1494.

[c] *Ancient Charters. Tempus edax rerum* the Cause of the Loss of the old Charters.

[d] *Elsewhere,* to wit at *Cadiz,* in *Spain* in the Year 1596. The Ships then set out by the Ports, as also in 1588. are before mentioned, *pag.* 29. whereof the Charge was not small, as might be made appear if occasion were.

[e] *Spaniards,* then Enemies to *England,* and the growing Monarchy in *Europe* in the beginning of this Queen *Elizabeth's* Reign, but since have declined in their Grandeur, lost part of the *Low Countries,* had their *Invincible Armada,* as they called it, spoiled in 1588. and other their Designs against the *English* blasted by special Providences: A Nation the less beloved of the *English* for their bloody Inquisition.

[f] *Rye* and *Winchelfea.* Before in this Page, and after throughout this Charter of Queen *Elizabeth,* where they are mentioned, *Rye* is placed first, whereas before, in King *Henry* VII's Time, *Winchelfea* is set before *Rye*; but about this Time, and somewhat after, the Decays of *Winchelfea* growing upon it, gave *Rye* leave to get the start of them, though since this follows apace after the others Ruins.

[g] *Towns.* And so several Times after being placed between the Ports and Members, must necessarily denote the *Two Ancient Towns.*

[h] *Part-*

CHARTERS.

and be Partners [h] of the said Discharge of 500 *l.* according to such Rate and Proportion as the *Cinque Ports, Towns and Members* be charged to us, our Heirs and Successors, in Service and in finding and maintaining of the Navy [i] of the said *Ports, Towns and Members*; in Consideration of the said Services, and for the better Maintenance and Sustentation of the Navy of the said Ports, and for divers other good Considerations us specially moving, of our special Grace, meer Motion, and certain Knowledge, do for us, our Heirs and Successors, grant unto the said Barons of the said *Cinque Ports,* and of the said Towns of *Rye* and *Winchelsea,* and of the Members of the same Ports and Towns, and every of them, and their Successors, Barons of the said *Cinque Ports, Towns and Members,* that at every Fifteenth heretofore to us granted and yet payable, and heretofore to us granted and hereafter to be paid, and also at every Fifteenth hereafter to us, our Heirs and Successors, to be granted, they the said Barons of the said *Cinque Ports,* and of the said Towns of *Rye* and *Winchelsea,* and of the Members of the said Ports and Towns, and of every of them, and their Successors, Barons of the said *Cinque Ports, Towns and Members,* for themselves and the Resciants of the said *Ports, Towns and Members,* and the Advocants [i] of the said Ports and Towns, shall have thereof, and be allowed in the *Exchequer* of us, our Heirs and Successors, at and of every such Fifteenth so granted or to be granted, as is aforesaid, the said Sum of 500 *l.* and no more. And therefore for us, our Heirs and Successors, we do will and charge the Treasurer, Chancellor, and Barons of the *Exchequer* of us, our Heirs and Successors, and of every of them for the Time being, for ever hereafter, that they do from Time to Time receive and take of the Collector and Collectors of any Fifteenth at any Time heretofore to us granted and yet payable, and heretofore granted to us and hereafter to be paid, and hereafter to us, our Heirs and Successors to be granted all such Bills and Billets for the Discharge of the said Barons of our said *Cinque Ports,* and of the said Towns of *Rye* and *Winchelsea,* and of the Members of them, and every of them, and of the Resciants of the said Ports, Towns and Members, and the Advocants of the same Ports and Towns, and of every of them for the Time being, of the Sum of 500 *l.* part or parcel of every such Fifteenth before this Time granted and yet payable, and heretofore granted unto us and hereafter to be paid, and hereafter to us, our Heirs or Successors to be granted, as well all those Bills and Billets that be, or hereafter shall be, under the Seals of any of the *Cinque Ports*
and

ANNOTATIONS.

[h] *Partners.* Here as before, p. 114. l. 16. is intended, that according to the Number of Ships they found, so should they have a proportional Allowance of this five Hundred Pounds, Port, Town and Member, every one accordingly.

[i] *Navy.* Generally throughout this Charter the Ports Ships are so termed, and therefore *Navigium* used in the foregoing Charters, and other *Latin* Records, may safely be so rendered.

[i] *Advocants,* both here and at divers other Places in this Charter the Advocants are mentioned of the *Cinque Ports* and Towns, that is the *Two Ancient Towns;* so as the Members it seems had no Advocants, but them that belong'd to some or other of the *Five Ports* and two Towns aforesaid.

I

[k] *Seals*

CHARTERS.

and Towns of *Rye* and *Winchelfea,* or any of them, as all thofe which be, or hereafter fhall be, under the Seals of any of the Members [k] of the faid *Cinque Ports* and Towns, or any of them. And if the faid Bills or Billets do or fhall, at any Time hereafter, of or for any Fifteenth, amount above the faid Sum of 500 *l.* then for us, our Heirs and Succeffors, we will and charge the faid Treafurer, Chancellor, and Barons of the fame *Exchequer,* and every of them, from Time to Time, to allow to the faid Collector and Collectors of us, our Heirs and Succeffors for the Time being, for the faid Barons of the faid *Cinque Ports,* and Towns of *Rye* and *Winchelfea,* and their Succeffors, and for their and every of their Members, and the Refciants of the faid Ports, Towns and Members, and the Advocants of the faid Ports and Towns, the faid Sum of 500 *l.* and no more : And then for us, our Heirs and Succeffors, we will and command, that the faid Treafurer, Chancellor, and Barons of the *Exchequer* of us, our Heirs and Succeffors for the Time being, make as hafty Procefs [l] as lawfully [m] may be made againft the faid Barons of the faid *Cinque Ports,* and of the faid Towns of *Rye* and *Winchelfea,* and their Succeffors, for the levying of the faid 1000 Marks by them to us, our Heirs or Succeffors, to be forfeited for their exceeding the faid Sum of 500 *l.* contrary to their faid Recognizance. And further, for us our Heirs and Succeffors, we do will and charge all and every Collector and Collectors of us, our Heirs and Succeffors, of every Fifteenth to us granted, or hereafter to us, our Heirs or Succeffors to be granted, that they and every of them do receive of the faid Barons of the *Cinque Ports,* and of the faid Town of *Rye* and *Winchelfea,* and their Succeffors, for them, their and every of their Members, and the Refciants of the faid Ports, Towns and Members, and the Advocants of the faid Ports and Towns, all and every fuch Bills and Billets as have been, or hereafter fhall be, tendred [n] unto the faid Collector or Collectors, or any of them, according to the Purport and true Meaning of thefe Prefents. And moreover, for us, our Heirs and Succeffors, of our meer Grace and certain Knowledge, we do grant to the faid Barons of the faid *Cinque Ports,* and
                                                                            Towns

ANNOTATIONS.

[k] *Seals of any of the Members.* The Seals wherewith the Billets were fealed being the Seals of Office of Mayoralty or Bailiage of the Towns refpectively, it follows of neceffity, that the Members not Corporate having no Mayor nor Bailiff, and fo confequently no fuch Seal to feal them with, could make no Billets; yet I find old *Romney,* not long before the making of this Charter, did attempt to make Billets; and feal the fame with fome Seal or other ; but being they were no corporate Member, they were reftrained by a Decree made at a Gueftling held at *Rye, January* 3, in the Fortieth Year of Queen *Elizabeth,* under the Penalty of one Thoufand Pounds, and ordered for the future to fetch their Billets at *New Romney* their Head Port, as other Members not corporate had ufed to do.

[l] *Procefs* upon a Recognifance is a *Scire Facias* to the Parties bound to fhew Caufe why Execution fhould not be awarded againft them for the Penalty of the Recognifance ; and if to two of them a *Nihil* be returned, there is ufually Judgment for Recovery and Execution thereupon againft the Recognifor.

[m] *Lawfully,* though in the King's Suit, yet the Proceedings therein muft be according to Law and Ufage in fuch Cafes.

[n] *Tendred.* The Bills or Billets, if tendred to the Collectors, ought by them to be accepted and received, and their Accompts to be charged therewith.

H h   [o] *Diftrain:*

CHARTERS.

Towns of *Rye* and *Winchelsea*, and of the Members of the said Ports and Towns, and their Successors, that neither they nor their Successors, nor any of them, nor the Resciants of them or any of them, nor the Advocants of the said Ports and Towns or of any of them, or their Successors, at any Time hereafter by us, our Heirs or Successors, or by the Treasurer, Chancellor, or Barons of the said *Exchequer* of us, our Heirs or Successors, or by any Collectors, or other Officers or Ministers of us, our Heirs or Successors, shall be distrained [o], impeached [p], impleaded or molested, in any Thing contrary to the Tenor and Purport of these Presents; although express mention of the true yearly Value [q] or Certainty of the Premisses, or of any of them, or of any other Gifts or Grants [r] by us or any of our Progenitors to the aforesaid Barons of the said *Cinque Ports*, or of the said Towns of *Rye* and *Winchelsea*, and their Members, heretofore made, in these Presents is not made, or any Statute [r], Act [s], Ordinance [t], Provision [u], or Restraint [v] to the contrary made, ordained or provided, or any other Thing, Cause or Matter to the contrary in any wise notwithstanding. In witness whereof we have caused these our Letters to be made Patents. Witness Our Self at *Westminster*, the six and Twentieth Day of *January*, in the three and Fortieth Year [w] of our Reign.

In-

ANNOTATIONS.

[b] *Distrained*, from the *Latin Distringo*, because the Goods or Cattle distrained, as for Rent, &c. are put into a Straight, which we call a *Pound* or *Pound*, whether Overt or Covert, Publick or Private. In the common Law it is taken for compelled, by which Compulsion a Man is brought, in certain real Actions, to appear in Court, or in other Cases to pay a Debt or Duty denied or neglected.

[p] *Impeached*, from the *French Empeschement*, that is, say some, *Impediment* or *Restraint*; but *Impeachment*, for which the Law uses *Impetitio*, is as much as an high Accusation or Charge for some Offence, as *Impeachment of Treason*, *Impeachment of Waste*, whereby Restraint ensues, as an Effect from the Cause.

[q] *True yearly Value*, Words of Course in Charters, where Lands, Tenements or Rents are granted, and so more formal than material here.

[r] *Gifts or Grants*. Want of mentioning this Allowance in any former Charter of the Ports, or any Thing mentioned therein to the contrary, or any Thing not fully mentioned here, to be no Hindrance or Obstruction to the Ports free Enjoyment thereof for the future.

[r] *Statute*, here for a Decree or Act of the High Court of Parliament. Sometimes the Word is used in the Law for a kind of Bond, as *Statute Merchant*, and *Statute Staple*, which are called *Statutes*, because made according to the Form of Statutes in that behalf provided.

[s] *Act*. Act of Parliament is all one with a Statute.

[t] *Ordinance* is sometimes taken for an Act of Parliament; but though every Act be an Ordinance, every Ordinance is not an Act, because it hath not the Consent of the three Estates, that is to say, King, Lords and Commons, for if any such Ordinance have, it passeth into an Act. An Ordinance of Parliament is reckoned binding so long as the Parliament sits that made it, and if executed in sitting of the Parliament is good; but an Act, perpetual, or for such Time as is limited therein. Sometimes Ordinance is taken for an Order of the Council Table, or some inferior Court.

[u] *Provision* is here a certain Condition or Limitation inserted in any Act or Ordinance of Parliament, upon Observance whereof the Validity of the whole consists, as a Deed wherein is inserted a Proviso. But if any Act be made to grant a Subsidy to the King, and a Proviso be therein, that he shall not give or grant any part thereof away to any Person or Persons, Bodies Politick or Corporate, by any Charter or Charters, yet may the King remit or release the same to them notwithstanding the Proviso.

[v] *Restraint*, sometimes taken for Imprisonment, but here for a Restriction, Straightning or Prohibition.

[w] *Three and Fortieth Year*. The Date of this Charter of Queen *Elizabeth* ending here is *Anno Domini* 1600.

[x] *Wi*

CHARTERS.	TRANSLATION.

CHARTERS.

Inſpeximus etiam literas patentes præchariſſimi avi noſtri Domini Jacobi, nuper Regis Angliæ, factas in hæc verba: Jacobus Dei gratia, Angliæ, Scotiæ, Franciæ, & Hiberniæ, Rex, Fidei Defenſor, &c. omnibus ad quos præſentes literæ prevenerint, ſalutem, &c. In cujus rei teſtimonium has literas noſtras fieri fecimus patentes. Teſte me ipſo apud Weſtmin. tricefimo die Januarii, anno Regni noſtri Angliæ, Franciæ, & Hiberniæ ſecundo, & Scotiæ triceſimo octavo. Inſpeximus etiam literas patentes chariſſimi patris noſtri Domini Caroli, nuper Regis Angliæ (beatæ memoriæ) factas in hæc verba: Carolus Dei gratia, Angliæ, Scotiæ, Franciæ, & Hiberniæ, Rex, Fidei Defenſor, &c. omnibus ad quos præſentes literæ pervenerint, ſalutem, &c. In cujus rei teſtimonium has literas noſtras fieri fecimus patentes. Teſte me ipſo

TRANSLATION.

We have ſeen [x] alſo the Letters Patents of our moſt dear Grandfather the Lord *James* [y], late King of *England*, made in theſe Words: *James* by the Grace of God, King of *England*, *Scotland*, *France*, and *Ireland*, Defender of the Faith, &c. to all to whom theſe preſent Letters ſhall come, Greeting, &c. In witneſs whereof theſe our Letters we have cauſed to be made Patents. Witneſs My Self at *Weſtminſter*, the Thirtieth Day of *January*, in the Year of our Reign of *England*, *France*, and *Ireland* the Second, and of [z] *Scotland* the Thirty eighth. We have ſeen [a] alſo the Letters Patents of our moſt dear Father the Lord *Charles* [b], late King of *England*, (of bleſſed Memory) made in theſe Words: *Charles* by the Grace of God, King of *England*, *Scotland*, *France*, and *Ireland*, Defender of the Faith, &c. to all to whom theſe preſent Letters ſhall come, Greeting, &c. In witneſs whereof we have cauſed theſe our Letters to be made Patents. Witneſs My Self at *Weſt-*

ANNOTATIONS.

[x] *We have ſeen.* This is another *Inſpeximus* of King *Charles* II. whoſe firſt was before the Confirmation of the old Charters by Queen *Elizabeth*, *pag.* 1. the ſecond before the *Engliſh* Charter of Queen *Elizabeth*, *pag.* 89. and this third comes before the Charters of his Grandfather and Father here mentioned, and afterward confirmed, but not recited *verbatim*, as others before them; becauſe as the Charter of King *Charles* the Firſt was in Subſtance nothing but a Repetition and Confirmation of the Charter of King *James*; ſo the following Charter of King *Charles* the Second contains the Subſtance of them both. Some Things indeed are more fully worded in the Charter of King *James* (which, as Occaſion ſerves, may be afterward noted) but ſome Things more ſlenderly than in this of King *Charles* II. otherwiſe this contains not only the Subſtance, but proceeds much in the ſame Method, as comparing them together will make appear. And ſeeing a Copy of the Charter of King *Charles* I. about twenty Years ſince, was printed and bound up with the Impreſſion of *Lambard*'s Perambulation of *Kent*, *Anno* 1656. I ſhall forbear to tranſcribe either of them at large, or any more than what may be uſeful; and that rather from a written Copy I have by me, than that printed one which is corrupt in very many Places, and as full of Errata as ever I ſaw any Copy of that bigneſs.

[y] *James*, who came to the Crown upon the Death of Queen *Elizabeth*, *March* 24, 1602. and reigned till his Death, which was *March* 27, 1625. He unites *Scotland* to *England*, as *pag.* 1. was before noted, and ſo his Title is different from his Predeceſſors.

[z] *Second, and of.* King *James* having been about Thirty ſix Years King of *Scotland* before he was King of *England*, makes the Date of his Charter different in the Stile, according to the Years of his Reign over each Kingdom, but both in the ſame Year of our Lord, *viz.* 1604.

[a] *We have ſeen.* This *Inſpeximus*, as the laſt, is of King *Charles* II. immediately preceding the mention of his Father's Charter, as the other that of his Grandfather.

[b] *Charles*, that is King *Charles* the Firſt, who came to the Crown at the Death of King *James*, his Father, *March* 27, 1625. and reigned till *January* 30, 1648.

† 2   [c] *Tenth*

CHARTERS.	TRANSLATION.
ipfo apud Weftmin. fexto decimo die Junii, anno Regni noftri decimo. Cunq; villa & Portus noftr. de Hafting in com. noftr. Suffex, ac	*Weftminfter* the fixteenth Day of *June*, in the tenth Year [c] of our Reign. And whereas [d] our Town and Port of *Ha-fting*, in our County of *Suffex*, and

ANNOTATIONS.

[c] *Tenth Year.* The Date of thefe Letters Patents was in the Year of our Lord, 1635.

[d] *And whereas.* Here, at thefe Words, beginneth the Charter of King *Charles* the Second, by which, as well as that of King *James* before, is not only plainly expreffed, which are the *Cinque Ports* and *two Ancient Towns*, but alfo the Names of their *Members*, and in what Counties they lie ; and by the fame may be gathered, which of the Members are corporate, and which not ; and to which of the Ports the Members feverally belong : Thofe not corporate are fometimes called *Limbs*, and fometimes *Members*, promifcuoufly, and have anciently, as well the one as the other, been added and united to fuch and fuch of the Ports, to help them the better to defray their chargeable Services to the Crown and Kingdom, as before noted.

The *Names of the* Cinque Ports, two Ancient Towns *and their* Members, *according to the laft mentioned Charters.*

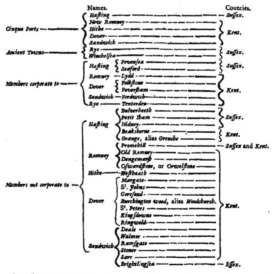

	Names.		Counties.
Cinque Ports	Hafting		Suffex.
	New Romney		
	Hithe		
	Dover		Kent.
	Sandwich		
Ancient Towns	Rye		Suffex.
	Winchelfea		
Members corporate to	Hafting	Pevenfea	Suffex.
		Seaford	
	Romney	Lydd	
	Dover	Folkftone	
		Feverfham	Kent.
	Sandwich	Fordwich	
	Rye	Tenterden	
Members not corporate to	Hafting	Bulverheeth	Suffex.
		Petit Iham	
		Hidney	
		Beakiborne	Kent.
		Orange, alias Grenche	
	Romney	Promehill	Suffex and Kent.
		Old Romney	
		Dengemarfh	
		Ofwardftone, or Orwelftone	
	Hithe	Weftheath	
	Dover	Margate	Kent.
		St. Johns	
		Gorefend	
		Burchington wood, alias Woodchurch.	
		St. Peters	
		Kingfdowne	
		Ringwold	
	Sandwich	Deale	
		Walmer	
		Ramfgate	
		Stoner	
		Sarr	
		Brightlingfea	Effex.

So as of the *Cinque Ports, Ancient Towns* and *Members corporate* there are now Fourteen, *viz.* five Ports, two *Ancient Towns*, and feven *Members*, whofe Situation, for the moft part, is along the Sea Coaft, from the Weft towards the Eaft, thus, *Seaford, Pevenfea, Hafting, Winchelfea, Rye, Lydd, Romney, Hithe, Folkftone, Dover* and *Sandwich*, the moft Eaftern Port : *Fordwich* more in the Country, on the River *Stowr*, that runs from *Sandwich* to *Canterbury* ; *Feverfham* further in the Country, yet hath fome benefit by a Creek of the Sea that cometh thereto on the Eaft fide of the Ifle of *Sheppey* ; and *Tenterden* lies Northward of *Rye* a Land Town, but by the Confines of its Liberty runs the ancient River of *Rother*, which now falls into the Sea at *Rye*. And according to the Situation of the faid *Cinque Ports* and *Ancient Towns* were they named before, in the Charter of Queen *Elizabeth* by themfelves, in their Letter of Attorney there recited, and ufually fo entered in the Records of their *Brotherhood*. But in all thefe

laft

CHARTERS.	TRANSLATION.
ac villæ & portus noſtr. de No- va Romney, alias Romene, Heeth, Dovor, & Sandwic, in com. noſtr. Kanc. ſunt, & a tempore cujus contrarii memor. hominum non exiſtit fuerunt, Quinque Portus noſtr. & progenitorum noſtrorum Regum & Reginarum Angliæ ; cumque etiam villæ noſtr. de Rye	and our Towns and Ports of *New Romney*, otherwiſe *Romene*, *Hithe*, *Dover*, and *Sandwich*, in our County of *Kent*, are, and time out of mind ᵉ have been ᶠ, the *Cinque Ports* of us and our Progenitors Kings and Queens of *England*; and whereas alſo our Towns of *Rye*

ANNOTATIONS.

laſt mentioned Charters of King *James*, King *Charles* I. and II. *Rye* is placed before *Winchelſea*, and both after all the *Five Ports* ; yet ſtill the Speakerſhip of the Courts of *Brotherhood* and *Gueſt-ling*, as aforeſaid, continue, as anciently, according to their Situation. Neverthelefs, neither according to their Nomination in their Charters, nor according to their Situation, do the Mayors, Bailiffs and Jurats of the ſaid Ports, Towns and Members corporate, ſit in the ſaid Courts, but take their Precedency thus, if *Haſting* be Speaker :

Haſting,	*Seaford,*
Sandwich,	*Pevenſea,*
Dover,	*Pordwitch,*
Romney,	*Folkſtone,*
Hithe,	*Feverſham,*
Rye,	*Lydd,*
Winchelſea,	*Tenterden.*

But if any other of the Ports befides *Haſting*, or any of the *Ancient Towns* be Speaker, then next the Speaker, on the right Hand, ſits the Mayor of *Haſting*, and on the left Hand the Mayor of *Sandwich* (if he be not Speaker) and after them the reſt in their Order. And becaufe fome-times *Dover* and *Romney* have contended for the upper Hand; as alfo *Rye* with *Winchelſea*; for quieting all Controverſies thereupon, it was at laſt ſettled by Order of the *Brotherhood*, *July* 25, 1615. in the thirteenth Year of King *James*.

ᵉ *Time out of mind.* *Verbatim* after the *Latin* here and in feveral other Places of this Charter It is, *From the Time the contrary whereof the Memory of Man is not*, for the printed Copy hath *hu-jufmodi* for *hominum*. This *Time out of mind*, by another Term, is called *Prefcription*, and is a Title that taketh Subſtance of Uſe and Time allowed by the Law, when no Man by word or writing can make the contrary appear. Hence it is that afterward, when *Tenterden* is menti-oned, That is not faid to have been Time out of mind a Member to the ancient Town of *Rye*, becaufe it appeareth by the Records of the Patents yet extant, when it was firſt annexed thereto.

ᶠ *Have been.* Of what Antiquity thefe Ports and Ancient Towns are, when enfranchifed, or at what Times their Members were annexed to them, are Things fo dark and difficult to be difco-ver'd, that without great labour and fearch (if then) little of Certainty can be had ; and ſhould any Certainty be found thereof, it would but contradict thefe Charters, which expreſs them to have been fo Time out of mind, and at moſt but render them the more aged (which too often is enough to render fome the more contemptible and defpifed with fome light and inconfiderate Fancies) nor would it at all advantage the Ports, ſeeing Prefcription is as good a Title to many Things as a Charter ; wherefore he that ſhall effay to determine thereof will fubject himſelf to be accounted either Negligent, if he omit any Thing that may be known thereof, or Igno-rant, if he miſtake in his Account or Report thereof, if not prefumptuous, to thwart the expreſs Words of the Charter, as alfo the Opinions of the Portſmen themſelves, who ſuggeſted fuch or the like Expreſſions in their Petition for the Renovation thereof; or perhaps all of them, if he content not himſelf with that for which he can bring good Authors and Vouchers; and there-fore I ſhall enter here this Proviſo, that room ſhall be left for any one to add hereunto what can hereafter be proved to make this Relation perfect.

The Lord *Coke*, in the fourth Book of his *Inſtitutes*, affirming * that *Dover*, *Sandwich* and *Romney*, were the Ports of ſpecial Note before the Conqueſt, and that to make the Five, King *William* the Conqueror added to them *Haſting* and *Hithe* †, and afterwards were annexed thereto the two Ancient Towns of *Winchelſea* and *Rye*, I ſhall look no further back, but con-clude them all alike enfranchifed and privileged ; and that though *Haſting* got the Precedency of the elder *Kentiſh* Ports, and be named before and fit above them, yet it was not becaufe either than they, or of greater Immunities or Grandeur, but either by fome Prenomination in the Charter or Confirmation of King *William* or his Succeſſors, or elfe from the Refpect that King had to *Haſting* for the Kindneſs ſhewed him there and free Reception; either at his firſt Landing, if he landed there, or ſuddenly after, if he landed at *Pevnſey* (a corporate Member of *K.* Ed. Will. I. *and* II. *and K.* Henry *his Great Grandfather*, An⁰. 7 *K.* Johii. *So if Johii's by this*, Hithe *was privileged before the Conqueror.*

Bract. lib. pag. 171. † *K.* John *in his Charter to Hithe, grants them certain Proe-doms, as they and their Ance-ſtors had them in the Times*

I i   now

ANNOTATIONS.

now to *Hasting*) or rather at *Bulverhithe*, somewhat nearer to *Hasting*, and an incorporate Member thereto, where then was an Haven called *Bolleside*, and afterwards *Bolcarhithe*, from whence came the Name it now hath; seeing all that make him land elsewhere than at *Hasting* agree, that he soon after his landing marched thitherward in order to the pitching of his Field in a convenient Place. And from some have thought that they had some such Charter from the Conqueror himself, because *Bratton*, who lived and wrote of the Laws of this Realm in the Time of King *Henry* III. in his third Book, and Treatise of the Crown, shewing the Articles inquirable before the Justices in *Eyre*, setteth forth a special Form of Writs, to be directed to the Bailiffs of *Hasting*, *Hithe*, *Romney*, *Dover* and *Sandwich*, to command Twenty four of their Barons to appear before the King's Justices at *Shepway* (as they were accustomed to do) there to inquire of such Points as should be given in Charge; conceiving, that a Man so learned in the Laws as he was would not have named the Ports in that order (which prefers them, said to be added by the Conqueror, before the rest) if he had not been warranted therein by some good Authority. But if I may add my own Conjecture, I rather think *Hasting* was and well deserved to be preferred by the other Ports and Ancient Towns to so small a Preheminence as the first Nomination and chief Seat in their Assemblies, because in the Service to *Yarmouth* they found two Bailiffs to any of the others one, and towards their Allowance paid double to any of the other Towns.

As to the Members, of what standing foever the Ports and Ancient Towns be, it must be presumed the Members are younger than they, seeing it is preposterous to speak of Members before there be an Head to whom they have relation. And though it be not certain how long they have been annexed to their respective Ports, or corporate, as now some of them are, yet it is certain they are not all of equal standing; for *Tenterden* was united to *Rye* but in the Reign of King *Henry* VI. viz. *August* the first, in the Twenty seventh Year of his Reign (which was in the Year of our Lord, 1449.) and though *Romney* now prescribe for *Dengemarsh* (as appears by this Charter, and those last before it) yet was it not (as I conceive) annexed thereto in the Time of King *Henry* I. for in the Time of that King it happened, that a Ship laden with the King's own Goods was wrecked within the precinct of that liberty, which his Officers would have seised and saved to his Use; but *Geffray*, then Abbot of *Battell* in *Suffex*, where King *William* the Conqueror had the Victory in his Battle with King *Harold*, and in Memory thereof built the Monastery of St. *Martin* there, and endowed the Monks thereof (as the Chronicles of that Abbey affirm) with the Wreck of the Sea falling in this *Dengemarsh*, so stoutly resisted, that the Matter by complaint came before the King, *Henry* I. who valuing his Father's Grant, yielded the Matter wholly into the Abbot's own Courtesy. By the Exemplification of the Services of the *Cinque Ports* before mentioned, besides *Winchelsea* and *Rye*, there then belonged to the Ports as Members, to *Hasting*, *Pevensea*, *Bulwenheth*, *Petit Iham*, *Beastborne*, and *Grench*, to *Romney*, *Old Romney*, and *Lydde*; to *Dover*, *Feversham*, *Feliftone*, and *Margate*; and to *Sandwich*, *Fordwich*, *Stoner*, *Dale*, and *Sarr*, as was then certified by *Stephen de Pencefter*, Constable of *Lover* Castle, and Warden of the *Cinque Ports*. And about Seventy three Years before this, in the

* Before this, An°. 10 H. III. Pevensey and Feversham have Writs sent to them with the Cinque Ports and Two Ancient Towns, to send their Ship to Portsmouth, Clauf. 10 H. III. in dorfo Rotuli, Memb. 18.

fourteenth Year * of King *Henry* III. by the aforesaid *Memorandum*, taken out of the Ports *Domesday* Book, specified as an Ordinance of the King touching the Service of Shipping. *Anno Domini* 1229. it appears the Ports had then more Men bers than are mentioned in the said Exemplification, viz. *Hasting* had *Seford* and *Northye*; which latter is not mentioned in the latter Charters, but probably is the Field yet called *Northey*, lying to the Westward of *Bulverbithe* towards *Bexbill*, being all the devouring Sea hath now left thereof, or else that which lyeth near *Crowding*, Westward of *Bexbill*. *Romney* had *Promboll*, *Ofwardstone*, *Dengemarsh*; *Heth* had *Westheth*; and *Sandwich* had *Reculver* (not mentioned in the latter Charters) and *Storey* (which I take to be for *Stoner*) And as they have been old Members, so have some of them been old Corporations; for by the Indenture recited in the before mentioned Decree of *Brotherhood*, it appears that *Pevensea*, *Fordwich*, and *Feversham*, were Bodies corporate at the making of that Indenture, in the Court of *Shepway* holden in the Thirty fifth Year of King *Edward* I. (which was the last Year of his Reign, and not long before his Death) by setting their Common Seals to the said Indenture. And when it was confirmed, with the additional Order thereupon, at the aforesaid *Brotherhood*, in the fifteenth Year of King *Richard* II. (*Anno* 1391.) there are found none other of the Members but *Pevensea*, *Fordwich*, and *Feversham*, which set their Common Seals to this Confirmation: So that though they had then, at both Times, more Members (as is plain by the Indenture it self, and Order also) yet it is questionable whether any more than those three were corporate, and yet there might be more, seeing sometimes there is a Default of Appearance at both Courts. But could I have seen the particular Charters at first granted to each

† It is questionable if there be any such, for the Charters of K. John are to every Town apart.

Town, or the old Charters to the whole Ports elder than † those of King *Edward* I. I should not only have been better satisfied as to the Point of Priority and Precedency before spoken to, but also concerning the present Prescription for their Usages and Customs, whether they had their Original from those Grants, or whether those Charters were only to corroborate and confirm what before time the Ports Men had used and accustomed and procured, the better to secure them and the joint Interest of the Ports therein. At present comparing some Records I have seen with the Charters yet extant, (the oldest of them, which are those of King *Edward* I.) I am induced to believe that most of the Ports Privileges, Usages and Customs, took not their Rise from the Charters (not even from those before his) but the Charters were rather Confirmations of what they had, than Grants of what they had not, at the Time when they were granted; and this for two Reasons:

First, From the Charter it self, to wit, that first of King *Edward* I. bearing Date at *Westminster June* 17, in the Sixth Year of his Reign, in which, besides the Grant of *Den* and *Strond* at *Yarmouth*, which he himself had granted to the Ports about a Year before (as before was observed) he seems to grant, that the Barons of the Ports should be quit of Shires and Hundreds; but withal added these Words, *So that if any would implead them, they should not answer nor plead other-*

CHARTERS.

Rye & Winchelfey, in dict. com. noftr. Suffex, funt, & à toto tempore fupradicto fuerunt, antiquæ villæ, & infra libertates præd. Quinque Port; cumque etiam villa & Leucata de Pevenfey, & villa de Sea-

TRANSLATION.

Rye and *Winchelfea*, in our faid County of *Suffex*, are, and from all the Time abovefaid have been, ancient Towns, and within the Liberties of the *Cinque Ports* aforefaid; and whereas alfo the Town and Lowey ⁱ of *Pevenfey* ᵏ, and the Town of Sea-

ANNOTATIONS.

otherwife than they were wont to plead in the Time of the Lord King Henry ⟨II⟩ *Great Grandfather*, which was King *Henry* II. who had been dead almoft Ninety Years before the Date of this Charter. And more plainly afterwards wills, *That they of the Ports aforefaid fhould not be impleaded but where they ought and were wont*, that is to fay, at *Shepway*. And that they fhould have their *Liberties and Freedoms as they and their Anceftors more fully and honourably had them in the Times of Edward*, William *the Firft and Second*, &c. *Kings of England, as the Charters* (which he fays) *the faid Barons have, and he had feen, do reafonably teftify*. And again, feemingly *De novo it granted*, That the Marriage and Wardfhip of their Heirs fhould not be in the King, by reafon of the Tenure of their Lands, yet it is expreffed to be of which he or his Predeceffors have not had the Wardfhip and Marriage [*temporibus retroactis*] in Times paft. So that, as may be plainly perceived in this, as alfo in other Charters, their elder Liberties and free Cuftoms are confirmed as before in *Magna Charta*, but in effect little, if any Thing, granted of new which they enjoyed not before, though expreffed therein to be now fo granted.

Secondly, From the Cuftoms themfelves, becaufe feveral of the Ufages and Cuftoms of the Ports were in ufe and practice amongft them before any mention is made thereof in their Charters; as to keep Courts, hold Cognifance of Pleas, take Fines of Lands, &c. None of their Charters mention any Thing thereof till that of King *Edward* IV. yet have I feen a Fine levied at *Rye*, in the fixteenth Year of King *Edward* II. before Paul *Fitz Robert*, then Mayor, and the Jurats there, from *John Rotherale* and *Goda* his Wife, to *Ralph Fitz John* and *Chriftian* his Wife, for feven Pence half-Penny Rent, &c. which was above one Hundred and forty Years before the Date of that Charter of King *Edward* IV. And in the Cuftomals of *Hafting* and *Winchelfea* (the former penned in the thirtieth Year of King *Edward* III. the other in the tenth Year of King *Henry* IV. both long before the Reign of King *Edward* IV.) is expreffly to be feen the Order and Manner of holding Pleas there by Prefcription even in thofe Days. And that Charter of King *Edward* IV. intimates as much, in that he wills them to hold their Pleas [*diebus & temporibus suidem confuetis*] the Days and Times there accuftomed. So for the Mayors being Coroners, and a Deputy Mayor acting for the Mayor, no mention is thereof in the Charters till that of King *James*; yet long before were both in ufe, and I have feen feveral Precedents thereof in the Records of the faid Town of *Rye*.

ⁱ *Lowey* or *Lowey*, q. l. *Lowway*, the Land thereabouts being Marfh and Low Grounds, as much noted for feeding of *Beeves*, as *Romney* Marfh for *Sheep*. The French Word *Launde* here kept, as alfo *Lenca* and *Leuga*, in the Chronicles of *Normandy* is ufed for a League (A Meafure in fome Countries containing more, in fome lefs, with us commonly three Miles). Upon what Occafion the *Lowey* of *Tunbridge* in *Kent*, from whence the Word came to be ufed here, was fet out, Mr. *Lambard* gives the beft Account that I have feen: He fays it was allotted firft on this Occafion, There was a Town in *Normandy*, and Land adjoining thereto, called *Bryonie*, which was of the ancient Poffeffion of the Dukedom, and had remained in the Hands of the Dukes there till *Richard*, the fecond Duke of that Name, gave it, amongft other Lands, to *Godfrey* his natural Brother, who enjoyed it all his Life, and left it to his Son *Gilbert*, who alfo held his Life-time; but after his Death, *Robert* Duke of *Normandy*, and eldeft Son of King *William* the Conqueror, being preffed to beftow it on *Robert* Earl *Mellent*, feifed it into his own Hands to unite it to the Dukedom again, which when *Richard*, the Son of *Gilbert* underftood, he put in his Claim of a long continued Poffeffion from *Godfrey* his Grandfather: fo that to ftop *Richard's* Mouth, by device of the Earl, and Mediation of Duke *Robert* with his Brother, *William Rufus*, it was brought to pafs, that *Richard* fhould receive in recompence the Town of *Tunbridge* in *England*, and fo much Land about it as *Bryonie* contained in *Chevile*; whereupon, *Bryonie*, and the Land about it, was meafured with a Line, which they afterward brought into *England*, and applying the fame to *Tunbridge* and the Land thereto adjoining, laid him out the very like in Precinct and Quantity; fo that long after, it was fo common and received Opinion in *Normandy*, that the Leagues of *Bryonie* and *Tunbridge* were alike in meafure and compafs.

ᵏ *Pevenfey*, *Pevenfea*, and vulgarly *Pemfey*, fortified once with a Caftle fuppofed of *Earl Robert*, Brother by the Mother to *William* the Conqueror; the Ruins whereof are yet to be feen. It is now like a Country Village, fave only the Corporation of Bailiff, Jurats and Commonalty there. It may feem to take the Name from the Scowring of the Haven by the Waters, it is now one of the Level pent in, having went through their Sluices here into the Sea. Here, fay fome, *William* the Conqueror firft arrived with his Fleet.

4 H. IILM.14.

Sea-

CHARTERS.

Seaford in præd. com. Suffex, &
villæ five loci vocati Bullver-
heeth, Petit Iham, & Hidney in
præd. com. Suffex, & villæ five
loci vocat. Bekesbourne &
Graunge, alias Grenche in præd.
com. Kanc. funt & à tempore
fupradicto fuerunt membr. ejufdem villæ & portus de Hafting;
ac villa de Bromehill in præd.
com. Suffex & Kanc. & vill. de
Lydd & veteri Romney in præd.
com. Kanc. & quæd. al. villæ
five loci vocat. Dengemarfh, Ofwardftone five Orwelftone in
prædict. com. Kanc. funt & à
tempore fupradicto fuerunt, membra ejufdem villæ & portus de
nova Romney, alias Romene;
&c

TRANSLATION.

Seaford[1] in the aforefaid County of *Suffex*, and the Towns or
Places called *Bulverbithe*[1]; *Petit Iham*[k], and *Hidney*[l], in the
aforefaid County of *Suffex*, and
the Towns or Places called
Beaksbourne[m] and *Graunge*, o-
therwife *Grenche*, in the aforefaid County of *Kent*, are, and
from the Time[n] abovefaid have
been, Members of the faid Town
and Port of *Hafting*; and the
Town of *Bromehill*[o] in the aforefaid Counties of *Suffex* and *Kent*;
and the Towns of *Lydd*[p] and
Old Romney[q] in the aforefaid
County of *Kent*, and certain other
Towns or Places called *Dengemarfh*[r], *Ofwardftone*[s] or *Orwelftone* in the aforefaid County of
Kent, are, and from the Time
abovefaid have been, Members
of the fame Town and Port of
New Romney, otherwife *Romene*;
and

ANNOTATIONS.

[i] *Seaford*, the only Town of all the Members that fends any Burgeffes to the Parliament;
whereby it appears to be an ancient Borough Town; and however *Provifion* be named before
it in this Charter, the Bailiff of *Seaford* taken place before the Bailiff of *Provifion* at the Gueftling, as was before noted.

[k] *Bulverbithe*, vulgarly *Bulverbide*; of this mention is made before, *page* 111. The greateft
part thereof is now eaten up by the Sea.

[k] *Petit Iham* or *Little Iham*, fo called, to diftinguifh it from another of the fame Name;
greater; of this fee before under the Word *Winchelfea*.

[l] *Hidney*. Unlefs this be the Lands called now the *Hidneius*, lying in, *Provifion* Kevel, between *Provifion* and *Romne*, I know not, nor can I fay, whether thofe Lands be in *Provifion*
Liberty, or yet owned by *Hafting*, as a Member.

[m] *Beaksbourne* and *Graunge*. I have nothing memorable to write of thefe; but that they are
ancient Members to *Hafting*, mentioned with the firft mentioned Members, there wrote *Bebyf-
borne* and *Greynche*.

[n] *From the Time*. Here and below, *l.* 11. again, *From the Time*, for, *From all the Time*; fo
in the Charter of King *James*, and both before and after in like cafe, in this Charter, which
makes me conceive, the Word *ane* in the *Latin* happened among the Erratas of the Prefs, or by
fome Miftake, was omitted in the Charter.

[o] *Bromehill*, in the Charter of King *James*, *Bromehill*, anciently (affirmed to be) a Parifh,
but now without Church, Houfe, or Inhabitant, been expreffed to belong to *New Romney*;
yet fo much thereof as lieth in the County of *Suffex* hath been taken to belong to *Winchelfea*,
and within their Liberty. And by an Order of the Lords of the Council, touching the levying
of Ship Money about the Year[*] 1638, as I mind, fo refolved to do, and is fuppofed to have
firft been a Member to old *Wine* elfe before the drowning thereof.

[p] *Lydd*. The Head Officer of this Corporation is yet a Bailiff. A Town not populous, yet
there are commonly on many Suits depending in Court as in any Court of the Ports or Members; the Church large, with a goodly Steeple, ferving for an ancient Sea Mark.

[q] *Old Romney*. Of this fomewhat was faid before.

[r] *Dengemarfh*[†], it lies near to *Lydd*, on the Extremity whereof (in taking) ftands the Light
called Dengenefs Light, for the Safeguard of Ships at Sea, firft projected by Mr. *Allen*, a Gold-
fmith of *Rye*, in the Reign of King *James*, and a Patent was defigned to have been got for the
Benefit of the Corporation of *Rye*, but it was begged of the King by another.

[s] *Ofwardftone*, near alfo to *Lydd*, near which, or on part thereof ftood one of the Wonders
of *England*, to wit, The many *Holm Trees* growing out of the *Stone* Beach not *Hilly* Land, where
nought but Space was feen, and was called the *Holmftone*, of late cut down, as —— to
there continued with Lydd to have the fame Liberties with Romney, and Members therein.

CHARTERS.

& etiam villa de Weſtheeth, in prædict. com. Kanc. eſt & à toto tempore ſupradicto fuit membrum ejuſdem villæ & Portus de Heeth ; & etiam villæ de Folkeſtone & Feverſham, in prædicto com. Kanc. & villæ & loci vocat. Margate, St. Johns, Goreſend, Birchington-Wood, alias Wood-church, & St. Peters in inſula Thannet, in prædicto com. Kanc. & Kingſdowne & Ringwolde in prædicto com. Kanc. ſunt & à toto tempore ſupradicto fuerunt membra prædict. villæ & Portus de Dover; ac etiam villæ ſive loci de Fordwich, Deal, Walmer,

TRANSLATION.

and alſo the Town of *Weſt-hithe*[t], in the aforeſaid County of *Kent,* is, and from all the time aboveſaid hath been, a Member of the ſame Town and Port of *Hithe*; and alſo the Towns of *Folkeſtone*[u] and *Feverſham*[w], in the aforeſaid County of *Kent*; and the Towns and Places called *Margate*[x], St. *John's,* *Gore-ſend,* *Birchington-Wood,* other-wiſe *Woodchurch,* and St. *Peters* in the Iſle of *Thannet*[y], in the aforeſaid County of *Kent*; and *Kingſdowne*[z] and *Ringwolde*[a] in the aforeſaid County of *Kent,* are, and from all the time above-ſaid have been, Members to the aforeſaid [b] Town and Port of *Dover*; and alſo the Towns or Places of *Fordwich*[c], *Deal*[d], *Walmer,*

ANNOTATIONS.

[t] *Weſthithe* or *Weſtheeth,* called *Weſt* in relation to the other *Hithe* lying Eaſt thereof; and *Hithe* (for which in the Charter *Heeth* is uſed, as before in *Balvenhithe*) becauſe here was a Port or Haven formerly, as was remembered before.

[u] *Folkeſtone,* famed in times of Popery for the Monaſtry of *Eufwide,* Daughter of *Eadbalde* Son of *Ethelbert,* King of *Kent,* long ſince ſwallowed up by the Sea, as a great Part of the Town beſides. For it is reported in the Time of King *Edward the Confeſſor* to have in it five Pariſh Churches; of which only one of St. *Peter* (as I take it) now remaineth. It had a Share of the Spoil Earl *Godwine,* in the time of his Baniſhment, did to the Sea Coaſts, and ſuffered by Fire from the *Scotch* and *French,* in the Time of King *Edward* III. but eſpecially being waſted by the Sea, was reduced to a low and inconſiderable Account, till of late, through the Induſtry of the Fiſhermen there, by the Quantities of freſh fiſh brought thither, it begins to thrive, and ſeems as likely as any Town of the Ports to be well traded and peopled, and may again deſerve the Name of *the Town of People, or Peoples-Town* (from its Popularity) though *Lambard* thinks it took the Name from the ſtone Cliff there, the reſt of the Cliffs between that and *Dover* being Chalk.

[w] *Feverſham* or *Feverſham,* and ſometime *Refreſham,* a pretty Market Town, noted of old [This, as is for the Parliament held there by King *Ethelſtane,* about the Year 903; and afterwards for the *before noted,* Abbey built there by King *Stephen,* wherein was buried, firſt, *Maude* his Wife, *Anno* 1151; *belonged to* and, in the next Year, *Euſtachius* their only Son; and, ſhortly after, King *Stephen* himſelf. *Dover, Anno* Towns that terminate in *Ham* ſeem to take their Original from ſome noted Houſe; for *Ham* 10 H. III. ſignifieth a Covering, and by a Metaphor, an Houſe that covereth us, which we call Home; and the Northern Men ſomething nearer the Original, *Heam.*

[x] *Margate* or *Mergate,* perhaps as a Gate or Inlet of the Sea, it being a Sea Town. The other Places here mentioned as Members to *Dover* were not memoriſed in that *Domeſday Book,* or Exemplification before mentioned, but *Margate* only.

[y] *Thannet.* An Iſland in the uttermoſt Part of *Kent* towards the eaſtern Part of the *Britiſh* Ocean. The Title whereof ſerveth to honour the Family of the Lord *Tuſton,* as Earl of *Thannet.*

[z] *Kingſdowne.* Not in that Iſland, but about *Midway,* between *Dover* and *Sandwich.*

[a] *Ringwolde,* vulgarly *Ringjole,* and ſometime hath been wrote *Kingwold,* but corruptly. It lieth near to *Kingſdowne.*

[b] *Aforeſaid.* So I find it in the Copy of King *James* his Charter I have by me; the printed Copy hath, *praced.* for *prædict.* foregoing for aforeſaid, a Word not uſual in this Caſe, nor uſed any where elſe in the Charter in ſuch Relation to any before named Place.

[c] *Fordwich,* as was ſaid before, on the River *Stoure,* between which and its Head Port, *Sandwich* hath been more Difference about their Compoſition, than hath happened between any other of the Ports and Members that I know of.

[d] *Deal* or *Dale*; becauſe built in a low Place, increaſed in the Buildings of late Years; ſo that of one Town there is now as it were two, called the *Upper* and the *Lower,* fortified with a Caſtle. It receiveth much Benefit by the Ships that lie in the *Deowe* juſt againſt it.

K k   *Walmer,*

CHARTERS.

Walmer, Ramfgate & Stoner, in præd. com. Kanc. & Sarr. in infula de Thannette, in dicto com, Kanc. & Brightlingfey in com. Effex, funt & à toto tempore fupradicto fuerunt membra dict. villæ & Port. de Sandwich; ac etiam villa & hundred. de Tenterden, in prædicto com. Kanc. eft membrum ejufdem antiquæ villæ de Rye. Cumque etiam Barones & Inhabitantes prædict. Quinque Portuum, antiquarum villarum & membrorum, eorum & prædeceffores fui; ac Major, Jurat. & Communitas villæ & Port. de Hafting prædict. in com. Suffex, & prædeceffores fui; ac Major, Jurat. & Communitas villæ & port. de Nova Romney præd. In dicto com. Kanc. & prædeceffores fui; ac Major, Jurat. & Communitas villæ & partus de Heeth præd. in dicto com. Kanc. & prædeceffores fui; ac Major, Jurat. & Communitas villæ & portus de Dovor. prædict. in dicto

TRANSLATION.

Walmer, *Ramfgate* and *Stoner*, in the aforefaid County of *Kent* and *Sarr*, in the Ifle of *Thanet*, in the faid County of *Kent*, and *Brightlingfey* in the County of *Effex* are, and from all the time abovefaid have been, Members of the faid Town and Port of *Sandwich*; and alfo the Town and Hundred of *Tenterden*, in the aforefaid County of *Kent*, is a Member of the fame ancient Town of *Rye*. And whereas alfo the Barons and Inhabitants of the aforefaid *Cinque Ports*, *Ancient Towns* and their Members, and their Predeceffors; and the Mayor, Jurats and Commonalty of the Town and Port of *Hafting* aforefaid, in the County of *Suffex*, and their Predeceffors; and the Mayor, Jurats and Commonalty of the Town and Port of *New Romney* aforefaid, in the faid County of *Kent*, and their Predeceffors; and the Mayor, Jurats and Commonalty of the Town and Port of *Hithe* aforefaid, in the faid County of *Kent*, and their Predeceffors; and the Mayor, Jurats and Commonalty of the Town and Port of *Dover* aforefaid, in the

ANNOTATIONS.

Walmer, not mentioned before the Charter of King *James*, fomewhat nearer to *Dover* than *Deal*, fortified alfo with a Caftle.

Ramfgate, fome have called *Romanefgate*, as being a Port frequented by them, lieth in the Ifle of *Thanet*, though not mentioned fo in this Charter.

Stoner, fo in the Charter of King *James*, of old *Stonor*; but in the printed Copy *Stonar*: I take the former to be righteft and beft agreeing with the Nature of the Place, as being fome-what more ftony than *Sandwich*, very near which it lieth, though in the Ifle of *Thanet*.

Sarr lieth in and near the weftern Part of the Ifland.

Brightlingfey, the only Place belonging to the Ports that lieth out of the Counties of *Kent* and *Suffex*, all the other being in one of them.

Effex, fo called from the *Eaft Saxons*.

Tenterden hath all the Hundred as well as the Town within the Liberty of the Ports; but cannot prefcribe; becaufe, as was before noted, it appears when it was feparated from the County and annexed to *Rye*. A country Town, hath been ftored with Gentry, wants not good Land about it, nor goodly Structures. The Church is adorned with a ftately Steeple, which, it feems was built about the time the Lands of Earl *Godwine* were fwallowed up by the Sea, which are now called *Goodwine Sands*; whence things co-incident, but not depending one upon another as the Effect on the Caufe, are proverbially made fimilar thereto. Neverthelefs, fome have thought, that feveral Workmen employed to repair the Sea Walls, and defend the faid Lands againft the Rage of the Sea, being drawn away and employed about the building of that Steeple, occafioned the Want of timely Reparations to prevent the inundation of the Sea, which once getting in was never recovered again; and if fo, then it may be faid, *Tenterden Steeple* was the Caufe of *Goodwine Sands*.

†   *Franchifes*.

CHARTERS.

dicto com. Kanc. & prædecessores
sui ; ac Major, Jurat. & Communitas villæ & portus de Sandwich
præd. in com. Kanc. & prædecessores sui ; ac Major, Jurat. &
Communitas antiquæ villæ de
Rye præd. in com. Suffex, &
prædecessores sui ; ac Major, Jurat. & Communitas antiquæ villæ
de Winchelsea prædict. in com.
Suffex, & prædecessores sui ; ac
Ballivus, Jurat. & Communitas
villæ & Leucatæ de Pevensey
prædict. in com. Suffex, & prædecessores sui ; ac Ballivus, Jurat.
& Communitas villæ de Seaford
præd. in com. Suffex, & prædecessores sui ; ac Ballivus, Jurat. &
Communitas villæ de Lydd præd.
in com. Kanc. & prædecessores
sui ; ac Major, Jurat. & Communitas villæ de Folkestone præd.
in com. Kanc. & prædecessores
sui ; ac Major, Jurat. & Communitas villæ de Feversham præd.
in com. Kanc. & prædecessores
sui ; ac Major, Jurat. & Communitas villæ de Fordwich præd.
in com. Kanc. & prædecessores
sui ; ac Major, Jurat. & Communitas villæ & hundred. de Tenterden. prædict. in com. Kanc. &
prædecessores sui, diversis libertatibus, franchesiis, privilegiis,
jurisdictionibus, quietanciis, &
immunitatibus temporibus retroactis,

TRANSLATION.

the said County of *Kent*, and
their Predecessors ; and the
Mayor, Jurats and Commo-
nalty of the Town and Port
of *Sandwich* aforesaid, in the
County of *Kent*, and their Predecessors ; and the Mayor, Jurats
and Commonalty of the ancient
Town of *Rye* aforesaid, in the
County of *Suffex*, and their Predecessors ; and the Mayor, Jurats and Commonalty of the
ancient Town of *Winchelsea*
aforesaid, in the County of
Suffex, and their Predecessors ;
and the Bailiff, Jurats and Commonalty of the Town and Lowey
of *Pevensea* aforesaid, in the
County of *Suffex*, and their Predecessors ; and the Bailiff, Jurats and Commonalty of the
Town of *Seaford* aforesaid, in
the County of *Suffex*, and their
Predecessors ; and the Bailiff,
Jurats and Commonalty of the
Town of *Lydd* aforesaid, in the
County of *Kent*, and their Pre-
decessors ; and the Mayor, Ju-
rats and Commonalty of the
Town of *Folkestone* aforesaid, in
the County of *Kent*, and their
Predecessors ; and the Mayor,
Jurats and Commonalty of the
Town of *Feversham* aforesaid, in
the County of *Kent*, and their
Predecessors ; and the Mayor,
Jurats and Commonalty of the
Town of *Fordwich* aforesaid, in
the County of *Kent*, and their
Predecessors ; and the Mayor,
Jurats and Commonalty of the
Town and Hundred of *Tenter-
den* aforesaid, in the County of
Kent, and their Predecessors, di-
verse Liberties, Franchises [m]
Privileges, Jurisdictions [n], Free-
doms and Immunities [o] in times
past,

ANNOTATIONS.

[m] *Franchises*. Freedoms or Liberties, from two French Words, *Franch*, *Free*, and *Chose*, a
thing.

[n] *Jurisdictions*. Power or Authority to administer Justice and execute Laws ; also a Court of
Judicature, and the Verge or Extent of it.

[o] *Immunities*. Freedoms or Liberties from any Charge or Burden ; equivalent to Exemptions.

The

CHARTERS.

actis, tam ratione literarum patentium prædict. superius recitat. ac seperalium aliarum cartarum & literarum patentium, per alios prædecessores nostros Reges & Reginas Angliæ, eis & prædecessor. suis antehac respective dat. concess. seu confirmat. quam ratione diversar. præscription. & consuetud. in eisdem portubus, villis & membris respective usitat. & consuet. habuerunt, tenuerunt, & gavisi fuerunt, & adhuc habent, tenent, & utantur: Nos considerantes quod Barones Quinque Portuum prædictor. ac Barones prædict. antiquarum villarum de Rye & Winchelsea, & membr. eorundem portuum & antiquar. villar. magna servitia cum navibus suis de tempore in tempus quamplurimis progenitoribus & prædecessor. nostris, Regibus & Reginis Angliæ, perimpleverunt & impenderunt, ad magnum eorum sumptum, & magnum progenitor. nostr. & Regni nostr. præd. honor. & commod. Ac gratiose pieque contemplantes, quod dict. Quinque Portus, antiquæ villæ & membra eorundem portuum & villarum, injuriis, violentiis, deprædationibus &

TRANSLATION.

past, as well by reason of the aforesaid Letters Patents above recited, and of several other Charters and Letters Patents, by other our Predecessors, Kings and Queens of *England*, to them and their Predecessors before this time respectively given, granted or confirmed, as by reason of diverse Prescriptions[p] and Customs, in the same Ports, Towns and Members respectively used and accustomed, have had, held and enjoyed, and yet have, hold and use : We considering that the Barons of the *Cinque Ports* aforesaid, and the Barons of the aforesaid ancient Towns of *Rye* and *Winchelsea*, and the Members of the same Ports and ancient Towns, great Services with their Ships from time to time[q] have performed and done to very many of our Progenitors[r] and Predecessors, Kings and Queens of *England*, at their great Cost, and to the great Honour and Commodity[s] of our Progenitors and of our Realm ; And graciously and piously contemplating[t], that the said *Cinque Ports*, ancient Towns and Members of the same Ports and Towns, lie subject continually to the Injuries[u], Violences, Spoils[w] and

ANNOTATIONS.

[p] *Prescriptions.* Prescription, as before noted, is usage time out of Mind ; Personal is, for the most part, applied to Persons ; but that which is local is alledged in some Manour or other Place. The Prescriptions here reach both the Ports and Portsmen.

[q] *From time to time.* Of this see before.

[r] *Progenitors,* are those of whose Line age any one descends.

[s] *Commodity* or Profit.

[t] *Contemplating* or considering, a serious Debate in the Mind.

[u] *N. B.* From the Word *Realm,* in the 19th Line of this Page, to the Word *Also* in the following Page, is much differing from the Charter of King *James,* where it runs thus : *And that the aforesaid* Cinque Ports *and ancient Towns aforesaid, and the aforesaid Members of the same Ports and ancient Towns do lie very dangerous to the first Entrances and continual Assaults and Invasions of our Enemies ; and in Times past, by Invasions, Spoilings and Burnings of such Enemies of our Realm aforesaid, have been greatly wasted and unpeopled. And also well and graciously considering, that the said* Cinque Ports, *ancient Towns, and the Members of the same Ports and Towns, do still lie subject to the like Injuries ; Violences and sudden Oppressions of our Enemies.* This makes me suspect another Error in the printed Copy, or in that Amanuensis that transcribed the Charter before it passed the Seal or afterward.

[u] *Injuries* or Wrongs ; such things as are done unjustly.

[w] *Spoils.* Spoils of warlike Enemies, after the *Latin, Depredations.*

[x] *Enemies.*

CHARTERS.

& fubitis oppreffionibus inimicorum noftrorum continue fubja-
cent ; necnon volentes & valde
cupientes, quod navigium portuum præd. & antiquar. villar.
prædict. ac membr. eorundem
portuum & antiquar. villar. non
pereat aut deficiat (quod abfque
magnis oneribus & expenfis fuftentari, onerari & manuteneri
non poterit) fed ad ferviend. nobis, hæredib. & fucceffor. noftris,
melius & promptius poterit inveniri ; & ut Quinque Portus &
antiquæ villæ ill. ac membr. eorundem portuum & antiquarum
villarum per recurfus frequen-
tiores & acceffiones populi vali-
diores & fortiores in ipforum &
patriæ adjacentis meliorem tuiti-
onem & defenfionem afficiantur ;
necnon confideratione habita ad
gratiffimum & exoptabil. fervitium, quod Barones Quinque Portuum & antiquarum villarum
præd. nobis in inauguratione noftra ad coronam hujufmodi Reg.
noftr. Angliæ fecerunt & impenderunt, ficut etiam temporibus
retroactis progenitoribus noftris,
Regibus & Reginis Angliæ, ad
eorum coronationes refpective, à
toto

TRANSLATION.

and fudden Oppreffions of our
Enemies [x] ; alfo willing and
greatly defiring that the Navy of
the aforefaid Ports and ancient
Towns aforefaid, and Members
of the fame Ports and ancient
Towns, may not perifh or fail
(which without great Charges
and Expences cannot be fuftained, charged [y] and maintained)
but may be found the better and
more ready to ferve us, our
Heirs and Succeffors ; and that
thofe *Cinque Ports* and ancient
Towns, and the Members of the
fame Ports and ancient Towns,
by more frequent Recourfe [z] and
Accefs of People, may be made
more ftrong and forcible, for
the better Safety [b] and Defence
of the fame and the Country adjacent [c] ; alfo in confideration [d]
of the moft grateful and acceptable [e] Service, which the Barons
of the *Cinque Ports* and ancient
Towns aforefaid have done to us,
in our Inauguration [f] to the
Crown of this our Kingdom of
England ; as alfo in times paft to
our Progenitors, Kings and
Queens of *England*, at their Coronations [g] refpectively, from all
the

ANNOTATIONS.

[x] *Enemies.* The *Cinque Ports*, lying along the Sea Coaft as they do, have been efteemed the Gates of the Kingdom ; for it is obferved, that in the Conquefts of the *Romans, Danes* and *Normans*, they ftill land at fome or other of the Ports.

[y] *Charged*, to wit, upon the Ports, or the Charge thereof born by them.

[z] *Frequent Recourfe.* This was doubtlefs the prudent Policy of State, and the true Reafon of the firft granting of the Liberties and Privileges, the better to people the Places that lie open to Invafion of foreign Enemies.

[b] *Safety*, Tuition or fafe keeping.

[c] *Adjacent* or lying near thereunto.

[d] *In confideration*, or having had confideration to the moft grateful, &c.

[e] *Acceptable.* After the *Latin*, defirable or to be wifhed.

[f] *Inauguration*, formerly taken in an ill Senfe, for confulting with Augurs or Soothfayers ; now taken for a folemn invefting one with an Office or Place of Honour or Eminence, and here all one with Coronation.

[g] *Coronations.* The Barons of the *Cinque Ports* and *Two Ancient Towns* have time out of mind had the Honour to carry the Canopy over the King and Queen at their Coronation, and dine with them the fame Day, as was before noted, and in the Charter of King *Edward* I. called *Their Honours at Court.* Touching which I find recorded, *fol.* 37. of the Cuftomal of *Winchelfea*, and *fol.* 51. of the Cuftomal of *Rye*, in *Latin*, as followeth, to which I have annexed the Tranflation.

L l   CUM

ANNOTATIONS.

CUM autem contigerit, quod aliquis Rex aut Regina Angliæ coronabitur, folent Barones Quinque Portuum, per breve dicti Domini Regis fummon. eis directi, ad coronationem illam venire, ad folita ferviria fua faciend. & honores fuos in curia ejufdem Domini Regis recipiend. videlicet, in die Coronationis Domini Regis, cum de camera exierit ut coronetur, & cum redierit a coronatione fua, folent Barones Quinque Portuum, prout de jure debent, portare fuper Regem ac Reginam pannos de cerico vel de auro, fcilicet, per triginta duos Barones Quinque Portuum: Ita de jure, quod nullus alius fit inter eos in dicto Officio exequend. Et folent, prout de jure deberent, mandari per breve Domini Regis folempniter per fummonition. quadraginta dierum ante coronationem prædictam, quod tali die veniant ad faciend. fervitium fuum Domini Regi debitum. Et folent ipfi triginta duo, vel plures nobiliores, venire ibidem de una fecta honorifice, folempniterque decenter veftiti & apparati de fuo proprio & fuis fumptibus propriis, fed expenfæ fuæ dummodo fuerint ad curiam folent effe de com.

Cum autem fecerint officium fuum portand. prædictos pannos, utrumque pannum fuper quatuor lanceas defuper deargentat qualit. lancea habens unam campanillam argenteam defuper deauratam, & de providentia Thefaurar. Domini Regis, ad quamlibet lanceam folent ire quatuor Barones. Ita quod uterque pannus porteetur per fexdecim Barones, & Dominus Rex fub unius panni medio, & Regina fub alterius panni medio. Et folent ipfi triginta duo, fimul cum omnibus aliis Baronibus qui adeffe voluerint, habere proximiorem menfam in magna aula Regia, & ad dextram ipfius Regis juxta menfam fuam de jure & antiquo libero ufu federe. Et ubicunque Dominus Rex invitaverit Barones Quinque Portuum, ut fecum comedant, femper habere folent de jure menfam propinquiorem menfæ fuæ in dextris ejus, & ibidem in prandio federe.

Cum vero licentiam dicti Barones à Domino Rege habeant redeundi, fecum habebunt prædictos pannos, cum lanceis & campanillis, & omnibus fuis pertinen. Et folent Barones de Haftyng cum fub membris habere unum pannum cum lanceis & campanillis & toto apparatu ejufdem, cæteri vero Portus alterum pannum cum toto fuo apparatu. Et Barones de Haftyng cum fuis membris folent dare pannum fuum fic habitum Ecclefiæ fancti Ricardi Ciceftr. & fic dederunt. Et Barones de Romen. Hethe, Dovorr. & Sandwych folent dare & dederunt pannum fuum fic habitum fancto Thomæ in Ecclefia Chrifti Cantuar. & diviferunt lanceas & campanillas inter fe.

Cum autem aliquis Rex decefferit & alius coronatur, folet proclamatio fieri in magna aula Regia, quod omnes magnati & alii quicunque cujufcunque ftatus, gradus feu dignitatis exift. qui aliquod fervitium jure vel hereditar. Domino Regi ad coronationem fuam facere deberent, feu honorem five beneficium ad coro-

AND when it fhall happen, that any King or Queen of *England* fhall be crowned, the Barons of the *Cinque Ports*, by Writ of Summons of our faid Lord the King t. them directed, are * wont to come to the Corona- * *Or were* tion, to do their wonted Services, and receive *want; and fo* their Honours in the Court of our faid Lord *it may be un-* the King, that is to fay, in the Day of the *derftood in a-* Coronation of our Lord the King, when he *ther Places.* fhall go forth of his Chamber that he may be crowned, and when he fhall return from his Coronation, the Barons of the *Cinque Ports* are wont, as of right they ought, to bear over the King and Queen Cloths of Silk or of Gold, that is to fay, by thirty two Barons of the *Cinque Ports:* So of right that none other be among them to execute † the faid Office. †*Or in execu-* And they are wont, as of right they ought, to *ting.* be fent for by Writ of our Lord the King folemnly, by Summons of forty Days before the aforefaid Coronation, that fuch a Day they may come to do their Service due to our Lord the King. And the fame thirty two, or the more noble, are wont to come there honourably, folemnly and decently clothe and apparelled with one Suit of their own proper Cofts; but their Expences whilft they fhall be at Court are wont to be of common.

And when they fhall do their Office to bear the Cloths aforefaid, each Cloth upon four Staves ‡ overlaid with Silver, every Staff ‡ *Or Launces* having one little filver Bell overlaid with *like the Staff* Gold, and of the providing of the Treasurer *of a Spear or* of our Lord the King, at every Staff are wont *Launce.* to go four Barons. So that every Cloth be born by fixteen Barons, and our Lord the King under the Middle of one Cloth, and the Queen under the Middle of another Cloth. And the fame thirty two, together with all the other Barons which will be prefent, are wont to have the next Table in the King's great ‖ Hall, and at the right Hand of the ‖ *Now called* King himfelf, according to his Table, to fit of Weftminfter right and ancient free Ufe. And whenfoever * Hall. our Lord the King fhall invite the Barons of * *Ubicunque,* the *Cinque Ports*, that they may eat with him, *ufed in the* they are wont always of right to have the Latin *for* Table neareft to his Table, at his right Hand, *quandocun-* and there to fit at Dinner. *que.*

But when the faid Barons have Licence of returning from our Lord the King, they fhall have the aforefaid Cloths, with the Staves and little Bells, and all their Appurtenances. And the Barons of *Hafting*, with their Members, are wont to have one † Cloth, with the † *That is,* Staves and little Bells, and all the Appurte- *when both* nance thereof; but the other Ports the other *King and* Cloth, with all its Appurtenance. And the *Queen are* Barons of *Hafting*, with their Members, are *crowned; fo* wont to give their Cloth fo had to the Church *that there* of S^t. *Richard* of *Chichefter*, and fo they have *were two Ca-* given. And the Barons of *Romney, Hithe, nopies; but* *Dover* and *Sandwich*, are wont to give, and now the Ba- have given their Cloth fo had, to S^t. *Thomas* † *vows divide* in *Chrift's Church* in *Canterbury*, and they have *equally,* divided the Staves and little Bells amongft ‡ *This was* themfelves. Tho. Becket,

And when any King fhall deceafe and an- *then a popifh* other be crowned, Proclamation is wont to be *Saint.* made in the King's great Hall, that all the Nobles and others whofoever, of whatfoever State, Degree or Dignity they be, which ought to do any Service by Right or hereditarily to our Lord the King at his Coronation, or claim to have any Honour or Benefit at the Coro-

CHARTERS.

toto tempore cujus contrarii memoria hominum non exiſtit, fecerunt & facere debuerunt; ac hæred.& ſucceſſor. noſtr. Regibus Angliæ, ad eorum coronationem, juxta privilegium & honorem ſua facere debent; noſque ſeperales literas patentes, tam præd. inclyti prædeceſſoris noſtr. Dominæ Eliⱬabethæ nuper Reginæ Angliæ, quam prædict. præchariſſimi avi noſtr. ac præchariſſimi patris noſtr. ſuperius mentionat. ac omnia & ſingula in eiſdem reſpective content. & ſpecificat; necnon omnes & ſingulas alias

TRANSLATION.

the time whereof the Memory of Man ʰ is not to the contrary, have done and ought to do; and to our Heirs and Succeſſors, Kings of *England,* at their Coronation, according to their Privilege ˡ and Honour, ought to do; and we the ſeveral Letters Patents, as well of our famous Predeceſſor, the aforeſaid Lady *Elizabeth* late Queen of *England,* as of the aforeſaid our moſt dear Grandfather, and our moſt dear Father above mentioned; and all and ſingular in the ſame reſpectively contained and ſpecified; alſo all and ſingular other

ANNOTATIONS.

coronationem Regis ſeu Reginæ habere clamant, venient coram ſeneſchallo Angliæ, ſeu ſuo locumtenente, ad certum diem aſſignat. ad monſtrand. & declarand. quod & quale ſervitium tent. ſeu clamant facere; ad quam diem ſolent Barones Quinque Portuum adeſſend. & ſervitium ad dictam coronationem pro Portubus prædictis faciend. electi miniſtrar. dicto Domino Seneſchallo quandam ſupplicationem ſub hac forma.

Coronation of the King or Queen, ſhall come before the Steward of *England* or his Deputy, at a certain Day aſſigned, to ſhew and declare what and what Manner of Service they hold or claim to do; at which Day the Barons of the *Cinque Ports* are wont to be, and thoſe elected to do the Service at the ſaid Coronation for the Ports aforeſaid, preſent to the ſaid Lord Steward a certain Petition * under this Form. *Or Supplication.*

The Petition here mentioned, in nature of a Claim, I have by me in the old French Language, as I copied it out of the ſame Cuſtomals; but ſince the Subſtance thereof is but according to the foregoing Records, I forbear to inſert it. And moreover I found there, at the Coronation of King *Richard* III. and Queen *Anne* his Conſort, ſuch a Petition or Claim was put in by the Ports to *John* Duke of *Norfolk,* then Steward of *England,* wherein they claimed theſe Honours as belonging to the Ports time out of mind; and received this Anſwer:

COnſideratum eſt, quod Barones Quinque Portuum, juxta eorum clameum, admittentur ad ſervitium ſuum faciend. videlicet, ad geſtand. pannos ſericos, quatuor haſtis deargentat. ſuſtentat. cum campanillis Argenteis deauratis, ultra Regem & Reginam in die coronacionis eorum, & poſt ſervitium impletum, ad eoſdem pannos cum ſuis apparat. & pertin. prædictis, tanquam feoda ſua conſueta, percipiend. & habend. Ac etiam ad ſedend. eodem die ad principalem menſam ad dextram partem Aulæ.

Per Johannem Ducem Norff. ſeneſc. Angl. hac Vice.

De Engliſh thus:

IT is conſidered, that the Barons of the *Cinque Ports,* according to their Claim, be admitted to do their Service, viz. to bear the ſilk Cloths ſuſtained by four Staves ſilvered over, with little ſilver Bells gilded, over the King and Queen in the Day of their Coronation; and after the Service performed, to receive and have the ſame Cloths, with their Appurtenances aforeſaid, as their accuſtomed Fees. And alſo to ſit the ſame Day at the principal Table at the right Side of the Hall.

By *John* Duke of *Norfolk,* Steward of England at preſent †. *† Or at this time.*

As to the forty Days Summons mentioned in the upper Part of this Record, it ſeems to be the old Cuſtom, but now hath long been diſuſed; for I find, in a Letter of Mr. *Edward Kellet* to the *Ports, July* 11, 1603. that he had ſearched the *Tower,* the *Rolls,* the *Petty-Bag,* the *Six-Clerks* and the *Crown-Office,* to find a Precedent for a Writ of Summons for the Barons of the *Ports* to do their Service at the Coronation, but could find none. So that now the *Ports* put in their Claim by way of Petition as aforeſaid.

ʰ *Man* or *Men.* The printed Copy here, as before, hath *hujuſmodi* for *hominum*; but I ſuppoſe corruptly, and ſo have adventured to alter it both here and there, *p.* 121.

ˡ *Privilege and Honour.* One Copy of King *James* his Charter reads it plurally.

ˡ *Dona-*

CHARTERS.

alias donationes, conceſſiones, cartas, confirmationes & literas patentes quaſcunque per aliquos vel aliquem anteceſſor. vel prædeceſſor. noſtrorum, Regum vel Reginarum Angliæ, Baron. Quinque Portuum ; ac BaronibusQuinque Portuum & hæred. ſuis ; ac hominibus de Quinque Portubus, vel aliquibus advocand. ſe de libertate eorundem ; ac Baronibus Quinque Portuum, hæred. & ſucceſſor. ſuis ; ac Baronibus Quinque Portuum & Membrorum eorundem ; ac Baronibus & probis hominibus Quinque Portuum & Membrorum eorundem ; ac Major. Ballivis & Jurat. Quinque Portuum & Membrorum eorundem ; ac Major. & Jurat. Ballivis & Jurat. ſive Jurat. Quinque Portuum & Membrorum eorundem, ac cujuſlibet & alicujus Portus & Membr. præd. ac Baronibus villæ & portus de Haſting ; ac Balliv. Jurat. & Communitat. villæ & portus de Haſting ; ac Major. Jurat. & Communitat. villæ & portus de Haſting ; ac Baronibus villæ & portus de Romney ; & Jurat. & Communitat. villæ & portus de Nova Romney ; & Major. Jurat. & Communitat. villæ & portus de Nova Romney ; & Baronibus villæ & Portus de Heeth ; ac Jurat. &

TRANSLATION.

other Donations [1], Grants, Charters, Confirmations and Letters Patents whatſoever, by any of our Anceſtors or Predeceſſors, Kings or Queens of *England,* to the Barons of the *Cinque Ports* ; and to the Barons [m] of the *Cinque Ports* and their Heirs ; and to the Men of the *Cinque Ports,* or to any calling themſelves of the Liberty of the ſame ; and to the Barons of the *Cinque Ports,* their Heirs and Succeſſors ; and to the Barons of the *Cinque Ports* and Members of the ſame ; and to the Barons and good Men of the *Cinque Ports* and their Members ; and to the Mayors, Bailiffs and Jurats of the *Cinque Ports* and their Members ; and to the Mayors and Jurats, Bailiffs and Jurats, or to the Jurats of the *Cinque Ports* and their Members, and of every and of any Port and Member aforeſaid ; and to the Barons of the Town and Port of *Haſting* ; and to the Bailiff, Jurats and Commonalty of the Town and Port of *Haſting* ; and to the Mayor, Jurats and Commonalty of the Town and Port of *Haſting* ; and to the Barons of the Town and Port of *Romney* ; and to the Jurats and Commonalty of the Town and Port of *New Romney* ; and to the Mayor, Jurats and Commonalty of the Town and Port of *New Romney* ; and to the Barons of the Town and Port of *Hitbe* ; and to the Jurats and

ANNOTATIONS.

[1] Donations are ſometimes taken for Benefices collated by the Patron to a Man, without Preſentation, Inſtitution or Induction ; but here for princely Gifts or Benevolences.

[m] And to the Barons. Here, and ſo along to near the Bottom of p. 133. are repeated the ſeveral Directions of ſeveral of the Charters, or the Names to whom, or Capacities by which ſuch Franchiſes and Immunities were granted, received and enjoyed. Yet there are others ; for *Tenterden* had a Bailiff for their head Officer, till about the latter End of Queen *Elizabeth,* albeit here is no Mention made of any Charter directed to them by the Name of the Bailiff, Jurats and Commonalty of *Tenterden,* as there is in the Charter of King *James.* And ſo had alſo *Hitbe,* for ſome time a Corporation, conſiſting of Bailiffs, Jurats and Commonalty, as before was noted, though no Notice be taken thereof here. However, all ſuch Charters are confirmed by the general Words following ; *by whatſoever Names, or by whatſoever Titles, &c.*

CHARTERS.

& Communitat. villæ & portus de Heeth; ac Major. Jurat. & Communitat. villæ & portus de Heeth; ac Baronibus villæ & portus de Dover, ac Major. Jurat. & Communitat. villæ & portus de Dover; & Baronibus villæ & portus de Sandwic, ac Major. Jurat. & Communitat. villæ & portus de Sandwic; & Baronibus antiquæ villæ de Rye, & Major. Jurat. & Communitat. antiquæ villæ de Rye; & Baronibus antiquæ villæ de Winchelsey, ac Majori, Juratis & Communit. antiquæ villæ de Winchelsey; & Baronibus villæ & Leucatæ de Pevensey, & Ballivo, Juratis & Communitat. villæ & Leucatæ de Pevensey; ac Baronibus villæ de Seaford, & Ballivo & Communitat. villæ de Seaford; & Baronibus villæ de Lydd, ac Ballivo, Juratis & Communitat. villæ de Lydd; & Baronibus villæ de Folkestone, & Majori, Juratis & Communitat. villæ de Folkestone; & Baronibus villæ de Feversham, & Majori, Juratis, & Communitat. villæ de Feversham; ac Baronibus villæ de Fordwich, ac Majori, Juratis & Communitat. villæ de Fordwich; ac Baronibus villæ & hundred. de Tenterden, ac Majori, Juratis & Communitat. villæ & hundred. de Tenterden; per quæcunque nomina, five per quodcunque nomen, vel per quafcunq; incorporationes, vel per quamcunq; incorporationem, vel prætextu cujufcunque incorporationis ante hac cognit. vocat. five nuncupat. fuerunt, modo fant, vel

TRANSLATION.

and Commonalty of the Town and Port of *Hithe*, and to the Mayor, Jurats and Commonalty of the Town and Port of *Hithe*; and to the Barons of the Town and Port of *Dover*, and to the Mayor, Jurats and Commonalty of the Town and Port of *Dover*; and to the Barons of the Town and Port of *Sandwich*, and to the Mayor, Jurats and Commonalty of the Town and Port of *Sandwich*; and to the Barons of the ancient Town of *Rye*, and to the Mayor, Jurats and Commonalty of the ancient Town of *Rye*; and to the Barons of the ancient Town of *Winchelsea*, and to the Mayor, Jurats and Commonalty of the ancient Town of *Winchelsea*; and to the Barons of the Town and Lowey of *Pevensea*; and to the Bailiff, Jurats and Commonalty of the Town and Lowey of *Pevensea*; and to the Barons of the Town of *Seaford*, and to the Bailiff and Commonalty of the Town of *Seaford*; and to the Barons of the Town of *Lydd*, and to the Bailiff, Jurats and Commonalty of the Town of *Lydd*; and to the Barons of the Town of *Folkstone*, and to the Mayor, Jurats and Commonalty of the Town of *Folkstone*; and to the Barons of the Town of *Feversham*, and to the Mayor, Jurats and Commonalty of the Town of *Feversham*; and to the Barons of the Town of *Fordwich*, and to the Mayors, Jurats and Commonalty of the Town of *Fordwich*; and to the Barons of the Town and Hundred of *Tenterden*, and to the Mayor, Jurats and Commonalty of the Town and Hundred of *Tenterden*; by whatfoever Names, or by whatfoever Name, or by whatfoever Incorporations, or by whatfoever Incorporation, or by pretext of any Incorporation; they have heretofore been, now are,

M m   or

CHARTERS.	TRANSLATION.
vel impofterum fuerint, omnia & fingula libertates, privilegia, franchefias, confuetudines, immunitates, acquietancias, exemptiones, jurifdictiones, ferias, nundinas, mercat. Tolnet. Theoſon. Stallag. Piccag. Cuftum, Eſiamenta, Fines, Amerciamenta & alia proficua & hæreditamenta in dictis literis patentibus, feu eorum aliquibus, feu aliqua (per præfentes minime revocat. diminut. five mutat.) content. feu fpecificat. eaque rata habentes, & grata ea omnia & fingula pro nobis, hæred. & fucceſſor. noftris (quantum in nobis eft) ratificamus, approbamus, acceptamus & confirmamus per præfentes, prout eis hactenus rationabiliter uſi fuerunt. Et ulterius de uberiori gratia noftra fpeciali,	or hereafter may be [n] known, called or named [o], all and fingular the Liberties, Privileges, Franchifes, Cuftoms, Immunities, Freedoms [p], Exemptions [q], Jurifdictions, Feafts [r], Fairs [f], Markets [t], Tolls, Tholls [u], Stallage, Piccage [w], Cuftom [x], Eafements [y], Fines, Amerciaments, and other Profits [z] and Hereditaments [a], in the faid Letters Patents, or any of them (by thefe Prefents not revoked [b], diminifhed [c] or changed) contained or fpecified, and the fame having ratified, and freely all and fingular the fame for us, our Heirs and Succeffors (as much as in us is) we do ratify, approve, accept and confirm by thefe Prefents, as hitherto they have reafonably ufed them. And of our more abundant fpecial Grace,

ANNOTATIONS.

[n] *May be* or fhall be.

[o] *Named* or expreffed.

[p] *Freedoms.* The *Latin* Word fo tranflated in the old Charters, *Quietancias,* is of the fame Force with the Word ufed here, which is *Acquietancias*; and becauſe it looks like Acquitances, fome have rendered it *Acquitments.* See before, page 8.

[q] *Exemptions.* To be exempt is to be freed from fome Burden, Charge, Incumbrance or other; as to be feparate from the reſt of the County, and not forced to go out of their Liberties to Mulcters, Seſſions, Aſſizes, &c.

[r] *Feafts,* fometimes termed Holy Days, as properly denoting fuch as are called Saints Days, but here feem efpecially to be fuch Days as every Parifh almoſt claims to have one for liberty of feafting, fporting or exercife of Youth in military Arts or feats of Arms, or fuch like.

[f] *Fairs.* Some Places have but one, others two or more in a Year, when and where there is free Traffick, though in Cities or corporate Towns, for the buying and felling of all forts of Goods, Wares and Merchandifes. A Fair is but a great Market.

[t] *Markets.* The fame Word that was ufed before for Merchandife in the Charter of King *Edward* I. is here rightly ufed for Markets; every Market is as it were a weekly Fair. The Markets in the Ports, moſt of them, are too fmall to be commended.

[u] *Tholls.* Both the *Latin Tolnetum* and *Theolonium* may be rendered *Toll,* of which already, *page* 8. fomething is noted, and if for difference fake *Theolonium* be read *Thol,* it fhall be differently underſtood from *Thol,* if *Thol* be freedom from Homage. See *page* 11.

[w] *Piccage,* the fame with *Picage* in the Charter of King *Edward* IV.

[x] *Cuftom.* This and the two Words before it, whether plural or fingular is uncertain, but though the *Englifh* ufe Cuftoms, yet *Stallage* and *Picage* are only fingular with them, albeit in the *Latin* they may be ufed in the plural. This Word *Cuftom,* in *Latin Cuftuma,* is the fame for which *Confuetudo* is ufed in the Charter of King *Edward* I. and is a Kind of Toll or Town Duty; and *Confuetudo,* though alfo tranflated *A Cuftom,* fignifieth an *Ufage,* and fuch Ufages as are accuftomed and of long ftanding.

[y] *Eafements* or *Eafiments* are fuch Services (faith *Kitchin*) as one Neighbour hath of another by Charter or Prefcription without profit, as a Way through his Ground, a Sink or Sewer, &c. and may here include the Highways, or ufe of Common Lands lying within the refpective Precincts of the Ports Towns and Members.

[z] *Profits,* a general Word for any Advantage arifing lawfully to the Receiver.

[a] *Hereditaments* are any Things that may be inherited, corporeal or incorporeal, real, perfonal or mixt.

[b] *Revoked* or recalled.

[c] *Diminifhed,* whereby any Liberty is leſſened, as the Liberty of electing Town Clerks is diminifhed afterward by this Charter; for the Words contained in this Parenthefis have reference to the Provifo's in the End of the Charter.

[d] *Con-*

CHARTERS.

ciali, ac ex certa fcientia &
mero motu noftris dedimus,
conceffimus, & confirmavimus, ac
per præfentes pro nobis, hæred.
& fucceffor. noftris damus, concedimus & confirmamus præfatis
Baronibus Quinque Portuum &
antiquarum villarum præd. &
membrorum eorundem portuum
& villarum, & fucceffor. fuis;
ac præd. Major. Jurat. & Communitat. villæ & portus de Hafting in com. Suffex, & fuccefforibus fuis; ac præd. Major. Jurat. & Communitat. villæ & portus de Nova Romney in com.
Kanc. & fucceff oribus fuis; ac
præd. Major. Jurat. & Communitat. villæ & portus de Heeth in
com. Kanc. & fucceff oribus fuis;
ac præd. Major. Jurat. & Communitat. villæ & portus de Dover. in com. Kanc. & fucceff oribus
fuis; ac præd. Major. Jurat. &
Communitat. villæ & portus de
Sandwic in com. Kanc. & fucceff oribus fuis; ac prædict. Major, Jurat. & Communitat. antiquæ villæ de Rye in com. Suffex,
& fucceff oribus fuis; ac præd.
Major. Jurat. & Communitat.
antiquæ villæ de Winchelfey in
com. Suffex, & fucceff oribus
fuis; ac prædict. Ballivo, Jurat. & Communit. villæ & leucatæ de Pevenfey in com. Suffex, & fucceff oribus fuis; ac
                              præd.

TRANSLATION.

Grace, and of our certain Knowledge and meer Motion, we have
given, granted and confirmed[d],
and by thefe Prefents for us, our
Heirs and Succeffors, do give,
grant and confirm, to the aforefaid
Barons of the *Cinque Ports* and
ancient Towns aforefaid, and
Members of the fame Ports and
Towns, and to their Succeffors;
and to the aforefaid Mayor, Jurats and Commonalty of the
Town and Port of *Hafting* in
the County of *Suffex,* and to
their Succeffors; and to the
aforefaid Mayor, Jurats and
Commonalty of the Town and
Port of *New Romney* in the
County of *Kent,* and to their
Succeffors; and to the aforefaid
Mayor, Jurats and Commonalty
of the Town and Port of *Hithe*
in the County of *Kent,* and to
their Succeffors; and to the
aforefaid Mayor, Jurats and
Commonalty of the Town and
Port of *Dover* in the County of
Kent, and to their Succeffors;
and to the aforefaid Mayor, Jurats and Commonalty of the
Town and Port of *Sandwich* in
the County of *Kent,* and to their
Succeffors; and to the aforefaid
Mayor, Jurats and Commonalty of the ancient Town of *Rye*
in the County of *Suffex,* and to
their Succeffors; and to the
aforefaid Mayor, Jurats and
Commonalty of the ancient
Town of *Winchelfea* in the
County of *Suffex,* and to their
Succeffors; and to the aforefaid
Bailiff, Jurats and Commonalty
of the Town and Lowey of *Pevenfea* in the County of *Suffex,*
and to their Succeffors; and to
                                the

ANNOTATIONS.

[d] *Confirmed.* The printed Copy reads it in the prefent Tenfe, which I conceive is erroneous,
becaufe the fame Word in the fame Tenfe is ufed but two Lines afterward, which makes a
Tautology: I have therefore ventured to alter it to the preterperfeft Tenfe, and make it *Confirmavimus.*

CHARTERS.

præd. Ballivo, Jurat. & Communitat. villæ de Seaford in com. Suffex, & fucceſſoribus ſuis; ac prædict. Ballivo, Jurat. & Communitat. villæ de Lydd in com. Kanc. & fucceſſoribus ſuis; ac prædict. Major. Jurat. & Communitat. villæ de Folke-ſtone in com. Kanc. & fucceſſoribus ſuis; ac prædict. Major. Jurat. & Communitat. villæ de Feverſham in com. Kanc. & fucceſſoribus ſuis; ac prædict. Major. Jurat. & Communitat. villæ de Fordwich in comitat. Kanc. & fucceſſoribus ſuis; ac prædict. Major. Juratis & Communitat. villæ & hundred. de Tenterden in com. Kanc. & fucceſſoribus ſuis reſpective; quod quilibet Major & Jurat. cujuſlibet Portus præd. Quinque Portuum & fucceſſores ſui reſpective infra quemlibet Portum prædictum, pro quolibet Portu prædicto, & quibuſcunque aliis locis ſive villis, & quocunque alio loco ſive villa, alicui Port. præd. pertinent. ſive exiſtent. Membr. alicujus Portus præd. & non habent. infra ſcipſos, ſive infra ſeipſum, Majorem vel Ballivum per Communitat. eorum locorum ſive villarum, ſive ejuſdem loci ſive villæ elect. ac etiam quilibet Major, & Jurat. cujuſlibet antiquarum villarum prædict. & fucceſſores ſui reſpective; ac quilibet Major. prædictæ villæ de Fever-

TRANSLATION.

the aforeſaid Bailiff, Jurats and Commonalty of the Town of *Seaford* in the County of *Suſſex*, and to their Succeſſors; and to the aforeſaid Bailiff, Jurats and Commonalty of the Town of *Lydd* in the County of *Kent*, and to their Succeſſors; and to the aforeſaid Mayor, Jurats and Commonalty of the Town of *Folkſtone* in the County of *Kent*, and to their Succeſſors; and to the aforeſaid Mayor, Jurats and Commonalty of the Town of *Feverſham* in the County of *Kent*, and to their Succeſſors; and to the aforeſaid Mayor, Jurats and Commonalty of the Town of *Fordwich* in the County of *Kent*, and to their Succeſſors; and to the aforeſaid Mayor, Jurats and Commonalty of the Town and Hundred of *Tenterden* in the County of *Kent*, and to their Succeſſors reſpectively; that every Mayor and Jurats of every Port of the aforeſaid *Cinque Ports*, and their Succeſſors reſpectively, within every Port aforeſaid, for every Port aforeſaid, and whatſoever other Places or Towns, and whatſoever other Place or Town, to any Port aforeſaid appertaining, or being a Member of any Port aforeſaid, and not having * within themſelves, or within it ſelf, a Mayor or Bailiff, by the Commonalty of thoſe Places or Towns, or of the ſame Place or Town, elected; and alſo every Mayor and Jurats of every ancient Town aforeſaid, and their Succeſſors reſpectively; and every Mayor, of the aforeſaid Town of *Fe-*

ANNOTATIONS.

* *Not having.* Thoſe Limbs or Members that have no Corporation within themſelves have ſome one deputed from the Chief Magiſtrates of the Head Port; who by virtue of his Dignitation acts in the Nature of an High-Conſtable, or rather of a Juſtice of the Peace, and takes care for the keeping of the Peace; but if any Cauſe criminal or other, between Party and Party, ariſe, the ſame is tried at the Head Port.

CHARTERS.

Feverſham, & ſucceſſores ſui reſpective; & quilibet Major. & Jurat. cujuſlibet al. Membr. Portuum & antiquarum villarum prædict. ubi Major. & Jurati exiſtunt, & ſucceſſores ſui reſpective infra quamlibet antiquam villam, & infra prædictam villam de Feverſham, ac infra quodlibet aliud membr. Portuum & antiquarum villarum prædict. pro qualibet prædict. antiquarum villarum, & pro prædicta villa de Feverſham, ac pro quolibet alio membro prædicto reſpective; & quilibet Ballivus & Jurat. & quilibet Ballivus ubi Jurat. non exiſt. cujuſlibet membri alicujus Portus prædict. ubi Ballivus hujuſmodi per Communitatem ejuſdem membri eſt elect. & Succeſſores ſui reſpective infra quodlibet tal. Membr. Port. prædict. pro quolibet tali Membro, prout ſuperius, ſeparaliter & reſpective limitat. de cætero imperpetuum, habeant & teneant, ac habere & tenere poſſunt coram eiſdem Major. & Jurat. & Major. & Ballivo & Jurat. & Ballivo reſpective loco infra quemlibet hujuſmodi Quinque Portuum, antiquarum villarum & Membrorum præd. magis convenient. diebus & temporibus ibidem reſpective conſuetis, unam curiam de record.
Et

TRANSLATION.

Feverſham[f], and their[g] Succeſſors reſpectively; and every Mayor and Jurats of every other Member of the Ports and ancient Towns aforeſaid, where Mayor and[h] Jurats are, and their Succeſſors reſpectively within every ancient Town[i], and within the aforeſaid Town of Feverſham, and within every other Member of the Ports and ancient Towns aforeſaid, for every one of the aforeſaid ancient Towns, and for the aforeſaid Town of Feverſham, and for every other Member aforeſaid reſpectively; and every Bailiff and Jurats, and every Bailiff, where Jurats[k] are not, of every Member of any Port aforeſaid, where ſuch Bailiff by the Commonalty of the ſame Member is elected, and their Succeſſors reſpectively, within every ſuch Member of the Ports aforeſaid, for every ſuch Member, as above, ſeverally and reſpectively limited from henceforth for ever, may have and hold before them, the ſaid Mayor and Jurats, and Mayor, and Bailiff and Jurats, and Bailiff reſpectively in the Place[l], within every ſuch of the *Cinque Ports*, Ancient Towns and Members aforeſaid, moſt convenient, in the Days and Times there reſpectively accuſtomed, one Court of Record[m].
And

ANNOTATIONS.

[f] *Feverſham.* It ſeems by this the Mayor of *Feverſham* may keep Court without the Jurats to aſſiſt him.

[g] *Their* or his.

[h] *And.* Next after Mayor is this *And* inſerted, and accordingly *Et* in the *Latin*, to ſupply the Defect of the printed Copy.

[i] *Town.* The *Latin* in the printed Copy has *villarum* for *villam*, the genitive Caſe plural for the accuſative Caſe ſingular, which is here amended.

[k] *Jurats.* It hath been ſaid, that the Bailiff of *Seaford* did anciently keep Court without the Aſſiſtance of Jurats (*tamen quare*) but now I know no Bailiff of any Member of the Ports that hath cognizance of Pleas without the Jurats to aſſiſt him.

[l] *Place.* This is now commonly called the Court Hall, ſometimes the Town Hall, and ſometimes, eſpecially in the Records themſelves, the *Guild Hall.*

[m] *Court of Record.* A Court of Record is the King's Court, though another have the Profits; and in all ſuch Courts (except within the Ports Towns and Members) a Writ of Error lieth for a Judgment given there, if the Judges ſhall err; and the Record ſhall be tried by it ſelf, and
not

N n

CHARTERS.

Et quod iidem Major. & Jurat. & Major. & Ballivi & Jurat. & Ballivi, & Succeffores fui refpe-&ive, in qualibet curia curiarum illarum feparaliter & refpe&ive, plenius & liberius quam ante hac in eifdem habuerunt, habeant & habebunt, habeat & habebit plenam poteftatem & authoritatem per præfentes audiendi & terminandi in feparal. cur. præd. refpe&ive, per querelam in eifdem levand. & tenere omnia & fingula placita de & fuper omnibus & omnimodis debit. compot. convention. contra&. transgref. vi & armis, feu aliter in contempt. noftr. hæred. & succeffor. noftr. fa&. convention. detention. contempt. deception. vetit - namio, ac de & fuper omnibus, &

TRANSLATION.

And that the fame Mayors [n] and Jurats, and Mayors, and Bailiffs and Jurats, and Bailiffs, and their Succeffors refpe&ively, in every Court of thofe Courts feverally and refpe&ively, may have and fhall have, more fully and more freely than heretofore [o] in the fame [p] they have had, full Power [q] and Authority, by thefe Prefents, of hearing and determining [r] in the feveral Courts aforefaid refpe&ively, by Plaint [f] in the fame to be levied, and to hold all and fingular Pleas of and upon all and all manner of Debts [s], Accompts [t], Covenants [u], Contra&s [v], Trefpaffes by Force and Arms [w], or otherwife, in contempt of us, our Heirs and Succeffors, done, Covenant [x], Detinue [y], Contempt, Deceipt, Withernam [z]; and of and upon all and

ANNOTATIONS.

not by Jury or Witneffes; and within the Ports fuch erroneous Judgments fhall be tried at *Shepway*. But the County Court, Hundred Court, Court Baron, and fuch like, are not Courts of Record, and there a Writ of Error lieth not, but a Writ of falfe Judgment, and the Proceedings there may be denied and tried by Jury. They are not Courts of Record, for they cannot hold Plea of Debt or Trefpafs, if the Debt or Damages do amount to forty Shillings, or of any Trefpafs *vi & armis*, &c.

[n] *Mayors* and Bailiffs, are plural here, but in the beginning of *p.* 137. feem to be in the fingular Number in the printed Copy.

[o] *Heretofore* or before this Charter.

[p] *The fame*, that is the fame Courts.

[q] *Power* when joined with Authority, as it is here, may import Strength, Force of Law, and Authority, as much as lawful Right, or legal Power fo to do.

[r] *Hearing and determining* or to hear and determine.

[f] *Plaint.* Suits in the Ports are brought into the Courts by Plaint, and not by original Writs out of the *Chancery.*

[s] *Debts*, as A&ions brought upon Specialties for Rent, Penalty in fome Statute, or the like.

[t] *Accompts.* Such as A&ions againft Bailiffs, Receivers, Guardians, &c. to render a reafonable Accompt of their Receipts, &c

[u] *Covenants*, properly by Writing to be made appear.

[v] *Contra&s*, fometimes the fame with Covenants, fometimes taken for any Bargain or Agreement, for not doing or performing whereof an A&ion of Trefpafs upon the Cafe lieth, the Confideration of the Bargain being good.

[w] *Force and Arms.* All fuch A&ions in the Declaration of the Caufe, whereof thefe Words, *By Force and Arms* (in *Latin, Vi & Armis*) are to be ufed, as in A&ions of Trefpafs, Affault, &c.

[x] *Covenant.* Seeing Covenants were mentioned before, *l.* 17. this may be Covenant broken, for I am jealous, that inftead of *fa&. convention.* in the printed Copy which I follow, it fhould be *fra&. convention.* and the Tranflation be read thus, — *and Succeffors, Covenant broken, Detinue,* &c.

[y] *Detinue* lieth where Goods delivered, to be kept for ufe of another, are refufed to be redelivered, when demanded.

[z] *Withernam.* If Goods diftrained and impounded be replevied, and Return thereof be adjudged, if it happen the Goods cannot be found, and thereupon the Officer return his Writ, that the Goods are elongated to Places unknown, &c. then fhall go forth a Writ of *Withernam* to take other Goods of the Party, &c. and this *taking*, for fo *Nam*, or rather *Næme*, after the *Saxon*, fignifies, *whither* of the one fort of Goods or of the other, made the Word up *Withernam*, as fome think. And this old Cuftom, derived from the *Saxon* Laws, gave being to the Ports ufage

CHARTERS.

& omnimod. al. actionib. real.
perfonal. & mixt. quibufcunq;
querel. de affif. novæ diffeifinæ,
five mortis anteceffor. vel de re-
'diffeifin. infra quemlibet hujufmodi port. ac fines, limit. & præcinct. portus ejufdem, & quoflibet alios locos five villas, &
quemlibet alium locum five villam alicui port. præd. pertinent.
five fpectant. five exiften. Membr.
alicujus hujufmodi port. portuum,
ubi nec Major nec Ballivus elect.
exiftit, refpective, & infra quamlibet antiquam villam prædictam,
& infra prædictam villam de Feverfham, ac infra quodlibet aliud
Membrum prædict. ac fines, limit.
& præcinct. hujufmodi antiquarum villarum, villæ de Feverfham prædict. & al Membr. præd.
refpective, quovifmodo emergent.
five emergend. five contingent.
vel contingend. Et quod iidem
Major. & Jurat. & Major. & Ballivi & Jurat. & Ballivi & Succeffores fui refpective, fuper hujufmodi placitis, action. querel.
de affif. novæ diffeifinæ five mortis anteceffor. vel de rediffeifin. in
dict.

TRANSLATION.

and all manner of other Actions,
real, perfonal and mixt, whatfoever Plaints of Affife [a] of
Novel Diffeifin, or [b] Mortdancefter, or of Rediffeifin [c], within every fuch Port, and the
Bounds [d], Limits and Precincts
of the fame Port, and all other
Places or Towns, and every o-
ther Place or Town to any of
the Ports aforefaid appertaining
or belonging, or being Member
of any fuch Port of the Ports,
where neither Mayor nor Bailiff
is elected refpectively [e], and
within every ancient Town
aforefaid, and within the a-
forefaid Town of *Feverfham*,
and within every other Member aforefaid, and the Bounds,
Limits and Precincts of fuch
ancient Towns, Town of *Feverfham* aforefaid, and other
Member aforefaid, refpectively,
in any wife arifing or to arife,
or happening or to happen.
And that the fame Mayors and
Jurats, and Mayors and Bailiffs,
and Jurats and Bailiffs, and their
Succeffors refpectively, upon fuch
Pleas, Actions, Plaints of Affife
of Novel Diffeifin, or Mortdancefter, or of Rediffeifin in the
faid

ANNOTATIONS.

ufage of fending Letters of Procefs to other Corporations, and taking *Withernam* of them for default of Juftice, a very ancient Ufage among them, and well may be called *Petit-namio*, or the *old taking* (if it be not mifprinted) in the Charter, of which I have feen much in their Records and Cuftomals, with Approbation of learned Lawyers Judges, Serjeants and others: However, of late fome conceive otherwife, and accordingly, againft that Ufage and Cu-ftom of the Ports, it was adjudged in *Paramor* and *Ferral's* Cafe [*]. But whether all Cuftoms of [*] *Anderfon's Rep.* Places, confirmed by fo many Charters, and practifed Time out of mind, ought to be conformable to the ftrict Rules of the Common Law of the Nation, is yet a Quere, and doubted by many; neverthelefs fince that Judgment the Ports fend no Procefs to foreign Corporations.

[a] *Affize of novel Diffeifin.* Diffeifin (derived from the *French* Word *Diffeifir*) is a wrongful putting out of Seifin, or difpoffeffing one that is actually feized of a Freehold. An Affize of no-vel Diffeifin is a Writ brought by fuch an one as is lately fo difpoffeffed to recover his Seifin.

[b] *Mortdancefter.* An Affize of Mortdancefter is a Writ one may have after the Death of his immediate Anceftor, when Father, Mother, Brother, Sifter, Uncle or Aunt die feized of Lands or Tenements, and a Stranger abateth, that is entreth into the faid Lands or Tenements, and keepeth out the Heir.

[c] *Rediffeifin.* Where Seifin is recovered upon an Affize of novel Diffeifin or Mortdancefter, and after that, the Diffeifor gets into Poffeffion again, a Writ of Rediffeifin may be had, accord-ing to the Statute of *Merton,* cap. 3. made *Anno* 20 *Henry* III.

[d] *Bounds,* Borders or Confines.

[e] *Refpectively.* By this it appeareth, that fuch Actions arifing or happening in the Members not corporate, may be tried in the Port to which they refpectively belong.

[f] *Faculty*

CHARTERS.   TRANSLATION.

dict. cur. five earum aliqua motis feu levat. movend. feu levand. habeant poteftatem, authoritatem & facultatem perfonam & perfonas verfus quam vel quas hujufmodi placita action. querel. de affif. novæ diffeifinæ five mortis antecefforis vel de rediffeifina, in præd. cur. vel earum aliquarum levar. vel mover. contiger. in placitum trahere & deducere per fummonition. attachiament. vel diftrictiones fervient. ad clavam ipforum Major. & Jurat. & Major. & Balliv. & Jurat. & Balliv. cujuflibet portus, antiquæ villæ & membri port. & antiquarum villarum præd. five alicujus eorundem refpective, feu al. Miniftr. per feipfos refpective ad id fpecialiter deputat. five deputand. five al. Miniftr. cur. prædict. feu alicujus earundem, dirigend. aut per attachiament. corporis perfonæ vel perfonarum per hujufmodi fervient. ad clavam feu al. Miniftr. faciend. fecundum legem & confuetudinem regni noftri Angliæ, vel confuetud. cujuflibet portus five antiquæ villæ prædict. & cujuflibet Membri portuum & antiquarum villarum prædict. refpective, vel fecundum confuetud. in aliquo Burgo, vel

faid Courts, or in any of them moved or levied, or to be moved or levied, may have Power, Authority and Faculty [f] the Perfon and Perfons againft whom fuch Pleas, Actions, Plaints of Affife of Novel Diffeifin or Mortdancefter, or of Rediffeifin, in the aforefaid Courts, or in any of them, fhall happen to be levied or moved, to draw and bring [g] to plead by Summons, Attachments or Diftreffes [h], to be directed to the Serjeants [i] at the Mace [j] of the fame Mayor and Jurats, and Mayors and Bailiffs, and Jurats and Bailiffs, of every Port, ancient Town, and Member of the Ports, and ancient Towns aforefaid, or of any of them refpectively, or other Minifters [k] by themfelves refpectively thereunto efpecially deputed or to be deputed, or to other Minifters of the Courts aforefaid, or of any of them; or by Attachments of the Body of the Perfon or Perfons by fuch Serjeants at the Mace, or other Minifters to be made, according to the Law and Cuftom of our Kingdom of *England*, or the Cuftom of every Port or ancient Town aforefaid, and of every Member of the Ports and ancient Towns aforefaid refpectively, or according to the Cuftom in any Borough [l], or

ANNOTATIONS.

[f] *Faculty* or Ability, all one with lawful Authority and Power.

[g] *Draw and bring*, force or compel by courfe of Law.

[h] *Diftreffes.* If thofe againft whom the Actions lie appear not in Court to anfwer to the Plaintiffs in perfonal, or Demandants in real Actions, upon the Summons or Attachments, then Diftreffes, as the Cafe requires, may iffue forth of the Court to compel them to appear.

[i] *Serjeants* or Servants, as the Word fignifies, the Officer to execute the Writs or Precepts of the Court, which is a Servant or Minifter of the Court.

[j] *Mace.* A filver Rod with a clubbed Head, born by the Serjeant before the Mayor or Bailiff, at his going to and from the Court.

[k] *Other Minifters*, fuch other Serjeants, befides the Serjeant at the Mace, as ufually make Arrefts; to thefe the Procefs of the Court may be directed to be executed.

[l] *Borough.* According as is done in other Corporations, Borough Towns, Cities, &c. for in the Charter of King *Charles* I. it is *City* where the printed Copy hath *comitas.* that is, *County*, but it muft needs be falfe, either in the Subftantive or the Adjective, feeing it is printed *aliqua comitat.* whereas it is well known that *comitatus* is the mafculine Gender and not the feminine.

CHARTERS.

vel aliqua civitate noftr. infra Regnum noftrum Angliæ ufitat. & confuet. Et præd. omnia & fingula placita, actiones, querel. & auif. novæ difleifinæ, mort. antecelfor. vel redifleifinæ audire & determinare in qualibet cur. curiarum præd. refpective, & per confimil. procef. confiderationes, judic. & executiones judiciorum, deducere & determinare, per quæ confimil. placita, actiones, querel. de aflif. novæ difleifinæ, mortis anteceffor. vel de redifleifina per legem regni noftri Angliæ in aliqua curia noftra, five per confuetud. in aliqua hujufmodi port. antiq. villa præd. aut in aliquo Membro portuum five antiquar. villarum præd. refpective, vel in aliquo burgo, aut civitate, vel libertate infra dictum regnum noftrumAngliæ,deducuntur & deterpminantur, vel deduci & determinari poflunt, ad libertatem ipforum Major. & Jurat. Major. Ballivi & Jurat. & Ballivi refpective, executionefque procef. & judic. fuper inde facere & exequi per prædict. fervient. ad clavam, vel al. Miniftr. fupradict. Et quod quilibet Major. Jurat. & Communitat. cujuflibet Quinque Portuum, antiquarum villarum & Membrorum præd. ubi Major. exiftit,

TRANSLATION.

or any of our Cities within our Kingdom of *England* ufed and accuftomed. And all and fingular the aforefaid Pleas, Actions, Plaints and Aflife [m] of Novel Difleifin, Mortdanceftor, or Redifleifin, to hear and determine in every Court of the Courts aforefaid refpectively, and by fuch like Procefs, Confiderations, Judgments and Executions of Judgments, to order [n] and determine, by which the like Pleas, Actions, Plaints of Aflife of Novel Difleifin, Mortdanceftet or Redifleifin by the Law of our Kingdom of *England* in any of our Courts, or by the Cuftom in any fuch Port, ancient Town aforefaid, or in any Member of the Ports or ancient Towns aforefaid refpectively, or in any Borough, or City [o], or Liberty within our faid Kingdom of *England,* are ordered and determined, or may be ordered and determined, at the Liberty [p] of the fame Mayors and Jurats, Mayors, Bailiffs and Jurats, and Bailiffs refpectively, and Executions and Procefs [q] of the Judgments thereupon to make and execute by the aforefaid Serjeants at the Mace, or other Minifters abovefaid. And that every Mayor [r], Jurats and Commonalty of every of the *Cinque Ports,* ancient Towns and Members aforefaid, where a Mayor is,

ANNOTATIONS.

[m] *And Aflize,* or of *Aflize,* for I fufpect & for *de* in the *Latin,* as it is in other Places before and after, Plaints of Allize.

[n] *Order,* deduce or guide.

[o] *City,* here as before, l. 1. of this Page, the printed Copy hath *comitat.* County, but the Charter of King *Charles* I. in both Places hath *City*; and feeing in the County Court none of thefe Actions can be tried, I have followed the former Charter and made it City.

[p] *Liberty,* or at the Will of the faid Mayors, &c. intending the Magiftrates within the Ports may be at their Choice, whether they will follow the Cuftoms ufed among themfelves in fuch Actions, or the Manner of Proceedings in other Corporations.

[q] *Procefs of the.* Et in the *Latin,* as in the printed Copy, I miftruft to be mifprinted for *de,* becaufe the Power to proceed to Judgment is given before, and fo were needlefs here to be repeated; but this Claufe gives Authority to make out judicial Procefs, and proceed to execute the Judgments given in the Actions aforefaid.

[r] *Mayor,* and fo Bailiff, p. 142. l. 1. may be read plurally.

[s] *Perceive,*

CHARTERS.

exiftit`, &. fucceffores fui re-
fpective, & quilibet Balliv. Jurat.
& Communitat. &. Balliv. &
Communitat. cujuflibet Membri
port. prædict. ubi hujufmodi Balliv. per Communitatem Membr.
prædict. eft elect. & fucceffores
fui refpective, habeant & percipiant, & habebunt & percipient
ad eorum proprium ufum & commodit. refpective, omnia & fingula fines, amerciamenta, redemptiones, exit. forisfactur. &
al. profic. quæcunq. de & in cur.
prædict. refpective, provenien. e-
mergen. acciden. feu contingen.
Ac omnia & fingula ill. fines, redemptiones, amerciamenta, exit.
forisfactur. & profic. ad eorum
proprium ufum & commodit. refpective, de tempore in tempus,
per Miniftros fuos levare, percipere, feifire & retinere poffunt
per actionem vel actiones debiti,
five tal. al. fectas, actiones, media,
vias & procef. in aliqua cur. vel
aliquibus curiis de recordo infra
Quinq. Port. aut antiquas villas
præd. feu Membr. eorundem
præd. vel eorum aliquid vel aliqua habend. & profequend. per
quas hujufmodi fines amerciament. Redemption. exit. forif-
factur. & profic. in aliqua cur.
noftr. hæred. & fucceffor. noftrorum per totum regnum noftrum
Angliæ levari, percipi & re-
cuperari folent aut poffint, fine
impediment. noftro hæred. vel
fucceffor. noftrorum aut aliquorum Miniftrorum noftrorum
quorumcunque. Et ulterius,
pro meliore regimine & gubernatione

TRANSLATION.

is and their Succeffors refpectively, and every Bailiff, Jurats and
Commonalty; and the Bailiff and
Commonalty of every Member
of the Ports aforefaid, where
fuch Bailiff by the Commonalty
of the Member aforefaid is elected, and their Succeflors refpectively, may have and perceive [f],
and fhall have and perceive to
their proper Ufe and Commodity refpectively, all and fingular
Fines, Amerciaments, Redemptions [g], Iffues, Forfeitures, and
other Profits whatfoever of and
in the Courts aforefaid refpectively, growing, arifing, happening or contingent. And all
and fingular thofe Fines, Redemptions, Amerciaments, Iffues,
Forfeitures and Profits to their
own Ufe and Commodity re-
fpectively, from time to time, by
their Minifters to levy [t], perceive,
feife and retain, by Action or
Actions of Debt, or fuch other
Suits, Actions, Means, Ways
and Procefs in any Court or
Courts of Record within the
Cinque Ports or ancient Towns
aforefaid, or Members of the
fame aforefaid, or any of them,
to be had and profecuted, by
which fuch Fines, Amerciaments,
Redemptions, Iffues, Forfeitures
and Profits, in any Court of us,
our Heirs and Succeffors, through
our whole Kingdom of *England*,
are wont, or may be levied, perceived or recovered [u], without
impediment of us, our Heirs or
Succeffors, or any of our Minifters whatfoever. And further,
for the better regulating [v] and governing

ANNOTATIONS.

[f] *Perceive*, ufed in the Law for to take or receive rather than difcern.

[g] *Redemptions* or Ranfoms.

[t] *To levy*, or they may levy, perceive, feize and keep to their proper Ufe and Behoof, that is
to the Ufe of their refpective Corporations, not to the Ufe of the Mayor and Jurats, or Bailiff
and Jurats.

[u] *Recovered* is to be reftored by the Sentence of a Judge to a Thing (or Satisfaction for it) ex-
torted or detained by wrong.

[v] *Regulating*, Rule or ruling.   I

[w] *Governing*

CHARTERS.

bernatione Quinque Portuum,
antiquarum villarum & Membr.
præd. de gratia noſtra ſpeciali,
ac ex certa ſcientia & mero motu
noſtris, dedimus, conceſſimus &
confirmavimus, ac per præſentes
pro nobis, hæred. & ſucceſſor.
noſtris, damus, concedimus &
confirmamus eiſdem Baron. &
probis hominibus Quinq. Portuum & antiquarum villarum
præd. & Membr. eorundem portuum & villarum, & ſucceſſor.
ſuis ; ac prædict. Major. Jurat.
& Communitat. villæ & Portus
de Haſting in com. Suſſex, &
ſucceſſoribus ſuis ; ac præd.
Major. Jurat. & Communitat.
villæ & portus de Nova Romney in com. Kanc. & ſucceſſoribus ſuis ; ac præd. Major. Jurat. & Communitat. villæ & portus de Heeth in com. Kanc.
& ſucceſſoribus ſuis ; ac præd.
Major. Jurat. & Communitat.
villæ & portus de Dover in com.
Kanc. & ſucceſſoribus ſuis ; ac
præd. Major. Jurat. & Communitat. villæ & portus de Sandwich in com. Kanc. & ſucceſſoribus ſuis ; ac præd. Major. Jurat.
& communitat. antiquæ villæ de
Rye in com. Suſſex, & ſucceſſoribus ſuis ; ac præd. Major. Jurat. & communitati antiquæ villæ
de Wynchelſey in com. Suſſex,
& ſucceſſoribus ſuis ; ac præd.
Balliv. Jurat. & Communitat.
villæ & Leucatæ de Pevenſey in
com. Suſſex, & ſucceſſoribus ſuis ;
ac

TRANSLATION.

verning * of the *Cinque Ports*,
ancient Towns and Members
aforeſaid, of our ſpecial Grace,
and of our certain Knowledge
and meer Motion, we have given,
granted and confirmed, and by
theſe Preſents for us, our Heirs
and Succeſſors, do give, grant
and confirm to the ſame Barons
and good Men of the *Cinque
Ports* and ancient Towns aforeſaid, and Members of the ſame
Ports and Towns, and to their
Succeſſors ; and to the aforeſaid
Mayor, Jurats and Commonalty
of the Town and Port of *Haſting*
in the County of *Suſſex*, and to
their Succeſſors ; and to the aforeſaid Mayor, Jurats and Commonalty of the Town and Port
of *New Romney* in the County
of *Kent*, and to their Succeſſors ;
and to the aforeſaid Mayor, Jurats and Commonalty of the
Town and Port of *Hithe* in the
County of *Kent*, and to their
Succeſſors ; and to the aforeſaid
Mayor, Jurats and Commonalty
of the Town and Port of *Dover*
in the County of *Kent*, and to
their Succeſſors ; and to the
aforeſaid Mayor, Jurats, and
Commonalty of the Town and
Port of *Sandwich* in the County
of *Kent*, and to their Succeſſors ;
and to the aforeſaid Mayor, Jurats and Commonalty of the
ancient Town of *Rye* in the
County of *Suſſex*, and to their
Succeſſors ; and to the aforeſaid
Mayor, Jurats and Commonalty
of the ancient Town of *Winchelſea* in the County of *Suſſex*, and
to their Succeſſors ; and to the
aforeſaid Bailiff, Jurats and Commonalty of the Town and Lowey
of *Pevenſea* in the County of
Suſſex, and to their Succeſſors ;
and

ANNOTATION.

* *Governing* or Government.

x *Keepers*

CHARTERS.

ac præd. Balliv. Jurat. & Communitat. villæ de Seaford in com. Suffex, & fuccefforibus fuis; ac præd. Balliv. Jurat. & Communitat. villæ de Lydd in com. Kanc. & fuccefforibus fuis; ac præd. Major. Jurat. & Communitat. villæ de Folkftone in com. Kanc. & fuccefforibus fuis; ac præd. Major. Jurat. & Communitat. villæ de Feverfham in com. Kanc. & fuccefforibus fuis; ac præd. Major. Jurat. & Communitat. villæ de Fordwich in com. Kanc. & fuccefforibus fuis; ac præd. Major. Jurat. & Communitat. villæ & hundred. de Tenterden in com. Kanc. & fucceffo008.ribus, fuis refpective, quod quilibet Major. & Jurat. de quolibet portu prædict. Quinque Portuum refpective, infra portus prædict. fines, limit. & præcinct. eorundem portuum, ac etiam infra quoflibet alios lo008.os & villas, & quemlibet alium loc008.um & villam, alicui portui prædict. pertinent. five fpectant. five exiftent. Membr. alicujus Portus præd. in quibus locis five villis, aut in quo loco five in qua villa Major. aut Ballivus non exiftit per Communitatem eorum locorum five villarum, five ejufdem loci five villæ elect. & fucceffon fui refpective ; & quilibet Major. & Jurat. de qualibet prædict. antiquarum villarum de Rye & Winchelfey, & de quolibet Membrorum Portuum & antiquarum villarum præd. ubi Major. exift. & fucceffores fui refpective; ac etiam quilibet Ballivus & Jurati de quolibet Membro Portuum prædict. ubi hujufmodi Balliv. per Communitat. ejufdem

TRANSLATION.

and to the aforefaid Bailiff, Jurats and Commonalty of the Town of *Seaford* in the County of *Suffex*, and to their Succeffors; and to the aforefaid Bailiff, Jurats and Commonalty of the Town of *Lydd* in the County of *Kent*, and to their Succeffors ; and to the aforefaid Mayor, Jurats and Commonalty of the Town of *Folkftone* in the County of *Kent*, and to their Succeffors ; and to the aforefaid Mayor, Jurats and Commonalty of the Town of *Feverfham* in the County of *Kent*, and to their Succeffors ; and to the aforefaid Mayor, Jurats and Commonalty of the Town of *Fordwich* in the County of *Kent*, and to their Succeffors; and to the aforefaid Mayor, Jurats and Commonalty of the Town and Hundred of *Tenterden* in the County of *Kent*, and to their Succeffors, refpectively, that every Mayor and Jurats of every Port of the aforefaid *Cinque Ports* refpectively, within the Ports aforefaid, the Bound, Limits and Precincts of the fame Ports, and alfo within all other Places and Towns, and every other Place and Town to any Port aforefaid appertaining or belonging, or being Member of any Port aforefaid, in which Places or Towns, or in which Place or Town a Mayor or Bailiff is not elected by the Commonalty of thofe Places or Towns, or of the fame Place or Town, and their Succeffors refpectively; and every Mayor and Jurats of every of the aforefaid ancient Towns of *Rye* and *Winchelfea*, and of every of the Members of the Ports and ancient Towns aforefaid, where a Mayor is, and their Succeffors refpectively; and alfo every Bailiff and Jurats of every Member of the Ports aforefaid, where fuch Bailiff by the Commonalty

of

CHARTERS.

ejufdem membri eft elect. & fucceffores fui refpective, infra antiquas villas & membr. prædict. ac
fines, limit. & præcinct. eorundem
feparaliter, prout fuperius limita-
tur, de cætero imperpetuum fint
& erunt cuftodes pacis ac jufticiar.
noftr. hæred. & fucceffor. noftrorum, ad pacem noftram, hæred. &
fuccefforum noftrorum confervand. Et quilibet eorum fit &
erit cuftos pacis & jufticiar. noftr.
hæred. & fuccefforum noftrorum,
ad pacem noftram, hæred. & fuccefforum noftror. infra quoflibet
Quinque Port. antiquas villas,
membr. & locos fupradict. ac libertat. & præcinct. eorundem &
eorum cujuflibet feparaliter & refpective confervand. Ac ipfos Majores, Ballivos & Jurat. & quoflibet eorum,& fucceffores fuos refpective, cuftodes pacis & jufticiar. noftros, hæredum & fuccefforum noftrorum, ad pacem noftrorum, hæred. & fucceffor. infra
quemlibet Quinque Portuum, antiquar. villarum membr. & loc.
præd. ac libertates, fines, limites
& præcinct. eorum refpective
confervand. creamus, conftituimus, facimus, ordinamus & confirmamus per præfentes; ac ad
omnia ordinationes & ftatuta pro
bono pacis noftr. hæredum &
fuccefforum noftrorum, ac pro
confervatione ejufdem & quieto
regi-

TRANSLATION.

of the fame Member is elected, and their Succeffors refpectively, within the ancient
Towns and Members aforefaid,
and the Bounds, Limits and Precincts of the fame feverally, as
above is limited, from henceforth
for ever may be, and fhall be
Keepers [x] of the Peace, and Juftices of us our Heirs and Succeffors, to keep [y] the Peace of
us, our Heirs and Succeffors.
And every one of them may be,
and fhall be a Keeper of the
Peace, and a Juftice of us, our
Heirs and Succeffors, to keep
the Peace of us, our Heirs and
Succeffors, within every of the
Cinque Ports, Ancient Towns,
Members and Places abovefaid,
and the Liberties and Precincts
of the fame, and every of them
feverally and refpectively. And
the fame Mayors, Bailiffs and
Jurats, and every of them, and
their Succeffors refpectively,
Keepers of the Peace, and Juftices of us, our Heirs and Succeffors, to keep the Peace of us,
our Heirs and Succeffors, within every of the *Cinque Ports*,
Ancient Towns, Members and
Places aforefaid, and the Liberties, Bounds, Limits and Precincts of them refpectively, we
do create [z], conftitute, make, ordain and confirm by thefe Prefents; and to keep, or caufe to
be kept, all the Ordinances and
Statutes, for the good of the
Peace of us, our Heirs and
Succeffors, and for Prefervation of the fame, and quiet
Rule

ANNOTATIONS.

[x] *Keepers* or Wardens; the *Latin Cuftodes* ferving for both. By virtue of this Claufe the
head Officers and Jurats of the Ports, Towns and Members, within their refpective Limits,
have like Power to fee the Peace to be kept as the Juftices of the Peace in the Counties have;
and this the Ports did before the Charter of King *James*, which is the firft that exprefly in
Words mentions this to be granted to them; and did take Security for the Peace and good Behaviour long before; and kept Seffions of the Peace alfo; and I have feen in the Records of
Rye feveral Seffions of the Peace held there in the Reign of King *Henry* VIII.

[y] *To keep*, preferve or conferve our Peace.

[z] *Create.* As much as make of new, or make them to be what they were not before.

[a] *Rule*

CHARTERS.	TRANSLATION.

regimine & gubernatione populi noftri, hæred. & fucceffor. noftrorum edit. feu impofterum edend. in omnibus & fingulis fuis articulis, infra quemlibet Quinque Portuum, antiquarum villar. membr. & locorum præd. ac libertates, fines, limit. & præcinct. eorundem feparaliter & refpective, juxta vim, formam & effectum eorundem, cuftodiend. & cuftodiri faciend. Et ad omnes contra formam ordinationum & ftatut. ill. & eorum alicujus ibidem refpective delinquent. caftigand. & puniend. prout fecundum formam ordinationum & ftatut. ill. fuerit faciend. Et ad omnes ill. qui alicui vel aliquibus de populo noftri, hæredum vel fucceffor. noftrorum, de corporibus fuis, vel de incendio domorum fuarum minas fecerunt, ad fufficientem fecuritatem de pace, vel de bono geftu fuo erga nos, hæredes & fucceffores noftros, & populum noftrum, hæredum & fucceffor um noftrorum inveniend. coram prædict. Major. Balliv. & Jurat. refpective venire faciend. Et fi hojuf-

Rule and Government [a] of the People of us, our Heirs and Succeffors, made [b], or hereafter to be made, in all and fingular the Articles [c] thereof, within every of the *Cinque Ports*, Ancient Towns, Members and Places aforefaid, and the Liberties, Bounds, Limits and Precincts of the fame feverally and refpectively, according to the Force, Form and Effect of the fame. And to chaftife and punifh [d] all Delinquents there againft the Form of thofe Ordinances and Statutes, and every of them refpectively delinquent [e], as after the Form of thofe Ordinances and Statutes fhall be to be done. And all thofe, which have threatned [f] any of the People of us, our Heirs or Succeffors, concerning their Bodies, or concerning the Burning of their Houfes, to caufe to come before the aforefaid Mayors, Bailiffs and Jurats refpectively, to find fufficient Security [g] for the Peace, or for their good Behaviour [h] toward us, our Heirs and Succeffors, and the People of us, our Heirs and Succeffors; and if they fhall

ANNOTATIONS.

[a] *Rule and Government*, or regulating and governing, as in *Page* 149.

[b] *Made*, &c. or *made and publifhed*. And in the next Line; or *hereafter to be made and publifhed*; for the Word *Edo*, from whence *Edit.* in the Charter, fignifies to give forth or make publick.

[c] *Articles*, that is, the Particulars of fuch Ordinances and Statutes as are or fhall be made for keeping the Peace.

* *Before the Reign of K.Ed. III. the Judgment for Petit Larceny was referred to the Difcretion of the Judge, and executed fometimes by the Pillory, Lofs of the Ear, Whipping, &c. but fince no Perfon by the Common Law for it lofs any Member,*

[d] *Chaftife and punifh*, to wit, according as the Law directs: Yet had the Ports among their old Cuftoms fome Punifhments rarely to be found elfewhere; as to put fcolding Women in an iron Collar faftened to a Poft in the Market Place, to ftand there with it about their Necks for an Hour; and for Larceny * to lofe an Ear, or be whipped and have a Billet nailed to the Ear, and fo to ftand in open Market the Space of an Hour; of which latter Punifhment I have feen fome Precedents, in the Reign of Queen *Elizabeth*, recorded to have been inflicted for diffolute and loofe living, the Offenders, after fuffering thereof were banifhed the Town.

[e] *Delinquent*, that is, tranfgreffing.

[f] *Threatned*, or have made Threatnings, or given threatning Speeches.

[g] *Security*, both for the Peace and good Behaviour, is taken by Recognifance, wherein the Party (if not a married Woman, for then others are bound for her) with two Sureties are to be bound to the King for appearance at the next Seffion of the Peace to be holden for the Place refpectively, and in the mean time to keep the Peace, or be of the good Abearing accordingly.

[h] *Good Behaviour*, often called *good Abearing*, that is, when the Party doth behave, carry or bear himfelf towards all Men, and efpecially towards the Officers of Juftice, as becometh, againft which latter properly any thing in Words or Deeds faid or done contrary to good Manners, deferveth Surety for the good Behaviour.

Coke 3d Part Inftitut. chap. 101. *yet the Ports after K. Ed. III. kept their old Cuftoms in this Kind of Punifhment.*

[i] *Prifon.*

CHARTERS.

hujufmodi fecuritatem invenire recufaverint, tunc eos in prifona, quoufq; hujufmodi fecuritatem invenerint, falvo cuftodiri faciend. Ac infuper volumus, & pro nobis, hæred. & fucceffor. noftris per præfentes concedimus & confirmamus præfat. Major. Jurat. & Communitat. Ballivis, Jurat. & Communitat. & Ballivis & Communitat. cujuflibet Quinque Portuum & antiquar. villar. & membrorum prædict. & fucceffor. fuis refpective, quod quilibet duo vel plures prædict. Major. & Jurat. de quolibet Portu præd. Quinque Portuum, & fucceffores fui refpective infra Port. prædict. ac libertates, fines, limit. & præcinct. eorundem, ac etiam infra quoflibet alios locos & villas, & quemlibet alium locum & villam, alicui Portui prædicto pertinent. feu fpectant. five exiftent. membr. alicujus Portus prædict. in quibus locis five villis, aut in quo lolo five in qua villa, Major aut Ballivus non exiftit per Communitat. eorundem locorum five villarum, five ejufdem loci five villæ, elect. (quorum Major. vel ejus deputat. pro tempore exiftent. femper unum effe volumus.) Et quod quilibet duo vel plures præd. Major. & Jurat. de qualibet prædict. antiquarum villarum de Rye & Winchelſea

TRANSLATION.

fhall refufe to find fuch Security, to caufe them to be kept fafe in Prifon [1], until they fhall find fuch Security. And moreover we will, and for us, our Heirs and Succeffors, by thefe Prefents grant and confirm to the aforefaid Mayors, Jurats and Commonalties, Bailiffs, Jurats and Commonalties, and Bailiffs and Commonalties of every of the *Cinque Ports* and Ancient Towns and Members aforefaid, and their Succeffors refpectively, that every Two or more [2] of the aforefaid Mayors and Jurats of every Port of the aforefaid *Cinque Ports,* and their Succeffors refpectively, within the Ports aforefaid, and the Liberties, Bounds, Limits, and Precincts of the fame, and alfo within all other Places and Towns, and every other Place and Town, to any Port aforefaid appertaining or belonging, or being Member of any Port, in which Places or Towns, or in which Place or Town a Mayor or Bailiff is not elected by the Commonalty of the fame Places or Towns, or of the fame Place or Town (of whom [k] we will the Mayor or his Deputy, for the Time being, always to be one). And that every two or more of the aforefaid Mayors and Jurats of every of the aforefaid ancient Towns of *Rye* and *Winchelſea*

ANNOTATIONS.

[1] *Prifon.* Such who fhall be ordered to find Sureties for the Peace or good Behaviour, in cafe of Refufal, fhall be committed to Prifon till they find them.

[2] *Two or more.* By this ftrictly taken, it may feem the Mayor and one Jurat may hold a Seffion of the Peace; but the Ufage every where in the Ports and Members (*Sandwich* as aforefaid excepted) hath been to keep the Courts of Record and Seffions of the Peace, alfo Hundreds and Affemblies, with no lefs than the head Officer and two Jurats; and fo was before this Charter, and is ftill continued.

[k] *Of whom.* The Mayor and Bailiff, or their refpective Deputies, muft be prefent at the Seffions of the Peace, as being of the Quorum. And by exprefs Words in the Charter of King *Charles* I. they were, as well as here, fo made, that fo being nominated and made there might be no Caufe of Demurer to any Act done by them and the Jurats as Juftices of the Peace, to the doing whereof there ought to be one of the Quorum.

CHARTERS.

chelſea præd. & quolibet Membro prædict. Quinque Portuum & antiquarum villarum prædict. ubi Major exiſtet & ſucceſſores ſui reſpective (quorum Major. vel ejus deputat. pro tempore exiſtent. ſemper unum eſſe volumus.) Ac quilibet duo vel plures præd. Ballivorum & Jurat. de quolibet Membro Portuum prædictorum, ubi hujuſmodi Ballivus per Communitat. ejuſdem Membri eſt elect. & ſucceſſores ſui reſpective (quorum Ballivum vel ejus deputat. pro tempore exiſtent. ſemper unum eſſe volumus) infra antiquas villas & membr. prædict. ac libertates, fines, limit. & præcinct. eorundem ſeparaliter & reſpective, de cætero imperpetuum ſint & erunt Juſticiarii noſtri & hæredum noſtrorum, & habeant de cætero imperpetuum plenam poteſtatem & autoritatem ad inquirendum per ſacramentum bonorum & legalium hominum de præd. Quinque Portubus, antiquis villis & membr. corundem reſpective, per quos rei veritas melius ſciri poterit, de omnibus & omnimodis felon. murdr. homicid. veneficiis, incantationibus, arte magic. tranſgreſ.

TRANSLATION.

chelſea aforeſaid, and of every Member of the aforeſaid *Cinque Ports* and Ancient Towns aforeſaid, where a Mayor is, and their Succeſſors reſpectively (of whom[k] we will the Mayor or his Deputy, for the Time being, always to be one). And every two or more of the aforeſaid Bailiffs and Jurats of every Member of the Ports aforeſaid, where ſuch Bailiff by the Commonalty of the ſame Member is elected, and their Succeſſors reſpectively (of whom[k] we will the Bailiff or his Deputy, for the Time being, always to be one) within the Ancient Towns and Members aforeſaid, and the Liberties, Bounds, Limits and Precincts of the ſame ſeverally and reſpectively, from henceforth for ever may be, and ſhall be Juſtices of us and our Heirs, and may have from henceforth for ever full Power and Authority to inquire by the Oath[l] of good and lawful Men[m] of the aforeſaid *Cinque Ports*, Ancient Towns and Members of the ſame reſpectively, by whom the Truth of the Thing[n] may the better be known, of all and all Manner of Felonies, Murders, Homicides[o], Sorceries[p], Inchantments[q], Art Magick[r], Treſpaſſes,

ANNOTATIONS.

[k] *From Sacra mente, becauſe to be done with a ſacred and religious Mind.*

[l] *Oath.* Called by the ſame Word commonly, in the Law, that is uſed for a Sacrament[k], as denoting both the holy Inſtitution and ſacred Obſervation thereof.

[m] *Good and lawful Men.* That is the Jury of twenty four or twelve, ſworn to deliver a Truth upon the Evidence delivered to them touching the Matter in queſtion. They are called *good and lawful*, that is, ſuch as the Law approves for honeſt Men, not attaint or convict of Perjury, or otherwiſe diſabled by Judgment of the Law to judge of the Facts of others; and ought to dwell near, be of competent Ability, and Indifferency to either Party concerned; ſo as no Cauſe of Challenge may be againſt them to ſet them by.

[n] *The Thing* or the Matter.

[o] *Homicides* or Manſlaughter, derived from the *Latin*, ſometimes taken for the killing of any Perſon by another, generally; but taken ſpecially, is to ſlay one voluntarily, but not with Malice prepenſed or forethought; and ſo is moſt commonly taken to difference it from Murder.

[p] *Sorceries*, Witchcrafts or Poyſonings.

[q] *Inchantments* or Charms by Incantation; for there is ſome Difference between Charms and Inchantments; and the Statute of 1 *Jac.* 12. reads them in the Diſjunctive; by which Statute both theſe, and that of Sorceries before, are made Felonies.

[r] *Art magick.* This is ſingular in the Charter, including as the *genus*, all Conjurations, Necromancy, &c. made Felony alſo by the Statute *Anno* 1 *Jac.* cap. 12.

CHARTERS.

gref. foreftall. regrat. ingroffar.
& extortion. quibufcunque, ac de
omnibus & fingulis al. malefact.
& offenf. quibufcunque, de quibus Jufticiarii pacis noftræ, hæred. vel fuccefforum noftrorum,
infra præd. Quinque Portus, antiquas villas & membr. eorundem
feu infra eorum aliquos, vel infra
aliquem com. regni noftri Angliæ,
legitime inquirere poffint aut debent, per quofcunque & qualitercunque infra quemlibet Quinque
Portuum, antiquarum villarum,
membrorum & locorum præd.
ac libertat. fines, limit. & præcinct. eorum feparaliter & refpective fact. five perpetrat. vel quæ
impofterum ibidem refpective fieri vel attemptari contigerint ; ac
etiam de omnibus illis, qui infra
Quinque Portus, antiquas villas,
membr. vel locos prædict. vel infra libertates, fines, limit. & præcinct. eorum refpective, in conventiculum contra pacem noftram,
hæredum vel fuccefforum noftrorum, in perturbatione populi
noftri, hæred. vel fuccefforum noftrorum, feu vi armat. ierunt vel
equi-

TRANSLATION.

paffes, Foreftallings, Regratings, Ingroffings[r], and Extortions whatfoever, and of all and
fingular other Crimes[s] and Offences whatfoever, of which the
Juftices of the Peace of us, our
Heirs or Succeffors, within the
aforefaid *Cinque Ports,* Ancient
Towns and Members of the
fame, or within any of them, or
within any County of our Kingdom of *England,* lawfully may
or ought to inquire, by whomfoever, and in what manner
foever, within every of the
Cinque Ports, Ancient Towns,
Members and Places aforefaid,
and the Liberties, Bounds, Limits and Precincts of the fame,
feverally and refpectively done
or committed[u], or which hereafter fhall happen there to be
done or attempted refpectively ;
and alfo of all thofe, who within the *Cinque Ports,* Ancient
Towns, Members or Places a-
forefaid, or within the Liberties, Bounds, Limits and Precincts of the fame refpectively,
have gone or rode in Troops[v],
or by Force, armed[w], or hereafter fhall prefume fo to go or ride,
to the Difturbance[x] of the People

ANNOTATIONS.

[r] *Ingroffings.* By the 6th *Edward* VI. *cap.* 14. may be feen, an Ingroffer fhall be accounted one that getteth into his Hands, by Buying, Contract, or Promife, and taketh (other than by Demife, Leafe or Grant of Land, or of Tithe) any Corn growing in the Fields, or other Corn or Grain, Butter, Cheefe, Fifh, or other dead Victual within *England,* to the latent to fell the fame again. But fuch as buy Barley and Oats (without Foreftalling) and turn the fame into Malt or Oatmeal ; and fuch Purveyors of Corn, or Victuallers, as being Licenfed, buy (without Foreftalling) are excepted. See *Stat.* 5 *Elizabeth,* 12 & 13 *Elizabeth* 25.

[s] *Crimes,* Evil Deeds, Mifdeeds or Mifdemeanors.

[u] *Committed,* acted or perpetrated ; and fo again, *page* 151. *l.* 22.

[v] *Troops.* Thus the Englifher of the Charter of King *Charles* I. rendered the Word, but *Con-venticulum* in this Charter being a diminutive of *Conventus,* properly is an Affembly or Conven-ticle, commonly ftiled in the Law an *Unlawful Affembly,* and being here in the fingular Num-ber, feems to be fuch a Meeting together of more than Two, and though under the Number of Twelve, as being affembled, have an Intention to kill, beat or maim any, or cut or caft down any lawful Inclofure, Conduit-pipe, &c. or enter upon a Poffeffion, or do fome fuch unlawful Act, though they be prevented and do it not ; and if after their affembling they have fet for-ward to attempt it, then is it called a *Rout,* though it were not effected, but if done, then is it a *Riot.*

[w] *Force armed.* This going or riding armed, to the Terror or Affrightment of the People, is to be underftood as a feparate Claufe from the foregoing, for this is punifhable in any fingle Perfon.

[x] *To the Difturbance* or in Difturbance.

Q q   *Y Have*

CHARTERS.

equitaver. feu impofterum ire vel equitare præfumpferint ; ac etiam de omnibus his, qui ibidem refpective ad gent. noftr. hæred. vel fuccefforum noftrorum, maimand. vel interficiend. in infidiis jacuer. vel impofterum jacere præfumpferint ; ac etiam de hoftellar. & iis omnibus & fingulis perfonis, qui abufu ponder. vel menfurarum five in venditione victual. contra formam ordinationum vel ftatut. vel eorum alicujus inde pro communi utilitate regni Angliæ feu populi noftri, hæredum vel fuccefforumnoftrorum edit. vel edend. deliquerunt vel attemptaverunt, feu impofterum delinquere vel attemptare præfumpfer. infra Quinque Portus, antiquas villas, membra five locos prædict. vel infra libertates, fines, limit. & præcinct. eorundem refpective ; ac etiam de quibufcunque conftabular. fubconftabular. cuftod. Gaolæ, ac

TRANSLATION.

ple of us, our Heirs or Succeffors, againft the Peace of us, our Heirs or Succeffors ; and alfo of all thofe, who refpectively there have [y], or hereafter fhall prefume to lie in wait to maim [z] or kill the People of us, our Heirs or Succeffors ; and alfo of Huckfters [a], and all and fingular thofe Perfons, who by Abufe of Weights and Meafures [b], or in the Sale of Victuals [c], againft the Form of the Ordinances or Statutes, or any of them made, or to be made [d] thereupon [e], for the common Profit [f] of the Kingdom of *England,* or the People of us, our Heirs or Succeffors, have trefpaffed [g] or attempted, or hereafter fhall prefume to trefpafs or attempt, within the *Cinque Ports,* Ancient Towns, Members or Places aforefaid, or within the Liberties, Bounds, Limits and Precincts of the fame refpectively ; and alfo of whatfoever Conftables, Petty Conftables [h], Keepers [i] of the Gaol [j], and

ANNOTATIONS.

[y] *Have* or have lain in wait.

[z] *Maim,* wrote after the Lawyers *French Mayheme,* is fuch a corporal Hurt properly, as whereby the Party loofeth the Ufe of the Member, whether Eye, Hand, Foot, or fuch like ; fome Finger of the Hand, or the Fore-Tooth, as fome fay. The Canonifts call it *Membri mutilatio.* See *Glanvile, lib.* 14. *cap.* 7. and *Ugolin. de irregul. cap.* 4.

[a] *Huckfters,* fuch Inn-Keepers, Victuallers and others, that fell Victuals by Retail, which they bought in Grofs, or buy in great Quantities and fell out by fmall Parcels. The Tranflation of the Charter of King *Charles* I. for this Word *Hoftellar.* hath *Duellers* ; but though Duellers are punifhable, and within the Ports, by the Magiftrates there, and that within the Purview, and by virtue of this Charter ; yet becaufe *Duellum* is commonly a *Duel,* and *Duellator* ufed for each of the Two that fight, with fome other Reafons, I have rendered *Hoftellar. Huckfters,* as before.

[b] *Weights and Meafures,* the Standard whereof, by the Statute made *Anno* 11 *Henry* VII. *cap.* 4. for the *Cinque Ports,* is to be kept in *Dover* Caftle.

[c] *Victuals,* fuch dead Victuals as a Man may be guilty of ingroffing.

[d] *Made or to be made,* to be underftood as before, *page* 146, *Note* [b], for made publick or fet forth.

[e] *Thereupon* or thereof, or concerning Weights, Meafures, fale of Victuals, &c.

[f] *Profit,* Utility or Benefit.

[g] *Trefpaffed,* tranfgreffed, been delinquent or faulty ; and *l.* 20. *trefpafs* in the fame Senfe.

[h] *Petty Conftables,* in refpect of whom the Conftable of the whole Hundred is called the High Conftable. Thefe petty, fub, or under Conftables, being within fome Borough or Part of the Hundred.

[i] *Keepers of the Gaol.* Jaylors or Gaol Keepers are the Officer or Officers which under the Head Officer of the Port, whether Mayor or Bailiff, hath the Charge of the Prifon, and is to fee the Prifoners fafely kept.

[j] *Gaol* is fometimes wrote *Jaile* and *Jeyle,* a Prifon or a Place of Durance, where Offenders are to be kept till delivered by Law.

[k] *Care-*

CHARTERS.

ac al. Officiar. & Miniftr. qui execution. officiorum fuorum circa præmiffa feu eorum aliqua indebit. fe habuerunt, aut impofterum indebit. fe habere præfumpfer. aut tepidi, remif. vel negligent. fuer. aut impofterum fore contigerint, infra Quinque Portus, antiquas villas, membra, five locos prædict. vel infra libertates, fines, limit. & præcinct. eorundem refpective; ac de omnibus & fingulis articulis, circumftant. & al. rebus quibufcunq; per quofcunq; & qualitercunq; infra Quinque Portus, antiquas villas, membra, feu locos prædict. vel infra libertates, fines, limit. & præcinct. eorundem refpective, fact. feu perpetrat. vel quæ impofterum ibidem refpective fieri vel attemptari contigerit qualitercunque præmiff. vel eorum aliquorum concernend. plenius veritatem; et ad indictament. quæcunque fic coram prædict. Major. & Ballivis vel eorum deputat. & Jurat. vel fucceffor. fuis refpective, capt. five capiend. aut coram al. nuper. Jufticiar. noftris pacis infra prædict. Quinque Portus, antiquas villas & membra eorundem feu eorum aliquibus refpective, fact. five capt. & nondum terminat. infpiciend. ac' ad procef. inde verfus omnes & fingulos fic indictat. vel quos coram prædict. Major.

TRANSLATION.

and other Officers and Minifters, which in the Execution of their Offices about the Premiffes, or any of them unduly have behaved themfelves, or hereafter fhall prefume unduly to behave themfelves, or have been, or hereafter fhall happen to be carelefs[k], remifs, or negligent, within the *Cinque Ports,* Ancient Towns, Members or Places aforefaid, or within the Liberties, Bounds, Limits and Precincts of the fame refpectively; and of all and fingular Articles, Circumftances, and other Things whatfoever, by whomfoever, and in what manner foever, within the *Cinque Ports,* Ancient Towns, Members or Places aforefaid, or within the Liberties, Bounds, Limits and Precincts of the fame refpectively, done or committed, or which hereafter there refpectively fhall happen to be done or attempted, in any manner of wife concerning the Truth of the Premiffes, or any of them more fully. And the Indictments[l] whatfoever fo before the aforefaid Mayors and Bailiffs, or their Deputies, and the Jurats, or their Succeffors, refpectively taken, or to be taken, or before other our late Juftices[m] of the Peace within the aforefaid *Cinque Ports,* Ancient Towns and Members of the fame, or any of them refpectively made or taken, and not yet determined, to infpect, and to direct, make, and continue the Procefs thereupon, againft[n] all and fingular fo indicted, or whom before the aforefaid Mayor

ANNOTATIONS.

[k] *Carelefs,* the *Latin Tepidi,* properly fignifies *Lukewarm.* For fuch Officers to be negligent, carelefs or remifs in Execution of their Offices is punifhable.

[l] *Indictments.* An Indictment or Inditement is an Accufation of twelve Men, or more, at the King's Suit, upon their Oath, wherein is declared the Crime with which fuch Perfon indicted is charged.

[m] *Late Jufices.* Change of a Mayor, Bailiff or Jurats, fhall not quafh an Indictment, but they may proceed to hear and determine fuch as they find depending undetermined at their Election.

[n] *Againft,* fo is the *Latin Verfus* ufed in the Law for *Adverfus.*

CHARTERS.

Major. vel ill. Deputat. & Jurat. Ballivo feu ill. Deputat. & Jurat. vel fuccefforibus fuis refpective, impofterum indictari contigerit, quofque capiant. vel reddant fe miniftris fuis propriis, dirigend. faciend. & continuand. & ad omnes & fingulas felonias, murdr. homicid. veneficia, incantationes, fortileg. arte magic. transgreffiones, foreftal. regratar. ingroffar. extortiones, conventiculum, indictament. prædict. cæteraq; omnia & fingula præmiffa, fecundum leges & ftatut. regni noftri Angliæ, edit. vel impofterum edend. audiend. & terminand. & ad eofdem delinquent. & quemlibet eorum, pro delictis fuis, per fines, redemptiones, amerciament. forifactur. & alio modo, prout fecundum legem & confuetudinem regni noftri Angliæ, aut formam ordinationum & ftatut. prædict. edit. vel impofterum edend. fieri confuevit aut debuit vel debebit, caftigand. & puniend. ac ad omnia alia agend. exequend. & peragend. infra prædict. Quinq. Portus, antiquas villas & Membr. eorundem & libertates, fines, limit. & præcinct. eorundem refpective, adeo plene, libere & integre, ac in tam amplis modo & forma, prout jufticiar. noftri, feu hæred. noftrorum, ad pacem noftram, hæredum vel fucceflorum noftrorum in comitat. Kanc.

TRANSLATION.

Mayor or his Deputy and Jurats, Bailiff or his Deputy and Jurats, or their Succeffors refpectively, hereafter fhall happen to be indicted, and thofe who may be taken or render themfelves to their proper Minifters; and to hear and determine all and fingular Felonies, Murders, Homicides, Sorceries, Inchantments, Divinations [o], Magick Art, Trefpaffes, Foreftallings, Regratings, Ingroffings, Extortions, unlawful Affembly [p] and Indictments aforefaid, and all and fingular other the Premiffes, according to the Laws [q] and Statutes of our Kingdom of *England*, made or hereafter to be made; and thofe Delinquent [r], and every of them, for their Crimes [f], by Fines, Ranfoms [s], Amerciaments, Forfeitures, and otherwife [t], as according to the Law and Cuftom of our Kingdom of *England*, or the Form of the Ordinances and Statutes aforefaid made, or hereafter to be made, hath been accuftomed, or ought or fhall be due to be done, to chaftife and punifh, and to do, execute and perform all other things within the aforefaid *Cinque Ports*, ancient Towns and their Members, and the Liberties, Bounds, Limits and Precincts of the fame refpectively, fo fully, freely and perfectly, and in as ample Manner and Form as the Juftices of us or our Heirs, to keep [u] the Peace of us, our Heirs or Succeffors, in the Counties of *Kent*,

ANNOTATIONS.

[o] *Divinations*, moft properly the Divination by Lots.
[p] *Unlawful Affembly* or Conventicle. See the Word *Troops*, *p.* 149, *Note* [v].
[q] *Laws*, when mentioned with Statutes, may be underftood the Common Law of the Nation. The Lord *Coke* reckons up fifteen Sorts of Laws in *England*, in the fift part of his *Inftitutes*.
[r] *Delinquent* or tranfgreffing, as before.
[f] *Crimes*, Faults or Offences.
[s] *Ranfoms* or Redemptions, as before is noted.
[t] *Otherwife* or in other manner.
[u] *Keep*. This Word is neceffarily fupplied in the Tranflation.

CHARTERS.

Kanc. Suffex & Effex, vel eorum aliquo, feu in aliquo al. com. infra regnum Angliæ, virtute alicujus commiffionis, act. parliament. ftatut. legis feu confuetud. vel aliquo alio legali modo quocunque, antehac fecer. perager. vel execut. fuer. feu impofterum facere, peragere vel exequi valeant feu poffint, ac in tam amplis modo & forma, prout fi ea omnia in his literis noftris patentibus fpecialiter, & per fpecialia verba content. declarat. recitat. vel expref. fuiffent. Et quod quilibet duo vel plures prædict. Major. & Jurat. de quolibet portu prædict. Quinque Portuum, & fucceffores fui refpective, infra portus prædict. ac infra libertates, fines, limit. & præcinct. eorundem, ac etiam infra quoflibet alios locos & villas, & quemlibet alium locum & villam, alicui port. prædict. pertinent. feu fpectant. five exiftent. Membr. alicujus portus prædict. in quibus locis five villis, aut in quo loco five in qua villa, Major. aut Ballivus non exiftit per Communitatem eorundem locorum vel villarum, five ejufdem loci five villæ, elect.
(quo-

TRANSLATION.

Kent, Suffex and *Effex,* or in any of them, or in any other County within the Realm of *England,* by virtue of any Commiffion [v], Act of Parliament, Statute, Law or Cuftom, or in any other lawful Manner whatfoever, heretofore have done, performed or executed, or hereafter [w] may or can do, perform or execute; and in as ample Manner and Form, as if all thofe things, in thefe our Letters Patents fpecially, and by fpecial Words, had been contained, declared, recited or expreffed. And that every two or more of the aforefaid Mayors and Jurats, of every Port of the aforefaid *Cinque Ports,* and their Succeffors refpectively, within the Ports aforefaid, and within the Liberties, Bounds, Limits and Precincts of the fame, and alfo within all other Places and Towns, and every other Place and Town, to any Port aforefaid appertaining [x] or belonging, or being Member of any Port aforefaid, in which Places or Towns, or in which Place or Town, a Mayor or Bailiff, by the Commonalty of the fame Places or Towns, or of the fame Place or Town, is not elected
(of

ANNOTATIONS.

[v] *Commiffion.* Such Writing as paffeth under the Great Seal of *England* to the Judges and Juftices of Affife and Gaol Delivery, whereby Power is committed to them to hear and determine the Offences of the Prifoners in the Gaols of the Counties in their Circuit, is called a Commiffion ; and this is the Commiffion here intended, notwithftanding feveral other Writings, wherein Power is committed to others, are called Commiffions.

[w] *Hereafter* By this it feems, that if after the Grant of this Charter any thing be made Felony by Act of Parliament, which before was not Felony, either by the Common Law or by any Statute, yet it is inquirable and punifhable within the Corporations of the Ports, Towns and Members ; which otherwife were queftionable : For Charters and Commiffions, as I take it, are to receive equal Conftruction ; and if the King grant a Commiffion to inquire of all Felonies and Pleas of the Crown, and after the Commiffion fome Offence is made Felony by Statute, the Commiffioners have not Power by that Commiffion to deal with the new made Felony. And in Leets Felonies are prefentable by the Common Law ; but in things made Felony by Statute fince the Erection of Leets, Book Cafes are no Prefentment, and fhall be made in Leets not as for Felony, but for Trefpafs.

[x] *Appertain ng,* and the Words *belonging, being,* in this Place, and the Word *being, p.* 154, *l.* 2, 14, 13. feeing they are Participles of the prefent Tenfe in other Places of the Charter, I have deviated from the printed Copy, which hath them in the Participle of the Future in *dus, as pertinend. fpectand exiftend.* but I reckon them among the Errata of the Prefs.

CHARTERS.	*TRANSLATION.*

(quorum Major. vel ejus deputat. pro tempore exiftent. femper unum effe volumus) & quod quilibet duo vel plures prædict. Major. & Jurat. de qualibet prædictarum antiquarum villarum de Rye & Winchelfea prædict. & de quolibet Membro prædict. Quinque Portuum & antiquarum villarum prædictarum, ubi Major exiftit, & fucceffores fui refpective (quorum Major. vel ill. deputat. pro tempore exiftent. femper unum effe volumus) ac quilibet duo vel plures prædict. Balliv. & Jurat. de quolibet Membro portuum prædict. ubi hujufmodi Balliv. per Communitatem ejufdem Membri eft elect. & fucceffores fui refpective (quorum Ballivum vel ejus deputat. pro tempore exiftent. femper unum effe volumus) de tempore in tempus, de cætero impertuum fint & erint jufticiar. noftr. hæred. & fuccefforum noftrorum, ad gaol. infra Quinque Portus, antiquas villas, Membra, & alios locos prædict. ac libertat. fines, limit. & præcinct. eorum refpective, de tempore in tempus, fecundum leges & confuetud. hujus regni noftri Angliæ, de prifon. in eadem exiftend. & effent. deliberand. Ac quoflibet duos vel plures ipforum Major. Balliv. & Jurat. & fucceffores fuos refpective (quorum Major. & Balliv. vel ill. deputat. pro tempore exiftent. femper unum effe volumus) jufticiar. noftr. hæred. & fuccefforum noftrorum, ad gaol. deliberand. infra præd. Quinque Portus, antiquas villas, Membr. &

(of whom we will the Mayor, or his Deputy for the time being, always to be one) and that every two or more of the aforefaid Mayors and Jurats, of every of the aforefaid ancient Towns of *Rye* and *Winchelfea* aforefaid, and of every Member of the aforefaid *Cinque Ports* and ancient Towns aforefaid, where a Mayor is, and their Succeffors refpectively (of whom we will the Mayor, or his Deputy for the time being, always to be one) and every two or more of the aforefaid Bailiffs and Jurats, of every Member of the Ports aforefaid, where fuch Bailiff by the Commonalty of the fame Member is elected, and their Succeffors refpectively (of whom we will the Bailiff, or his Deputy for the time being, always to be one) from time to time from henceforth for ever, may be and fhall be Juftices of us, our Heirs and Succeffors, to deliver the Gaols [y] within the *Cinque Ports*, ancient Towns, Members and other Places aforefaid, and the Liberties, Bounds, Limits and Precincts of them refpectively, from time to time, according to the Laws and Cuftoms of this our Kingdom of *England*, of the Prifoners in the fame being and to be : And every two or more of the fame Mayors, Bailiffs and Jurats, and their Succeffors refpectively (of whom we will the Mayor and Bailiff, or his Deputy for the time being, always to be one) Juftices of us, our Heirs and Succeffors, to deliver the Gaols within the aforefaid *Cinque Ports*, ancient Towns, Members and

---

ANNOTATIONS.

[y] *Deliver the Gaols.* In Imitation of the Commiffion to the Juftices of Affife in the Counties, who befides that of *Oyer* and *Terminer*, have another Commiffion to deliver the Gaols of Prifoners found therein.

[z] *Being.*

CHARTERS.

& locos prædict. ac fines, limit. libertat. & præcinct. eorum respective, de tempore in tempus, secundum confuetudinem hujus regni Angliæ, de prison. in eadem exiftent. deliberand. creamus, conftituimus, facimus, ordinamus & confirmamus per præsentes ; ac ad omnia quæcumque, de tempore in tempus, agend. exequend. & peragend. infra prædict. Quinque Portus, antiquas villas, Membr. & locos prædict. ac fines, limit. libertat. & præcinct. eorundem refpective, adeo plenè, liberè & integrè, ac in tam amplis modo & forma, prout jufticiar. noftr. hæredum & fucceflorum noftrorum, in prædict. com. Kanc. Suffex & Effex, & eorum aliquo, feu in aliquo alio com. infra regnum Angliæ, ad gaol. deliberand. virtute alicujus commiffionis, act. parliament. ftatut. legis feu confuetud. vel aliquo alio legal. modo quocunque antehac fecer. perager. vel execut. fuer. feu impofterum facere, peragere, & exequi valeant feu poffint ; ac in tam amplis modo & forma, prout fi ea omnia in his literis noftris patentibus fpecialiter, & per fpecialia verba content. declarat. recitat. vel expreff. fuiffent. Quodque nullus al. jufticiar. noftri, hæred. vel fucceflorum noftrorum,
                                    ad

TRANSLATION.

and Places aforefaid, and the Bounds, Limits, Liberties and Precincts of them refpectively, from time to time, according to the Cuftom of this Kingdom of *England,* of the Prifoners in the fame being ⁱ to deliver, we do create, conftitute, make, ordain and confirm by thefe Prefents ; and to do, execute and perform all things whatfoever, from time to time, within the aforefaid *Cinque Ports,* ancient Towns, Members and Places aforefaid, and the Bounds, Limits, Liberties and Precincts of the fame refpectively, fo fully, freely and perfectly, and in as ample Manner ᵃ and Form, as the Juftices of us, our Heirs and Succeffors, in the aforefaid Counties of *Kent,* *Suffex* and *Effex,* and in any of them, or in any other County within the Realm of *England,* by virtue of any Commiffion, Act of Parliament, Statute, Law or Cuftom, or in any other lawful Manner whatfoever, heretofore have done, performed or executed, or hereafter may or can do, perform and execute, to deliver the Gaols ; and in as ample Manner and Form, as if all things ᵇ in thefe our Letters Patents fpecially, and by fpecial Words, had been contained, declared, recited or expreffed. And that none other Juftice of us, our Heirs or Succeffors, affigned, or to be affigned ᶜ, to keep

ANNOTATIONS.

ⁱ *Being.* In the printed Copy *exiftint.* for the Reafon before mentioned I have made *exiftent.*

ᵃ *Ample Manner.* As fully and effectually as other Juftices in other Places can hear and determine fuch Matters, their Authority fo to do being by virtue of the Commiffion to them directed ; equivalent to which is the Charter of the Ports to the Magiftrates thereof, as a ftanding Commiffion.

ᵇ *All things,* or all thefe things.

ᶜ *Affigned.* From the *Latin, affignamus,* ufed in their Commiffion. An Affignee (in the *Latin, affignatus*) is he that is appointed or deputed by another to do any Act, or perform any Bufinefs, or enjoy any Commodity. An Affignee may be either in Deed or in Law ; Affignee in Deed, is he that is appointed by a Perfon ; an Affignee in Law, is he that the Law makes
                                                              fo

CHARTERS.

ad pacem noftram hæred. vel fuccefforum noftrorum, infra præd.
comitat. Kanc. Suffex & Effex,
feu eorum aliquem, affignat. feu
affignand. nec aliquis jufticiar. noftri, hæred. vel fucceffor. noftrorum, ad diverfas felonias tranf-
greff. & al. malefact. inquirend.
audiend. & terminand. vel ad
Gaol. deliberand. affignat. vel
affignand. infra com. Kanc. Suffex
& Effex, vel eorum aliquo ; nec
ullus vicecomes, fub vicecomes,
coronator, efcaetor, nec aliquis
al. officiar. noftr. vel hæred. vel
fucceffor. noftrorum, prædict. com.
Kanc. Suffex & Effex, vel eorum
aliquis, ad aliquod vel aliqua infra prædict. Quinque Portus, antiquas villas, Membra vel locos
fupradict. vel libertates, fines,
limit. feu præcinct. eorum faciendum, agendum vel peragen-
dum impofterum aliqualiter fe
intromittat feu intromittant, nec
aliquam autoritatem five jurif-
dictionem habeat feu exerceat,
habeant feu exerceant, de aliquibus caufis, rebus vel mater. quibufcunque ad jufticiar. noftros,
hæredum & fucceflorum noftro-
rùm, ad pacem confervandum,
vel ad diverf. felon. tranfgref. &
al. malefact. inquirend. audiend.
& terminand. vel ad gaol. deliberand. affignat. five affignand.
quovifmodo pertinen. fpectan. five
incumben. vel quæ impofterum
pertinere, fpectare, vel incum-
bere contiger, infra dictos Quinque Portus, antiquas villas
Membr. & loc. prædict. five infra
liber-

TRANSLATION.

keep [d] the Peace of us, our Heirs
or Succeffors, within the aforefaid Counties of *Kent, Suffex* and
Effex, or any of them ; nor any
Juftice of us, our Heirs or Succeffors, to inquire, hear and determine divers Felonies, Trefpaffes and other Crimes [e], or
affigned, or to be affigned, to deliver the Gaols within the aforefaid Counties of *Kent, Suffex*
and *Effex,* or in any of them ;
nor any Sheriff, Under-Sheriff,
Coroner, Efcheator, nor any
other Officer of us, or our Heirs
or Succeffors, of the aforefaid
Counties of *Kent, Suffex* and
Effex, or any one of them, to
do, act or perform any thing or
any things within the aforefaid
Cinque Ports, ancient Towns,
Members or Places abovefaid, or
the Liberties, Bounds, Limits or
Precincts of them, may hereafter
in any wife intermeddle, nor have
or exercife any Authority or Jurifdiction of any Caufes, Things
or Matters whatfoever, to the
Juftices of us, our Heirs and Succeffors, affigned, or to be affigned,
to keep the Peace, or to inquire,
hear and determine divers Felonies, Trefpaffes and other Offences [f], or to deliver the Gaols, in
any wife appertaining, belonging or incumbent [g], or which
hereafter fhall happen to appertain, belong or be incumbent,
within the faid *Cinque Ports,*
ancient Towns, Members and
Places aforefaid, or within the
Liber-

ANNOTATIONS.

fo without appointment of any Perfon by Deed. *Dyer, fol.* 6. *num.* 5. *Perkins, Tit. Grants,* faith,
an Affignee is he that ufeth or enjoyeth a thing in his own Right ; and a Deputy, he that
doth what he doth in the Right of another.
  [d] *Keep.* Supplied in the Tranflation, as before *p.* 152. *Note* u.
  [e] *Crimes,* Offences or evil Deeds, as moft properly the Word fignifies.
  [f] *Offences,* evil Deeds or Crimes, as the fame Word *malefact.* is above rendered, *l.* 8. and fo
p. 157. *l.* 27.
  [g] *Incumbent,* leaning, lying or refting upon. An Incumbent, in the Common Law, is he
that is prefented, admitted and inftituted to any Church or Benefice with Cure, who is therefore called the Incumbent of that Church ; becaufe he depends thereupon, and bends all his
ftudy to the Difcharge of the Cure there.   i

CHARTERS.

libertates, fines, limit. & præcinct. eorundem, vel eorum alicujus, ex quacunque causa, five
quovifcunque tempore emergend.
five contingend. Et quod quilibet Major. Jurat. & Communitas cujuflibet Quinque Portuum, antiquarum villarum &
Membr. prædict. ubi Major. exiftit, & fucceffores fui refpective ;
& quilibet Ballivus, Jurat. &
Communitas, & Ballivus & Communitas cujuflibet Membri port.
prædict. ubi hujufmodi Balliv.
per Communitatem Membr.
præd. eft elect. & fucceffores fui
refpective, habeant & percipiant,
habebunt & percipient, ad eorum
proprium ufum & commodum refpective, omni. & omnimod. fines,
exit. redemptiones, amerciament.
forisfactur. & profic. quæcunque,
coram præfatis jufticiariis noftris,
hæred. vel fucceforum noftrorum, ad pacem confervand. necnon ad diverf. felon. tranfgref. &
al. malefact. inquirend. audiend.
& terminand. feu ad gaol. noftr.
hæred. vel fucceffor. noftrorum,
deliberand. infra dictos Quinque
Portus, antiquas villas, Membr.
& loc. fupradict. & coram eorum
quolibet five aliquo refpective,
de tempore in tempus, perpe-
tuis futuris temporibus affidend.
forisfaciend. adjudicand. prove-
niend. accidend. five emergend.
& ea omnia per eorum pro-
prios & feparal. Miniftr. ad eorum ufum proprium refpective,
levare & percipere poffint &
poffit, abfque aliquo extract.
inde

TRANSLATION.

Liberties, Bounds, Limits and
Precincts of the fame, or any of
them, for whatfoever [h] Caufe,
or in whatfoever time they fhall
arife or happen. And that every
Mayor, Jurat and Commonalty
of every of the *Cinque Ports,*
ancient Towns and Members a-
forefaid, where a Mayor is, and
their Succeffors refpectively ; and
every Bailiff, Jurat and Commonalty, and Bailiff and Commonalty, of every Member of the
Ports aforefaid, where fuch Bailiff by the Commonalty of the
Member aforefaid is elected, and
their Succeffors refpectively, may
have and perceive, and fhall
have and perceive, to their proper Ufe and Commodity refpectively, all and all manner of
Fines, Iffues, Redemptions, A-
merciaments, Forfeitures and Profits whatfoever, before the aforefaid Juftices of us, our Heirs or
Succeffors to keep the Peace,
alfo to inquire, hear and determine divers Felonies, Trefpaffes
and other Offences, or to deliver the Gaol of us, our Heirs
and Succeffors, within the faid
Cinque Ports, ancient Towns,
Members and Places abovefaid,
and before every or any of them
refpectively, from time to time,
for ever hereafter [j] to be affeffed [j],
forfeited, adjudged, growing,
happening or arifing, and all the
fame [k] by their proper [l] and feveral [m] Minifters, to their proper
Ufe refpectively, they may [n] levy
and perceive, without any Eftreat [o]
thereof

ANNOTATIONS.

[h] *For whatfoever.* Of or from whatfoever Caufe, or what time foever arifing or happening ;
that is, fuch Caufes, &c. fhall arife or happen.
[j] *Ever hereafter,* or at all times to come.
[j] *Affeffed* or fet down.
[k] *All the fame,* to wit, the Fines, Iffues, Redemptions or Ranfoms, &c.
[l] *Proper* or own ; and fo in feveral other Places.
[m] *Several.* The Officers or Minifters of one Corporation not to intermeddle in another, but
each to act diftinctly and apart within their Limits.
[n] *They may,* or they and every of them may.
[o] *Eftreat.* That is a Writing or Copy of the feveral Fines, Iffues, Amerciaments, &c. ex-
tracted or drawn out of the Records of the Seffions or Courts where fuch Fines, &c. are fet,
and

CHARTERS.   TRANSLATION.

inde in Scacarium noftrum, hæred. vel fuccefforum noftrorum, fiend. & abfque aliquo impedimento noftro, hæredum vel fuccefforum noftrorum, aut miniftrorum noftrorum quorumcunque. Volumus tamen, ac intentio noftra eft, ac per præfentes pro nobis, hæred. & fuccefforibus noftris, concedimus & confirmamus præfatis Major. Jurat. & Communitat. Balliv. Jurat. & Communitat. & Balliv. & Communitat. cujuflibet portus, antiquarum villarum, prædict. & Membr. prædict. & fucceffor. fuis refpective, quod quilibet Major. Balliv. & Jurat. prædict. qui nunc eft, vel impofterum erit refpective, antequam ad executionem officiar. jufticiar. pacis, infra aliquem prædict. Quinque Portuum, antiquarum villarum, Membr. vel loc. prædict. aut libertat. fines, limit. vel præcinct. eorum refpective, virtute harum literarum noftrarum patentium, vel præd. literarum patentium dicti præchariffimi avi noftri Jacobi, admittant. aut admittat. tal. facrament. corporal. fuper facrofanctis Dei Evangeliis, ad offic. ill. in omnibus & per omnia fideliter exequend. de tempore in tempus, præftabit & præftare poffit & valeat, qual. & prout per conftitut.& ordinat. inde per præfat. Major. Jurat. & Communitat.

thereof to be made into the *Exchequer* of us, our Heirs or Succeffors, and without any Impediment of us, our Heirs or Succeffors, or our Minifters whofoever. We will notwithftanding, and our Intention is, and by thefe Prefents, for us, our Heirs and Succeffors, we do grant and confirm to the aforefaid Mayors, Jurats and Commonalties, Bailiffs, Jurats and Commonalties, and Bailiff and Commonalty, of every Port, ancient Towns aforefaid, and Members aforefaid, and their Succeffors refpectively, that every Mayor, Bailiff and Jurat aforefaid, which now is, or hereafter fhall be refpectively, before he or they be admitted to the Execution of the Office *p* of Juftice of the Peace, within any of the aforefaid *Cinque Ports,* ancient Towns, Members or Places aforefaid, or the Liberties, Bounds, Limits or Precincts of them refpectively, by virtue of thefe our Letters Patents, or of the aforefaid Letters Patents of our faid moft dear Grandfather King *James,* fuch corporal Oath upon the Holy Evangelifts *r*, to execute that Office in and by all things faithfully, fhall and may make from time to time, in fuch Manner *s*, and as by the Conftitution *t* and Ordinance thereupon to be made by the aforefaid Mayors, Jurats and Commonalties,

ANNOTATIONS.

and returned into the Exchequer, that fo from thence Procefs may be taken out to levy them ; but in the Ports they may be levied, and before the making of this Charter were, without eftreating them into the Exchequer.

p *Office.* In the printed Copy it is *officiar.* that is Officer, but I take it for *Office.*

q *King.* Is fupplied in the Tranflation.

r *Evangelifts* or Gofpels of God, verbatim after the *Latin.*

s *Such Manner,* fuch Sort, or fuch Oath.

t *Conftitution.* This and *Ordinance* following in the next Line, may be read plurally. After the Charter of King *James,* the Ports, at their Brotherhood at *Romney, July* 16; 1668. in the fixth Year of the Reign of that King over *England,* &c. did agree upon the Form of an Oath for the Mayors, Bailiffs and Jurats to take as Juftices of the Peace, and appoint the fame to be taken accordingly.

u *Commiffion,*

CHARTERS.

munitat. Balliv. Jurat. & Communitat. & Balliv. & Communitat. cujuflibet port. antiquarum villarum & Membr. prædict. & fucceffor. fuorum refpective, vel eorum majorem partem refpective, in hac parte faciend. conftitut. & ordinat. fuerit, abfque aliquo al. warrant. brevi vel Commiffione à nobis, hæred. vel fucceffor. noftris, procurand. feu obtinend. videlicet, quod quilibet Major. & Balliv. præd. qui nunc eft, vel impofterum erit refpective, de tempore in tempus, hujufmodi facrament. ut fupradict. eft, præftabit & præftare poffit & valeat coram prædict. Jurat. qui nunc funt, vel impofterum erunt, vel duobus feu pluribus eorum refpective ; quodque quilibet prædict. Jurat. qui nunc eft vel impofterum erit, de tempore in tempus, hujufmodi facrament. ut prædict. eft, coram prædict. Major. & Balliv. qui nunc funt vel impofterum erunt, refpective præftabit & præftare poffit & valeat, abfque aliquo al. warrant. brevi vel commiffione à nobis, hæred. vel fucceffor. noftris, procurand. feu obtinend. ad quas quidem conftitut. & ordinationes, de tempore in tempus condend. & faciend. iifdem Major. Jurat. & Communitat. Balliv. Jurat. & Communitat. & Ballivo & Communitat. cujuflibet port. antiquarum villarum & Membr. prædict. & fucceffor. fuis refpective, plenam

TRANSLATION.

monalties, Bailiffs, Jurats and Commonalties, and Bailiff and Commonalty, of every of the Ports, ancient Towns and Members aforefaid, and their Succeffors refpectively, or the greater part of them refpectively, in this Behalf fhall be conftituted and ordained, without any other Warrant, Writ or Commiffion [t] to be procured or obtained from us, our Heirs or Succeffors; that is to fay, that every Mayor and Bailiff aforefaid, which now is, or hereafter fhall be refpectively, from time to time fuch Oath as is abovefaid fhall and may make before the [u] aforefaid Jurats which now are, or hereafter fhall be, or two or more of them refpectively; and that every of the aforefaid Jurats, which now is, or hereafter fhall be, from time to time, fuch Oath as is aforefaid, before the aforefaid Mayors and Bailiffs which now are, or hereafter fhall be refpectively, fhall and may make, without any other Warrant, Writ or Commiffion, from us, our Heirs or Succeffors to be procured or obtained; to which faid [v] Conftitutions and Ordinances, from time to time to be ordained and made to the faid Mayors, Jurats and Commonalties, Bailiffs, Jurats and Commonalties, and Bailiff and Commonalty, of every of the Ports, ancient Towns and Members aforefaid, and to their Succeffors refpectively, full

ANNOTATIONS.

[t] *Commiffion.* *No dedimus poteftatem* to any to adminifter the Oath, as there is for the Juftices of the Peace in the County, Commiffioners of Sewers, &c. but the fame may be adminiftred by virtue of the Charter.

[u] *Before the,* &c. The Head Officer to be fworn before the Jurats, and the Jurats before the Head Officer, and this was the Cuftom long before; for the Oath to any new Mayor or Bailiff, on their Election to their Office, was adminiftred by the old Mayor or Bailiff refpectively; and if he happened to be elected again, or dying in the time of his Office, another was chofen to fupply his Place for the reft of the Year; then was the Oath adminiftred by the eldeft Jurat to fuch new elect or re-elect Mayor or Bailiff.

[v] *The which faid,* &c. or thus, the which faid Conftitutions and Ordinances from time to time to ordain and make, &c.

CHARTERS.

plenam poteſtatem & autoritatem pro nobis, hæred. & ſucceſſor. noſtris, damus & concedimus per præſentes. Ac inſuper volumus, ac per præſentes, pro nobis, hæredibus & ſucceſſorib. noſtris, damus, concedimus & confirmamus eiſdem Major. Jurat. & Communitat. Balliv. Jurat. & Communitat. & Balliv. & Communitat. cujuſlibet Port. antiquarum villarum & Membrorum præd. & ſucceſſor. ſuis reſpective, quod præd. Major. Balliv. & Jurat. qui nunc ſunt vel impoſterum erunt reſpective, de tempore in tempus, de cætero imperpetuum habeant & habeat plenam poteſtatem & autoritatem adminiſtrand. tale ſacramentum, ut præfertur, omnibus & ſingulis perſonis in offic. Major. Balliv. vel Jurat. Quinque Portuum, antiquarum villarum vel Membrorum prædict. ſeu eorum aliquorum vel alicujus reſpective, modo elect. vel impoſterum eligend. abſque aliquo al. vel ulterior. warrant. brevi vel commiſſione à nobis, hæred. vel ſucceſſor. noſtris, in ea parte procurand. ſeu obtinend. Et ulterius volumus, ac per præſentes pro nobis, hæred. & ſucceſſor. noſtris, concedimus præfat. Major. Jurat. & Communitat. Balliv. Jurat. & Communit. & Balliv. & Communitat. cujuſlibet Quinque Portuum, antiquarum villarum & Membr. eorundem & ſucceſſor. ſuis reſpective, quod ſi contigerit aliquem Major. de aliquo Portu, vel de aliqua antiqua villa, ſeu Membr. Quinque Portuum & antiquarum villarum præd. ubi Major. exiſtit

pro

TRANSLATION.

full Power and Authority for us, our Heirs and Succeſſors, we give and grant by theſe Preſents. And moreover we will, and by theſe Preſents, for us, our Heirs and Succeſſors, do give, grant and confirm to the ſaid Mayors, Jurats and Commonalties, Bailiffs, Jurats and Commonalties, and Bailiff and Commonalty, of every of the Ports, Ancient Towns and Members aforeſaid, and to their Succeſſors reſpectively, that the aforeſaid Mayors, Bailiffs and Jurats, which now are, or hereafter ſhall be reſpectively, from Time to Time, from henceforth for ever, and every of them [w], may have full Power and Authority to adminiſter ſuch Oath as aforeſaid to all and ſingular the Perſons now elected, or hereafter to be elected into the Office of Mayor, Bailiff or Jurat of the *Cinque Ports*, Ancient Towns or Members aforeſaid, or any of them reſpectively, without any other or further Warrant, Writ or Commiſſion from us, our Heirs or Succeſſors, in that behalf [x] to be procured or obtained. And further we will, and by theſe Preſents, for us, our Heirs and Succeſſors; grant to the aforeſaid Mayors, Jurats and Commonalties, Bailiffs, Jurats and Commonalties, and Bailiff and Commonalty, of every of the *Cinque Ports*, Ancient Towns and Members of the ſame, and to their Succeſſors reſpectively, That if it ſhall happen any Mayor of any Port, or of any Ancient Town or Member of the *Cinque Ports* and Ancient Towns aforeſaid, where a Mayor

is

ANNOTATIONS.

[w] *And every of them.* So it may be read, conſidering in the *Latin* it is *habeant & habeat.*
[x] *Behalf* or *Part*; and ſo before, *p.* 159, *l.* 8.

[y] *Being*

CHARTERS.

pro tempore exiftend. aut aliquem Ballivum de aliquo Membro Portuum præd. ubi hujufmodi Ballivus per Communitat. Membr. præd. eft elect. pro tempore exiftend. ad aliquod tempus five aliqua tempora impofterum fic ægritudine aut infirmitat. laborare, aut ex aliqua alia juft. & rationabili caufa ita detiner. feu inhabilem reddi, quod offic. Major. & Balliv. & neceffar. eorum negotia ad præfens intendere non poterit vel poterit, vel Port. antiqu. vill. vel Membr. præd. pro aliqua caufa rationabili egredi, quod tunc & toties bene liceat & licebit cuilibet Majori & Ballivo aliquorum præd. Quinque Portuum, antiquarum villarum & Membrorum eorundem, pro tempore exiftend. refpective facere & conftituere unum Jurat. ejufdem Portus, antiquæ villæ, & Membri prædict. refpective, ubi ipfe Major. aut Balliv. pro tempore exiftend. extiterit, fore & effe Deputat. ejufdem Majoris aut Ballivi, fic, ut præfertur, ægritudine aut infirmitate laborant. aut fic pro caufa rationabili abfent. detent. five inhabil. reddit. ut fupradict. eft; qui quidem Deputat. in offic. Deputat. Majoris vel Ballivi præd. fic faciend.

TRANSLATION.

is, for the Time being [y], or any Bailiff of any Member of the Ports aforefaid, where fuch Bailiff by the Commonalty of the Member aforefaid is elected, for the Time being, at any Time or Times hereafter fo labour with[a] Sicknefs or Infirmity, or of any other juft and reafonable Caufe fo be detained or rendered unable, that they or he cannot intend[x] the Office of Mayor and Bailiff, and the neceffary Affairs[a] thereof at prefent[b], or for any reafonable Caufe go forth of the Port, Ancient Town or Member aforefaid, that then, and fo often[c], it may and fhall be lawful to every Mayor and Bailiff of any of the aforefaid *Cinque Ports*, Ancient Towns and Members of the fame, for the Time being refpectively, to make and conftitute one of the Jurats[d] of the fame Port, Ancient Town and Member aforefaid refpectively, where the fame Mayor or Bailiff for the Time being fhall be, to be the Deputy of the fame Mayor or Bailiff, fo, as aforefaid, labouring with Sicknefs or Infirmity, or for Caufe reafonable fo abfent, detained or rendered unable, as is abovefaid; which faid Deputy, fo to be made and conftituted into the Office of Deputy of the Mayor or Bailiff aforefaid, may be,

ANNOTATIONS.

[y] *Being*, or to be, ftrictly after the *Latin, exiftend.* and fo again afterward, *l.* 6, 21, 26.
[a] *Labour with, &c.* or be fick, weak or infirm.
[x] *Intend* or attend upon.
[a] *Affairs* or Bufineffes of the fame.
[b] *Prefent* or to the prefent neceffary Affairs of the fame.
[c] *Then and fo often.* The Cuftom of *Rye*, long before the Charter of King *James*, was, in the Abfence or Sicknefs of the Mayor, for the eldeft Jurat prefent at Court, Seffions, Affembly, &c. to act as Deputy of the Mayor, and in his Stead to do all that the Mayor might do if he were prefent, although fuch Jurat had no Deputation in writing, under the Hand and Seal of the Mayor, to authorize him thereunto. And that Courts, &c. might be held before a Deputy Mayor and Jurats, although no fuch exprefs Words were then in the Charters; I have feen the Opinion of Sir *Roger Manwood*, in Queen *Elizabeth's* Time, delivered pofitively in the Cafe, with confiderable Reafons for the fame. The like Cuftom I prefume was in other of the Ports and Members, for the eldeft Jurat to act as Deputy for the Head Officer, Mayor or Bailiff, without a written Deputation.
[d] *One of the Jurats*, or one Jurat; that is, any one; for the Mayor or Bailiff now is not tied to the Cuftom, but may conftitute any one of the Jurats, though not the eldeft, to be his Deputy.

T t   [e] *During*

CHARTERS.

faciend. & conftituend. fit & erit
Deputat. ejufdem Majoris feu
Ballivi refpective, de tempore in
tempus, toties & quoties prædict.
Major. feu Balliv. refpective fic
ægritudine vel infirmitate laborare, aut ex alia rationabili caufa detineri feu inhabil. reddi vel
abeffe, ut præfertur, contigerit, durant. toto tempore quo prædict.
Major. feu Balliv. in offic. Major. feu Balliv. refpective continuaverit, nifi interim prædict.
Major. feu Balliv. alium Jurat.
ejufdem Port. antiquæ villæ feu
Membri prædict. refpective, ejus
Deputat. fecerit aut conftituerit.
Et quod quilibet hujufmodi Deputat. prædict. Major. feu Balliv.
ficut præfertur, fiend. & conftituend. omnia & fingul. quæ ad offic.
Major. vel Balliv. refpective pertinent feu pertinere debent, faciend. & exequend. de tempore in
tempus, toties & quoties prædict.
Major. feu Balliv. refpective fic
ægritudine vel infirmitate laborare, aut fic detineri feu inhabilem
reddi vel abeffe contigerit, durant.
tali tempore quo Deputat. præd.
Major. feu Balliv. refpective erit
& continuaverit, facere & exequi
valeat & poffit vigore harum literarum patentium, adeo plenè, liberè & integrè, ac in tam amplis modo & forma, prout Major.
aut Balliv. prædict. fi præfens
effet

TRANSLATION.

be, and fhall be Deputy of the
fame Mayor or Bailiff refpectively, from Time to Time, fo often
and as often as the aforefaid
Mayor or Bailiff refpectively
fhall happen fo to labour with
Sicknefs or Infirmity, or of other
reafonable Caufe to be detained
or rendered unable, or be abfent
as aforefaid, during all the Time ᵉ
in which the aforefaid Mayor or
Bailiff fhould have continued in
the Office of Mayor or Bailiff refpectively, except in the mean
Time the aforefaid Mayor or
Bailiff fhall make or conftitute
another Jurat ᶠ of the fame Port,
Ancient Town or Member aforefaid refpectively, his Deputy.
And that every fuch Deputy of
the aforefaid Mayor or Bailiff, fo,
as aforefaid, to be made and conftituted, all and fingular the
Things which to the Office of
Mayor or Bailiff refpectively appertain, or ought to appertain, to
be done and executed from Time
to Time, fo often and as often
as the aforefaid Mayor or Bailiff
refpectively fhall happen fo to
labour with Sicknefs or Infirmity, or fo to be detained or rendered unable or be abfent, during fuch Time in which he
fhall be and continue Deputy of
the aforefaid Mayor or Bailiff
refpectively, may do and execute
by force of thefe Letters Patents,
fo fully, freely and perfectly,
and in as ample Manner and
Form, as the Mayor or Bailiff
aforefaid, if he were prefent,
might

ANNOTATIONS.

ᵉ *During all the time.* The Deputy, by Cuftom, upon the Abfence of the Mayor, and no longer, was reputed Deputy ; and for Matters out of Court, always the eldeft Jurat in Town ; but for holding Courts, the eldeft there prefent : But the Deputy by Charter, acting by virtue of his written Deputation, if not difplaced by the new Appointment of another, as after is mentioned in the Charter, may be continued to the End of the Year of the Mayoralty or Bai- liage of fuch Mayor or Bailiff refpectively.
ᶠ *Another Jurat.* The Deputations of this Sort, like Letters of Attorney, are revocable at Pleafure, and a New one makes the former of no Force.

ᵍ *Them*

CHARTERS.

effet, ill. facere & exequi valeat aut
poffit (facrament. corporal. fuper
fanctum Dei Evangel. per hujufmodi Deputat. ad omnem & fin-
gulam, quæ ad officium Deputat.
Major. vel Balliv. prædict. pertinent, bene & fideliter exequend.
coram uno vel pluribus al. Jurat.
prædict. Port. antiquæ villæ feu
Membr. prædict. refpective, prius
præftand.) & toties quoties cafus
fic acciderit.   Ac infuper volumus, ac per præfentes, pro nobis,
hæred. & fucceffor. noftris, concedimus & confirmamus eifdem
Major. Jurat. & Communitat.
Balliv. Jurat. & Communitat, ac
Balliv. & Communitat. cujuflibet Port. antiquæ villæ & Membr.
prædict. & fucceffor. fuis refpective, quod quilibet hujufmodi
unus vel plures Jurat. de tempore in tempus, de cætero imperpetuum, habeat & habeant plenam poteftatem & autoritatem
dand. & adminiftrand. tal. facrament. corporal. fuper fanct. Dei
Evangel. ut fupradict. eft, cuilibet
Deputat. Major. vel Balliv. in
hujufmodi cafu, ut præfertur, conftituend. abfque aliquo brevi,
commiffione five ulterior. warrant. in ea parte à nobis, hæred.
vel fucceforibus noftris, procurand. feu obtinend.   Et ulterius,
ut Barones Quinque Portuum
prædict. & prædictarum antiquarum villarum de Rye & Winchelfey & Membrorum eorundem
Portuum, & antiquarum villarum, fervitium fuum de navibus
fuis præd. nobis, hæred. & fuccefforibus noftris, commodius facere
va-

TRANSLATION.

might or could do them [s] (a corporal Oath [h] upon the Holy E-
vangelift by fuch Deputy firft
to be taken, before one or more
of the other Jurats of the aforefaid Port, Ancient Town or
Member aforefaid refpectively,
well and faithfully to execute all
and fingular the Things which
appertain to the Office of Deputy
of the Mayor or Bailiff aforefaid) and fo often and as often as
the Cafe fhall fo happen.   And
moreover we will, and by thefe
Prefents, for us, our Heirs and
Succeffors, grant and confirm to
the fame Mayors, Jurats and
Commonalties, Bailiffs, Jurats
and Commonalties, and Bailiff
and Commonalty, of every Port,
Ancient Town and Member
aforefaid, and to their Succeffors
refpectively, that every fuch one
or more of the Jurats, from Time
to Time, from henceforth for ever,
may have full Power and Authority to give and adminifter [i] fuch
corporal Oath upon the Holy E-
vangelift [j], as is abovefaid, to
every Deputy of the Mayor or
Bailiff in fuch cafe as aforefaid to
be conftituted, without any Writ,
Commiffion, or further Warrant
in this behalf, from us, our Heirs
or Succeffors, to be procured or
obtained. And furthermore, that
the Barons of the *Cinque Ports*
aforefaid, and the aforefaid Ancient Towns of *Rye* and *Winchelfea*,
and the Members of the fame
Ports and Ancient Towns, their
Service of their Ships aforefaid,
to us, our Heirs and Succeffors,
more commodioufly [k] may do in
Times

ANNOTATIONS.

[s] *Them* or the fame, that is, the Things which belong to the Office of Deputy.
[h] *Corporal Oath.* Deputies by Cuftom took no Oath, but fuch Deputy as is made according
to the Charter ought to be fworn well and truly to execute the Office, as is fpecified in the
Charter.
[i] *Give and Adminifter*, or of giving and adminiftring.
[j] *Evangelift,* here and above, *l.* 3. in both it may be read, *The Holy Gofpel of God.*
[k] *Commodioufly* or profitably, or fitly.

[l] *Oppor-*

CHARTERS.

valeant temporibus opportunis; ac etiam pro meliori regimine, gubernatione & fuſtentatione prædict. Quinque Portuum & prædict. antiquar. villarum & Membrorum cujuſlibet eorum Quinque Portuum & antiquarum villarum, concedimus & confirmamus eifdem Baronibus Quinque Portuum & antiquarum villarum præd. & Membrorum eorundem Portuum & villarum, & fucceſſoribus fuis, ac præd Major. Jurat. & Communitat. villæ & Portus de Haſting, & fucceſſor. fuis ; ac prædict. Major. Jurat. & Communitat. villæ & portus de Nova Romney, & fucceſſor. fuis; ac prædict. Major. Jurat. & Communitat. villæ & portus de Heth, & fucceſſoribus fuis; ac prædict. Major. Jurat. & Communitat. villæ & portus de Dover, & fucceſſoribus fuis ; ac prædict. Major. Jurat. & Communitat. villæ & portus de Sandwich, ac fucceſſoribus fuis; ac ·prædict. Major. Jurat. & Communitat. antiquæ villæ de Rye, & fucceſſoribus fuis; ac prædict. Major. Jurat. & Communitat. antiquæ villæ de Winchelfey, & fucceſſoribus fuis; ac prædict. Balliv. Jurat. & Communitati villæ & leucatæ de Pevenfey, & fucceſſoribus fuis; ac prædict. Ballivo, Jurat. & Communitati villæ de Seaford, & fuc-

TRANSLATION.

Times opportune [l] ; and alſo, for the better ruling [m], governing, and ſupporting [n] of the aforeſaid *Cinque Ports*, and the aforeſaid Ancient Towns and Members of every of the ſaid *Cinque Po, ts* and Ancient Towns, we do grant and confirm to the ſame Barons of the *Cinque Ports*, and Ancient Towns aforeſaid, and Members of the ſame Ports and Towns, and to their Succeſſors, and to the aforeſaid Mayor, Jurats and Commonalty of the Town and Port of *Haſting*, and to their Succeſſors; and to the aforeſaid Mayor, Jurats and Commonalty of the Town and Port of *New Romney*, and to their Succeſſors; and to the aforeſaid Mayor, Jurats and Commonalty of the Town and Port of *Hithe*, and to their Succeſſors ; and to the aforeſaid Mayor, Jurats and Commonalty of the Town and Port of *Dover*, and to their Succeſſors; and to the aforeſaid Mayor, Jurats and Commonalty of the Town and Port of *Sandwich*, and to their Succeſſors; and to the aforeſaid Mayor, Jurats and Commonalty of the Ancient Town of *Rye*, and to their Succeſſors; and to the aforeſaid Mayor, Jurats and Commonalty of the Ancient Town of *Winchelfea*, and to their Succeſſors; and to the aforeſaid Bailiff, Jurats and Commonalty of the Town and Lowey of *Pevenfea*, and to their Succeſſors; and to the aforeſaid Bailiff, Jurats and Commonalty of the Town of *Seaford*, and to their Suc-

ANNOTATIONS.

[l] *Opportune*, fitting or fuitable to the Occaſion.

[m] *Ruling, governing*, Rule, Government or Regulating, &c. as before in other Places of the Charter.

[n] *Supporting*, Upholding or Suſtentation, as well of the Service of Shipping aforeſaid, as of the Liberties, Charters, and Cuſtoms of the *Cinque Ports*, Ancient Towns and their Members, as is afterwards ſpecified in the Charter.

. †

[o] *Charges.*

CHARTERS.

fuccefforib. fuis ; ac prædict.
Ballivo Jurat. & Communitat.
villæ de Lydd, & fuccceffori-
bus fuis; ac prædict. Major.
Jurat. & Communitat. villæ de
Folkeftone, & fuccefforibus fuis;
ac prædict. Major. Jurat. & Communitat. villæ de Feverfham, &
fuccefforibus fuis; ac prædict.
Major. Jurat. & Communitat.
villæ de Fordwich, & fuccceffori-
bus fuis; ac prædict. Major. Jurat. & Communitati villæ & hundred de Tenterden, & fuccceffo-
ribus fuis, pro fervitio fuo navium fuarum prædict. nobis, hæredibus aut fuccefforibus noftris, faciend. aut pro libertate, franchef. confuetud. privileg. & oneribus cujuflibet Portus & antiquæ
villæ præd. & cujuflibet Membri
Portuum & antiquarum villarum
prædict. refpective manutenend.
& defend.   necnon etiam pro
quibufcunq; neceffitat. & offic.
cujuflibet Portus antiquæ villæ,
& cujuflibet Membri Portuum &
antiquarum villarum præd. five
alicujus eorundem refpective,
prout fuperius limitat. quod quilibet Major. Jurat. & Communitas cujuflibet Portus præd.
Quinque Portuum refpective, in
& fuper feipfos & quoflibet alios
inhabitantes & refidentes infra
quemlibet hujufmodi Port. fines,
limit. & præcinct. ejufdem
Port.   ac   infra   quofcunque
                              alios

TRANSLATION.

Succeffors ; and to the aforefaid
Bailiff, Jurats and Commonalty of
the Town of *Lydd,* and to their
Succeffors; and to the aforefaid
Mayor, Jurats and Commonal-
ty of the Town of *Folkeftone,*
and to their Succeffors; and to
the aforefaid Mayor, Jurats and
Commonalty of the Town of
Feverfham, and to their Succeffors; and to the aforefaid Mayor,
Jurats and Commonalty of the
Town of *Fordwich,* and to their
Succeffors; and to the aforefaid
Mayor, Jurats and Commonalty
of the Town and Hundred of
Tenterden, and to their Succeffors, for the Service of their
Ships aforefaid, to us, our Heirs
and Succeffors, to be done, or
for the Liberty, Franchife, Cuftoms, Privileges and Charges [o] of
every Port and Ancient Town
aforefaid, and of every Member
of the Ports and Ancient Towns
aforefaid refpectively, to be maintained [p] and defended; as alfo
for whatfoever Neceffity [q], and
Officers [r] of every Port, Ancient
Town, and of every Member of
the Ports and Ancient Towns
aforefaid, or of any of them refpectively, as above limited;
that every Mayor, Jurats and
Commonalty of every Port of
the aforefaid *Cinque Ports* refpectively, in and upon themfelves, and all other [f] the Inhabitants and Refidents within every fuch Port, the Bounds, Limits, and Precincts of the fame
Port, and within whatfoever
                              other

ANNOTATIONS.

[o] *Charges.* A general Word, including all Sorts of Services, in doing whereof Charge and
Expence accrues, or fuch Offices as are burdenfome, for the *Latin Onus* fignifies *Burden or
Charge.*

[p] *Maintained,* &c. or for the Maintenance and Defence of the Liberty, *&c.*

[q] *Neceffity.* Such as repairing the Town Walls, Defences againft the Sea, Provifion of Powder and Ammunition for Defence againft any foreign Enemies, *&c.*

[r] *Officers* or Offices. The Word in the *Latin* is abbreviated, and fo may be either. The
Charge of publick Offices to be maintained at the publick Charge.

[f] *All other* or all other whatfoever, and fo afterward.

CHARTERS.	*TRANSLATION.*

alios locos five villas, & quemcunque alium locum five villam, alicui portui præd. pertinent. five exiftent. Membr. alicujus hujufmodi port. ac non haben. five non habentes inter feipfos Major. aut Balliv. per Communitat. eorundem five ejufdem, ut præfertur, elect. & fuper omnia & fingula terr. reddit. & hæreditament. quæcunq; infra quemlibet hujufmodi port. fines, limit. & præcinct. ejufdem, & infra quoflibet alios locos five villas, & quemlibet alium locum five villam, alicui portui portuum præd. pertinent. five exiftent. Membr. alicujus portus non haben. five non habentes Major. aut Balliv. ut præfertur, elect. exiftend. refpective ; ac etiam infuper omnia & fingula bona, catalla & merchandizas omni. & fingul. inhabitantium & refident. five occupatorum five tenent. aliquarum hujufmodi terrarum five hæreditament. quorumcunque, infra quemlibet hujufmodi port. fines, limit. & præcinct. ejufdem, ac infra quemlibet alium locum five villam, five quoflibet alios locos five villas, alicui portui prædicto pertinent. five exiftent. Membr. alicujus hujufmodi portus, non haben. five non habentes de feipfos Major. aut Balliv. ut præfertur, elect. refpective ; ac quilibet Major. Jurat. & Communitas cujuflibet antiquarum villarum prædict. ac cujuflibet Membr. portuum & antiquar. villarum prædict. ubi Major. exiftit, refpective,

other Places or Towns, and whatfoever other Place or Town, to any Port aforefaid appertaining, or being a Member of any fuch Port, and not having among themfelves a Mayor or Bailiff by the Commonalty of the fame, as aforefaid, elected, and upon all and fingular Lands, Rents and Hereditaments whatfoever, within every fuch Port, the Bounds, Limits and Precincts of the fame, and within all other Places or Towns, and every other Place or Town, to any Port of the Ports aforefaid appertaining, or being a Member of any Port, not having a Mayor or Bailiff, as aforefaid, to be elected, refpectively ; and alfo in and upon all and fingular Goods, Chattels and Merchandizes of all and fingular the Inhabitants and Refidents, or Occupiers or Tenants [1] of any fuch Lands or Hereditaments whatfoever, within every fuch Port, the Bounds, Limits and Precincts of the fame, and within every other Place or Town, or other whatfoever Places or Towns, to any Port aforefaid appertaining, or being a Member of any fuch Port, not having of themfelves a Mayor or Bailiff as aforefaid elected, refpectively ; and every Mayor, Jurats and Commonalty of every of the ancient Towns aforefaid, and of every Member of the Ports and ancient Towns aforefaid, where a Mayor is, refpectively,

ANNOTATIONS.

[1] *Tenants*, from *Teneo* to hold, proper to the Defendant in a real Action. *A Tenant*, faith the Lord *Coke*, hath *five Significations*. 1. *The Eftate of the Land, as when the Tenant in a Præcipe of Land pleads*, quod non tenet, &c. *as much as to fay*, That he hath not feifin of the Freehold of the Land in queftion. 2^ly. *The Tenure or Service whereby the Lands and Tenements are holden, and in this fenfe it is faid in the Writ of Right*, quæ clamat tenere de te per liberum fervitium, &c. 3^ly. *Performance, as in the Writ of Covenant*, quod teneat conventionem, *that is, that he hold or perform his Covenant.* 4^ly, *To be bound, and fo in an Obligation it is faid*, teneri. 5^ly. *To deem or judge, as in* 38 Edward III. *cap.* 4. It fhall be holden for none, that is, *deemed or judged for none.* So a Tenant in Fee Simple, 1. Hath the Eftate of the Land. 2. He holdeth the fame of fome fuperior Lord. 3. And is to perform the Services. 4, and 5. And he is thereto bound by Doom or Judgment of the Law, *Hac ille.*

[t] *Upon*

CHARTERS.

refpe&ive, in & fuper feipfos, & quoflibet al. inhabitant. & refident. infra quamlibet hujufmodi antiquam villam, fines, limit. & præcinct. ejufdem, & infra quodlibet hujufmodi Membr. fines, limit. & præcinct. ejufdem Membri refpe&ive, in & fuper omnia & fingula terras, reddit. & hæreditamenta quæcunque, infra quamlibet hujufmodi antiquam villam & quodlibet hujufmodi Membr. ac fines, limit. & præcinct. ejufdem, exiftent. refpe&ive ; ac etiam in & fuper omnia & fingula bona & catalla & merchandizas omnium & fingulorum inhabitant. five refident five occupator. five tenent. aliquarum hujufmodi terrar. five hæreditament. quorumcunque, infra quamlibet hujufmodi antiquam villam, & quodlibet hujufmodi Membr. ac fines, limit. & præcinct. & cujuflibet eorundem, exiften ; & quilibet Balliv. Jurat. & Communitas, & Balliv. & Communitas cujuflibet Membr. port. præd. ubi hujufmodi Balliv. per Communitatem ejufdem Membr. eft elect. refpe&ive, in & fuper feipfos, & quoflibet alios inhabitant. & refident infra quodlibet hujufmodi Membr. fines, limit. & præcinct. ejufdem, & in & fuper omnia & fingula terras, reddit. & hæreditament. quæcunque, infra quodlibet hujufmodi Membr. ac fines, limit. & præcinct. cujuflibet hujufmodi Membr. exiftent. refpe&ive ; ac etiam in & fuper omnia & fingula bona, catella & merchandizas, omnium &

TRANSLATION.

refpe&ively, in and upon themfelves [t], and all other the Inhabitants and Refidents within every fuch ancient Town, the Bounds, Limits and Precincts of the fame, and within every fuch Member, the Bounds, Limits and Precincts of the fame Member refpe&ively, in and upon all and fingular Lands, Rents and Hereditaments whatfoever, within every fuch ancient Town, and every fuch Member, and the Bounds, Limits and Precincts of the fame, refpe&ively ; and alfo in and upon all and fingular Goods and Chattels and Merchandizes of all and fingular the Inhabitants or Refidents, or Occupiers or Tenants of any fuch Lands or Hereditaments whatfoever, within every fuch ancient Town, and every fuch Member, and the Bounds, Limits and Precincts of them, and every of them being ; and every Bailiff, Jurats and Commonalty, and Bailiff and Commonalty, of every Member of the Ports aforefaid, where fuch Bailiff by the Commonalty of the fame Member is elected, refpe&ively, in and upon themfelves, and all other Inhabitants and Refidents within every fuch Member, the Bounds, Limits and Precincts of the fame, and in and upon all and fingular Lands, Rents and Hereditaments whatfoever, within every fuch Member, and the Bounds, Limits and Precincts of every fuch Member being, refpe&ively ; and alfo in and upon all and fingular Goods, Chattels and Merchandizes of all and

ANNOTATIONS.

[t] *Upon themfelves*, in their perfonal Capacity, by their Abilities, Lands or Goods, as well as upon other the Inhabitants and Refciants that are not Freemen. And if any Lands belong to the Corporation (for the Corporations of the Ports may purchafe Lands or Tenements, notwithftanding the Statute of *Mortmaine*) thefe Lands and Tenements are alfo to be taxed. In like fort, thefe Words, *in and upon themfelves*, are ufed before p. 165, l. 37. and again afterward, l. 33. of this Page.

[u] Or

CHARTERS.

& singulorum inhabitantium sive occupator. sive tenent. aliquarum hujusmodi terrarum sive hæreditament. quorumcunque, infra quodlibet tale Membrum, ac fines, limit. & præcinct. ejusdem, exiftent. respectivé, affidere, affeffare, & imponere poffint, de tempore in tempus quotiefcunque eis neceffar. videbitur, rationabil. & ratabil. taxationes, fcott. fhott. & lott. tallag. & rationabil. taxationes, communiter vocat. common fines, impofitiones & pecuniarum fumhas folvend. infra certa tempora, five infra certum tempus, per ipfos refpective ad id limit. & ordinat. & percipiend. & per ipfos refpective levand. de inhabitantibus & refident. prædict. five de bonis, catallis & merchandifis, terris, reddit. tenement. & hæreditamènt. præd. refpective, per diftrictiones & venditiones ejufdem, five imprifonament. corporum perfonarum prædict. & eorum cujuflibet, fuper quos hujufmodi taxationes, fcott. lott. fhott. tallag. taxation. vocat. common fines, impofitiones & pecuniarum fummas, ut præfert. appofit. impofit. vel affeffat. fint vel erunt

TRANSLATION.

and fingular the Inhabitants, or Occupiers [u] or Tenants of any fuch Lands or Hereditaments whatfoever, within every fuch Member, and the Bounds, Limits and Precincts of the fame being refpectively, may fet down, affefs and impofe [v], from time to time, as often as to them it fhall feem neceffary [w], reasonable and ratable [x] Taxations [y], Scot [z], Shot and Lot [a], Tallage, and the reafonable Taxations, commonly called Common Fines [b], Impofitions and Sums of Money to be paid within certain times, or within a certain time, by them refpectively limited and ordained thereunto, and to be perceived and levied by them, refpectively, of the Inhabitants and Refidents aforefaid, or of the Goods, Chattels and Merchandizes, Lands, Rents, Tenements and Hereditaments aforefaid refpectively, by Diftrefs and Sale of the fame [c], or Imprifonment [d] of the Bodies of the Perfons aforefaid, and every of them, upon whom fuch Taxations, Scot, Lot, Shot, Tallage, Taxations called Common Fines, Impofitions and Sums of Money as aforefaid, may be or fhall be put, impofed or affeffed, or other-

---

ANNOTATIONS.

[u] *Or Occupiers.* Here is omitted *Refidents*, which is expreffed before, p. 166. l. 23. p. 167. h 19.
[v] *Impofe* or put upon.
[w] *Neceffary.* The Taxes to be made muft be neceffary and reafonable.
[x] *Ratable*, that is proportionable, according to fome Rate or Rule, by the Pound Rent, or the like.
[y] *Taxations* or Taxes.
[z] *Shot*, all one with Scot.
[a] *Lot*, the fame with Scot and Shot, as in the Statute 33 *Henry* VIII. *cap.* 19.
[b] *Common Fines.* Thus the Taxes of old levied in the Ports, towards the Defence of their Liberties and Franchifes, were called, as appeareth by a Decree of Brotherhood made the *Tuefday* next after the Clofe of *Eafter*, in the firft Year of the Reign of King *Richard* III.
[c] *Diftrefs and Sale*, or by Diftreffes and Sales.
[d] *Imprifonment* is the Reftraint of a Man's Liberty, whether it be in the open Field or in the Stocks, or Cage in the Streets, or in a Man's own Houfe, as well as in the common Gaol, whenever he hath not his Liberty to go freely at all Times whither he will, without Bail or Mainprize, or other Authority. For default of Payment of fuch Taxes as aforefaid in the Ports, Imprifonment is hereby permitted, and fo alfo fometimes hath been ufed; but the Law being very tender of the Liberty of every Perfon, it is good to be cautious herein; and the better Way, in my Opinion, is to proceed for the Levying of fuch Taxes by Diftrefs and Sale, as before mentioned, or by Action of Debt, as after fpecified in the Charter.

[e] *Legal*

CHARTERS.

erunt vel aliter per actionem &
actiones debit. in aliqua curia de
Recordo prædictorum Quinque
Portuum, aut antiquarum villarum prædict. feu Membrorum eorundem, verſus hujuſmodi perſonam & perſonas reſpective, pro-
ſequend. vel alio legali modo
quocunque recuperand. & obtinend. prout melius eis videbitur,
abſque aliquo impedimento noſtro, hæredum vel ſucceſſorum
noſtrorum, juſticiar. aut al. miniſtr.
noſtr. aut hæred. vel ſucceſſorum
noſtrorum quorumcunque, habend. tenend. & gaudend. omnia
& ſingula præmiſſa prædicta ſuperius, per præſentes conceſſa aut
confirmata, feu mentionata fore
conceſſa ſeu confirmata præfatis
Baronibus Quinque Portuum &
antiquarum villarum, & Membrorum eorundem portuum &
villarum, & ſucceſſoribus ſuis;
ac prædict. Major. Jurat. &
Communitat. Balliv. Jurat. &
Communitat. & Balliv. & Communitat. eorundem Quinque Portuum, antiquarum villar. & Membrorum eorum, & ſucceſſoribus
ſuis reſpective imperpetuum, red-
dendo & faciendo nobis, hæred.
& ſucceſſoribus noſtris, tot, tanta,
talia, eadem & hujuſmodi ſeod.
firm. ſervitia, redditus, denariorum ſummas & demand. quo-
cunq; quot. quant. qualia & quæ
nobis aut prædeceſſor. noſtris
antehac debit. conſuet. ſive ſo-
lub. ſuerunt vel ſunt.   Quare
vo-

TRANSLATION.

otherwiſe by Action and Actions
of Debt, in any Court of Record
of the aforeſaid *Cinque Ports* or
ancient Towns aforeſaid, or
Members of the ſame, againſt
ſuch Perſon and Perſons reſpectively, to be proſecuted, or in
other legal [a] Manner whatſoever
to be recovered and obtained, as
to them ſhall ſeem beſt, without
any Impediment of us, our Heirs
or Succeſſors, Juſtice or other
Miniſter of us, or our Heirs or
Succeſſors whatſoever [f], to have,
hold and enjoy all and ſingular
the Premiſſes aforeſaid above, by
theſe Preſents granted or confirmed, or mentioned to be
granted or confirmed to the a-
foreſaid Barons of the *Cinque
Ports* and ancient Towns, and
Members of the ſame Ports and
Towns, and to their Succeſſors;
and to the aforeſaid Mayors, Jurats and Commonalties, Bailiffs,
Jurats and Commonalties, and
Bailiff and Commonalty of the
ſame *Cinque Ports*, ancient
Towns and their Members, and
to their Succeſſors reſpectively
for ever; rendering and doing to
us, our Heirs and Succeſſors, ſo
many, ſo much, ſuch, the ſame
and ſuch like Fee-Farms [g], Services, Rents, Sums of Money
and Demands [h] whatſoever, as
to us or our Predeceſſors heretofore have been or are due, accuſtomed or payable.   Wherefore

ANNOTATIONS.

[a] *Legal*, or in any other lawful Manner.

[f] *Whatſoever*, or whomſoever.

[g] *Fee-farms*. Fee-farm is properly when a Tenant holdeth of his Lord in fee-ſimple, paying
to him the Value of half, or the third Part or fourth Part, &c. of the Land by the Year; and
he that ſo holdeth ought not to pay Relief, or do any other thing than is contained in the
Feoffment, but Fealty. Here it ſeemeth to be Rents for ſuch Lands as were holden of the King,
after the nature of Fee-farms; and whether the Ports have any ſuch or no, it is uſually inſerted
in Charters of like ſort as Words of Courſe.

[h] *Demands*. A large Word in the Law, and is either in Deed expreſs, or in Law implied.
In the firſt Senſe it includes real Actions, and in the latter perſonal Actions, Appeals, Judgments,
Executions, Right or Title of Entry, Rent-Service, Rent-Charge, Rent-Serk, common of
Paſture, mixt Actions, Warranty, &c. ſo as a Releaſe under Hand and Seal of all Demands
will bar the Party releaſing from the ſame. Here *Demands* is for any Due to the King from the
Ports and Portſmen.

CHARTERS.

volumus, ac per præsentes pro nobis, hæred. & succeffor. noftris firmiter injungendo, præcipimus quod ipfi prædict. Barones prædictorum Quinque Portuum & antiquar. villarum, & Membrorum corundem, & fucceffor. fui, & quilibet corum & fucceffores fui ; necnon Major. Jurat. & Communitas villæ & portus de Hafting prædict. & fucceffores fui ; necnon Major. Jurat. & Communitas villæ & portus de Nova Romney prædict. & fucceffores fui; necnon Major. Jurat. & Communitas villæ & portus de Hoeth prædict. & fucceffores fui; necnon Major. Jurat. & Communitas villæ & portus de Dover prædict. & fucceffores fui ; necnon Major. Jurat. & Communitas villæ & portus de Sandwic. prædict. & fucceffores fui ; necnon Major. Jurat. & Communitás antiquæ villæ de Rye, & fucceffores fui ; necnon Major. Jurat. & Communitas antiquæ villæ de Winchelfey, & fucceffores fui ; necnon Balliv. Jurat. & Communitas villæ & leucatæ de Pevenfey prædict. & fucceffores fui ; necnon Balliv. Jurat. & Communitas villæ de Seaford prædict. & fucceffores fui ; necnon Balliv. Jurat. & Communitas villæ de Lydd prædict. & fucceffores fui ; necnon Major. Jurat. & Communitas villæ de Folkeftone prædict. & fucceffores fui ; necnon Major. Jurat. & Communitas villæ

TRANSLATION.

fore we will, and by thefe Prefents for us, our Heirs and Succeffors firmly enjoyning, command that they, the aforefaid Barons, of the aforefaid *Cinque Ports* and ancient Towns, and Members of the fame, and their Succeffors, and every of them and their Succeffors ; alfo the Mayor, Jurats and Commonalty of the Town and Port of *Hafting* aforefaid, and their Succeffors ; alfo the Mayor, Jurats and Commonalty of the Town and Port of *New Romney* aforefaid, and their Succeffors; alfo the Mayor, Jurats and Commonalty of the Town and Port of *Hithe* aforefaid, and their Succeffors ; alfo the Mayor, Jurats and Commonalty of the Town and Port of *Dover* aforefaid, and their Succeffors ; alfo the Mayor, Jurats and Commonalty of the Town and Port of *Sandwich* aforefaid, and their Succeffors ; alfo the Mayor, Jurats and Commonalty of the ancient Town of *Rye* [i], and their Succeffors ; alfo the Mayor, Jurats and Commonalty of the ancient Town of *Winchelfea*, and their Succeffors ; alfo the Bailiff, Jurats and Commonalty of the Town and Lowey of *Pevenfea* aforefaid, and their Succeffors ; alfo the Bailiff, Jurats and Commonalty of the Town of *Seaford* aforefaid, and their Succeffors; alfo the Bailiff, Jurats and Commonalty of the Town of *Lydd* aforefaid, and their Succeffors; alfo the Mayor, Jurats and Commonalty of the Town of *Folkeftone* aforefaid, and their Succeffors ; alfo the Mayor, Jurats and Commonalty
of

ANNOTATIONS.

[i] *Rye* here, and *Winchelfea* three Lines lower, is not followed by *aforefaid* in the printed Copy, as in all the other here mentioned, which argues it an Omiffion ; but though omitted, fhall be underftood to be the fame Towns before mentioned. Here may be further noted, that from the 9ᵗʰ Line of this Page to the 5ᵗʰ Line of the following, the Words *Mayor* and *Bailiff* feem to be plural in the *Latin*.

†   [k] *Tolls*,

CHARTERS.

villæ de Feverſham prædict. &
ſucceſſores ſui; necnon Major.
Jurat. & Communitas villæ de
Fordwich prædict. & ſucceſſores
ſui; necnon Major. Jurat. &
Communitas villæ & hundred de
Tenterden prædict. & ſucceſſores
ſui, & quilibet eorum & ſucceſſorum ſuorum reſpective, habeant,
teneant, utantur, & gaudeant,
ac habere, tenere, uti & gaudere valeant & poſſunt imperpetuum omnes & ſingulas libertat.
authoritat. juriſdiction. franche-
ſias, quietan. terr. ten. fer. nun-
din. mercat. tolnet. theolo. cu-
ſtum. & privileg. præd. ſecun-
dum formam & tenorem harum
literarum noſtrarum patentium,
& al. conceſſion. eis confectarum
ſine actione vel impediment. noſtro, aut hæred. ſive ſucceſſor.
noſtrorum, juſticiar. vicecomit.
eſcaetor. ſive al. Balliv. ſive Miniſtrorum noſtror. hæred. & ſucceſſorum noſtrorum quorumcunque. Nolentes quod ipſi. vel
ſucceſſores ſui, vel eorum aliquis
vel aliqui, per nos vel hæredes
noſtros, juſticiar. vicecomit. eſcaetor. aut al. Balliv. ſive Miniſtros noſtros, hæred. ſeu ſucceſſorum noſtrorum quorumcounq. actio-
one verſus libertat. vel franchef.
præd. vel eorum alicujus actio-
nentur, moleſtentur, vexentur ſeu
graventur, occaſionentur, ſeu in
aliquo perturbentur; volumus, ac
per præſentes mandantes & præ-
cipient. tam Theſaurar. Cancellar.
&

TRANSLATION.

of the Town of *Feverſham* aforeſaid, and their Succeſſors; alſo
the Mayor, Jurats and Commonalty of the Town of *Fordwich*
aforeſaid, and their Succeſſors;
alſo the Mayor, Jurats and Commonalty of the Town and Hundred of *Tenterden* aforeſaid, and
their Succeſſors, and every of
them and their Succeſſors reſpectively, may have, hold, uſe and
enjoy for ever, all and ſingular
the Liberties, Authorities, Juriſdictions, Franchiſes, Freedoms, Lands, Tenements, Feaſts,
Fairs, Markets, Tolls, Tholls,
Cuſtoms [k] and Privileges aforeſaid, according to the Form and
Tenor of theſe our Letters Patents, and other Grants to them
made, without Action [l] or Impediment of us, or our Heirs or
Succeſſors, the Juſtices, Sheriffs,
Eſcheators, or other Bailiffs or
Miniſters of us, our Heirs and
Succeſſors whatſoever [m]. Unwilling [n] that they or their Succeſſors,
or any of them, by us or our
Heirs, the Juſtices, Sheriffs,
Eſcheators, or other Bailiffs or
Miniſters of us, our Heirs or
Succeſſors whatſoever, by Action
againſt the Liberties or Franchiſes aforeſaid, or any of them
ſhould be actioned [o], moleſted,
vexed or grieved, occaſioned [p], or
in any thing diſturbed by us
will, and by theſe Preſents
commanding and charging, as
well our Treaſurer, Chancellor
and

ANNOTATIONS.

[k] *Tholls, Cuſtoms.* See before, p. 134.

[l] *Action.* No Action maintainable againſt the Portſmen for what they do according to their
Charters and Liberties; neither by *Quo-warranto* at the King's Suit, or Action at the Suit of other
Party: Nevertheleſs ſometimes *Quo-warranto's* have been brought, beſides other Actions, before
the Judges in the Foreign (who ſeldom love the Ports) whereby their Liberties have been often
called in queſtion, contrary to their Charters; ſo as the Ports have been forced to defend their
ancient and juſt Rights and Privileges at their great Charges and Expences.

[m] *Whatſoever,* or whomſoever.

[n] *Unwilling;* that is as much as *forbidding,* as *willing* is all one with *commanding* in a
Charter, though in a Teſtament it be differently underſtood.

[o] *Actioned;* that is, have Actions brought againſt them.

[p] *Occaſioned,* in this Place, is as much as *troubled.*

[q] *Diſturbed* or troubled.

[r] *Claimes.*

CHARTERS.

& Baron. noftris de fcaccario noftro Weftminft. ac al jufticiar.
noftris, hæred. & fuccefforum noftrorum, quam attornat. & foli-
citator. noftris general. pro tempore exiftent. & eorum cuilibet,
ac omnibus aliis officiariis & miniftris noftris quibufcunque, quod
nec ipfi feu eorum aliqui ivel aliquis aliquid breve five fummonition. de Quo-warranto, five aliquid al. breve five brevia aut
proceffe noftr. quæcunq. verfus
ipfos vel eorum aliquem pro aliquibus caufis, rebus, mater. clam.
aut offenfis prædict. aut eorum
aliquem vel aliquos refpective,
debit. clamat. attempt. ufitat. habit. feu ufurpat. tempore nuper
apoftafiæ & defectionis, feu ad
aliquid aliud tempus ante diem
confectionis præfentium, profe-
quantur aut continuant. aut profequi aut continuari faciant aut
caufabunt, feu eorum aliquis fa-
ciet aut caufabit. Volentes etiam,
quod ipfi vel fucceffores fui, vel
eorum aliquis vel aliqui, per aliquem vel aliquos jufticiar. officiar. vel miniftr. noftr. hæred.
vel fucceffor. nofttrorum in aut
pro debit. ufu, clameo vel abufu
tiliquarum libertat. franchef. aut
jurifdiction: præd. tempore apoftafiæ & defectionis præd. feu ad
aliquid aliud tempus ante diem
confectionis harum literarum noftrarum patentium, minime im-
pediantur aut moleftentur, aut ad
ea vel eorum aliquid refpondere
compellantur. Provifo femper,
& intentio noftra regia eft, quod
hæ literæ noftræ patentes, feu aliquod in eis content. non fint in
aliquo

TRANSLATION.

and Barons of our *Exchequer* at
Weftminfter, and other Juftices
of us, our Heirs and Succeffors,
as our Attorney and Solicitor
General for the time being, and
every of them, and all other our
Officers and Minifters whatfoever, that neither they or any of
them, any Writ or Summons of
Quo-warranto, or any other
Writ or Writs, or Procefs of us
whatfoever, againft them or any
of them, for any Caufes, Things,
Matters, Claims ʳ or Offences
aforefaid, or any of them refpectively, due, claimed, attempted, ufed, had or ufurped ˢ
in the time of the late Apoftafy ᵗ
and Defection, or at any other
time before the Day of the
making of thefe Prefents, may
profecute or continue, or may
or fhall, or any of them may or
fhall, make or caufe to be profecuted or continued. Willing
alfo, that they or their Succeffors, or any of them, by any
of the Juftices, Officers or Minifters of us, our Heirs or Succeffors, in or for the due Ufe,
Claim or Abufe of any the Liberties, Franchifes or Jurifdictions aforefaid, in the Time of
the aforefaid Apoftafy and Defection, or at any other Time before the Day of making thefe our
LettersPatents, be not hindered or
molefted, or compelled to anfwer
to the fame, or any thing thereof.
Provided always, and our Royal Intention is, that thefe our
Letters Patents, or any Thing
in them contained, may not in
any

ANNOTATIONS.

ʳ *Claims.* Claim is a Challenge by any Man of the Property or Ownerfhip of a Thing
which he hath not in Poffeffion, but which is detained from him wrongfully.

ˢ *Ufurped.* Ufurpation feems in law to be two-fold; 1ſt, For a Stranger that hath no Right
to prefent to a Church, and his Clerk is admitted; 2dly, For any Subject to ufe royal Franchifes without lawful Warrant; and in this Senfe the Word *ufurped* is here ufed.

ᵗ *Apoftafy.* Falling away, and fometime rendered *Rebellion*, intending the Time from January 30, 1648, to May 25, 1660. And this Claufe in the Charter is tantamount to a Pardon
for any Act then done unduly.

ᵗ *Pre-*

CHARTERS.

aliquo prejudicial. Gardiano five Cuftod. pro tempore exiftent. præ-dict. Quinque Portuum, antiqua-rum villarum & Membrorum eorundem, quoad aliquas Jurifdicti-ones, authoritates, libertates, vel privilegia infra prædict. Quinque Portus, antiquas villas & Membr. eorundem, per Gardianos five Cuftod. dict. Quinque Port. anti-quar. villar. & Membror. eorundem antehac legitime ufitat. & exercit. Provifo etiam, quod hæ literæ patentes, aut aliquod feu aliqua in eifdem content. aut mentionat. non aliqualiter exten-dant vel extendat. ad confir-mand. corroborand. ftabiliend. approband. five ratificand. quaf-dam literas patentes, aut aliquid feu aliqua in eifdem content. feu mentionat. per Dom. Henricum fextum, nuper Regem Angliæ, fub magno figillo fuo Angliæ confect. gerend. dat. vicefimo octavo die Novembris, anno Reg-ni fui vicefimo quinto, Major. villæ de Feverfham, ac Baron. & Communitat. ejufdem villæ & fucceffor. fuis aut per quodcun-que al. nomen incorporationis an-tehac fact. five conceff. feu men-tionat. fore conceff. nec ad con-firmand. corroborand. ftabili-end. approband. five ratificand. aliquas libertat. franchef. immu-nitat. privileg. exemptiones, con-ceffiones, rem aut res quafcunque vel quamcunque in eifdem literis patent. dicti nuper Regis Henrici fexti dat. conceff. confirmat. con-tent. fpecificat. five mentionat. nec aliquas alias literas patentes quafcunque, quoad confirmat. cor-roborat.

TRANSLATION.

any Thing be prejudicial ' to the Warden or Keeper for the Time being of the aforefaid *Cinque Ports*, Ancient Towns and Members of the fame, as to any, Jurifdictions, Authorities, Li-berties or Privileges within the aforefaid *Cinque Ports*, Ancient Towns and Members of the fame, by the Wardens or Keepers of the faid *Cinque Ports*, Ancient Towns and Members of the fame, heretofore lawfully ufed and ex-ercifed. Provided alfo, that thefe Letters Patents, or any Thing or Things in the fame contained or mentioned, extend not, or in any wife be extended, to confirm, ftrengthen, eftablifh, approve or ratify, certain Letters Patents, or any Thing or Things in the fame contained or menti-oned, made by the Lord *Henry* ᵛ late King of *England* the Sixth, bearing Date under his Great Seal of *England* the Twenty Eight Day of *November*, in the Twenty fifth Year of his Reign, to the Mayor of the Town of *Feverfham*, and to the Barons and Commonalty of the fame Town, and to their Succeffors, or by whatfoever other Name of Incorporation heretofore made or granted, or mentioned to be granted; nor to confirm, ftrength-en, eftablifh, approve or ratify any Liberties, Franchifes, Immunities, Privileges, Exemptions, Grants, Thing or Things whatfoever, in the fame Letters Patents of the faid late King *Henry* the Sixth, giv-en, granted, confirmed, contain-ed, fpecified or mentioned, nor any other Letters Patents whatfoever, as to the Confirmation, Cor-roboration,

ANNOTATIONS.

ᵗ *Prejudicial* or hurtful. So as by this Provifo the Rights of the Lord Warden are faved, and what Authority he had before the making of this Charter he ftill hath.
ᵛ *Lord Henry.* This fecond Provifo excepts the Confirmation of the Letters Patents of King *Henry* VI. granted to *Feverfham*, as was before in the Charter of King *James*. Thefe I never faw, but have heard the Tenor thereof was not correfponding to the general Ufages and Cuftoms of the Ports.

Y y   ᵘ *Cor-*

CHARTERS.

roborat. feu approbat. prædict. literarum patentium dicti nuper Regis Henrici fexti, aut alicujus feu aliquorum in eifdem literis patentibus dicti nuper Henrici fexti content. feu mentionat. aliquo in patentibus in contrar. inde non obftant. Et ulterius volumus, ac per præfentes pro nobis, hæred. & fucceffor. noftris ordinamus & firmiter injungend. præcipimus, quod omnes & quilibet Major. Balliv. Jurat. Recordator. Coronator. communis Clericus, Conftabular. & omnes alii Officiarii & Miniftri prædictorum Quinque Portuum, antiquarum villarum & Membrorum eorundem, & eorum cujuflibet refpective, & eorum Deputati; necnon omnes Jufticiar. noftri ad pacem noftram, hæred. & fucceffor. noftrorum, infra eofdem Quinque Portus, antiquas villas, feu Membr. eorum feu eorum alicujus vel aliquorum, virtute aut fecundum tenorem harum literarum noftrarum patentium, feu aliquarum aliarum literarum patentium five cartarum antehac fact. modo conftitut. feu impofterum nominand. eligend. feu conftituend. antequam ipfi ad executiónem five exercitium officii vel officiorum, loci vel locorum, cui vel quibus fic refpective nominat. appunct. nat. elect. five conftitut. modo

TRANSLATION.

roboration[u], or Approbation, of the aforefaid Letters Patents of the faid late King *Henry* the Sixth, or of any Thing or Things in the fame Letters Patents of the faid late *Henry* the Sixth contained or mentioned, any Thing in the Patents to the contrary thereof notwithftanding. And furthermore we will, and by thefe Prefents for us, our Heirs and Succeffors, ordain, and firmly injoining, command, that all and every the Mayors, Bailiffs, Jurats, Recorders[w], Coroners, Common Clerks[x], Conftables, and all other Officers and Minifters of the aforefaid *Cinque Ports*, Ancient Towns and Members of the fame, and every of them refpectively, and their Deputies; alfo all our Juftices, to keep the Peace of us, our Heirs and Succeffors, within the fame *Cinque Ports*, Ancient Towns or their Members, or any of them, by virtue or according to the Tenor of thefe our Letters Patents, or of any other Letters Patents or Charters heretofore made, now conftituted, or hereafter to be nominated, elected or conftituted, before they, to the Execution or Exercife of the Office or Offices of the Place[y] or Places to which they are now fo refpectively nominated, appointed[z], elected or conftituted, or here-

ANNOTATIONS.

[u] *Corroboration* or ftrengthning.

[w] *Recorders.* Where fuch an Officer is, he ufeth to fit on the Bench with the Juftices, to direct the Court as to Matters of Law; and taketh Care the Records of the Procefs and Judgment of every Caufe be well drawn up and entered by the Clerk of the Court. But in moft of the Ports this Place is fupplied by the Town-Clerk.

[x] *Common Clerks.* Thus are the Town-Clerks called in the old Records, as being a Commoner or Freeman, and Clerk in common both to the Court of Record holden before the Mayor and Jurats, and of the Seffions and Hundred Courts; and alfo of all Affemblies of the Mayor, Jurats and Commoners, or Bailiff, Jurats and Commoners refpectively, where he is fo Clerk, as by the Cuftomals and Records of each Town fully appeareth. In the *Latin* it is fingular, *Common-Clerk,* and fo may the other Officers here mentioned be read without any Damage to the Senfe.

[y] *Of the Place.* *Of the* may be omitted, and it may be read *Office* or *Offices, Place* or *Places.*

[z] *Appointed.* In the *Latin* printed Copy it is *appunct. nat.* if it be not mifprinted, as I fuppofe it is, for *appunctunt.* then between *appointed* and *elected* in the Tranflation muft be fupplied the Word *born,* for which *nat.* is ufed by Abbreviation.

†   [a] *Behalf.*

CHARTERS.

modo exiftunt, aut impofterum nominat. elect. five conftitut. fuerint. admittat. feu aliqualiter in ea parte intromittant, feu eorum aliquis refpective intromittat, tam facramentum corporale communiter vocat. *The Oath of Obedience,* quam facramentum corporale communiter vocat. *The Oath of Supremacy,* fuper facrofanct. Dei Evangeliis præftabunt, & eorum quilibet præftabit coram tali perfona five talibus perfonis, qual. & quæ ad hujufmodi facramenta dand. & præftand. per legem & ftatutum hujus Regni noftri Angliæ ad præfens appunctuantur & defignantur, aut impofterum appunctat. & defignat. fuerit vel fuerint. Et ulterius volumus, ac per præfentes pro nobis hæred. & fucceffor. noftris, ordinamus & declaramus, quod cum aliqua electio de cætero facta fuerit de aliqua perfona vel aliquibus perfonis quibufcunque in officium Recordator. feu in officium communis Clerici aliquorum Portuum, villarum, Membrorum five locorum prædict. al. quam de tal. & hujufmodi perfona & perfonis, quæ modo in hujufmodi officio & officiis, feu eorum altero, electæ & præfectæ funt, & in eifdem, feu eorum altero, refpective modo deferviunt, fi nos, hæred. vel fucceffor. noftri per aliquid fcriptum five warrantum fub figno manuali noftro, hæredum vel

TRANSLATION.

hereafter fhall be nominated, elected or conftituted, be admitted, or in any wife intermeddle in that behalf [a], or any of them intermeddle refpectively, they fhall take, and every of them fhall take, as well the corporal Oath commonly called, *The Oath of Obedience* [b], as the corporal Oath commonly called, *The Oath of Supremacy* [c], upon the Holy Evangelifts [d], before fuch Perfon or fuch Perfons as to give [e] and take fuch Oaths by the Law and Statute [f] of this our Kingdom of *England* are at prefent appointed and defigned, or hereafter fhall be appointed or defigned. And furthermore, [g] we will, and by thefe Prefents, for us, our Heirs and Succeffors, ordain and declare, that when from henceforth any Election fhall be made of any Perfon or Perfons whatfoever into the Office of Recorder, or into the Office of Common Clerk of any of the Ports, Towns, Members, or Places aforefaid, other than fuch and fuch like Perfon and Perfons, which now is fuch Office and Offices, or in either of them, are elected and ferve [h], and in the fame, or in either of them, refpectively now officiate [i], if we, our Heirs or Succeffors, by any Writing or Warrant under the Sign Manual of us, our Heirs or

ANNOTATIONS.

[a] *Behalf* or part, as before and after.
[b] *Obedience* or Allegiance. This Oath is to be found among the printed Statutes, *Anno* 3 *Jac.* cap. 4.
[c] *Supremacy,* This Oath was ordained by a Statute made *Anno* 1 *Elizabeth,* and may there be feen, *cap.* 1.
[d] *Evangelifts* or Gofpels of God, as before noted.
[e] *Give and take,* or adminifter and receive.
[f] *Law and Statute.* It may be read plurally, becaufe the Oaths here mentioned are ordained by feveral Statutes ; but the printed Copy being in the fingular Number, I kept thereto in the Tranflation.
[g] *And furthermore.* The Claufe here following about the Election of a Recorder or Common Clerk, was not in any Charter of the Ports before ; and is a Reftriction to the ancient Liberty of the Ports in that cafe.
[h] *Serve,* rule or officiate.
[i] *Officiate* or ferve, and fo again in the following *page, l.* 18.

J *Mem-*

CHARTERS.

vel fucceffor. noftrorum declarabimus & fignificabimus Baronibus Quinque Portuum præd. aut Majori, Juratis & Communitati, feu Ballivo, Juratis & Communitati, feu Balliv. & Communitat. Portuum & antiquarum præd. villarum & Membror. eorum, feu aliis officiariis & Membris Portuum & villarum illarum & Membrorum eorundem refpective, cui vel quibus hujufmodi electio & electiones refpective pertinent fiend. improbationem noftri, hæred. vel fucceforum hujufmodi perfonæ five perfonarum refpective fic elect. ad deferviend. in hujufmodi officio five officiis, cui vel quibus fic, ut præfertur, refpective elect. fuerit vel fuerint ; quod tunc & toties & ab & poft hujufmodi declarationem & fignificationem in forma præd. factam, electionem & electiones hujufmodi perfonæ & perfonarum, perinde fic, ut præfertur, improbat. vacuæ fint & nullius effectus. Et quod abinde licitum fit & erit Baronibus Quinque Port. prædict. & Membr. eorundem, feu Major. Jurat. & Communitat. Portuum & antiquarum villarum prædict. & Membrorum eorundem, feu Balliv. Jurat. & Communitat. feu Balliv. & Communitat. Portuum & villarum illarum & Membrorum eorundem, feu eorum alicui vel quibus refpective, cui vel quibus hujufmodi electio & electiones refpective pertinent fiendæ, alium probum & difcretum virum, five alios probos & difcretos viros, habiles pro exercitio officii vel officiorum præd.

TRANSLATION.

or Succeffors, fhall declare and fignify to the Barons of the *Cinque Ports* aforefaid, or to the Mayor, Jurats and Commonalty, or Bailiff, Jurats and Commonalty, or Bailiff and Commonalty, of the Ports and Ancient Towns aforefaid, and their Members, or to the other Officers and Members [j] of the Ports, and thofe Towns and Members of the fame refpectively, to whom fuch Election and Elections refpectively appertain to be made, the Non-Approbation [k] of us, our Heirs or Succeffors, of fuch Perfon or Perfons refpectively fo elected, to officiate in fuch Office or Offices, to which he or they fhall be fo as aforefaid refpectively elected ; that then, and fo often, and from and after fuch Declaration and Signification in Form aforefaid made, the Election and Elections of fuch Perfon and Perfons, even fo as aforefaid not approved, are void [l] and of none effect. And that from thenceforth it may and fhall be lawful to the Barons of the *Cinque Ports* aforefaid, and Members of the fame ; or to the Mayors, Jurats and Commonalties of the Ports and Ancient Towns aforefaid, and Members of the fame ; or to the Bailiffs, Jurats and Commonalties, or Bailiff and Commonalty of the Ports, and thofe Towns and Members of the fame, or to any or which of them refpectively, to whom fuch Election and Elections refpectively appertain to be made, another good and difcreet Man, or other good and difcreet Men, able for the Exercife of the Office or Offices afore-

ANNOTATIONS.

[j] *Members*, it feems to be mifprinted for *Minifters*.
[k] *Non-Approbation* or Difallowance, and fo *not approved, l.* 27. and in the following *page* may be read, *difallowed*.
[l] *Are void*, may or fhall be void.

Any

CHARTERS.

TRANSLATION.

præd. cui vel quibus refpective nominatum & electum fuerit vel fuerint, in locum five locos hujufmodi perfonæ five perfonarum fic, ut præfertur, electum, & poftea improbat. eligere, nominare & jurare, juxta tenorem præfentium, & aliarum literarum patentium & conceffionum aliquorum progenitorum noftrorum in hac parte antehac fact. Et fic toties quoties cafus acciderit (aliquo in præfentibus contentó aut aliqua alia re, caufa vel materia quacunque in contrarium inde in aliquo non obftante.) Eo quod expreffa mentio de vero valore annuo, vel de certitudine præmifforum five eorum alicujus, aut de aliis donis five conceffionibus per nos feu per aliquem progenitorum five prædecefforum noftrorum, præfatis Baronibus Quinque Portuum, & Major. Jurat. & Communitat. Ballivis, Jurat. & Communitat. & Balliv. & Communitat. eorund. Quinque Portuum, antiquarum villarum & Membrorum eorundem, & fuccefforibus fuis, ante hæc tempora fact. in præfentibus minime fact. exiftit, aut aliquò ftatuto, actu, ordinatione, provifione, proclamatione five reftrictione, in contrar. inde ante hæc habit. fact. edit. ordinat. five provif. aut aliqua alia re, caufa vel materia quacunque, in aliquo non obftante. In cujus rei teftimonium has literas noftras fieri fecimus patentes.
Tefte

aforefaid, to which he or they fhall be refpectively nominated and elected, into the Place or Places of fuch Perfon or Perfons fo as aforefaid elected, and afterward not approved, to elect, nominate and fwear, according to the Tenor of thefe Prefents, and of other Letters Patents and Grants of any of our Progenitors in this behalf heretofore made ; and fo often as the Cafe fhall happen (any Thing in thefe Prefents contained, or any other Thing, Caufe or Matter whatfoever to the contrary thereof in any wife [m] notwithftanding.) Although [n] that exprefs mention of the true yearly Value, or of the Certainty of the Premiffes, or of any of them, or of the other Gifts or Grants by us, or by any of our Progenitors or Predeceffors, to the aforefaid Barons of the *Cinque Ports,* and to the Mayors, Jurats and Commonalties, Bailiffs, Jurats and Commonalties, and Bailiffs and Commonalties, of the fame *Cinque Ports,* ancient Towns and Members of the fame, and to their Succeffors, before thefe Times [o] made, in thefe Prefents be not [p] made, or any Statute, Act, Ordinance, Provifion [q], Proclamation [r] or Reftriction [s] to the contrary thereof heretofore had, made, fet forth, ordained or provided, or any other Thing, Caufe or Matter whatfoever, in any wife notwithftanding. In witnefs whereof thefe our Letters we have caufed to be made Patents.
Witnefs

ANNOTATIONS.

[m] *Any wife* or any Thing, fo *l.* 39. of this Page.
[n] *Although.* This is of as much force as a *notwithftanding.*
[o] *Before thofe Times,* or heretofore.
[p] *Be not,* or is not made.
[q] *Provifion* or provifo.
[r] *Proclamation,* a Declaration of the King's Pleafure with the Advice of his Privy Council.
[s] *Reftriction.* Under this Word may be included a Prohibition, or fuch like Reftraint.

CHARTERS.	TRANSLATION.
Tefte me ipfo apud Weftmin. vicefimo tertio die Decembris, anno regni noftri Caroli fecundi, &c. vicefimo.	Witnefs My Self 'at *Weftminfter*', the Twenty third Day of *December*, in the Twentieth Year" of the Reign of Us, *Charles* the Second, *&c.*
Per breve de privato figillo.	By Writ of Privy Seal.
Pigott.	*Pigott.*

ANNOTATIONS.

ˢ *My Self,* fo ftrictly after the *Latin,* and accordingly here, and before in divers Places, as, *p.* 20, 40, 41, 45, 50, 51, 87, 89, 119, is fo tranflated; but is commonly read *Our Self.*
ᵗ *Weftminfter,* in the old Charters, hath the *Latin* abbreviated, or elfe wrote *Weftmonafterium*; but in this Charter *Weftmin.* as the printed Copy hath it here and twice before, *p.* 119, 120.
ᵘ *Twentieth Year.* The Date of this Charter is in the Year of our Lord 1668.

☞ After the Word [*freely*] *p.* 41, 53, 89, 134, *&c.* may be read or underftood the Word [*confirmed.*]

THE

TABLE.

Bbb   Margate,

Parti.

F I N I S.

BOOKS printed for BERNARD LINTOT, at the Cross-Keys between the *Temple-Gates* in *Fleet-Street*.

	l.	s.	d.
THE Works of *Chaucer*, published by Mr. *Urrey*. In Quires	1	10	0
————ditto on Royal Paper	2	10	0
The Works of Mr. *Pope*, in 7 Vol. Royal 4to, bound and gilt	10	10	0
————ditto Second Royal (Subscribers Books)	8	8	0
————ditto Large Paper in *Folio*, bound and gilt	7	7	0
————ditto Small Paper in *Folio*, bound and gilt	4	4	0
————ditto in 12mo with Dr. *King*'s History of the Heathen Gods and Heroes: Necessary for the Readers of *Homer*	1	1	0
Mr. *Pope*'s *Homer*'s Odyssey, in Five Volumes, large Paper, *Folio*, bound and gilt	5	5	0
————ditto Small Paper	3	3	0
————ditto in 12mo	0	15	0
Monf. *Wicquefort* of the Functions of an Ambassador. On large Paper, bound and gilt	1	15	0
————ditto Small Paper	1	5	0
Mr. *Farquhar*'s Comedies. On Royal Paper	0	12	0
History of the *Saracens*. On Royal Paper, 2 Vol.	1	1	0
Dr. *King*'s Art of Love. Royal Paper	0	6	0
Mr *Fernou*'s Chancery Cases. Large Paper, bound	1	15	0
————ditto on Small Paper	0	17	6
N. B. The Second Volume is preparing for the Press.			
Reports taken by *Robert Skinner*, Esq; and publish'd by his Son, *Mathew Skinner*, Esq; Serjeant at Law, will speedily be publish'd.			
Dr. *Fiddes*'s Body of Divinity, 2 Vol.	2	10	0
————ditto on Royal Paper	4	0	0
Joannis Seldeni jurisconsulti Opera omnia, tam edita quam inedita. Collegit ac recensuit, Vitam Auctoris, Præfationes & Indices adjecit, David Wilkins, S. T. P. In 6 Vol. Charta Mag. in Sheets	10	10	0
————Min. in Sheets	6	14	0
Capt. *Breval*'s Remarks on several Parts of *Europe*, with above 45 Plates, 2 Vol.	2	10	0
England's newest Way in all Sorts of Cookery and Pastry. The Fourth Edition	0	2	6
Phædra and *Hippolitus*, by Mr. *Ed. Smith*	0	1	6
Lord *Lansdown*'s Plays	0	3	0
Sir *Richard Steele*'s Comedies	0	3	0
————Confscious Lovers	0	1	6
Mr. *Farquhar*'s Comedies, 2 Vol.	0	6	0
Mr. *Cibber*'s Plays, 4to Royal Paper	1	5	0
Mr. *Southern*'s Plays, 2 Vol.	0	5	0
Mr. *Gay*'s Plays	0	4	6
Moliere's Comedies, *Engl.* 6 Vol.	0	15	0
Letters of Love and Gallantry, by *Aristænetus*	0	2	0
Mrs. *Philips*'s Letters to Sir *C. Cotterell*	0	3	0
Rapin of Gardens, a Poem, by Mr. *Gardiner*	0	4	0
Mr. *Pope*'s *Homer*'s Iliad and Odyssey, 11 Vol. 12mo	1	13	0
————His Essay on Criticism	0	1	0
————Windsor Forest	0	1	0
————Messiah.			
————Ode for Musick.			
————Rape of the Lock, with Key	0	1	6
————Temple of Fame	0	1	0
————Eloisa to Abelard	0	1	0
Dean *Parnel*'s Poems, by Mr. *Pope*	0	3	6
Earl *Lauderdale*'s Virgil, 2 Vol.	0	5	0
Horace, with Notes upon Notes	0	10	0
————Ditto without Notes	0	2	0
Dacier's Homer, 5 Vol.	0	12	6
Mr. *Somerville*'s Poems	0	5	0
Rev^d Mr. *Broome*'s Poems	0	4	0
Rev^d Mr. *Pitts*'s Poems	0	3	6
Mr. *Harte*'s Poems	0	4	0
Mr. *Fenton*'s Poems	0	3	6
Oxford and *Cambridge* Poems	0	5	0
Shakespear's Poems	0	2	6
Mr. *Pope*'s Poems	0	12	0
————Miscellany, 2 Vol.	0	5	0
Mr *Gay*'s Poems, 4to Royal	1	5	0
Lady *Chudleigh*'s Poems	0	2	0
Miscellany of Poems	0	3	6
Dr. *King*'s Art of Cookery	0	2	6
————Art of Love	0	3	6
————Transactions	0	3	0
————Useful Miscellanies	0	0	6
Bezæ Poemata Juvenilia	0	1	0
Landeni Poemata	0	1	0
The Assembly, by Mr. *Barford*	0	1	6
La Motte upon *Homer*	0	1	0
Homer's Battle of the Frogs and Mice	0	1	0

Dr.

9 780274 697489